WORLD CULTURES
AND WORLD RELIGIONS

Books by
HENDRIK KRAEMER
Published by The Westminster Press

The Communication of the Christian Faith
Religion and the Christian Faith
A Theology of the Laity
World Cultures and World Religions

WORLD CULTURES
AND
WORLD RELIGIONS

The Coming Dialogue

by
HENDRIK KRAEMER

THE WESTMINSTER PRESS
PHILADELPHIA

CONTENTS

PREFACE

AT THE END of March 1958 I had the privilege of delivering the Stone Lectures of that year. I treated the subject of this book in five hours. The book, therefore, tells much more than could be said in Princeton. The enthusiasm with which the audience received these Lectures has encouraged me to publish them as a book.

I have purposely dealt with the subject in a strictly historical fashion. There may be readers or competent non-readers of this book who disagree with this line of presenting the subject. I have done it for two reasons.

The first is that, in my opinion, it is impossible to talk intelligently and *situationally* on "the coming dialogue" without being deeply aware of the historical background. Not for curiosity's sake but because this whole history determines the *mood* (a highly important thing) in which East and West are approaching this "coming dialogue". Unless we keep this in view, the whole matter is conceived in a too exclusively theoretical cast of mind. Especially indispensable is a fair knowledge of the facts since the beginning of the 19th century. Not in the first place out of historical interest, but for the same reason I have tried to give in Chapter 2 a careful analysis of the cultural relations between Christian Europe and the Muslim World in the Middle Ages, as the remembrance of this highly important event plays a considerable rôle in the *mood* of the Arab Muslims of to-day and their self-understanding. Therefore this mediaeval event is a contemporary factor and has meaning for the "coming dialogue".

Everybody to-day speaks about the meeting of Christianity and the great non-Christian religions, half-educated, educated and academic people alike. In my opinion this speaking is far too vague and general. Academically trained people, especially most theologians, imagine too often that they can approach this "meeting" with handbook-knowledge about these religions.

This is a fallacy. The fundamental and the concrete must, in such an important situation, combine.

Therefore, and this is my second reason, my extensive historical analyses are meant as a modest attempt to provide those who are called to fulfil a responsible rôle in this eventful "dialogue" with a fair knowledge of the facts, of the concrete and its significance as an indispensable basis for the fundamental aspect.

Only in the first and the last chapters have I tried—it is only an attempt—to indicate the deeper issues behind this awesome meeting of cultures and religions and implied in the "coming dialogue". Again on purpose. Therefore I have not included a more specified and systematic description of these great non-Christian cultures and religions, because each of them requires a special book if one realizes how formidable a task such a description is. Moreover, scattered through the chapters one can find many observations pertinent to it.

I have taken care to announce that these special books are on my programme. I request future reviewers to take due notice of this announcement, if they feel inclined to criticize the absence of a systematic description.

The main aim of this book is to provide those who are truly interested in the "meeting" and "dialogue" with concrete knowledge of how it grew, and so to enable them to *see*, for knowledge and information are not enough.

In closing I want to express my sincere gratitude to Miss Adrienne Boerwinkel, a Dutch student, for her great help to me in typing my often complicated written manuscript.

I gladly and gratefully add my warm thanks to the Rev. Cecil Northcott and Miss Hilda Wilson of the Lutterworth Press for the care they have devoted to making this book by an "alien" more readable for Anglo-Saxon readers. To those readers I offer my apologies for my un-English idiosyncrasies of thought and style.

H. KRAEMER

Chapter One

WHY THIS SUBJECT?

THE motivation of this book lies in the situation in which and through which we are living at present. Orient and Occident as different worlds of existence and expression, and their relation to each other, have been one of the great themes of historical reflection since the days when Aeschylus wrote his *Persae* and Aristotle defined the self-understanding of the Greek over against the barbaroi as the free man filled with intellectual curiosity versus the slave with brains.[1] Throughout history this major theme, in act as well as in reflection, has occupied the minds of thinkers, statesmen and great soldiers.

Up to the present day this has remained the case, and in the last 150 years especially the two great hemispheres have entered into a close and all-comprehensive contact such as was never known before. A meeting, an encounter, of the different cultural and religious worlds is inevitable. In fact, it has already been on the move for quite a long time. Apart from the more strictly scientific production of books on the great theme, the output of cultural-philosophic writing on the meeting or conflict of Orient and Occident is already immense. Their mutual influence and irradiation is one of the conspicuous aspects of the world situation. We can safely assert that this process of mutual influence, interpenetration and permeation

[1] It is interesting to see that Pope Gregory the Great, the outstanding personality of the Occident of his dismal time, expressed in a letter written in 603 to the Emperor Phocas in Byzantium (which was then the capital of Occidental, i.e. Greek civilization) this same feeling of superiority of the Greek-stamped Mediterranean West in regard to the Germanic "barbarians". The words are: "Hoc namque inter reges gentium et reipublicae imperatores distat quod reges gentium domini *servorum* sunt, imperatores vero reipublicae domini *liberorum*" (italics mine. "This is the difference between the tribal kings and the state emperors: the tribal kings are lords of *slaves*, but the state emperors are lords of *free men*." Quoted from H. Pirenne: *Mohammed and Charlemagne*, p. 144). Equally interesting is it that the great Spanish Muslim, Ibn Hazm (994-1046) who was, in spite of his rigid orthodoxy, an heir to Greek civilization (cf. our next chapter) opined that slaves and European peoples were unfit for culture.

is one of the cardinal events of our time. Many gifted minds grow wings and are stirred towards speculating or prophesying about the coming world civilization[1] or the one world religion in the making.

The most daring author in this respect is the great theorist and systematizer of the "civilizations" of mankind in the last 6,000 years, Arnold Toynbee, who has become more and more also a religious and cultural prophet. In one of the essays of his *Civilization on Trial* he even behaves as a grand-style soothsayer about the future religious-cultural physiognomy of mankind. The essay bears the title "Encounter between Civilizations", and affords us the startling experience of meeting a soothsayer who predicts the still-hidden pattern of mankind's religious-cultural life not only from the hand-lines of contemporary history, but also from those of future world history.

He suggests that the future historians of A.D. 2047 will say that the great event of the 20th century was the impact of Western civilization upon all the other living societies of that day. Those of 3047 will be chiefly interested in the tremendous counter-effects from the foreign (Eastern) worlds on the Western world, which is at present in the 20th century trying to engulf the Eastern worlds. The historians of 4047 will say that the impact of Western civilization on its contemporaries to-day was so epoch-making because it was a first step towards the unification of mankind in one single society. And Toynbee then adds the significant remark that the importance of this social unification will be found to lie not in the field of technics, economics, war or politics, but in that of *religion*.[2]

My reason for referring to Toynbee at some length is not to draw attention to his visionary treatment of history, his futurology, which contains abundant material for ardent discussion, especially when compared with Orwellian or Huxleyan visions of far shorter range. It is particularly his last point: religion. This book is concerned, as the title says, about the coming dialogue of world religions, and therefore has continuously to touch upon religion. Although I take issue with nearly every aspect of Toynbee's idea of religion,[3] I am at one

[1] Cf. e.g. the title of W. E. Hocking's book: *The Coming World Civilization*, 1956.
[2] Italics are mine.
[3] Cf. his remarkable book: *An Historian's Approach to Religion*.

with him that the religious issue is the deepest in the total meeting of Orient and Occident.

On the background, however, of Toynbee's wide-roaming soothsaying, I want to stress and to explain why my motivation in presenting this vast subject of world cultures and world religions moves within more modest limits. Without denying or minimizing the degree and amount of encounter between world religions and world cultures which has already occurred in the last 150 years and certainly will occur increasingly in the future, nor even rejecting totally the value of Toynbee's "proleptic" thinking, I steer on purpose a more modest course. I hope, however, that it therefore has at least the advantage of affording opportunity for a deeper probing and a more concrete elaboration of extremely vital issues, which call for perspicacious and resolute dealing in our generation.

Most of the many writers on the meeting of East and West, (or, to put it more precisely, on the meeting of the great Western-"Christian", Muslim, Indian, Buddhist, Chinese and Japanese civilizations and religions) whether optimist or pessimist, whether profound or shallow, take it for granted that the meeting in the proper sense of the word is not coming, but is already happening. I have already indicated that this attitude contains a great element of truth. There can be, and is, an eloquent case for it. The growing interdependence of the world forces it upon us. There is no possibility for the existing world cultures and world religions to run away from one another, even if they wanted to. It is again Toynbee who hammers that undeniable fact into the contemporary mind in sentences like this: "The annihilation of distance through the achievements of a Late Modern Western technology has brought all the living higher religions all over the world into a much closer contact with one another than before."[1]

SUPERFICIAL "MEETING" OF EAST AND WEST

My contention, however, is that, true and undeniable as this may be, the words "meeting" and "encounter", even the word "interpenetration" that may rightly be used (as I myself will show later on in this book), suggest too much; suggest more than they should when we make a closer examination of the

[1] *op. cit.*, p. 263.

facts. Leaving aside the unification of mankind into one single society, which is essentially a desirable or undesirable ideal according to one's philosophy of man and the world; equally leaving aside the future of Religion, which can be an interesting matter of speculation but never of any sure knowledge; the main point in my contention is that the contemporary encounter or meeting of Orient and Occident in cultural and religious respect, truly impressive and fascinating as it may be in many senses, is fundamentally speaking still a superficial matter.

After many blind, groping, preparative, often rather disconnected stages of meeting, in which these civilizations and religions contacted each other superficially or more thoroughly, the last 150 years manifest an increasingly close contact, the varied causes of which I will deal with more substantially later in this book. The recent nature of this more intense contact appears from the fact that the History of Religions is a young branch of systematic learning and research. The first chair of the History of Religions in Geneva dates back only to 1873. It was only in 1867 that the famous Max Müller in his *Chips from a German workshop* labelled his pioneer work Science of Religion (*Religionswissenschaft*). All the famous reviews or encyclopedias started after 1880.

The contact is not only increasing but continuous, and short of a cosmic or planetary disaster we can confidently assume that this continuity will go on. Yet, however important this growing contact as an event of world-historical importance may be, I insist that the words "meeting" and "encounter", although their use is understandable, suggest a deeper meaning than the facts warrant. In my view the immense scale on which contact takes place and develops does not yet really involve a "meeting" or "encounter". These constitute, it seems to me, *foreshadowings* of a still approaching meeting, interpenetration and *Auseinandersetzung* of cultural attitudes and orientations contained in these civilizations, and of inevitable mutual religious influence and stimulus. The real play has not yet begun; it is in process of being staged. They meet mainly because they can't help it. They meet partly in conative attempts towards conscious "meeting".

The attempts of philosophical or theological minds to chart,

already, synthetic maps of the new emerging spiritual continents, and determine the desirable solution of ingredients, are
undoubtedly interesting and significant, but they necessarily
must remain individual rough drafts, which stimulate and
fructify thinking. It is, however, still wholly undecided whether
the present rather confused multilogue of cultures and religions
will issue in mutual communication or in competitive self-
assertion. This amounts to saying that the essential meaning of
"meeting", i.e. real communication on the basis of real understanding of self and the other, and not on that of self-assertive
competition or premature "unitarianism" which confounds the
real issues, is still in the balance.

Because of this all-important and fundamental point of
orientation I have given to this book the title: The *coming
dialogue* of world cultures and world religions. The words
"coming" and "dialogue" are equally important. As I regard
it, speaking from the standpoint of facts, the issues are still
entirely undecided; the title therefore expresses a hope and a
deep desire rather than a confident prophecy.

THE PROCESS OF RE-EVALUATION

We have become accustomed to speaking about the Western
invasion of the Orient, politically, economically, culturally,
religiously. It is true that we are for the time being living through
a drastic modification of the mode of Western invasion,
especially in a political and economic respect. The result is that
the Western world is thrown into an agonizing attempt at
getting rid of its spontaneous thinking and striving in terms
of Western hegemony in the world and of a Western-centred
view of the world. Equally is the Eastern world thrown into a
not less agonizing attempt to get rid of its "underling" resentment and adjust itself to a quite new position of power, possibilities and responsibility in the world cacophony of to-day.
The two situations can be summed up in a single phrase which
sounds harmless but is full of explosive and auspicious
possibilities: Orient and Occident are both in a process of re-
evaluation of themselves and of one another.

The understandable tendency to dwell on the significance of
the "Western invasion" and its still incalculable effects in the
Orient should, however, not induce us to forget that we have

more and more cause for being aware of the "Eastern invasion" in the West, especially from the cultural and religious point of view. Perhaps for a good long time—let us say till the end of the First World War—we were entitled to speak of a skirting of the Occident by the Orient. Nowadays, however, we should speak of a growing "Eastern invasion". An invasion occasioned by increased activity taken on Eastern initiative, and not less by a subterranean sensitivity of Western minds to Eastern modes of thinking and reacting. In the development of the theme of this book I will return to both aspects in greater detail.

These two different modes of cross-current "invasion" are happening within a context which has world dimensions and which lends it a peculiar acuteness. The great rendezvous of different cultures and religions, of social and economic structures, of races and peoples, with their different standards, norms and conceptions of truth and value, necessarily implies a deep feeling of relativity and distortion of judgment in regard to truth and value. This feeling of relativity and distortion pervades the whole spiritual atmosphere of our day and insinuates itself into everybody's mind, either as a paralysing or as a broadening factor in the outlook of the children of our time. It is, in many cases, experienced as a dark menace against an impregnable position one has tried to build for oneself, leaving it to the "experts" of one's own persuasion to meet the difficulties. Even the huge paroxysms of totalitarianism, with their ferocious dogmatisms, are to a great extent a response to this general atmosphere, and so witness to its all-pervasiveness.

Plurality of religions has always been a fact, but has only very rarely been realized not simply as a concrete, evident reality but also at the same time as a relativization of all standards. In short, as a tormenting philosophical questioning of the tenability of ultimate, universally valid norms. It is the great and painful privilege of our period of history that the plurality of religions and normative standards of truth and value in other fields than religion proper presses itself upon us in an inescapable way. However, not only in regard to its massiveness, but also in regard to its intensity, this phenomenon manifests an unprecedented degree of power. The majority of people sense it and give evidence of it in different ways, sometimes patently significant, sometimes seemingly insignificant, but nevertheless on closer inspection often highly significant. Many, in the mood of a would-be tolerance, of indifference, throw out the question whether it is not absurd to keep confidently to the truth of one's own religion as inherited by the accident of birth, whereas it is a patent fact that when adherents of alien cultures and religions live in our own neighbourhood, different "truths" and standards of value are upheld as *the* truth.

Most of the leading writers to-day, particularly when they treat human problems, for the solution of which they lean heavily on the industrious investigations of "scientific" workers, start from this relativity as a self-evident assumption. So everybody may be said to inhale this relativist atmosphere. The revival of determined attempts to find a new world of universally valid, normative reality, is in my view mainly an effort to exorcize the pernicious, and ultimately nihilistic, consequences, to which this atmosphere logically tends.

With special regard to religion it cannot be denied that many of those who are considered authorities in the Science of Religion, or in ethnology, or cultural anthropology, either assume or inculcate in their books the validity of this relativity as a thing taken for granted. Everything conspires to make our time a storm-centre for a revolution of mankind. In the West it is still more complicated by the fact that often this pervasive relativity, which fosters more an attitude of placid superiority than of anxious concern, coalesces with an often ill-concealed resentment against and criticism of Western culture and religion, i.e. Christianity. It behaves like a kind of delicious self-castigation.

Another feature of the general context in which the meeting of cultures and religions moves is a striking difference in attitude between Orient and Occident in this whole matter. It is important to pay special attention to it, because it is relevant to our main contention. Although a grand-scale dialogue is of the essence of real meeting, it is still undecided within the configuration of our time whether we are heading for a genuine attempt at dialogue or are in for a competition in self-assertiveness.

The peculiar thing about the West, alongside a large amount of ignorance and indifference, is that one cannot but remark a growing interest in alien cultures and religions. The magnificent exhibitions in modern museums, displaying all forms of art, are provided with clear, succinct descriptions of the religious and cultural background of these alien art-forms. They represent education in the history of religion and culture in capsule form. Henri de Lubac in his noteworthy book: *La rencontre du Bouddhisme et de l'Occident* (1952),[1] rightly adduces, as a sign of Europe's ripeness for a spiritual colonization by the East, a fact which he expresses in the words: "To give only one example of it, easily verifiable: there is no shelf more patronized in bookshops, even sometimes in Catholic bookshops, than the shelf of books on 'Indian' spirituality at all levels, and no bookshops more frequented than those that specialize in this same field."

This publishing activity is mainly a result of Western initiative, and to a great extent the efforts at spreading trustworthy information and fair understanding are also Western. The Western quest for truth and knowledge, which is such an outstanding characteristic of Western culture, is certainly one of the motive forces in this striking movement.[2]

There are also, within the general atmosphere of relativity, other factors. A weariness with one's own cultural and religious world; a nostalgia for the exotic; a vague, nomadic, cultural and religious cosmopolitism of the spiritual isolationists from the West. There is, however, something far more puzzling and important, which has greater significance than the bookshop shelves to which Father de Lubac has pointed. There is evident in the fields of pictorial art, of novels, of thinking and of depth-psychology, a kind of premonition. They manifest a spontaneous openness, *a readiness to be invaded*, to become "spiritually colonized" by the Orient. There are open "gates" for an Eastern invasion, a *pénétration pacifique*, in the forms of dispositions and needs of mind, of intuitions, which are transparently expressed in the thinking of the Orient. I have already hinted once at this trend. In the course of the argument of this book I will deal specifically with it, and at length, as it seems to me that this remarkable fact has not yet been appreciated in its true and profound significance.

[1] p. 274, note 46.
[2] Cf. Denis de Rougemont's stimulating book: *Man's Western Quest*, 1957 (the French title is *L'aventure occidentale*).

ATTITUDE OF THE ORIENT

Compared with what has been said so far about the kind and manifestations of the spiritual *curiosité* of the Occident in regard to the Orient, it is not unfair to say that the attitude of the Orient is, generally speaking, quite different. The reasons for this difference are inherent in the situation of the Orient, which is not, like the Occident, in the crisis of a critical re-appraisal of its fundamental bases and concepts. The Orient is in the crisis of an expectant re-appraisal of its own spiritual resources as the means for a brighter future of self-respecting statehood and nationhood in the great concert of peoples. Western civilization is to the East mainly a quarry of usable materials for its own benefit, not a world of spiritual discovery. This also is inherent in its peculiar situation, just as is the rather aggressive cultural and religious self-assertion the Orient manifests at present. The political predicament which now exists in regard to Occident and Orient, although for the time being extremely embittering, is, in the wider context of the theme of this book, of a secondary nature.

For all these reasons there is great activity in the Orient to gain further information about, and understanding of, its own cultural and religious resources, and of its vital, immediate, social and economic problems. The severe self-criticism in the West, which often develops even morbid tendencies, does not find at present any parallel in the East. Taking things as they are, this relative lack of receptivity, in the deeper sense, is wholly understandable. Consequently there is hardly any Oriental activity or initiative to furnish trustworthy information about and fair understanding of Western culture and religion, i.e. Christianity. In so far as it exists, it is accomplished either by the publishing efforts of Christian Missions or by the many private or Western-governmental organizations for information and propaganda.

This book is written from a definitely Christian standpoint and therefore ultimately will make an endeavour to offer a Christian interpretation. This needs to be said with some emphasis, because most books which attempt an understanding evaluation of the meeting of cultures and religions are written from a humanist background of whatever variety of humanism, for humanism is a house with many mansions, just as the Christian Church is. I hope to show that to write and interpret from a distinctly Christian background, with a fair knowledge of the facts, about this fascinating meeting of cultures and religions is as biased or unbiased an effort as any humanist attempt pretends to be. Because of this consciously Christian attempt to deal with the matter, some fundamental remarks for the sake of clarification of my concern and purpose are still essential in this opening chapter.

THE DIFFERENCE BETWEEN EASTERN RELIGIONS AND CHRISTIANITY

My whole view will be pervaded by two dominant ideas, not always expressed or stressed. The first is that, in my opinion, it must always be kept in mind that in the great Asian religious-cultural systems (particularly of India and China, and consequently of Japan) the organic indissoluble unity, or, to put it somewhat differently, the symbiosis of culture and religion belongs to their essence, and determines their fundamental character.

The ultimate reason for this fact is that these systems are colossal and imposing outgrowths of the archaic or primitive systems of cosmic naturalism, which we find through the whole of South and South-Eastern Asia even as far as the remote islands of Indonesia and Melanesia (especially New Guinea). In Christianity we find a quite different situation. Of course, it is undeniable that we can point out in the history of Western-Christian civilization many instances of a far-reaching symbiosis of religion (in these cases some form of Christianity) and culture. Yet, when we penetrate to the core of the Christian faith and observe closely the cultural-religious history of the West, it is evident that in Christianity itself there is hidden a fundamental stubbornness and aloofness, which makes for an unavoidable tension; a detached "distance" in regard to culture as the field of human creativity.[1]

This essential, given tension is the cause of the many conflicts

[1] This innate detachment has its cause in the prophetic-apostolic nature of biblical revelation in which Christianity has its roots. Everything creaturely, however sublime, is under the perennial judgment of God, condemning as well as healing and blessing, which implies the relativity of everything human and historical before God's tribunal. This is a relativism of a purely religious kind, utterly different from the cultural and philosophical relativism referred to above.

between Christianity and culture in the course of history. These conflicts may have been the result of a misunderstanding of itself by a concrete form of Christianity, or of a right self-understanding; but in both cases their deepest cause was hidden in Christianity's essential nature, which implies —in contradistinction from the great Eastern religions—a complete emancipation from or a complete loss of cosmic naturalism.

In stressing this deep difference between the Eastern systems and Christianity it is not in the least intended to maintain that Christianity, when taken in its essential meaning, has no positive relation to culture, as the words about inherent "stubbornness" and "aloofness" might suggest. It certainly has a very positive relation to culture, as innate as the detachment referred to, and for the same reasons. This positive relation even is a peculiar aspect of its fundamental critical tension, because its critical salt if true to its nature is at the same time creative judgment and creative invigoration. If this peculiar salt in Christianity is half or wholly insipid, the tension between Christianity and culture is a false, unfruitful tension, harmful both to Christianity in its essence and historical manifestation and to culture. In these harmful cases the Christian Church has misunderstood its own real nature and misinterpreted its "distance" from the universe of culture.

NEW IMPACT OF WESTERN CULTURE

In the second place, the other guiding idea in the theme of this book is that Western culture, as far as I can see, is not at the end of its impact on its contemporary confrères, but is entering on a new lease of impact. At the moment it seems rather preposterous to make this assertion. There is at present in the Oriental world quite clearly a kind of revulsion from the impact of Western civilization and a harking back to its own roots and heritage. Taking into account the political tensions and the resentments against Western dominance in the colonial past, this revulsion is not at all strange or a matter for dismayed amazement. This revulsion against the Occident does not diminish the desire in the Orient to acquire those Western skills and achievements, especially in the field of technology and social techniques. This may seem contradictory to the rather vociferous revulsion. Yet I am inclined to maintain my thesis about the advent of a deeper-going effect of Western culture and its dominant principles in the future, particularly on the ground that the real dialogue between the great cultures and religions has still to begin.

In this book I propose to touch more than once upon the question in what sense and measure Western culture, in its essential meaning, has been received and digested by the great Oriental peoples under the hateful shadow of Western political and economic dominance. It is not too sanguine to expect, when the irritations and resentments of to-day have subsided, that a new curiosity, a new openness for the true "secret" of Western culture and its peculiar dynamism will awaken unhampered by the hateful shadow. It would seem not unnatural that thoughtful people in the Orient should begin to understand that one cannot in the long run merely *use* certain typical achievements of Western civilization as mere tools without understanding and acquiring the *spirit* out of which they were born.

This consideration is corroborated by the fact that the "crisis" in the West inevitably impels towards self-examination, and a re-interpretation of its meaning and significance for the world at large. Such re-interpretation will receive much light from the West's encounter with the East in the last 150 years. The singularity and universality of Western culture as it has developed in Europe has still a very significant rôle to play, if it remains faithful to its peculiar genius. America, which is, at the same time, an autonomous and very significant *mutation* of European culture (quite a different thing from the current superficial conception of it as an offshoot of European culture) has also to be taken into full consideration. Particularly because America shows a special type of reaction on its meeting with Oriental cultures and religions, and is itself searching for an entirely new type of culture.

QUESTIONS FOR CHRISTIANITY

Our special concern is twofold. First, to find some answers to specific Christian questions such as: *what* is it that the Christian Church, with her peculiar message and calling, will have to face? *How* should she face this coming dialogue? And also, *how* should she express in that situation her inherent missionary nature, which under no condition can she ever surrender?

It is necessary to formulate and answer these questions un-equivocally, because as yet they have not risen above the horizon of the Church(es). Nor have they really entered into the perspective of the Churches' professional thinkers, the theologians, who have not yet realized that the thing they have to face in a near future is something else and something more than coming somehow to terms with the results of the Science of Religion and having done that (either along an orthodox or a liberal line) turning to what they consider· their proper occupation. Here, to use Toynbeean terms again, arises for the Church and the theologians the imperious demand to leave all parochialism and regionalism aside and ascend to a yet unknown dimension of world-embracing mundial thinking.

Second, to show the specific Christian ferment and dynamism in Western culture, even in its present secularized form, and to find out the fundamental orientation of the Eastern religious-cultural patterns with their patent contrasts and hidden affinities to the "Christian" West.

The central issue in this coming dialogue with the grand, elusive Eastern systems of *humanist* thinking will, it seems, be to vindicate the *personal* conception of the living God as manifest in Jesus Christ, and the meaning and purpose of Man and the World in the light of God's self-disclosure in the historical Jesus Christ. The keyword of Oriental humanistic philosophies is Harmony. In this respect they betray again that they are impressive elaborations of the fundamental aspirations and tendencies of the universal, primitive, archaic systems of life and the.world, centring around the harmony of man, nature and cosmos and glossing over the glaring disharmonies in man's inner and outer life.

This vindication in the face of, and in dialogue with, the fascinating religious philosophies of the East is a far more arduous enterprise than Christianity has ever experienced in its meeting in history with so-called classical Humanism. Classical Humanism is in comparison with the Humanisms of the East a respectable but rather pale affair. The only point of comparison to be found in Church history is the renowned struggle of the Church with Gnosticism. In my opinion the coming dialogue will, if anything, most certainly imply a new dialogue and combat with Gnosticism, but in a wholly new setting. It is worth while to note that the Gnosticism of the past was of an essentially Eastern temper.

To preclude misunderstanding I stress the point that in using the words "the personal conception", etc., I have not at all in mind an apology of a so-called theism over against the impersonal conceptions of the East. That would simply mean that the biblical conception of the living qualitative God as manifest in Jesus Christ is one form of Theism. In fact it is a category of its own. This implies, in contradistinction to the impersonal quality-less Eastern "Divine Ultimate", the super-personal character of God.

In saying this I am not making the same point as Paul Tillich makes with his category of the "trans-personal", in the interest of his ontological bias. What I mean by saying "super-personal" is, though maintaining unequivocally the personal character of God, to show due awareness of the fact that we only know God as He has revealed and disclosed Himself. We do not know Him in His essential being. The only thing we can say about it is, not that He is the supreme or ultimate ὄν, but that God the Hidden, who sustains and gives life to all, is a holy Mystery of Adorableness. The philosophical τὸ ὄν and the impersonal *nirguna* (quality-less) Brahma of the Orient are a different category.

I have also purposely inserted the expression "the historical Jesus Christ", to indicate the unsurrenderable historical character of Christianity over against the emphatically non-historical bias of the Eastern religious philosophies; a fact which (and we should face this unflinchingly) *philosophically* speaking seems to put Christianity at the outset in a weak position. In regard to Harmony and Disharmony it is the peculiar trait of biblical religion to face the Disharmony in man and the world realistically. Islamic religion and culture are a quite different proposition. Islam, by its origin and by its development as a religious-cultural and political factor of great magnitude, moreover by its propinquity with the Western "Christian" world, has with Christianity a contradictory relation of kinship and deep difference and animosity. This fact makes the problem and the "dialogue" of Islam and Christianity a difficult and intricate one, which calls for great discernment and understanding, and consequently for a treatment wholly different from that of the great Asian cultures and religions.

Chapter Two

THE RELATIONS OF EASTERN CULTURES AND RELIGIONS WITH THE WEST IN THE PAST

THE meeting and interpenetration of cultures as specific expressions of human life, creativity and mood, and as specific ways of living together, is one of the most fascinating subjects in the field of historical study. It is a meeting and crossing of different *curricula vitae* with their material substratum and their metaphysical orientation.

This phenomenon of the meeting of cultures belongs to the life-blood of mankind, in spite of the many factors in human history which seem to hamper and frustrate it and yet have often stimulated it. Such factors are geographical barriers, political conflicts, or the strong introvert tendency which is inherent in all peoples and their cultural attitude. That tendency produces the kind of spontaneous xenophobia which is such a universal human trait. Without this exchange of material goods and spiritual seeds and patterns, without this spiritual free trade, civilization would ossify into forms of human community resembling the buried cities that have been excavated and brought to light in reasonably undamaged condition. Toynbee, in his classification of cultures, has rightly reserved a place for the category of "arrested civilizations".

CULTURAL CONTACTS IN HISTORY

The occurrence and importance of cultural contact in the course of history have been far greater than we often know or imagine. The methodical investigations of the so-called *kulturgeschichtliche* school in cultural anthropology (formerly known as ethnology) have shown the great significance of migrations and reception of foreign material and spiritual

26

cultural elements even in prehistoric times, taking place on a grand scale between all the five continents. These fascinating movements took place in a period when the distinction between East and West as two different, representative types of apprehension and orientation did not yet operate in the sense in which it came to be conceived, after the conflict of Greece and the Persian Empire. Archaeological research, which has especially in the last fifty years been conducted so successfully in Central Asia and different parts of Europe, that modest promontory of Asia (cap de l'Asie), has demonstrated the existence of trade contacts and of artistic and idea export from Asia to Europe and vice versa.[1]

These interactions of great civilizations across land- or sea-routes, particularly in the field of ceramics, point to a regular contact. Occasional Western-influenced objects appear, for instance in China in the late Chou period (between 1000 and 700 B.C.).[2] To keep to China, the penetration of Nestorian Christian missionary activity in Central Asia and in China during the T'ang Dynasty, which was one of the highlights of Chinese civilization in the days of the European "Dark Ages", and later on, in the 13th century, of Franciscan missionary activity during the Mongol Dynasty, are remarkable feats of daring. To mention some examples from antiquity, it is appropriate to remind ourselves e.g. of Herodotus (484-425 B.C.), who evinced already the typical Western intellectual curiosity in his interesting accounts of "barbarian" religions (Egypt, Persia, Scythia, Thrace) and speculated on their origin and their relation to Greek myths and cults. One of the greatest historical achievements in cultural and religious contact and interaction between East and West was, as is well known, accomplished by the conquest and genius of Alexander the Great. It caused the emergence of the great melting-pot of Eastern, Greek and Mediterranean cultures and cults, which lasted in its effects till the 5th century of our era. Oriental Hellenistic culture remained for nearly seven centuries the culture pattern in the context of which the huge trend of religious syncretism in the Roman Empire of the Caesars arose,

[1] Compare for instance the two interesting Bulletins of the Royal Ontario Museum of Archaeology of Toronto (No. 19 in 1952 and No. 21 in 1953) respectively called: "East-West" and "West-East".

[2] Cf. Bulletin No. 19, p. 1.

27

and the great rival of Christianity, viz. Mithraism, spread everywhere over Europe where the Roman legions maintained peace and order.

Both Christianity and Islam were born and developed within the realm of Oriental-Hellenistic culture. Here lies the reason why Islam as a religious and cultural structure of life, which at present is commonly felt as belonging to the "East" and put, fundamentally speaking, outside the "Western" orbit, is, historically speaking, closely related to the Greek heritage, which is one of the main basic sources of the "West".

Another remarkable result of a synthesis of "East" and "West" in artistic respect, of Greek and Oriental, presents itself in Buddhist iconography, particularly in the statue of the Buddha, which has spread all over the Buddhist world—even as far as Indonesia by the influence of the so-called Gandhara art, which originated in the Kingdom of Gandhara on the confines of India. Although the origin and growth of the Mahayanist wing of Buddhism are still in many respects obscure (a fact which should caution us against too speculative conclusions about religious and cultural contacts, above all between India and the West in the ages around the beginning of the Christian era) it is nevertheless not at all improbable that in the melting-pot of Alexander's making, Western (in this case Christian) influences may have contributed to various elements and peculiar tones of religious emphasis in Mahayanism.[1]

The opinion, often stressed, that Christianity—notwithstanding the strong Western imprint it received in the course of its development—is by birthright a fruit of the East, is justified in relation to geography and to the growing up of

[1] A daunting example of too easy speculation and of a slipshod handling of the subtle matter of cultural and religious interaction is to be found in Arnold Toynbee's *Study of History* and particularly in *Civilization on Trial* (p. 219). Just because of the authority attributed to Toynbee in these matters, a word of protest is required. It is nothing less than careless and inexact to assert that Christianity was born "from a marriage between two [Graeco-Roman and Syrian] cultures". Leaving all other criticism aside, the simple fact that he is absolutely silent about Israel's place in the genesis of Christianity reveals the levity of this construction. It is misleading when in the same context Toynbee declares Christianity, Islam, Hinduism and Mahayanism products of the encounter of Greek-Roman civilization and its contemporaries, and it is really preposterous to characterize Christianity and Mahayanism as non-violent and Islam and Hinduism as violent responses to Greek-Roman civilization. This is bad history and an even worse treatment of cultural and religious problems.

Christianity in the Mediterranean world, of which the Eastern basin was the cultural pivot of the Roman Empire. (Israel is situated in this respect on the borderline of East and West.) As an exhaustive explanation it is tenable only from an immanent view of history. Its authentic nature escapes the categories of East or West.

The long period of cultural and spiritual interaction inaugurated by Alexander's adventures came in most respects to a standstill after the downfall of the Roman Empire. The period of the barbarian invasions (5th-8th centuries), which preceded the time-span known as Europe's Dark Ages (8th-12th centuries), does not, however, show a complete breakdown of East-West relations in the orbit of Oriental-Hellenistic-Roman civilization centred around the Mediterranean, consciously called *mare nostrum*.

H. Pirenne in his book *Mohammed and Charlemagne* has irrefutably proved this thesis: that although the barbarian invasions and settlements, especially in the Western part of the Roman Empire, caused politically a curtailment of the direct political power of the Roman Emperor, the idea of his all-comprising sovereignty remained intact (except in the Vandal Kingdom in the Western part of North Africa) and the interactions between East and West in economic, cultural and religious respect functioned nearly as well as before the 5th century. With the Mediterranean world on all its four sides, the Roman Empire constituted one world, an oecumenè of East and West, of which Constantinople was the natural and recognized centre.

In an equally brilliant way Pirenne has established his second thesis that the catastrophic end of Late Antiquity (*die Spätantike*) with its cultural ecumenity transcending all national and racial differences, did not happen by a process of decadence (although there was decadence) but was caused suddenly and abruptly by the lightning-like appearance of Islam in the 7th century. This lightning-like character is vividly portrayed in the fact that by Heraclius' victory over Persia after a long struggle, in 627, Byzantium's prestige and future seemed assured. Ten years later, by the Muslim onrush, which nobody could have foreseen, the Roman Empire had lost Syria, Palestine, and Mesopotamia. Five years later Egypt and North

Africa were lost to them also. A formidable rival, impelled by the force of a political religion and lust for booty, turned the world upside down.

The Mongol invasions were as lightning-like, but they were short-lived. Islam was, however, not to be a passing meteor, but stayed and still lasts. It meant a complete break-up of the unified Mediterranean world, and the equally complete change of the religious, political and economic map of those days. *Mare nostrum* as a cultural and political entity sank into oblivion. It became a field of fierce conflict and piracy. Through Islam's extraordinarily rapid conquests the Roman Empire shrank together into a Byzantine Empire, limited to the North-Eastern basin of the Mediterranean. Christianity virtually lost its territories in Asia Minor and North Africa, and this great orbit which comprised its spiritual centre no longer gravitated towards Byzantium but towards Baghdad, the capital of the Muslim Empire.

The world-historical significance of Islam is that it broke forth from the deserts of insignificant Arabia and for religious and political reasons arose as the implacable opponent of the European "Christian" world. The sudden emergence and progress of Islam was the cause of Christianity's practical confinement to Europe, which has had such momentous consequences for its development as a seemingly "Western" religion and culture. Except that Byzantium within its shrinking borders acted till the fall of Constantinople in 1453 as the bastion of Christendom and the shield of Europe against an increasing submergence of Europe by Islam, the Western Christian world abandoned (had to abandon) its orientation towards the Mediterranean and replaced it by an orientation towards North-Western Europe, with the Carolingian Empire as its initial nucleus. The Middle Ages began on an agrarian and feudal basis, which religiously and culturally gave to the Church a tutorial and paternalist stamp.

ISLAM AND CHRISTIANITY—FRATERNAL ENEMIES

The *corpus Islamicum* and the *corpus Christianum*, each according to its own genius and to its peculiar historical situation, constituted two blocs, in a religious and political sense necessarily antagonistic. Nevertheless in a cultural and even religious respect they were, in a way, fraternal enemies, because as cultural-religious systems they had been nourished in the orbit of Oriental-Hellenistic civilization. As religion they comprised, within their irreconcilable fundamental difference and contrast, cognate elements, because Islam originated in an atmosphere determined by Christian and Jewish notions and ideas. Hence the Church Father John Damascene, who lived in the 7th century under Muslim dominance, regarded the new, successful religion as a Christian heresy. Harnack[1] concluded, after having in his youth conceived it equally as a Christian sect, that closer comparison had to lead to a modification of this view; viz. Islam is in his opinion a transformation of Judaism as altered by the influence of gnostic Judaistic Christianity, reproduced by a great prophet in Arabian form. Others regard it as a mutation of Judaism. These opinions are only mentioned here to substantiate the idea that Islam, Christianity and Judaism are undeniably fraternal enemies, that is to say fundamentally different and inimical, but fraternal because of many traits of family likeness.

The historical considerations and comparative endeavours which have led to these conjectures are certainly not devoid of value, but they do not indicate in any measure the mystery which is hidden in these three religions of revelation, and in their mutual relations. However, it is not the place here to enter into this riddle, which is inaccessible as well to history as to philosophy, and which can only be approached with some profit along the path of theology.

The *corpus Islamicum* and *Christianum*, as they appeared in what is commonly called the Middle Ages, can be characterized not only as fraternal enemies but as participators in a community of fate (*Schicksalsgenossen*). Although both enclosed in their respective "worlds", they could not but be aware of and count with one another, by political and religious compulsion. Till the opening of the Gaman period in Asia, which was the beginning of the Great Discoveries of the 15th and 16th centuries and which in fact began, through the Portuguese expeditions of Henry the Navigator, by circumventing the huge Islamic barrier between Europe and India, the Muslim world represented, for the Western world, "the East" in the

---

[1] *Lehrbuch der Dogmengeschichte*, II⁴, pp. 529-538. (E.T. *History of Dogma*.)

sense it is used in this book, unaware of the fact that by its likeness of structure the Western world itself resembled more the
East than the West in the classical Greek sense.

The Western world for the time being was mainly confined
to North-Western Europe and Italy. The Muslim world on the
one hand was a broad belt, shutting off Europe from the
Farther Eastern world. Only occasionally some daring individuals slipped through, such as the Franciscan Wilhelm
Rubruk and the Dominican di Monte Corvino in the 13th
century to convert the Mongol Khans in Karakorum, hesitating
between Islam, Christianity and Buddhism; or the layman
Marco Polo; all bringing back their wondrous tales. On the
other hand the Muslim world constituted the only possibility
for a meeting of East and West.

The causes which led to some extremely important contacts
are manifold. The most important were the inroads of Muslim
power and culture in the Iberian Peninsula, in Sicily and some
parts of Italy; the Crusades, which paradoxically were in
motive a Christian "Holy War" (*Gesta Dei per Francos*), but also
a military and political conflict, yet engendering an amount of
cultural contact as a by-product which had great consequences
for the future; the acquisitive economic instinct which drove
mercantile republics like Venice and Genoa to trade with this
inimical world, which was the transit-region for the greatly
coveted spices and luxuries of India and the Far East; the
sporadic but intense feeling of missionary responsibility in men
like Francis of Assisi and Raymond Lull, and which produced
centres of prodigious Oriental learning.

It is important to mention the striking fact that, although the
"West" in the confined sense just indicated was by its historical
configuration, generally speaking, the inferior of the Muslim
East in cultural respect, nevertheless this meeting and contact
of East and West took place, in the main, on the initiative and
out of the *curiosité* of the European Westerners. The rather
uncouth Europeans in their state of adolescence met with the
more urbane but supercilious East as represented in the
Islamic world.

This meeting of West and East (almost exclusively in the
form of the "house of Islam" in the Middle Ages) has had a
particular significance. For this reason it is necessary to look

at it with special attention and discernment. Europe and the Muslim world are perennially one another's opposite neighbour. We have at present entered a stage of history in which the Muslim world has to play, in a different setting from before, a rôle of world importance in which the European West and Islam will be confronted with one another in a way which requires that "meeting" becomes "dialogue". The mediaeval contact and meeting, though its cultural effects were of great value, at any rate for the West, never became a dialogue. It could not become one, because the political and religious or rather (in this case) ideological conflict went too deep and had to be carried out in an atmosphere too heavily laden with emotion and fanatic passion.[1]

THE MEDIAEVAL MEETING

By way of introduction to our analysis, a question of terms must first be settled. It is customary to speak about this mediaeval event of contact in terms like: the influence of Islam, or of Muslim culture (words we have been using ourselves) or of Arab civilization on mediaeval Europe. Contemporary Muslim apologists especially do this with great emphasis and satisfaction. This emphasis is quite understandable in the light of the fact that these apologists, after a long period of decadence and degradation of the "house of Islam", are sincerely happy to rediscover the ancient cultural glory of the Muslim world and its superiority over the West in the Middle Ages. Often they go to the length of implying that modern science and all the achievements of the West in the last centuries are, historically speaking, due to the cultural impulse of Islam in the Middle Ages. However, non-Muslim writers as well often write in a kindred vein, not as in the case of many modern apologists out of their joy of regaining new self-confidence and self-respect, but from the need they feel to do historical justice to the Muslim world and to impress upon the intellectuals of the West its indebtedness to the Muslim world and its inordinate feeling of superiority. For these two reasons a clarification of terms is necessary in order to know what we are talking about in

[1] The impasse between the Muslim and "Christian" worlds has much similarity with that between "East" and "West" in the sense in which these terms are now used for the present great political division.

regard to the highly interesting cultural meeting of the "Christian" and Muslim world, especially in the 13th century.

In the Preface to the volume "The Legacy of Islam" the following passage shows the right way to accomplish this necessary clarification:[1]

> In the Legacy of Islam we do not treat of the Legacy of the religion of Muhammad qua religion; the reader will learn from this book that there is little that is *peculiarly* Islamic in the contributions which occidental and oriental Muslims have made to European culture. . . . Islam is the fundamental fact which made the Legacy possible. It is under the protection and patronage of the Islamic Empire that the arts and sciences which this book describes flourished.

To express it more explicitly: the terms Muslim or Arab civilization, as the donor of stimulants to mediaeval Europe in a cultural respect, convey the wrong impression—as if it were Islam as a religion[2] or the Arabs as a people that were the real carriers of the cultural influences.

It is just as if the present influence of Western civilization in the East were to be ascribed to Christianity as a religion, because Christianity is the dominant religion of the West, or to the Anglo-Saxon peoples because English is the main language-vehicle of the West as Arabic was the language-vehicle of the Muslim Empire. In fact, Islam as a religion was not the producer or bearer of the cultural influences and contributions that came from the territory where Islam was the dominant religion. The Arabs were only a small minority of the men who influenced mediaeval Europe.[3] What these men transmitted was Hellenistic learning and philosophy in Arab form, enriched or modified in some respects by their own labours, which represented more than merely digested material. The only qualification that must be made to this statement is that Muslim theological thinking, as the reader will see below,

---

[1] p. v. In the "Legacy" series, Oxford University Press.

[2] Philosophy was in the orbit of the "house of Islam" an *esoteric* affair and the philosophers exercised it as such, because state and religion required this attitude. This esoteric conception of philosophy implied that religion was exoteric and inferior.

[3] In the later part of this chapter it will become clear that pure Arabs were few and far between in the band of Muslim scholars and philosophers. The most prominent was al-Kindi, called the Arab philosopher (d. 873).

certainly became known in Europe and played, through the keen intellectual avidity of the scholastics of Europe, a rôle in the development of Western scholastic theology. The Arabic version of Neo-platonism was for a short time stimulating and disturbing European theological/philosophical discussion in the 13th century.[1]

In order to get as firm a grasp as possible on this particular instance of cultural contact, it must be kept in mind that besides the Crusades, which set in motion a stream of culture-contact and of receptivity and efforts to acquire the tools for studying Arab books on the European side, the main centres from which this cultural and philosophical/theological fertilization of mediaeval Europe irradiated were Sicily and the Iberian Peninsula. The Crusades meant culturally a contact of the West with Palestinian and Syrian Islam, but this contact was inferior in results compared to those with Spain and the culture-bridge, Sicily.

CULTURAL CONTACT IN LANGUAGE

The most convenient way to start a short essay on the vital and portentous meeting of the mediaeval "Christian" West with the Oriental and Occidental Islam is to take a quick glance at international words in European languages, which vividly illustrate this cultural contact.[2]

They point to material goods, imported from the Muslim Orient and becoming universally used; to military equipment, quite understandable from the continuous conflicts on sea and land; to the arts and craftsmanship; to commercial and financial transactions, in which is manifest that the Islamic world was heir to the high development of Hellenistic-Roman business forms and of the arts, introduced in the backward society of the time, following the higher techniques of the 8th century. They point also to the care with which inquisitive Europeans of those days studied the Arabic works on astronomy and mathematics. Our word "coffee" derives from *qahwa*,

[1] *The Legacy of Islam* leaves this point on one side in the sentence quoted from its Preface, although in the book itself there is a chapter on "Philosophy and Theology".

[2] In this matter and in what follows I am greatly indebted to the careful studies collected in *The Legacy of Islam*, to De Lacy O'Leary's *Arabic Thought and its Place in History*, G. E. von Grünebaum, and many more. There are, however, still masses of material on this subject hidden in unpublished manuscripts.

originally meaning wine, but in Yemen applied to the drink which came to be called coffee; the beverage "punch", which gets its name from Persian "punch" = 5, because of the 5 ingredients of which it was composed; "tea", originally a Chinese word and product, found its way to Europe in Turkish garb. The well-known word "arsenal" stems from Arabic *alsina'a*, i.e. handicraft. Our admirals take their name from the abbreviated title of the Commander of the Faithful, viz. *amir al-mu' minīn*.

Paper, a Chinese invention, came to Europe by the intermediary of Muslim Samarkand, Baghdad and Spain (in that country there were paper-factories) and is delivered in a quantity called a "ream". This word directly derives from mediaeval Latin *risma*, which goes back through Spain to Arabic *rizma*. Our "lute" has its original form in Arabic *al'ūd* (=piece of wood); our "guitar", although the original word for it is Greek *kitharon*, got its name through Spanish *guitarra*, which was derived from the Arabic form *gitāra* for *kitharon*; our "tambourine" and "tambour" hail back to Arabic *tanbūr* and can be traced back to Provence (Southern France), which has been an interesting meeting-place of the West with the finer arts of life from the Muslim Orient, as is proved also by "troubadour" (from Ar. *tarrūb*) and our word "mask" which comes from Spanish *mascara* and represents in its Spanish form Ar. *maschara*, i.e. a minstrel, a jester.

In astronomy and mathematics the following remarks may suffice: our word "cipher" is Ar. *sifr*=nought, zero[1]; our figures are derived from the Arabic ones, which had their origin in India; "algebra" is Ar. *al-jabr*; "logarithm" is a term made from the name of the famous Muslim mathematician al-Khwarizmi (from Turkestan); our "x" for an imaginary, unnamed number is the Ar. word (through the mediaeval form *xei*) *shay'*=thing; "cheque" is a Persian word and is with many others, which we still use in our financial vocabulary, an indication of the fact that the Eastern merchants in the Middle Ages introduced many simplifying devices in financial transactions into Western Europe; "zenith" and "nadir" are

[1] "Zero" is an alteration of the same word, which was so significant because the o added to the ordinary numbers heightened their value ten times, and was therefore an astounding and simple device.

alterations of the Ar. words *assamt* (= the way) and *nādir*, i.e. the opposite (viz. of "zenith"); the word "azimuth" equally derives from the Ar. plural of *assamt* (viz. *assumūt* = the ways). The game called *Schach* in German and "chess" in English goes back to Persian *shāh* = king, the principal piece of the play. It came to Europe from India (called there *caturangga* = square) through Persia (where it was called *shatranj*, a distortion of Sanskrit *caturangga*) and by the Arabic-speaking world was transmitted, through Spain, to mediaeval[1] Europe.

To these examples could be added many more. They are merely adduced to suggest in an illuminating way the great, enriching influence which the superior world of material, scientific and artistic culture in the garb of the Arabic language exercised on mediaeval Europe.

WHENCE ISLAM'S INFLUENCE?

Taking all this into account, there emerges a question which will lead us to an awareness of the intricate and fascinating ways the history of cultural contacts often takes. The question is: if (as has been said above) Islam as a *religion* and as a religious system with a definite thought and behaviour pattern, is only in a very restricted sense responsible for the indelible cultural influence of the Muslim world on Western Europe in its formative, mediaeval period, whence did this capacity for influence come? The answer to this question requires some detailed attention and an expansion of some views expressed already in general terms above.

Islam arose in Arabia, a culturally backward and insignificant country. When it burst forth from this barren peninsula and flooded within two decades (one of the most astonishing events in world history) the greater part of the Near and Middle East and North Africa, annihilating in the victorious marches of its armies the Persian Empire of the Sassanids, and reducing the Byzantine Empire to less than half its former size, it was a religion whose sole basic document was the Koran.

This book, containing the Prophet's revelations, which set this movement of world-historical significance in motion, is from the standpoint of systematic, dogmatic or mystical

---

[1] King Alfonso the Wise of Toledo in the 13th century wrote the first handbook on chess.

theology only a book of raw materials. In cultural and ethical respect it reflects the urban and Beduin background of Arabian life, but strongly marked by the uplifting and remoulding influence that sprang from Muhammad's endeavours as a religious prophet. As an extraordinarily dynamic leader he shaped a new, religiously-motivated community, to which he proclaimed a legislation based on absolute divine authority.

This movement, as it were blindly impelling its armies towards world conquest, plunged into two highly civilized worlds, that of Persia and that of Byzantium, both based on age-old magnificent cultural traditions. Historically speaking, it did not create a culture but it inherited the Oriental-Hellenistic culture of which Byzantium was the embodiment as building material for creating, within the space of four centuries, Islam as a religious-cultural-social system. Or, to put it differently: the civilization which grew up in Asia and North Africa around the Mediterranean as a result of Alexander the Great's meteoric career, entered through Islam into a new metamorphosis, of which Persian culture became an ingredient also.

The means by which this was done were an extensive activity of translation of the rich Greek heritage in philosophy and the sciences. The Muslim conquerors left the administrative and scientific institutions in Persia and Byzantium intact. For this reason Jundeshapur, Nisibis, Edessa and the Byzantine schools of Alexandria and other places remained centres of scientific activity and of translation. The Umayyad Khalifate of the 7th and 8th centuries took no initiative in this field, but the first century of the Abassid Khalifate, centred in Baghdad (c. 750-850) saw a great activity in the field of translation under the impulse of the first Abassid Khalifs. The first stage was the translation into Arabic of works on Greek philosophy and science from Syrian (or Aramaic), because before the advent of Islam the Eastern-Syrian Nestorians and the Western-Syrian Monophysites had absorbed the Hellenistic heritage by translation into Aramaic. The second stage was direct translation from Greek into Arabic, beginning in the 9th century.

The translators were nearly all Christians, who became the real culture transmitters and so enabled scholarly-minded "Muslims" to deploy their gifts, using as their basis and material

the legacy of Oriental-Greek learning and thought, and adding
their own contributions and apprehension. Eagerness was great.
Men searched sometimes the whole Near and Middle East for
a single Greek manuscript, and the Khalifs paid for it.

Three observations press themselves upon the mind of the
interested student of this fascinating process of the absorption
of Ancient Civilization by the "Muslim" Empire. First, every
aspect of this ancient post-classical civilization embodied in the
great treasure of Greek manuscripts, viz. philosophy, mysticism
or philosophical mysticism, medicine, chemistry, mathematics,
optics, astronomy, geometry, musical theory, etc. was assimi-
lated, digested, and rendered into Arabic, with one important
exception—the great Greek writers and tragedians remained
unnoticed, just as they had been by the Christian Syrian
translators. Greek humanism in its most genuine expression got
no chance to leaven the growing "Muslim" civilization.
Second, the "Arab" scholars and philosophers (belonging to
various nationalities) were in the main transmitters and interpreters of the given material. They were no creators. They kept
to the theoretical productions of the Greek imaginative
creators or interpreters of the sciences and philosophy. They
were continuators. The "Arab" thinkers and scholars (generally
speaking both were combined in one man) added an often
valuable contribution to the inherited store of knowledge and
thought by their striking gifts of observation. For example in
the field of optics the "Arabs" (e.g. al-Hazm) attained to a
degree of excellency far above that of the Greeks. Their
peculiar achievement is the use of figures, algebra as a science,
the development of trigonometry.

Third: Islam as a religion was thus also enabled to build up
a system of ethics and dogmatics founded on the Koran, in
what is called the *fiqh* or Divine Law (*Shari'a*) and *kalām*
(theology proper); a great theological achievement. This
achievement was possible through the intellectual tools the
pre-Islamic Hellenistic civilization afforded. Dogmatics or
kalām is an intellectual fashioning of the Muslim creed by
Greek philosophical means and partly born out of a confrontation with Eastern-Orthodox theology. Christian mysticism played the main rôle in the impressive elaboration of
Muslim mysticism. Theology as such by reason of its primary

39

orientation on Revelation, although it went a long way in rationalist treatment of its problems, naturally lived in tension with all intellectual and spiritual expressions, which made Reason, often combined with mystical intuition, the main norm.

Hence even before, in the 12th century, the heavy hand of stagnation began to weigh on the life of the Muslim peoples, orthodox Islam assumed an attitude of distrust towards the representatives of speculative philosophy, which was in varied forms an Arabic version of Neo-platonist Aristotelianism, and also towards the sciences and their servants. This distrust had as its main ground the philosophical conception of the eternity of the world with its consequences of evaporating the faith in God the Creator and in the divine creation of the world, and the fear that philosophy would undermine religious certitude. Theologians and popular opinion often held the scholars in suspicion, for many scholars had free, critical minds, even nibbling at Ptolemy's authority. This explains why the stimulating "Muslim" cultural influence cannot be identified with Islam as a religion and its theological system.

What has been said up to now proves clearly that the cultural fertilization process of the "Muslim" East on mediaeval Western Europe is a really unique case of cultural contact with great consequences. The only other case which can be put in parallel with it in importance, without minimizing the enormous cultural influence of India in Central, Eastern and South-Eastern Asia, is that of China's cultural stimulus on Japan since the 7th century.

CULTURAL MEETING—THE CRUSADES AND SICILY

On account of its uniqueness (and also for the sake of rectifying the many distorting views which are constantly expressed on this matter by Eastern and Western authors) it is nevertheless necessary to focus it more closely. It has been said above that the irradiation of the "Muslim" East in the mediaeval West had three source areas: the "Muslim" East proper, through the agency of the Crusades; Sicily and Spain, which were the great centres of the "Muslim" West. Here some clear distinctions must be made. There is a tendency to attribute this fertilization process almost entirely to the Crusades. This view is far from historical truth in regard to this whole very complicated case of culture transmission, which was not at all a one-way traffic, but shows innumerable cross-currents and zigzags. To be sure, the Crusades were very important. They brought in their wake not only a manifold cultural fertilization, but also prosperous trade, a new system of credit and finance, a vague presentiment of tolerance and independence from a closed, ideologically bound society and a far-reaching change in the economic and social structure of Western Europe (the decline of feudalism, the growing strength of urban centres and of their leading citizenry). Yet the most fruitful vehicles of cultural influence in its more restricted and elevated sense (philosophy, sciences, letters, etc.) were not the Crusades, but the display of cultural superiority and refinement in Muslim Sicily and Spain, which attracted many Westerners, eager to learn the *artes Arabum*.

The Crusades did not do very much in the transmission of "Arabic" science or philosophy to the West. Western scholastic philosophical theology got especially from Spain the stimulus of the Aristotelianism of the "Arab" philosophers. Sicily and Spain became, particularly after the reconquest of Sicily from the Muslims by Roger the Norman and in Spain after the Christian *reconquista* of Toledo by Alfonso VI in 1087, remarkable areas of cultural meeting and symbiosis. The many names of great "Arab" scholars and philosophers came to the keen, thirsty adolescent minds of Western Europe through Spain. Sicily was above all, after the Norman *reconquista*, mediator of art, as well of the rich "Arab" novelistic literature, in this way stimulating the emergence of the genre of the knightly romances and of poetry, as of the exquisite craftsmanship of the "Muslim" East, which continued in this respect the rich heritage of pre-Muslim Hellenistic-Persian culture.

All this brought refinement of life. Under the Norman dynasty, for example Roger II in Palermo, the court was a centre of cultural symbiosis. "Christian" and "Arab" scholars and artists had a constant encounter with one another. Eastern Muslim patterns of life were incorporated. The court had two harems. The great Hohenstaufen Emperor Frederick II (1215-1250) realized in his court a still more thorough form of cultural symbiosis, even drawing personally, it seems, one of its possible conclusions, that is to say philosophical religious relativism and agnosticism. Through his education he had grown up in an atmosphere of commingling culture ("Arab", Greek-Roman, Norman) and was himself, by his great gifts, a many-sided personality. Public opinion called him *stupor mundi* (the wonder of the world) and suspected him of atheism. He was in regular correspondence with "Arab" philosophers and scholars. He had for instance Aristotle translated into Latin and stimulated in the peninsula of Italy the establishment of academic institutions, teaching "Arab" sciences. He also kept two harems and was buried in a tunic on which were written Arabic inscriptions.

THE SPANISH CULTURAL LABORATORY

Even more enthralling than the story of the cultural and artistic brilliance of Sicily is what happened around Toledo, under the impetus of Alfonso VI. Before entering briefly into the fascinating Spanish cultural laboratory, a few points of great importance should be made by way of preface.

In Toledo, and particularly also in Cordova, the most effective culture transmitters were the "Mozarabs", viz. the *Christians* under Muslim rule in Cordova who led a life preponderantly in "Arab" style and whose language was Arabic. They kept harems, practised circumcision, applied themselves to Arab literature and sciences. Many of them went to the North, to Toledo, and exercised there the same influence as cultural transmitters. Corresponding to the progress of the Christian *reconquista* it was on the contrary the "Mudejar", viz. the Muslims under Christian rule, who spread "Arab" influence in dress, commerce, agriculture and craftsmanship. The Jews were equal or often even superior to the "Mozarab" and "Mudejar" in this process of cultural meeting and syncretism. The time in which all this developed and took place between Occidental "Islam" and Europe was (contrary to what one would expect) also the period of the beginning of the degeneration and stagnation in the Oriental "Muslim" world (12th and 13th centuries) in general respect.[1]

Whereas "Muslim" and "Arab" culture by its superiority

[1] Cf. *Classicisme et déclin culturel dans l'histoire de l'Islam*, Symposium de Bordeaux, 1956.

(owing to its being the heir of late classical civilization) had in this mediaeval culture-contact the rôle of fructifier and donor, it should be kept in mind that this fructifying rôle in fact was mainly the result of Western keenness and initiative. What happened around Cordova and Toledo is the most vivid illustration of this fact. Of course new configurations in various fields of life came into being through the Crusades, which were not and could not be consciously planned. In regard to culture in its higher dimensions, it holds true that the dominating power in the whole process of culture contact was a determinate quest and adventure of Western Europe, which smelt the significance of the *artes Arabum*, the hidden treasures of the East. It is, moreover, appropriate to remind oneself that the Europe of the 11th and 12th centuries is not rightly described by the epithet "barbarian". The Latin West of that time was full of seething powers, evident in such men as Abelard, Anselm, Gregory VII and others. E. Barker in *The Legacy of Islam* pointedly observes that it was "a new and growing West which[1] burst upon an old and waning East".[2]

"ARABISM IN EUROPE"

We can now grasp the true significance of what happened in Spain after the end of the 11th century. Toledo, the capital of Northern Christian Spain under Alfonso VI, became a vast laboratory of translation, compilation and commenting on the Arabic translations of Hellenistic philosophy and sciences, and of Hebrew works of the same sort, into Latin. Alfonso VI and Archbishop Raymond, aided by Domenico Gundisalvi, stimulated this undertaking, which made Toledo at the same time a bustling meeting-place and an abode of intellectual co-operation between excellent minds and between different religions and cultures.

In this period Gerard of Cremona (d. 1187) was one of the greatest translators at Toledo (he translated more than 80 works) and so became one of the great "fathers" of Arabism in Europe. Raymond founded after the Christian *reconquista* of Toledo (1085) a regular institute of translation, by which for example the Arabic versions of Aristotelian philosophy as conceived by al-Farabi and Ibn Sina (Avicenna), who belonged to

---

[1] In spite of its position of receiver.   [2] p. 52.

Oriental "Islam", became known in Latin. In this way these "Arab" commentators[1] on Aristotelian philosophy influenced the development of European scholasticism. Before this permeation process began to function, scholasticism in its earlier form had mainly lived, as to source-material from antiquity, on Pseudo-Dionysius and Boëthius. Muslim theology proper became mainly known by translations in Toledo of works of the great al-Ghazzali (d. 1111).

This curiosity about Muslim theology as distinguished from "Muslim" or "Arab" philosophy had two roots. The one was a genuine missionary interest in Islam (very rare in the Middle Ages) amongst small bands of Dominicans and Franciscans.[2] The other was an insatiable desire for a thorough knowledge of Islam so as better to refute this formidable opponent, whose domain was at the same time the habitat of a culture they sincerely admired. The Dominicans, in 1250, founded in Toledo the first School of Oriental Studies. Arabic and Hebrew were studied there by theologians with great zeal and success. Raymond Martin was the main luminary of this School. He possessed a solid knowledge of philosophy and theology, in Arabic and Hebrew garb—Hebrew, because the missionary interest of these Dominicans extended also to the Jews. His best-known work is: *Pugio fidei adversus Mauros et Judaeos*, in which a great wealth of Arabic sources in respect to philosophy (e.g. the famous *Tahāfūt* of Ghazzali) and theology was contained. In 1143 at Toledo a Latin version of the Koran was completed, and during Alfonso the Wise's reign two more Latin versions were added.

The intensity of meeting and co-operation between adherents of the three religions was very much furthered by the intolerance of the Almohad princes in Cordova of the 12th and 13th centuries. Christians (Mozarabs) were persecuted and took refuge in Northern Spain, Southern France and Sicily. One unexpected and unintended result was an intenser cultural insemination in Western Europe, particularly in regard to philosophy, than ever before. For instance, the great Averroes, who lived in Cordova and had never had any

[1] al-Farabi was, properly speaking, a Turk, who had studied under Christian philosophers and scholars; Ibn Sina was from Turkestan.

[2] Francis himself went on a missionary errand to Egypt, to the court of the great Saladin (end of 12th century).

significant influence by his philosophy on his Muslim co-religionists, found his most devoted disciples amongst the Jews, who even formed an Averroist school of thought, of which the equally great Maimonides (d. 1204) was the propagator. The dispersion of the Jews through Almohad persecution in those parts of the Christian world which were the fermenting places of culture-crossing made them the transmitters of "Arab" Aristotelianism in the Christian world. Through these and other causes, amongst which is the Christian *reconquista* of Cordova (1236)[1], Alfonso the Wise deployed a new vigour in stimulating the labours of translation, compilation and absorption. Archbishop Rodrigo of Toledo wrote a *Historia Arabum* drawing on Arabic sources.

EUROPE'S "MUSLIM" AND "CHRISTIAN" ORBIT

The way in which philosophical and theological "Arab" authors influenced Western Europe demands special attention, because this avid reception by the West of Greek philosophy and Muslim theology, particularly in the 13th century when scholasticism reached its crowning achievements, meant very much for the development of philosophical/theological thinking and controversy in mediaeval Europe. Some fundamental points must be kept in mind for the sake of an adequate understanding of what really happened.

The first point is that one should not forget the way in which this profuse philosophical material was introduced into Western Europe. The "Arabs" acquired it by translating from the Syrian (Aramaic) versions, as made by Christians in the pre-Islamic period, into Arabic, whereas the Jews (especially in Spain) did the same in Hebrew, or, on the basis of the Greek heritage, composed Hebrew philosophical works. All this literature became available to Western Europe through the Latin translations made in Toledo.[2] It therefore represented classical philosophy as it had been modified by Oriental Hellenism in the Roman Empire of the first centuries A.D.

The second point is, however, the more important. We

[1] Followed in 1248 by the fall of Seville and Murcia, both, like Cordova, being centres of cultural activity and symbiosis.

[2] The few Aristotelian works translated directly from Greek into Latin were Aristotle's *Politics* and *Ethics*, accomplished by the Archbishop of Carinthia, W. van Moerbeke, and his colleague, H. van Brabant.

usually regard philosophy mainly as a special discipline, practised by a definite class of men. The Middle Ages both in its "Muslim" and its "Christian" orbit had a quite different idea. Philosophy and theology were always indissolubly combined into one religious philosophy, which dominated thought and life. It is, therefore, more accurate to say that philosophy meant an eclectic mystical religious philosophy, i.e. Aristotelianism and Platonism interpreted in a Neo-platonist spirit.

The "Arabs", in this respect, took over what the Christian Syrian translators had offered them, and so continued a philosophical attitude which the Christians before the advent of Islam had acquired from Oriental Hellenism.

Very significant in this connection is the fact that the Arabic translation of the resumé of the three last books of Plotinus' *Enneads*[1] ran its course and exercised its influence in the Middle Ages, in East and West, under the title: *Theology of Aristotle* (!) and was considered to be Aristotle's own work. The psychology of Plotinus about the "material *nous*" (Ar. *'aql hayyūlāni*), part of the individual soul, and the "active *nous*" (Ar. *'aql fa'āl*), which was eternal, as it was considered an emanation of the First Cause, enabled the philosophers (who were mostly mystical rationalists) and the theologians (who regarded the eclectic modification of classical philosophy also as authoritative but had to reconcile it with the unphilosophical data of Revelation, Faith and Dogma) to have their common ground in rational Metaphysics. Both, philosophers and theologians, were consequently mainly attracted by metaphysics, logic and psychology and regarded the eclectic Aristotelian-Platonist-Neo-platonist version of these three main aspects as authoritative.[2]

This cardinal fact is of crucial importance for understanding the development and meanderings of Western scholasticism in its final stages. Before the 12th century scholasticism was chiefly Augustinian-Platonist. As to philosophical sources it was confined to the *Logic* of Aristotle, as mediated by Boëthius. As to

[1] The Syrian translator, Najma of Edessa (from which the Arabic rendering was made) followed Alexander Aphrodisias' Neo-platonist interpretation of Aristotelian psychology.

[2] The Arian, Nestorian and Monophysite controversies were, philosophically speaking, deeply influenced by different interpretations of Neo-platonist psychology.

Plato, it knew him through Cicero and the *Timaeus,* and as to Neo-platonism, Pseudo-Dionysius was their man. The grand-scale acquaintance with Greek philosophy through the "Arabs" and the small-scale acquaintance with Aristotle's *Politics* and *Ethics* by van Moerbeke's direct translation from Greek into Latin (cf. note on page 45), caused a powerful new fermentation of the keen mind of mediaeval Europe and also deep divergences of approach and understanding.[1]

Without grasping this cardinal fact just mentioned, it is impossible to understand Averroes' (Ar. Ibn Rushd) philosophical habitus, the conflicting repercussion Averroism had in Western Europe, Aquinas' pivotal significance in the whole matter, the rôle of men of the stature of Ghazzali and Dante. It is, from the standpoint of cultural history, irrefutable that the study of mediaeval European philosophy and theology requires, strictly scientifically speaking, a competent knowledge not only of the Latin and Greek sources, but also of the Syriac and Arabic translations of the eclectic mystical religious philosophies of Oriental Hellenism.

It is one of the ironies of history that Averroes (d. 1198), who was a *Qādi* (judge) in Cordova and the last great "Arab" philosopher, elaborated his philosophy under the fanatically-orthodox Almohads, inimical to all thinking deviating from Muslim Orthodoxy. In the great and ancient controversy about the primacy of *gnosis* (knowledge) and *pistis* (faith), he opted for the former and, though not denying agreement between *gnosis* and *pistis,* accorded the latter a subordinate place, from the standpoint of the philosopher. "*Pistis*", as embodied in a positive religion of Revelation like Islam, is the imperfect form of truth of authoritative character, adapted to the needs of the lesser breed, the "people". Philosophy on the contrary is the apprehension of truth, founded on Reason and proof, of which Aristotle is the greatest prophet and revealer. Averroes exercised in Western Europe an enormous influence, especially by his commentaries on Aristotle (in Neo-platonist colouring), which he composed on the basis of the Arabic

---

[1] Those still keeping to the Augustinian line taught the primacy of the will and the necessity of divine illumination to attain to certainty in faith and knowledge; those who were Averroists put knowledge as higher, above faith, as lower (the old controversy about *gnosis* and *pistis*); and there were those who wanted to be Christian Aristotelians as for instance Thomas Aquinas.

translations of what went as Aristotelian philosophy in the "Arab" world, as he did not know Greek. This is an important point to note in order to appreciate rightly what kind of material and Aristotelianism (viz. Averroism) Thomas Aquinas worked upon in constructing his famous reconciliation of Reason and Revelation.

A special point in Averroes' philosophy deserves emphasis, because it yielded the material for one of the crucial debates in Western scholasticism. This point is that, contrary to traditional philosophical opinion, Averroes maintained in his Commentaries that the material soul (*'aql hayyūlāni*, see above) was part of the Universal Soul and therefore was nonexistent in individual form. This Averroistic exegesis made (for example) immortality and prayer fictitious.

FERTILIZING THE WEST

Ghazzali had great significance for the development of philosophical-theological thinking in mediaeval scholasticism, for two reasons. This towering figure in Muslim theology, who went through a stormy inner crisis, made his peace with orthodox Islam by interpreting it in a mystical way,[1] thereby securing a legitimate place for mysticism in Islam; a problem which had remained for many centuries undecided. In the second place, in a very remarkable work, the *Tahāfūt al-falāsifa* (i.e. destruction of the philosophers) he broke through the eclectic philosophical syncretism, which was (see above) inherent in the Neo-platonist Aristotelianism, as current in the "Arab" world, by demonstrating its disastrous tendency towards the dilution of virile intellectual and religious discernment, and by delimiting the proper boundaries of philosophy and faith. Ghazzali's personal crisis had been a shaking of the foundations in his personal life, because it turned on the agonizing question of unshakable, absolute certitude in regard to Truth.

[1] In his famous work, also known in the Latin West, the *Ihyā' 'ulūm addīn* (i.e. revivification of the Science of Religion, that is to say Islam). The great Spanish Orientalist Asin Palacios therefore interprets Ghazzali as having produced in his works, written after his crisis, a Christianized version of Islam (cf. Asin's *Islam cristianizado*). This very interesting attempt is fully understandable in a Roman Catholic theologian, who is at the same time a great scholar in Arabic and Islam, because the mediaeval theologians who still have great standing in R.C. theology are all pervaded by a spirit deriving from a latent or patent synthesis of "Faith" (revelation) and mysticism.

Thus he flung in the face of the philosophers, who were all "gnostics", the affirmation that Revelation and not philosophical Reason is the authentic source of certitude, whereas philosophical Reason ultimately must remain the abode of incertitude. Averroes, who had, under the political-religious régime at the time, to hold his real idea of Truth as an esoteric opinion, was to such a degree provoked by Ghazzali's *Tahāfūt* (destruction) that he took the risk of lifting his esoteric visor and wrote a "Destruction" of his opponent's "Destruction".[1]

So Ghazzali, as well in his philosophical as in his theological production, fertilized the Latin West, and not least the great Aquinas. Averroes the philosopher and Ghazzali the theologian were not, however, the only "Arab" thinkers who influenced and aided Thomas, the philosophical-theological pole-star of the Roman Catholic Church, in constructing his grand synthesis. He joined the great Franciscans (e.g. Alexander of Hales, d. 1245) and the other great Dominicans (e.g. his teacher Albertus Magnus, d. 1280) in studying assiduously the "Arab" commentaries on Aristotle in Latin translations. He was conversant with Avicenna (Ibn Sina, d. 1037), the greatest philosopher and scholar of Oriental Islam, the Jewish Aristotelians Maimonides and Ibn Gabirol (d. 1058, called in Latin Avencebrol), the second of whom had strong Neo-platonist leanings; the first "Arab" philosopher in Occidental Islam, Ibn Bajja, in Latin called Avempace (d. 1138), to mention only a few. Moreover, in order to grasp the concrete cultural situation in which men like Albertus Magnus and Thomas Aquinas were reared and breathed, and to avoid reducing this living reality to a dry-as-dust genealogy of commentaries and manuscripts, one should always realize that Thomas came from and studied in Southern Italy (Naples), a region not only quite near to the brilliant centre of culture-cross-breeding under the impulse of Frederick II, viz. Sicily, but itself saturated with "Arab" cultural influences and institutions.

It is therefore striking, when comparing Thomas's and

---

[1] Cf. S. van den Bergh: *Averroes' Tahāfūt al-Tahāfūt* (translated from the Arabic with introduction and notes). An interesting short review appeared in the *Times Literary Supplement*, 21 Dec. 1956. The writer of the review remarks justly that neither mediaeval nor 17th-century Oxford would have had to explain to the educated reader, as is necessary in our day, why it was important to read a "Muslim" book of philosophy.

Ghazzali's theological/philosophical production, to note the great similarity in habitus and structure, the problems they wrestle with and the cognate solutions they propose, e.g. in the pivotal problem of the right relation of Reason and Revelation. Thomas has gratefully used Ghazzali, the "destroyer" of the philosophers, in order to defend himself against the seductive allurements of the admired philosophy of Averroes. They each produced a *Summa*, in which rational thinking and mysticism have married: a marriage which enables both to maintain the superiority and authority of Revelation above Reason. Except for the absence of Incarnation and Trinity in Ghazzali's works, it is easy to have the feeling that in reading either Ghazzali or Thomas (leaving aside their individual peculiarities) one moves in the same world, under the same heaven and in the same climate.

MUSLIM AND CHRISTIAN MYSTICISM

The relation of Muslim and Christian mysticism and the turbulent Averroistic controversy, centring around Paris University, require a special word, even were there no other reason for it than this: that we at present live through a growing impact of Eastern mysticism on the West and a decisive controversy in the East on the inescapable impact of Western civilization on the East, particularly felt as a challenge by the Islamic world.

Muslim mysticism has absorbed Hellenistic (of which Eastern Christian mysticism was the most valuable variety) and transposed it within a Koranic and Islamic context. The same channels which secured, through Spain and Sicily and partly through the Crusades, concrete contacts with Islamic life—the influence of philosophy and theology—opened the way for irradiations of Muslim mysticism into the West. Though it was not accompanied in this case by grand-scale translation. But the similarity and affinity of background, of psychology and of the structure of mediaeval Christian and Muslim *Weltanschauung* is unmistakable. Similarity and affinity are not due to either Christianity or Islam as religions, but to the common heritage of late classical antiquity, for which the Muslim world became the transmitter and the eagerness of the Latin West the catalyst.

Averroes and Thomas were the great protagonists of the harmony of Reason and Faith. Whether Averroes in the depth of his heart really aimed at that goal is uncertain. One is dealing with "Arab" thinkers who had to live under the sway of an intolerant orthodoxy, supported by the State; one is never certain whether they ultimately clung to an esoteric truth, which in their own opinion transcended the limitations of contradictions of Faith to Reason. Even with a man like Ghazzali one is not certain. This uncertainty is the more justified because in the Muslim world a remarkable theory was widespread (and practised too with good conscience)—the theory of *taqiyya*. This is a religious-political tenet, by which in many circumstances people tried to combine inner intellectual and spiritual freedom with outer submissiveness to the official, state-protected religio-political ideology. *Taqiyya* means: to behave and speak "as if", to conceal.

It seems to me that Averroes kept to the line of the harmony of Faith and Reason and the ultimate identity of prophetic Revelation and philosophical Truth as formulated by the greatest teacher of Truth, Aristotle. It is rather pedantic to say, as is often said, that the Averroists of the West, who solved the knotty problem of the harmony or disharmony of Faith and Reason by the doctrine of "the dual Truth" (theology and philosophy), were deviating from the great Master Averroes, and that this deviation was due to errors in translation. This procedure betrays a too guileless philological approach to a problem that has far deeper roots. It ignores the wide spiritual and cultural context in which these intellectual storms went on. There are irrefutable indications in this context that Averroes was rightly understood by the "Averroists" of the West.

Averroes is quite clear on the point that faith and theology represent a lower order of Truth, fit for the masses; Ghazzali's fundamental attack on philosophy (see above) was evidently felt by Averroes as an attack on his own position, and his answer shows the signs of irritation and of the contempt of the aristocratic philosopher. The theory of *taqiyya*, just mentioned, offered him all possibilities of self-justification. Siger of Brabant, the leader of the Parisian Averroists, seems to me to have defined in clear, unambiguous terms what was inherent in the position of the "Arab" philosophers, but what they said only by way of allusion and suggestion, and not as a clear-cut standpoint. To take one instance out of many: Ibn Tufail (d. 1185), the famous author of the philosophical Robinson-Crusoe-tale *Hayy ibn Yaqzān*, is such an example of allusive suggestion. The gist of the tale is that a contemplative hermit lives on an isolated island, trying to reach union (*ittisāl*, a key-term in all "Arab" philosophy) with Ultimate Reality and so attain to truth. He is happy. Another island is inhabited by people who live accordingly to Muslim Divine Law (*Shari'a*). They are happy too. The hermit intends to convert them to his higher Truth, but learns by experience that it is better to leave them happy with their conventional Truth.

Siger of Brabant (d. 1284) stoutly declared the double-Truth doctrine: there is the theological truth, different from and inferior to the only true philosophical Truth, which recognizes Aristotle as the supreme authority and maintains, amongst other points, the eternity of the world and the denial of individual immortality. This contradictory doctrine was the farthest limit rationalist thinkers could go to under the conditions of mediaeval society and its *corpus Christianum*. It combined loyalty to Truth as one saw it and loyalty to the ideology of the community. Maybe, therefore, Siger's doctrine is not only a defiance of the mediaeval system but also the cry of men who saw no other way to honour their two loyalties.

DANTE AND THE "ARAB WORLD"

Dante in his *Divine Comedy* is probably the most interesting and fascinating demonstration of the cultural contact with the "Arab" world in the Middle Ages. The word "probably" is used deliberately, because some critical reserve must be preserved in view of much research which is still needed. It is again the great Spanish Orientalist, Asin Palacios,[1] who by his investigations has put Dante in such a central place on the map of cultural cross-currents, and it is worth while to summarize his proposition as a fitting postlude to the illuminating story of what happened between the "Arab" East and the Latin West in the Middle Ages.

Asin's thesis starts from the Koranic data on Muhammad's nocturnal journey to the Mosque in Jerusalem (*Sūrat al-isrā*,

[1] *Islam and the Divine Comedy.*

S. 17) and the tales about his Ascension to heaven (mi'rāj) in S. 53, linked to S. 17. These Ascension-tales have a definite place in the oldest Arabic biographies of Muhammad, and are widespread up to the present day in the popular mawlid literature (mawlid = birth). In Spain the Christians came to know these tales from the Muslim books of ḥadīth (Tradition), in which they were incorporated. Sicily was the region from which all kinds of stories and tales from the Orient penetrated into the West, including those about Muhammad's mi'rāj. Dante lived in the orbit of great admiration for "Muslim" or "Arab" culture, Italy being penetrated by "Arab" influences. Brunetto Latini, who had been ambassador to the Court of Alfonso the Wise at Toledo and was Dante's beloved teacher, assembled in his *Tesoro* an encyclopedic store of knowledge from the "Arab" East, in which also a biography of Muhammad was contained.

Looking at this evidence it would indeed not be astonishing to suppose a Dante acquainted with and touched by this cultural stream, and to conjecture the borrowing of literary elements.

In the *Divine Comedy* Dante gives Muhammad a place in Hell, and beside him sets his son-in-law Ali, because both are creators of schism by conquest. Ibn Sina (Avicenna) has also his place in Hell, but Averroes (Ibn Rushd) gets a habitat in Limbo, the precinct of Hell. As I see it, this could reflect the attitude in mediaeval Christian Spain: on the one hand a true appreciation of "Arab" cultural superiority out of youthful hunger and thirst for knowledge, mixed with contempt for Islam with its anti-Christian bias and destructive consequences for Christendom. So for example Peter Paschal, bishop and martyr in Granada (1300), is known for his anti-Islam book *Impunazion de la seta de Mohamah*, testifying to his great knowledge of the Koran and of Tradition (ḥadīth). Yet he knew and appreciated "Muslim" culture.

It is not without interest to note that Siger of Brabant, the Averroist opponent of Thomas Aquinas, has a place in Heaven *beside* Thomas. This might suggest a peculiar philosophical viewpoint on Dante's part. Asin suggests that Dante's philosophy has affinity with the illuminationist (ishrāqī) philosophy of Ibn Masarra and of the famous mystic Ibn Arabi, both living in Spain. There is similarity in their and Dante's use of images, numerical symbolism and astrological beliefs. Asin points also to a remarkable similarity of the *dolce stil nuovo* (sweet new style) and Ibn Arabi's love-hymns, meant as allegories for the divine mysteries of Beauty and Love. Dante gave an allegorical interpretation of 14 love-hymns, composed by himself. This Platonic love for a woman who is angel and symbol is probably of "Muslim" origin, as Ibn Arabi seems to suggest. Asin goes even so far as to suggest that Ibn Arabi's mystical work *al-Futūḥāt* is the prototype of the *Divine Comedy* on account of the basic idea, the images, the geometrically-planned universe with Heavens and Hells, etc. Asin reasons in this way: the ascension of the mystic's soul in the *Futūḥāt* is an adaptation of the bodily Ascension, told about Muhammad in popular and semi-canonical Muslim literature, which circulated also in Christian Spain and Italy. This served as the inspiring element for Dante's descent into Hell and for his and Beatrice's ascent to Heaven.

Asin's suggestive tableau contains undoubtedly many conjectural elements, difficult to substantiate. But at any rate he has made a case for the extraordinary spread of Muslim eschatological lore in the Latin West, and for its influence and that of Muslim mystical philosophy on the greatest literary achievement of the Middle Ages. The establishment of Turkey in Europe (fall of Constantinople 1453) and the flowering of the Renaissance, which was nourished not only by the more direct contact in the 14th and 15th centuries with classical Greek antiquity through the Byzantines but also by the revival of interest in the Roman past (cf. the rôle of Virgil in Dante's Comedy, and Petrarch), put a stop to the fascinating mediaeval cultural influx from the East. The stagnation of Oriental Islam since the 13th century and the rolling up of the Moorish Empire in Spain since the same century had already slowed it down. Europe, so to speak, well fed by intoxicating stimulants wrung from the "Arabs", went the way of its own genius with reborn vigour. Turkey became a wall of separation between East and West rather than a thoroughfare. It is not our aim to write a cultural history of Europe, and therefore we will finish this exposition of the remarkable effect of the "Legacy of Islam" on the mediaeval Latin West with an evaluation of the worth and significance of this cultural event and of what is properly called the Renaissance.[1]

NEW MEETINGS OF NEW WORLDS

The effect of the "Legacy of Islam" on the Latin West of the Middle Ages was, in fact, a fertilization of Europe's adolescent life by Eastern-Hellenistic civilization, mediated by "Arab" scholars and philosophers. It afforded a closed "Christian" society the opportunity for philosophical foundation and synthesis. The direct knowledge of Plato and Aristotle and of authentic Greek and Roman thinking, art and science, through the Byzantines, meant a re-diffusion of classical antiquity as a whole in the blood-stream of Europe. As classical antiquity embodies one of the great *representative* ideas and ideals of man and his place in the universe, it meant at the same time that all the dominant expressions of its life in thought and endeavour again became ferments of Western life, all going under the name of Humanism in general or Christian Humanism, this time by direct studious contact, and not only as in the Middle Ages through the indirect medium of Augustine's discussion with classical culture.[2] The European Renaissance, in contrast to the Muslim world and mediaeval Christianity, appropriated to itself not only the sciences and philosophy but also the great poetry and drama of antiquity.

The over-arching facts which have determined the meeting of cultures since the end of the 15th century are the discovery of the whole earth by Western initiative and the growing hegemony of Western Europe over the globe. India, the Far East, the Americas and their cultures and religions entered into the orbit of European interest and curiosity. This was done by circumventing the Islamic bloc, symbolized in Vasco da Gama's voyage round the Cape of Good Hope. Two poles dominate this unfolding of events. On the one hand, a mysterious explosion of dynamism, of human willpower and vitality, of conquest of the world in all fields of life. On the other hand, an introvert, seemingly lethargic Eastern world, yet filled with latent vitality, into which this onrush of will-to-conquest penetrated.

[1] It is still a matter of controversy how to define the Renaissance.
[2] Cf. C. N. Cochrane: *Christianity and Classical Culture.*

In regard to Asia, Panikkar calls this the Gaman period.
Africa remained mainly virgin territory till the 19th century.
As to the Americas, in the North it seemed only as if huge
forests were waiting to be turned into cultivable land. In
Central America it was different. There, one of the dramas of
history was enacted. The *conquista* met with pre-Columbian
civilizations of real grandeur, in many respects amazing, the
more so because they had a primitive social organization and
rather scanty technical means. They broke down under the
victorious raids of the *conquistadores*, because the heirs of those
civilizations were stunned by these strange, strong-willed dare-
devils. The motive forces of this world-wide conquest were a
strange, inextricable mingling of missionary urge and thirst for
gold and adventure.

This meeting of two opposite worlds had a still sharper accent
of *coincidentia oppositorum* because the aggressive West, being in
a stage of mobile and growing creativity in material and
spiritual respects, was, particularly in military means, provided
with more effective instruments than the peoples the Westerners
encountered. Creativity met stagnation. A culturally rich and
saturated, introvert world was confronted with restless dynamism. Here are the roots of the growing Western hegemony, in
the 19th century, with a rather cacophonic prelude in the 17th
and 18th centuries. The pushing power of vigorous dynamism
was in these ages still retarded by two causes: the colossal
distances and surface of these unknown continents and the
small operation-basis in Western Europe. Yet in the Americas
a new civilization, beginning as an offshoot of European
civilization, set out on its uncharted career. In South America
a mixed civilization grew up under the aegis of the Roman
Catholic Church. Asia responded by self-chosen isolation
(Japan, China) or by gradual breakdown (India, Java). The
19th century[1] brought a great acceleration of this formidable
conquest.

Such, in broad lines, was the background of new meetings
of wholly different cultural worlds. Necessarily, under these
circumstances, the meeting had to remain superficial; quite
different from the intensive meeting of Oriental and Occidental
Islam with the mediaeval West, though the Muslim and the

---

[1] See next chapter.

Christian world remained inimical political and religious, or rather ideological, blocs. Asia had no interest in the West, with the exception of the stealthy interest some Japanese in the hermetically closed Japan manifested in the arts and sciences of the West, which they could glean from their contacts with the Dutch on the small islet of Deshima. Or the interest the Jesuit Fathers in the 17th and 18th centuries aroused in some Chinese circles by their learning and technical ability.

Though the majority of the Western invaders were supremely indifferent to the countries and peoples they came in contact with, the Western "curiosity"-impulse appeared nevertheless as evidenced by the works on cultures and religions in unknown Asia written by a select minority of *dilettanti*. The *hommes curieux* were mainly missionaries and in the second half of the 18th century especially in India the great prototypes of the "civil servant" of later days (e.g. William Jones in India, Stamford Raffles and Th. Crawfurd in Indonesia). On the missionary side should be mentioned in the period before the 19th century the famous work of the Protestant missionary B. Ziegenbalg (d. 1719), *Malabarisches Heidentum*; the invaluable book by Abbé J. A. Dubois, *Hindu Manners, Customs and Ceremonies;* and the *Lettres curieuses et édifiantes* or the *Relations* of Jesuit missionaries in America and Asia.

THE "ENLIGHTENMENT" AND RELIGION

This genre of information by *Lettres* and *Relations* became of real significance especially in 18th-century France, because the Jesuits gave full and laudatory descriptions of China as a political, cultural and religious body. This information coincided with a Western society in cultural and religious ferment, and full of criticism of the existing order. The "Enlightenment" imagined finding in the China as pictured by the Jesuits the near-fulfilment of their rationalist ideals and their moralist optimism. The picture derived from the descriptions by the erudites,[1] who were enthusiastic about the peculiar religious nature of the Chinese, their pure monotheism, their knowing the true God, Shangti, even before Abraham, their pure, sublime ethics, older than the foundation of Rome. They imagined that their ideal deistic Religion and ethics, free from

[1] Cf. Leibniz's *Novissima Sinica*.

57

miracles and revelation, founded on Reason, had been realized in China.

Of course, this enthusiasm, which appeared also in their interest in Chinese art (of which interest the Rococo style is a demonstration) was far from being purely disinterested cultural enchantment.[1] It suited the fighting position of the Enlightenment extremely well to use this "Chinese miracle" as a weapon against a decadent Society and an authoritarian Church. Voltaire in his *Essai sur l'esprit et les moeurs des nations* purposely played off China against "Christian" Europe, writing the first cultural history from a great fund of knowledge and aiming consciously at the destruction of the Christian view of history.

The simple monotheism of Islam and the genius of Muhammad, its creator, evoked also in the atmosphere of the Enlightenment a feeling of congeniality, and caused the publication of books describing Islam in favourable contrast with Christianity. Here again the same combination occurred in the enthusiastic estimate of Islam: congeniality and the discovery of a good weapon in their own battle with the powers of cultural and religious conservatism and retrogradation. Edward Gibbon, one of the exponents of this "enlightened" mood, reduces it in his famous book[2] to the simple formula of a rationalist sceptic: "The faith which under the name of Islam, he [i.e. Muhammad] preached to his family and nation is compounded of an eternal truth and a necessary fiction, THAT THERE IS ONLY ONE GOD AND THAT MAHOMET IS THE APOSTLE OF GOD".[3]

So in regard to China and Islam we have in the 18th century the same spectacle as before: a keen Western élite of forerunners using Eastern cultural elements, yielded by an unwilling and uninterested East, for its own spiritual struggle. The threshold of the 19th century is near.

As we step over it, we see the mutual "blind" meeting in the preceding centuries turning into some kind of perspicacity.

[1] Cf. A. Reichwein: *China und Europa im 18en Jahrhundert* (E.T. *China and Europe*, "History of Civilization" series), and N. Söderblom: *Das Werden des Gottesglaubens*, particularly chapter 19 entitled "Die Urheberreligion in Europa", pp. 324-360.

[2] *The History of the Decline and Fall of the Roman Empire*, Vol. V, p. 397.

[3] Capitals are Gibbon's.

Chapter Three

THE NEW SITUATION IN THE NINETEENTH CENTURY

FOR the "meeting" of East and West three factors have been of decisive importance.[1] These are: the Western dominance, the work of the Western Orientalists, and Christian Missions.

During the 17th and 18th centuries, the cultural meeting between Asia and Europe was, as we have seen, an extremely marginal and one-sided affair. A great change took place in the 19th century. The real invasion and penetration of the West into the East, particularly Asia, began. This great episode is at present in Chinese Communist parlance even called "the cultural aggression of the West", in which America is included. This evaluation, as is evident from many convulsive reactions, e.g. in India, Burma, and particularly Ceylon, virtually corresponds to deep-seated sentiments everywhere in Asia and Africa. In Africa the Mau-Mau rebellion is an outstanding example, although political and economic causes are, just as in Asia, playing a great rôle too.

This Western invasion deserves its name particularly in comparison with the two preceding centuries, when "the West" lived and acted on the fringes. It became possible by the amazing and rapid development of theoretical and applied science, by the constantly growing body of knowledge, and technical and organizational equipment, made imperative by the industrial revolution, which was as well the result as the impetus of these causes. The total process led to one of the prominent features of 19th century history—Western imperialism; or, in other words, the political, economic and cultural dominance of the West in the Eastern hemisphere. This whole

---

[1] A fourth factor of equal importance is the response of the Eastern cultures. Chapter 5 is devoted especially to that aspect.

dramatic event was sustained by a strong feeling, a deep conviction of innate Western spiritual and cultural superiority, in many cases even soaring to a belief in being charged with a divine vocation and right.[1]

WESTERN IMPERIALISM

Looking back to the event, this whole drama unfolding under the aegis of Western imperialism is incontrovertible and was inevitable. On the one hand was a creative, dynamic West, thirsty for enterprise, hungry for markets, impelled to burst its bounds; on the other hand a defenceless, spacious and populous East. *It could not but happen.* Morally speaking, Western imperialism was and is, without any doubt, very much open to criticism on account of the unscrupulous and vehement fierceness which often marked its way. Yet, though this should be said without any whittling down, the same retrospective look at the history of the last 200 years requires us also to state clearly that this same great event has appeared to be a means to a greater end; that is, the painful welding of a number of provincial worlds into a universe. This is not to say that this universe is already achieved. Far from it. But there is a chance that man of to-day is on the road to it, and, what is still more important in regard to our subject of the coming dialogue of Eastern and Western culture and religion, the journey from the confinement in our provincial worlds towards the still uncertain and distant goal of a world-embracing mutual understanding and a greater solidarity in responsibility for one another's life, beckons mankind to-day imperatively towards an unknown and thrilling future.

As so often, comparison with comparable happenings in the past may help in understanding what happened through Western dominance in the 19th century in Asia. Therefore it is worth while to ask: In what respect do Western dominance and imperialism differ from former imperialisms (Babylon, Egypt, Alexander the Great's conquest, Rome)? The answer that offers itself seems to be: in the case of the imperialisms of the past, speaking in general terms, peoples of a cognate type

---

[1] André Siegfried's *La Crise de l'Europe* (E.T. *Europe's Crisis*, 1935), and Meredith Townsend's *Asia and Europe* are excellent helps towards realizing the significance of this element.

of culture, social organization and economic implementation came to be related to one another as rulers and ruled, as dominators and subjected. In spite of the many differences, and varieties in the levels of dominators and various subjected peoples, on the whole it holds true. This is particularly true in regard to the pivotal point of Religion as the life-centre and basic foundation of these societies. Different as the religions of all the peoples contained in these former empires may have been as to names and ceremonies and emphases, they were all rooted in one common apprehension of Man, the World, Life and the Divine.

In the case of modern Western imperialism the situation is utterly different. The European peoples who established their dominance in Asia and Africa represented a wholly different type of culture and civilization, a social and political order, poles apart from the feudal structure of the agrarian East, imbued with a different economic spirit and implementation. They were in manners, habits of life, attitude towards life and the world, and in their methods and ideas of government a truly alien reality. And above all, the religion of the Europeans differed deeply from the Eastern religions of their new subjects. Moreover, the Europeans whether believers or not had received through Christianity an ethico-religious orientation and apprehension, in many, if not in most, respects opposite to the attitude bred into the fibre of the Asian peoples by their age-old religions.

A TOTALLY ALIEN DOMINATION

The contrast, in a word, was staggering. The triumphant optimistic faith of the 19th century however was not well-suited to gauge its depth. Although endlessly quoted, Kipling's "East is East and West is West and never the twain shall meet" only reflected the serious view of a small minority. The progressive and dynamic mood was prepared either to leave the East alone and to be happy with one's own self-realization at the expense of the East, or to tie it to its car of triumph and thereby modify it. For the Easterners the Western dominance was the *first totally alien* dominance in their memory. In the past they had repeatedly lived under foreign subjection, but always by Asians, who were culturally and religiously vanquished and absorbed by the peoples of the higher civilizations, though these latter had to submit to the political and military power of the foreign Asian invaders. The history of China and India is full of examples of this kind.

The Western invaders, however, were not only foreign, i.e. from abroad, but were truly *alien*. Besides that, they were not only superior in political and military respect as for example the Mongols were, when invading India and China. They were undeniably superior in technical and economic equipment, and instead of being food for absorption by the Eastern cultures, so absorptive by nature, they came with a strong feeling of their own cultural superiority and of Asia's backwardness, bound in the shackles of tradition, oblivious of any true dynamism. The epithet "foreign devil" for all whites did not primarily express hatred, but was a spontaneous aversion to this *eo ipso* unacceptable *alien* world, which could not be digested, but only ignored or despised.[1]

This mutual alienness, the one as it were stimulating the other to an acuter consciousness of it, explains the deep-seated, mostly unconscious, widespread feeling that this Western invasion was in fact an aggression, an insult, an uncalled-for attack on authentic Asian life. To be sure, the meeting of East and West in the last 150 years has gone through many vicissitudes of attraction and repulsion, the tale of which undoubtedly is not covered by what has been said in the preceding sentence. Yet it is nevertheless true as a basic reaction, and it is striking to find it as such clearly stated in K. M. Panikkar's *Asia and Western Dominance*.

This is not said to make the gulf between East and West as wide and deep as possible. Nor as an expression of a pessimistic view. But it must be said, because if one wants to be serious about the possible "coming dialogue between world cultures and world religions" as this book purports to be, this aspect[2] is

---

[1] Useful books for giving some understanding of this fact are Pearl Buck's *East Wind: West Wind*, and *The First Wife*.

[2] We have already mentioned the violent revulsions, long concealed, now released, as apparent in Ceylon, and the Mau-Mau rebellion, which bear testimony to what we are trying to make clear about the alienness and aggression of the West. The Boxer uprising had the same pattern. A mass of literature has appeared in regard to "primitive" peoples and peoples of the great Asian civilizations and their contact with the West, under this angle. Cf. e.g. Pitt-Rivers: *The Clash of Culture and Contact of Races;* Meredith Townsend: *Asia and Europe.*

highly important and a realistic approach is indispensable. There certainly is also another side of the medal, but that will be treated at its due place. We must, however, pay adequate attention here to the cardinal fact that East and West represent two great different structures of mentality in mankind, fortified by a long historical tradition; and that to-day, in our time, the first real and inescapable meeting of these two structures seems to be emerging as one of the dominant factors in world history. To ignore it or pay it a scanty attention would evince a lack of wisdom.

The East during a large part of the 19th century suffered and underwent the rising deluge of the Western invasion as one suffers a natural catastrophe. Japan was the sole exception. Whether it were primitive peoples or populations living under the sway of a great civilization, as India and China, they stood, in their heart of hearts, stupefied by this Western orgy of energy, ambition, passionate pursuit of exploitation and material progress. Although the current fashion of contrasting East and West as spiritual over against materialistic is one of the most misleading and false theories for grasping the difference, it is fully understandable that the West has the reputation in the East of being materialistic to the core. The Easterners could not know that they were in contact with the projection of one of the aspects of Western civilization, and moreover its most ambiguous and demonic one: its acquisitive urge. They were so to speak the world-proletariat, who just like the labour-proletariat in Europe tasted the bitter dregs of the liberalist wine of *laisser-faire*.

Europe, bursting with vitality and energy, hurried on along the road of exploitation, dominance and increasing prosperity. The surpluses of this prosperity impelled towards new attempts at forcing Asia and Africa to yield manpower, productive power and markets, and like a vicious circle this resulted in a feverish scramble for political power and economic exploitation and penetration. André Siegfried summarizes the matter very clearly when he says:[1] "Thus there existed in the 19th century a complete European system, comprising a world-wide economic régime controlled by Europe" and[2] "What wonder that Europe felt imbued with pride? World-empire, in very truth, was hers."

[1] In *La Crise de l'Europe*, p. 37.　　[2] *ibid.*, p. 41.

It is in this way that "colonialism" has grown to its full stature. Europe, hardly, or not at all, knowing what she did, chased Asia and Africa towards a way of radical revision in all spheres of their life (social, cultural, moral, religious), which bore in its womb the seeds of gigantic unrest and crisis. To-day we live in the midst of it. Only after the process had started and moved forward did the colonial powers entertain the idea of Westernizing the East, and even then never whole-heartedly and resolutely. Europe, or the West,[1] till the end of "colonialism" abruptly came, kept wavering between two possibilities: Westernization or not.

It is therefore interesting to notice that nevertheless the virus of the West has worked violently in the lifeblood of Asia. And still more interesting (a fact, even, of consequences still incalculable) is that, just because of the deep contrast between East and West, the East faced for the first time in its long and glorious history the challenge to make a radical change. At least in principle, it meant a radical break with all the time-honoured bases of its existence. The history of Asia and Africa shows a great number of dramatic vicissitudes and changes. But, spectacular as they may have been, properly speaking they were surface events. They happened within the framework and in continuance of the inherited normative bases and patterns of their existing apprehension of life and the world. These bases and patterns were felt as eternal and unchangeable. The meeting of East and West in our time is the first occasion in Asian and African history when the very bases and elemental metaphysically grounded attitudes towards life and the world have been called in question, or at least have to be thoroughly revised.

BREAK IN EASTERN CONTINUITY

Unbroken continuity was till this challenging event the hallmark of the East. But it cannot now get on its feet again and take a fruitful and vigorous part in contemporary international life if it does not make up its mind about, and take into account, the unprecedented break that has occurred in this continuity

[1] In this case not America, which in the Philippines followed a determined policy of Westernization; but in this regard it stands unique among all the types of colonial policy that have been practised.

and its consequences. The West of the 19th century, which in most respects played a blind and reluctant rôle in bringing about this unprecedented revolution in the life of the East, would have been horrified at the very idea of being instrumental to such a colossal re-evaluation of powers, interests and spiritual values. It would have considered it sheer madness, because it only dreamt of and confidently lived on the expectation of the unbroken and unbreakable continuity of its world primacy, just as the East was assured of the unbroken and unbreakable continuity of its Tradition.

A good illustration of this point is given by the acutest observer of Indian culture and religion who ever lived, Father H. Dubois. He says[1] of the first quarter of the 19th century, when British dominance in India had become firmly established:

> The European Power which is now established in India is, properly speaking, supported neither by physical force nor by moral influence. It is a piece of huge, complicated machinery moved by springs which have been arbitrarily adapted to it. Under the supremacy of the Brahmins the people of India hated their government, while they cherished and respected their rulers; under the supremacy of Europeans, they hate and despise their rulers from the bottom of their hearts, and they cherish and respect their government.

One question is pertinent: What have been the constituent marks of "colonialism"? I would, on the basis of study and a long experience of living in "colonial" countries, venture to answer by the following condensed formula.

A country is a "colonial" country, where the real dynamic economic activity is in *foreign* hands, nourished by *foreign* capital, directed by *foreign* personnel, inspired by a *foreign* spirit of enterprise, primarily directed towards *foreign* interests. A "colonial" country is therefore a country which lives, objectively speaking, in a state of helotism; a country of which people and land are, in the last instance, instruments and means for *foreign* purposes, and where *foreign* decisions determine those peoples' destiny.

This is not said out of lust for denunciation, but to lay bare

---

[1] pp. 4f. in his *Hindu Manners, Customs and Ceremonies.*

the *essence* of the colonial relation. Nor is it said as meaning that this is all that can and should be said about it. Many a reader may well be amazed at this definition, in exclusively economic terms; the more so because most discussions during the time of colonialism's undisputed rule and its decline, and also after its recent fall, stress very strongly its political aspect. Westerners and Easterners agree in this respect. It is of course as patent as daylight that political subjection is a very conspicuous trait of "colonialism". Who would or could deny it? Yet, true as this is, for a right understanding of "colonialism" it is appropriate to stress the point that political dependence and subjection are not *necessarily* part of "colonialism". They very often are; but South America proves this point. Until recently the South American republics, though politically speaking independent countries, were (as André Siegfried maintains quite rightly in his book, *L'Amérique Latine*) a "colonial" region because of their deep-rooted economic subservience to powers and interests from abroad. Political dependence and subjection help greatly, of course, to ensure that a "colonial" country exists primarily to serve foreign, and not its own, interests and ends, but this is not indispensable for making a country "colonial".

The truth of this thesis is proved by one of the main factors behind what is called the neutralism of the new independent states in Asia, which only a short time ago still lived in colonial status. This factor is their evident (and not unjustifiable) fear that, although they themselves still think mainly in political terms about "colonialism", their economic dependence and subservience to the potent West remains too strong if they take sides in the "Great Power Contest" of to-day, or too naïvely accept financial support as "underdeveloped countries", in dire need of help.

Still another qualification must be made in order to avoid wrong conclusions from the given definition. In spite of the central significance of the economic aspect of "colonialism", it is in the interest of a true, concrete historical picture of Western "colonialism", free of distortion, also appropriate to state that the colonial relation does not necessarily mean mere exploitation, in which the human and material resources of a "colonial" country are exclusively objects of such exploitation. There have been such times, or times when it was prevalent in definite

66

sectors of colonial Government policies.[1] But to generalize in this way along the whole line would be contrary to the facts. It is a rather striking peculiarity of Western colonialism that, although there are many flagrant episodes of "naked imperialism", it has had in various directions a stimulating influence on the East, to a quite amazing degree. Panikkar[2] describes it with genuine recognition in many of its aspects and states with great conviction that the massiveness of the changes, brought about by the West in the East, has modified the outlook of the ancient Eastern societies to such an extent that it involves a "qualitative break" of a revolutionary character. This should never be forgotten when speaking about "imperialism" and "colonialism".

WESTERN IMPERIALISM—"A SPIRITUAL CONQUEST"

This leads us on to the other side of the medal, which is of direct interest to the theme of this book. Western imperialism had a Janus head. The one face represented its conquest by power and subjection. The other face, however, reflects a quite different thing, viz. a spiritual conquest, which was source and stimulant of unexpected developments. Magnificent as the Eastern cultures in many respects are, they would never have been able to develop from their own spiritual resources the peculiar dynamism which alone can generate such happenings as we witness at present. Their fundamental apprehensions and attitudes could not generate the new visions and aspirations, which by the mysterious dispensation of history rather paradoxically proved to be the unintended gifts of Western "colonialism". This spiritual conquest again has two sides, which each need separate treatment. The first is what I propose to call the unbroken epic of Western Oriental studies; the second may be called the broken epic of transmitting Western liberal culture and idealism, combined with the work of social and economic uplift which became, besides administration, an integral part of the colonial governmental machinery. In a certain sense these two kinds of epic could be considered the *redeeming* touches in the total "colonial" picture.

---

[1] e.g. the *Cultuurstelsel* in Java; the Congo in the past; British tariff-politics in India in the interest of English textiles; the Opium War against China, etc.
[2] *Asia and Western Dominance*, pp. 479ff.

The word "epic" suggests itself automatically when one contemplates the scene of the origins and growth of Oriental studies in Europe, beginning about 1800.[1] Western 19th century imperialism made possible also a vast spiritual conquest. As a rule people are mainly mindful of the amazing progress of the Natural Sciences, as these have, by their results and applications, such an enormous impact on the life and structure of society. And, moreover, as they contain revolutionary consequences in regard to what is called the modern *Weltbild* (world image) and a new estimate of man and life. Generally speaking, people are not aware in the same manner of the large-scale development in the 19th century of the Science of History, although it too has had consequences for the moulding of the "modern" mind which mean as great a break with the past as the Natural Sciences have accomplished. Never before in history has there been such a methodical and systematic search and criticism of the sources, on the basis of which historians try to build up a coherent, intelligible picture of the past in order to elucidate the present, and, in interpreting it, design attempts at self-understanding. The same century (the 19th) which broke the bounds of tradition, also produced a new historical approach to the adventures of mankind which never existed before in this analytical, critical way.

One of the most thrilling parts of this development of historical study is the field of Oriental studies, mainly active in the field of archaeology and in assembling and studying the astounding masses of material in numerous, very difficult Oriental languages. These masses of material have been digested (the process is still going on and will go on for a long time to come), translated, analysed and interpreted in ever new attempts. In combination with the findings of archaeology, these learned Oriental studies have enabled the Orientalists to map out the long history of Eastern cultures and religions in a way which some years ago would not have been supposed possible, and to formulate their meaning and significance. The History of Religion and Culture has thus become a powerful element in the moulding of the attitude and outlook of "modern" man on life and the many-sided significance of man.

[1] The 17th and 18th centuries give a splendid record too, but do not enter into our subject.

To anyone who knows this whole development of Oriental studies, especially in respect to religion and culture, it really is a marvellous unfolding. Two points which concern our theme need to be made.

In the first place it should be stressed that these Oriental studies and their magnificent results (leaving wholly alone the great consequences they have had and continue to have for man's outlook in Western culture) are rooted in a sheer thirst for knowledge, understanding and truth. This is their source and their abiding inspiration.[1] Speaking in general, it is no exaggeration to say that this development of Natural and Historical Science is one of the glories of Western humanism.

THE WEST AWAKENED THE EAST

The second point needs explanation at greater length. One of the finest results of the excavation and restoration of buried cities and temples in the Orient, of the assiduous learning of unknown languages and the study of dead and living cultures and religions, has been the colossal impetus this has exercised on the awakening of the East and its entering into a reborn self-consciousness. In short, in acquiring a new self-understanding and self-respect, built on the previously unknown historical range of its religions and cultures as unearthed by the labours of Western Orientalists, the East has been provided with a new vision and motivation.

In other words, nationalism (to which we will turn presently) as the great motive force in "colonial" days for a radical change of the existing political relationship, owes much of its inspiration and enthusiasm to Western Oriental scholarship, in most cases exercised in quiet libraries, in the retirement of private studies, or on journeys of arduous fieldwork. Western scholarship never consciously intended any such result. This outcome of its labours was entirely unlooked-for.

Western Orientalism, by all its work of investigation, interpretation and restoration, gave to the East—i.e. India, the Muslim world (Egypt, Iraq, Iran) and in a somewhat different

---

[1] Just as Natural Science, e.g. by its discovery of nuclear fission, finds itself now in an inner crisis in respect to its dominant, normative inspiration, so also is this the case at present in the field of historical study, because of the danger of substituting ideological, totalitarian motives for its only legitimate abiding inspiration.

sense to China and Indonesia also—a sense of history and of cultural pride and happiness. The Eastern intelligentsia learned to think, as never before, in terms of historical continuity. In Muslim countries the glories of the pre-Muslim past, brought to light by the ingenuity and perseverance of Western Orientalists, have thus entered again into the orbit of mind and influence.[1]

The famous French Orientalist Sylvain Lévi has made this crystal clear in his excellent booklet: *L'Inde et le Monde*. He describes there what he calls the *provincial* brahmanic civilization (Hinduism proper) and the "humanisme bouddhique *universel*". He says,[2] characterizing the amazing, unexpected rôle of Western Orientalism in the affairs of the world of to-day: "By an anomaly without parallel among the rest of mankind, it is by teachings from abroad that she [i.e. India] has begun to know her true greatness."

Although it sounds to us now incredible, it is nevertheless an undeniable fact that up to the beginning of the 20th century India had practically effaced Buddha from her memory. Now, thanks to the painstaking work of the Western Orientalists, she rightly extols him as one of her greatest sons. Asoka, one of the most remarkable emperor-figures that ever lived (3rd century B.C.) had sunk into complete oblivion. The decipherment of his Rock Edicts, which had stood for two millennia unnoticed on India's soil, by the Englishman Prinsep in the 1830's was the beginning of the unveiling, to India and to the world at large, of one of the most fascinating religio/political stories that exist. Alexander the Great, who first established contact between Greece and India, whose Diadochs had ambassadors at the court of Candragupta (3rd century B.C.) in Patna, and from whose daring expeditions sprang Indo-Grecian kingdoms, left not even his name in India, except in popular tales introduced by the Muslim invaders. Lévi summarizes it briefly: "It is Europe who has given back Buddha, Asoka, to India."

He advances another example, the great Buddhist thinker and poet Asvaghosa (*c.* 100 A.D.), whom Lévi himself made

[1] Think e.g. of the pyramids and tomb temples in Egypt, the remnants of Babylonian civilization in Iraq, the Buddhist Borobudur and the Hindu Prambanan in Indonesia.

[2] *op. cit.*, p. 15.

known to Europe and India in 1892 by editing his *Buddhacarita*. Asvaghosa, whom Lévi considers a genius of the first rank, reminding us of Milton, Goethe, Voltaire and Kant in one, "is completely a conquest of Western learning". One could make a long list, to show "what India [and many other Eastern countries] owes to its contact with Europe *in the awakening of its consciousness*" (italics mine). Lévi closes his striking account by saying:[1] "To such conquests, disinterested triumph of the human intelligence over ignorance, the East has no objection to raise." Indeed, India (and other Eastern countries, in varying degrees) would never have known a coherent picture of her political, cultural and religious history and significance, if Western Orientalism had not reconstructed it.

In the present overheated atmosphere of sensitiveness and resentment between Orient and Occident, it is pertinent to observe that a chivalrous recognition of this whole matter on the Oriental side, and absence of boasting in respect of it on the Western side, would be a real and deeply needed contribution to the possibility of a "coming dialogue". It would also be a healthy antidote to much high-sounding but unconsciously hypocritical talk on the unity of all religions as the elixir for the ills of our present storm-tossed world.[2]

[1] *ibid.*, p. 136. Lévi was a great friend and admirer of India. In his case it should be superfluous to remark that he does not speak like this to deprecate India.

[2] A splendid example of this chivalrous recognition is shown in the following quotation from an article on Kenneth Cragg's *The Call of the Minaret* by Dr. Muhammad Daud Rahbar, a Pakistani Muslim, in *The Muslim World*, Jan. 1958, p. 45. Dr. Rahbar says:
"Chairs in Islamic learning have existed in Universities of the Christian world for centuries. Scholars of various Christian countries have rendered immeasurable service to Muslim learning, with their innumerable editions of the classics of Islamic lore, sometimes of massive proportions. They have collected great libraries of Muslim literature and catalogued them most methodically. Apart from thus preserving this literature and making it accessible to scholars everywhere, they have spent hundreds of lifetimes in writing systematic grammars and lexicons of Islamic languages, in producing commentaries on our classics in modern languages, and in the translation of those classics. The Leyden Encyclopedia is but one exemplary achievement. . . . We are certain that we do not possess teams of Islamic scholars able to produce an original encyclopedia of the same quality, nor shall possess for years and years to come. Can any Muslim scholar in the whole Islamic world claim with conviction that he knows more about Christianity than the average Christian Islamicist in a Western University knows about Islam? Do not we Muslims rather talk about Christianity from ignorance than from adequate knowledge?"
Panikkar (*op. cit.*, p. 492) also says expressly that European scholars and thinkers enabled India, Ceylon and Indonesia to think in terms of historic continuity, and that from these same scholars they learnt to rationalize the belief they always held, viz. that their inherited cultures are superior to others.

THE TRANSMISSION OF WESTERNISM

Having treated the "unbroken epic", we now turn to the "broken epic" of transmitting modern Western liberal culture and idealism, new political institutions, moral and social uplift work.

As with Orientalism, it does not fit into our plan to describe all aspects and effects of this complex process, which has awakened new energies, hopes and demands in the Eastern peoples and introduced quite new principles and methods for managing the human problems of society. In short, it has helped to create an Asia with a new face. We will touch only on some points, which seem to us essential.[1]

Once a colonial Government was well established, it soon became apparent that efficient administration, the maintenance of peace and order, the exploitation of the resources of a "colonial" country, could not stay within its well-defined borders. Even with the strict principle of leaving people as much as possible alone, one could not build up an administration without using indigenous people to run the machinery. Administration as well as exploitation (stimulating commerce and transport, etc.) required the creation of new, unknown institutions, especially a new kind of training and education for indigenous personnel in the Administration.

India is in this respect a good example. In the first quarter of the 19th century one sees there cropping up amongst the Western rulers a difference of opinion as to policy, which already betrays forebodings of the "split conscience" of Europe on account of its cultural and spiritual background. The "occidentalists" among the Europeans asked for education in English and European knowledge. Voices in favour of a determined policy were raised by some of the best civil servants, who then pronounced as the goal of the British Raj to educate India towards self-government. For instance, in European and Indian circles a violent discussion took place on the abolition of *sati* (burning of widows with their dead husband). The "Orientalists", amongst whom there were perhaps (besides

[1] Panikkar's closing chapter is very profitable reading, the more so because it is by an Asian with excellent training in history and economics and experience in diplomatic service in Egypt and China. The literature on this subject is so immense that its bibliography would itself make a book.

conservatives, who prized above all the preservation of the *status quo*) men who had some inkling of the shock an initiation into the principles and ideals of an utterly different world might produce in India, pleaded for education within the existing Indian framework. Dubois,[1] who wrote in that period, echoes these stirrings in the words: "If it be possible to ameliorate the condition of the people of India, I am convinced that this desirable result will be attained under the new régime", and: "I for one cannot believe that this nation [i.e. the British] will ever be blind enough to compromise its own noble character by refusing participation in these benefits [i.e. of Western civilization] to a subject people which is content to live peaceably under its sway."

Macaulay in 1838 in his famous Minute on the problems of the language-vehicle (English or Sanskrit) for higher education gave his verdict in favour of English. A momentous decision indeed. The motives behind this decision were a compound of mainly three elements: the strong 19th-century belief in the victorious march of Progress for the whole of mankind; a deep conviction of the excellence and superiority of Western civilization, and a profound ignorance of Indian culture.[2] Macaulay's decision leads us to the heart of the matter. The educational policy of a country is always a strategic point of prime importance. This is still more the case in a colonially governed country. So the most portentous step of the British Government in India has been its decision to build up a system of education, which at its top (colleges and universities) was almost wholly Western in content and modelled on the prototype of English college education.

This brings us back to the "split conscience" of Europe, which lies at the bottom of the *inevitable* downfall of Western "colonialism" and imperialism. "Colonialism", subjection of alien peoples for one's own benefit, was secretly or openly tormented by an ambiguity inherent in the spiritual make-up of Europe. Unscrupulous as the behaviour of Western imperialism often has been, this undeniable fact cannot

[1] *op. cit.*, p. 5.

[2] In his conceit Macaulay used the famous flamboyant phrase that one shelf of a European library was of more worth than a whole library of Sanskrit books. He was unaware of the labours of the Western Oriental scholars, who were on the way to expose the hollowness of this assertion.

minimize in the least another fact of capital and creative importance. The moral conscience of Europe has through a long educative process by Christianity acquired a peculiar sensitivity, which runs counter to the strong but unregenerate impulses of imperialism. Moreover, and particularly so in the 19th century, the *humanitarian* outlook and emphasis of the Enlightenment, which was included in the democratic ideology in politics and in society, determined the moral idealism of the élite. This synthesis of Christian sensitivity and humanitarian idealism and enthusiasm, which constituted, besides Progress and the mastery of Nature, the (at least officially) recognized elements of the hypostasized "Western way of life", was the hidden axe at the root of the flourishing tree of triumphant colonialism.

This is what I mean by "split conscience". Objectively speaking, the West could ultimately not justify its colonial dominion in the face of its own normative ideal of the "Western way of life". The ultimate basis of this dominion was power, which may have its place in our relative, confused human relations[1] but cannot stand up before the tribunal of mercy and justice which in the "Western way of life" were in moral respect acknowledged as the sovereign lights of life.

To be more concrete, it was impossible to educate generations of young Indians in Mill, Shakespeare, Milton, the Bible (the many Christian colleges certainly did so), etc., to inculcate into them the glorious excellence of Liberty and Justice, to permeate them with new ideals of citizenship and social responsibility, and yet to expect them not to apply all this moral and political idealism to their own situation; if not yet in practice, then at any rate in theory and carrying it in their minds as a ferment. The slogans which many Westerners, particularly the responsible statesmen, used to elevate the whole "colonial"

---

[1] It must always be kept in mind that the *absolute* power-view and the *absolute* justice-view are always theoretical abstractions, never concrete realities. Human life as it is, is always a mixture of relativisms, inherent in human imperfection and sin. The problem is to watch always when Power follows its inherent instincts of unscrupulousness and ruthlessness, and is not heedful of the powers that rather restrain its daemon; and also to watch always when Justice as a principle follows its inherent tendency of inhumaneness, not heedful of the only power that can restrain its daemon (i.e. subserviency to itself as a Principle *in abstracto*) viz. that its real meaning is to be there *for* man, not for its own sake (*fiat justitia pereat mundus*, let justice be done though the world perish); to *serve* human needs for the sake of human solidarity.

drama to a higher level than naked power and self-interest—
such as "the white man's burden" and "*mission sacrée*", are a
perfect expression of the inner ambiguity in the West's "split
conscience". They are hybrid expressions, combining real
sincerity and not less real hypocrisy. One or other of the two
elements preponderated according to whether a genuine
attempt was made to understand the situation on the highest
possible level under the unalterable circumstances, or whether
it was simply whitewash to smooth over, in high-sounding
terms, the inner ambiguity.

The dynamic Western penetration into the life of ancient
Eastern societies and cultures could, *logically* speaking, only end
in raising and nourishing the one outstanding fruit of all
"colonialisms" of our time: nationalism. Logic became
actualized. Nationalism in the long run, aggressive militant
nationalism, was a natural, morally inescapable, outcome.

NATIONALISM BORN OF COLONIALISM

It could not but come. It is the only answer to colonial
servitude, even the most beneficial, especially when, as in the
case of the West, the rulers themselves taught their colonial subjects the way towards a new self-respect and dignity inculcated
in their minds in the name of Western idealism. Therefore it is
no exaggeration to put the whole drama into the somewhat startling assertion: it is not the Asian or African nationalists, however much they may behave in a vociferous, emotional and
unbalanced way, who are the great disturbers of the world of
to-day. Rather the West itself is the disturber, because it is the
centre from which the world-embracing earthquake in all
realms of life has emanated and still emanates, and at the same
time the dynamic powerhouse which fed and feeds it. To shake
the foundations of "ancient" societies, to pulverize numberless
"primitive" societies, to violate and question brutally their
deep-rooted apprehensions, to change forcefully their whole
world outlook and world image, to pour into them new desires
and "myths", cannot but have revolutionary consequences, and
it is obvious that the turbulent waters will need time to carve
out new river-courses.

The "colonial" meeting of the West with the East, which
seems on the surface so aloof (and in fact was) is by its

unintended dynamic consequences a very important concomitant in the cultural and religious encounter of East and West. And the reason it became so dynamic was exactly that "split conscience", that peculiarly Western sensitivity to moral and social responsibility which introduced into government an ingredient which had its origin in a different, even antithetical dimension. It was a compound of Christian and, in the sense of Enlightenment idealism, humanitarian feelings and principles.

It is wholly in line with this "philanthropic" inspiration that Christian Missions, either privately or as substitutes for the Governments, made such a great and stimulating contribution to education, social service, medical care, moral welfare. There were also, especially in the first half of the 19th century, many outstanding civil servants in India, who synthesized in their own persons a sincere Christian faith and humanitarian idealism. The dynamic hidden in this "philanthropy" (also hidden to those who were its protagonists or instruments) has been the leaven in the momentous "meeting" of West and East, which has worked in it with silent, unobtrusive, but relentless logical force.

It is interesting to quote here again H. Dubois[1] as it demonstrates that even this sagacious man did not foresee this development. In the quotations given above from his book are passages in which he expresses his sympathy with the colonial Government's endeavours of his day to ameliorate the condition of the people of India, and expresses the hope that the Government would continue on that road in spite of much negative criticism. He continues, however, by saying:

At the same time I venture to predict that it [i.e. the Government] will attempt in vain to effect any considerable changes in the social condition of the people of India, whose character, principles, customs and ineradicable conservatism will always present insurmountable obstacles. To make a people happy, it is essential that they themselves should desire to be made happy and should co-operate with those who are working for their happiness. Now, the people of India, it appears to me, neither possess this desire nor are anxious to co-operate to this end.

This remarkable passage shows that the writer, who had lived for decades *within* the pattern of India's tradition-bound

[1] *op. cit.*, p. 5.

society, was so deeply (and rightly) impressed by the massive immobility of such a huge system of custom and belief that his shrewd sagacity forbade him to entertain the possibility of any substantial change; but at the same time he nevertheless lauded and encouraged the Government in obedience to the humane leanings of his heart. At that time he could not suspect that in these humane and Christian "by-products" of the Western invasion lay the explosive dynamic which would accomplish just the thing he deemed impossible, and even more. It not only engendered the "desire", which Dubois rightly deemed indispensable in this land of "ineradicable conservatism", but even by-passed in its effects the desire for "co-operation" which Dubois rightly saw as the second indispensable condition. To be sure, that "co-operation", not believed in by Dubois as possible, became for a time a reality, but this stage was passed and the thing happened of which Dubois would not even have dreamt. The Asians themselves, sons of these civilizations of "ineradicable conservatism", took the task of radical change into their own hands. The leadership was, of course, provided by the Westernized men and women of these regions. The West equipped and aroused them to this act of self-assertion.

IS THE EAST ONLY TEMPORARILY GALVANIZED?

This is a good place to devote attention to a question which is a matter of discussion amongst Western observers as well as Eastern intellectuals. Many Western writers, often so-called experts, are still so deeply imbued with the idea of the extreme "otherness" of the East and its determining life-apprehensions in regard to the world, man, and man in his relationships and social structures, that they regard the dynamic shock received by the East as still a superficial affair which will gradually diminish in its effects, especially as Western political dominion has now abdicated. In the depth of Asia's soul, they reason, there has not taken place any change, and, though seemingly dormant for the moment, it is unbroken as to its identity. They are far from regarding it as impossible that after a certain period of turbulence, uncertainty and feverish attempts to try its hand at the political and social "forms" of the West, the East will revert to type. The present so-called resurgence of Eastern religions and cultures seems to corroborate this view of the ultimate inalterability of the East, in spite of its present frenzied dynamism.[1]

This view amounts in fact to saying that the contact with the West will appear not to have dynamized the East as a permanent, incontrovertible event, but to have only temporarily galvanized it. Panikkar in the "Conclusion" of his book already often quoted is evidently much concerned about this opinion and rejects it, pointing to what he considers the lasting effects of the Western invasion. Yet in the more specific fields of cultural typology he is convinced that, even if vaster changes occur through the influences the West has introduced than are visible already at present, "Asian civilizations will continue to develop their marked individuality and remain spiritually and intellectually separate from Christian Europe".[2]

The strength, the uniqueness and tenacity of the peculiar dominant Asian apprehensions of life and the world cannot easily be over-estimated. Neither can its capacity for resilience, which paradoxically has become strengthened by the touch of the magic wand of Western infiltrations. The Western propounders of the "revert-to-type" theory seem, however, to over-emphasize the indispensability of Western *political* dominion for keeping Asia sufficiently long under a psychosomatic treatment that can guarantee a radical change. They leave out of account the possibility that the ever-increasing political and economic interdependence, which releases still unforeseeable powers, will multiply the efficacity of the Western injection beyond what the West did by its political dominion.

Panikkar seems also to ignore this aspect, and consequently to leave too much out of consideration the fact that the end of Western political dominion is not the end of Western cultural and spiritual influence, nor the beginning of an era in which the digestion and manipulation of the Western influence is furthermore an exclusive affair of the Asians. To be sure, they have in the determination of their cultural and spiritual selfhood a great say, but not an exclusive one. Moreover, we are standing only at the *beginning* of a cultural confrontation and meeting of unprecedented and incalculable dimensions, in which the conscious running and willing of man, be he Western or Eastern, is not necessarily the decisive factor.

[1] This resurgence will be discussed in Chapter 10.   [2] *op. cit.*, p. 506.

THE AMBIGUITY IN PHILANTHROPY

The word philanthropy was used above to characterize the "liberal" policies of education, social uplift, moral welfare, etc., which were part of Western colonialism. This word is here used in its original sense of human sympathy, humanitarian love of mankind. Now, however, it needs to be said that this "philanthropy", because part of colonial *policy*, contained an ambiguity. This ambiguity is inherent in all acts of political governments in dealing with "foreign" affairs.[1] A political Government, *any* political Government, if it performs in the field of "foreign" politics an act which is inspired by idealist motives and altruistic aims, never acts (nor can act) out of pure cosmopolitan love of man (=*philanthropia*[2]). Its motives and aims inevitably are always bound up with substantial considerations of self-interest and self-regard. That is because a *government,* even if it is generous, can never deny its primary nature, viz. that it represents the power and interests of a given people and country. This is the ambiguity inherent in political Governments and their "foreign" policies, which, if at certain times they involve actions having an undeniably idealistic tinge, do give to naïve idealists so much food for over-abundant praise and hope, and to cynics occasion for mordant sarcasm and derision.

The ambiguity in the special matter of "liberal" Western colonial policy in fulfilling its averred "sacred mission" lay as well in a reversal as in a specific combination of motives. These were especially operative in the motives for the vast educational policy that was in many cases developed. Officially the primary motive was to initiate an upper layer of the Eastern world into the knowledge, ideals and life principles of the West, making them sharers in these excellent, elevating benefits. Also officially the secondary motive was that such a high-level education, either locally or in the metropolis, would yield as a by-product men who would be more efficient instruments for the administration and rule of the colonial country. More efficient and adapted, because they could understand better the why and

[1] Remember the definition of colonialism given above as being the rule of "foreigners" over peoples regarded as "foreigners".

[2] The word *philanthropia* derives from the Bible, but there it signifies the philanthropy of God, His love of men. Titus 3: 4.

how of the spirit and technique of the governmental machinery. In fact, the secondary motive mostly became primary,[1] and the primary descended to secondary rank. This is what is meant by "reversal" and "combination". Even in the "reversal" the two motives each made their contribution.

These considerations, however, lead us to the rather startling fact that the colonial Governments themselves have been the creators of a new Asian "intelligentsia". This they meant to be their more efficient and understanding *instrument* in establishing and continuing their dominion, but instead it became the bearer of an ever-increasing vehement nationalism, insisting on getting an answer to the unanswerable (at least for a Government which after all was related to the background of Western Christian humanitarian ideology): an answer to the question by what right—if not by power—their country was kept in subjection. Unanswerable also because as good pupils of Western higher education they knew that "colonialism" and the West's moral-religious conscience were incompatible. They indicted the West in the name of the supreme Norm of the West.

To put it differently: the colonial Governments by creating a Westernized "intelligentsia", destined to be loyal instruments, created the judges and grave-diggers of colonialism.

The ambiguity which was at the bottom of this whole para-doxical process is the reason why I have proposed to call this aspect of "colonialism", in contradistinction to the disinterested spiritual conquest of Asian cultures and religions by Western Orientalists, the "broken epic" of Western dominance.

THE UNFORESEEN BECOMES THE PRINCIPAL RESULT

This drama of colonialism, its faults and achievements, its growth and disappearance, is a telling example of what the German philosopher and psychologist, Wilhelm Wundt, has termed *"die Heterogonie der Zwecke"* (the diversity of the goals). He tried to express in this formula one of the main character-istics of the course of human history, which lends to history an aspect of mystery and teaches great modesty as to man's

---

[1] I must leave it at this assertion, because it would take too much space to illustrate it by examples which I observed in various colonial countries when living there.

capacity to *explain* history (a claim made so often by modern historians). Wundt meant to say: man as agent in history finds as a continuous experience that he is nearly always transcended by the outcome of his deliberate acts and undertakings. The more impressive and deliberate they are, the more he experiences that their main results are not what he consciously intended by them, but are the so-called by-products, which happened as *unforeseen* and *unforeseeable* consequences and in fact became the principal result.

The whole history of colonialism, including too the disinterested, a-political study of the Orient, the creation of a "liberal" colonial policy with many aspects, is a striking illustration of Wundt's "*Heterogonie der Zwecke*", which after all reduces to a compact, neat formula the awe-inspiring mystery of human history. It reveals the great limitations of the modern conception of history, which proposes to treat history as self-explanatory.[1]

[1] Cf. R. Niebuhr: *Faith and History*.

Chapter Four

THE SIGNIFICANCE OF CHRISTIAN MISSIONS

IN the preceding chapter the two facets of the colonial period in the meeting of West and East, the labours of Western Oriental Science with their effects and the "liberal" policies, which were also features of Western "colonialism", were called redeeming factors. I do not hesitate to propose Christian Missions as the third "redeeming factor".[1]

I am fully aware that, in the company of writers on the cultural and spiritual meeting of East and West, this is not a popular thing to do. The prevailing custom is to mention it in passing, often with condescension and a hardly concealed scorn, if not with harsh condemnatory irritation. Hermann Keyserling's notable book: *Das Reisetagebuch eines Philosophen*,[2] written in 1912, is a good example of this way of dealing with Missions and missionaries as a factor in the Eastern ferment. It is to be found in most books dealing with the cultural and spiritual meeting of East and West.

Behind this condemnatory or unsympathetic attitude is hidden not only a deep misunderstanding of the Gospel, but also a curiously inhibited view of the Western Invasion. The argument one meets everywhere, in able writers and in the mouths of Western business men and civil servants, runs as follows: "Why do Missions disturb and penetrate into these Eastern structures and religions, introducing an alien element? They have no right to do so."

The simple answer is first that the whole Western Invasion, cultural, economic and political, represented in civil servants, business men, teachers etc., perpetrates the same thing by

---

[1] By Christian Missions we mean the missionary activity of the Roman Catholic Church as well as of the non-Roman Christian world.
[2] E.T. *The Travel Diary of a Philosopher*, 1925.

disturbing as an alien element the Eastern structures of culture and religion. Yet these agents of the great disturbance do not dream of applying the demand to quit, which they direct towards Missions, to themselves. Second: if Christianity on this argument had stayed in the Mediterranean, it would never have become the great educative power of Europe, of which every Westerner is a product and a debtor. This whole kind of reasoning is at bottom rather childish, because logically speaking it excludes all spiritual free trade, which is the life-blood of true cultural life. At the same time it betrays the modern fallacy of the West: that is, treating religion as an isolated sector of human life.

HUMANISTIC REVULSION AGAINST MISSIONS

For all these reasons it is left to specific missionary literature to accentuate the significance of Missions to the whole scope of this complicated event. The public reached by this literature is, however, mainly the body of supporters of Missions. In so far as it catches the attention of people amongst the culturally interested, who do not belong to these supporters but often are antagonistic to Missions, it is read as a specimen of specious pleading by people who have their own axe to grind. It is rarely used as material for getting a full-sized picture of the Western Invasion and the Eastern responses. Therefore, to term Missions a third "redeeming factor" cannot count on much sympathy and understanding amongst the writers on the great theme of Eastern-Western contact in the last 150 years, whose names usually occur in the extensive bibliographies on this subject.

It does not take very deep reflection to understand this curious phenomenon, however much one may consider it—and with reason—as a symptom of blind prejudice, sailing under the flag of objective presentation of the subject. It does not take deep reflection because it is simply an exemplification of the general phenomenon of current writing of history, including the history of the West itself. The guiding spirit in modern history-writing and interpretation, and therefore the whole orchestration of selection and emphases, is (leaving on one side the dogmatic Marxist interpretation) humanistic.

Christopher Dawson[1] has rightly emphasized the point that

[1] In *Making of Europe*, p. 249.

since the break-up of mediaeval unity and since the religious divisions which, resulting from the Reformation, split the West, the cultural unity of Europe has been "based on a common intellectual tradition and a common allegiance to the classical tradition rather than on a common Faith". In the preceding chapter I have stressed with sincere conviction and grateful recognition the excellent and undoubted merits of—to use again the words of that truly great humanist Sylvain Lévi—the "disinterested triumph of human intelligence over ignorance". Therefore, in saying that the usual tendency to take scant notice of the significance of Missions in the matter of East-West culture contact is an exemplification of the prevailing humanistic method of writing and interpreting history, I do not want to seem lacking in genuine appreciation of the great achievements and merits of Humanism in the field of historical research. These achievements and merits cannot easily be exaggerated.

And yet it seems unmistakable to a fair-minded observer, who rejoices in the feats of Humanism, that the prevailing humanistic approach has one blind spot in its interpretation of cultural history.[1] It excels in the field of culture proper, and of the arts, whether Eastern or Western. Even in the field of foreign religions. But as soon as Christianity comes on the scene (which is clearly the case with Missions) it seems as if a certain inhibition, a conscious or semi-conscious revulsion, becomes operative and distorts the picture. Not only does there appear a strange inability to understand Christianity or Missions adequately from within—as one rightly tries to do in regard to foreign religions—on its own merits as it were, but also, in regard to Missions particularly, a propensity to evaluate it first and foremost according to its faults (which are indeed many) and to misunderstand it as to its intention and rôle. Current hearsay is often used as a sufficient basis for judgment.[2]

It is very striking that many Eastern writers on the subject of East-West cultural relations are often fairer in their dealing with the significance of Christianity and Missions in the Eastern

[1] A magnificent example of a writer who is chiefly concerned about the problem of culture, free of this blind spot, is Denis de Rougemont in his book *Man's Western Quest*.

[2] From a long personal experience in various Asian countries I could give many illustrations.

scene. This may be said even when one recognizes that Eastern writers react to Christianity with great antipathy. The instances of fairness are the more striking because these writers are as non-Christians more justified in having a definite bias against Christianity and Missions. Panikkar, who has a special section in his book on "The failure of the Christian Missions"[1]—and he clearly and understandably rejoices in this failure as he sees it—shows a far more balanced judgment in this matter. In his "Conclusion"[2] he aptly reminds his readers that "the European expansion towards the East began as a crusade", and that "the crusading spirit was replaced . . . by a spirit of evangelization".[3]

This is true, and pertinent to the subject of the momentous East-West culture contact, because this was its beginning. Panikkar should have made it clearer that not only (in so far as the religious motive was the dominant one in the whole undertaking) was anti-Islamic crusading spirit the impulse, but at least as much a positive missionary urge. Mexico and Cortez' letters to his King are one of the clear proofs; also the whole position of a great figure such as Francis Xavier, to mention only a few examples.

Panikkar, however, goes further in his estimate of the West's influence in Asia by stating: "It may indeed be said that the most serious persistent and planned effort of European nations in the 19th century was their missionary activity in India and China".[4] "All that need be said here is that *in surveying the influences of Europe on Asian countries* [italics mine] it is necessary to keep in mind the unbroken religious urge of European expansion, and take into consideration the immense non-official and voluntary effort that it represented." Most Western writers on the same subject could learn a lesson in giving due place to an obvious fact from this anti-missionary and anti-Christian Indian author.

A NON-OFFICIAL AND VOLUNTARY EFFORT

The "immense *non-official* and *voluntary* effort" (to use Panikkar's words) was carried out under auspicious and adverse conditions alike as an act of joyful obedience to what was felt as a divine commission and obligation to spread the

---

[1] *op. cit.*, pp. 454-460. [2] pp. 479-509.
[3] pp. 480, 481. [4] pp. 481, 482.

Message of world-salvation through Jesus Christ, "unto the ends of the earth". Whoever does not seize this point in its biblical plenitude of universality and of reserveless committal, not to a dogma, but to the living Lord Jesus Christ, cannot but misinterpret Christian Missions by reducing them to an annoying proselytism or an exasperating arrogance in forcing one's own limited truth down the throats of others.

This is not to deny that in the history of Missions there have been amongst those who represented them, either as missionaries or as advocates of Missions, people who in their human zeal and narrow-mindedness disguised[1] the primary motive and source in a way which suggested the attitudes just mentioned. Neither do we gloss over the undeniable fact that secondary motives of a different calibre and nature mingled with the primary motive in its biblical purport and sometimes, in practice, took the first place. To acknowledge this frankly in the interest of the missionary concern itself should not, however, make us forget that even these distortions cannot efface the fact that the Christian missionary movement represents one of the most amazing human phenomena in world history as a whole. Distorted or not, acting according to its true nature as a disinterested service out of surrender to Jesus Christ, the Lord and Saviour of the world, or affected by the poison of spiritual imperialism, it is unique (this word is not too strong and is used deliberately) by the power with which it has inspired and sustained through the ages numberless men and women to lives of devotion, service, danger, loneliness. They were sensitive to the needs of the lowliest and most despised and downtrodden mass of humanity, faithfully persevering when often results or success did not ensue. It is also a unique fact that especially in the period called "Modern Missions", i.e. from the beginning of the 18th century till to-day, this outpouring of lives and money, these triumphs and defeats, have been carried by the

---

[1] To this offensive disguise Han Suyin clearly reacts when she says: "How difficult it must be to become a missionary. In order to convince others, one must be so completely indoctrinated with the superiority of one's own brand of belief. To understand, to tolerate, to condone is incompatible with the very idea of being in possession of a higher truth, a better explanation of the spiritual life." See *A Many Splendoured Thing*, p. 13. The ultimately agnostic bias regarding Truth expressed in these words is evident, and a misunderstanding of the Christian truth. Yet the author cannot be blamed for her view, because there are undeniably types of Mission that give this impression.

sustained, voluntary effort of people all over the world, rich and poor, wise and ignorant, educated or uneducated, most of whom never knew the country or the people or the individuals which were the aim of their contributions.

Everyone who knows the Christian Churches and the missionary activity in the domain of these Churches from the inside cannot but agree that, while again frankly acknowledging that even in this case there is of course unholy fire on the altar, Christian Missions have represented for centuries the concern for the spiritual and bodily needs of the "unknown" and "far-off" neighbour, which is at present, by the totally new world set-up, thrown upon the nations as a world responsibility. The fact that Christian Missions have done this for centuries when no incentive whatever, issuing from the world situation, was operative, manifests the spontaneous religious urge which created and sustained it. Both for its uniqueness and its significance it deserves more in the books on history, even on Church history, than the silence or scanty notice generally accorded to it.

This whole state of affairs is particularly evident in the origins of the period of "Modern Missions". For this reason, and above all for the reason that these "Modern Missions" run parallel with and have intertwined with the rise and growth of Western colonialism with its political and economic consequences and the Western invasion in the cultural sense, it is appropriate to look at it more closely.

When writing about the period of the origins of "Modern Missions" it has to be noted that this is an affair happening in the non-Roman Christian world, because Roman Catholic Missions started simultaneously with the Age of Discoveries and have continued uninterruptedly to the present day. When studying this period a truly amazing spectacle unfolds itself. It is impressive evidence of the peculiar nature of Christianity amongst the religions and philosophies of the world, and an equally impressive manifestation of the dynamic nature of the biblical faith in Jesus Christ, the Lord and Saviour of the world, not as a principle, a spirit or an ideal, but as an ever-active reality.

Historically speaking, this new upsurge of missionary zeal is an aspect of what is known in the Anglo-Saxon world as the

"Great Awakening", in which Jonathan Edwards of New England and John Wesley of Old England are the focal personalities, and in the Continental European world as "Pietism", in which August Hermann Franke with Graf Ludwig von Zinzendorf are the leading figures. The amazing spectacle consists in the unbelievable outburst of burning concern for the salvation of the world for the sake of Jesus Christ. Not in the official institutional Churches, nor amongst the wise and the mighty, but amongst the simple, ignorant and unknown. They had no considerable knowledge of the world, but spontaneously saw the world in its entirety as their parish. It is probably the most authentic illustration in Church history of the words[1] of the Apostle Paul: "For the love of Christ constraineth us . . . God . . . has given to us the ministry of reconcilation, to wit, that God was in Christ reconciling the world unto himself . . . and has committed unto us the word of reconciliation . . . Now then we are ambassadors for Christ, as though God did beseech you by us: we pray you in Christ's stead, be ye reconciled to God". The missionary development which resulted from these beginnings, from whose impetus all present missionary activity is still deriving, is in many respects a "hidden epic", which could provide material for many exciting pages.[2]

AMBIGUITY IN THE 19TH CENTURY "COLONIAL" PERIOD

The 19th century, though in most respects like the 18th century a pioneering period in Missions, brought for Christian Missions nevertheless a great change. The cause is obvious. Missions had to happen and operate in a quite new world context of political and economic relations. To put it differently, they had to operate in the context of Western imperialism and (originally unintended but gradually more planned) Western cultural invasion in the East.

In the 19th century, although the fundamental inspiration and motive remained the same, nevertheless there entered into Missions an ambiguity which calls for explanation. This

[1] 2 Cor. 5: 14, 18, 19, 20.
[2] The literature on this subject is immense. I can refer only to J. Richter: *Missionskunde*, and J. van den Berg: *Constrained by Jesus' love, an enquiry into the motives of the missionary awakening in Great Britain in the period between 1698 and 1815*, and the bibliographies there.

ambiguity was due to various causes. Missions had mainly to function in the realm and atmosphere of Western colonialism or semi-colonialism. There were various Mission fields in regions of the world (New Guinea, the Batak countries, in Sumatra, other parts of Indonesia, big parts of Africa etc.) where Missions did their work for a long time unprotected by any Western political power, because these regions were either purely nominally part of a colonial area or still independent. But in the most conspicuous parts of the Eastern world where Missions of sundry sections of the Christian Church exercised their activity, they did so under the protection and with the assent of the colonial governments. The legal motivation was the principle of religious neutrality which the colonial governments in the multi-religious countries of the East had adopted, a somewhat different but in principle equivalent application of the attitude of the Western Home Governments in their multi-confessional countries. This neutrality because of its own inherent ambiguity and questionableness[1] had in its application, in Western countries as well as in Eastern, many shades and varieties, depending on the different situations in which it had to function. On the whole it worked rather well, and under its wings missionary activity could deploy quietly, provided it did not come into conflict with public law and order.

This régime opened a wide opportunity for the activity of Missions and was from this point of view a real blessing. Missions became, not in the political but in the general sense of the word, closely allied to the colonial machinery in its educational and medical and social service facets. Having always been active on their private initiative in these fields as pioneers, they now, to a great extent, became integrated in this part of the machinery by the grant-in-aid system. Missions clearly profited in that way very much as to the expansion of this service aspect of their work, touching a great number of people, the majority of whom were non-Christians. A considerable number of the leading Westernized intelligentsia received their

[1] This is not its own fault, but was caused by the fact that within the framework of democratic states in the West, in which all citizens are equal before the law and have liberty of conscience and of expression, the difficulty of a multi-religious society found its emergency solution in the principle of neutrality as the least harmful and workable hypothesis in regard to the touchy subject of Religion. In theory and practice, as everybody knows, pure neutrality does not and cannot exist.

training in missionary schools and colleges, which were often preferred by non-Christians above other institutions because of their quality. It can be said without exaggeration that Christian Missions have been great agents in the East-Western culture contact which took place in this dimension. Not less in the field of medical care and social service, which also should be taken into account when considering the matter of meeting of cultures. Missions have made a great contribution in permeating the Eastern societies in which they worked with new Christian-humanitarian ideals; in short, in humanizing the whole outlook.

This is not to say that these Eastern societies did not have humane institutions and feelings of their own. Far from it. They had, but wholly group-bound and tradition-bound. Christian Missions were an important instrument (together with other agencies) for inculcating a humanization which transcended the traditional limits and opened people's eyes to entirely new channels of service. To mention only a few examples: Missions were the first to tackle the outcaste problem of India, although they never could hope, being foreigners, to solve it. An important activity such as the Ramakrishna movement is in its orientation and devoted activity unthinkable without the stimulus derived from Christian Missions. In Java the Muhammadiyya movement, which has grown into a vast organization of Muslim religious education and propagation of the Muslim faith in modern form, with several grades of school education, medical work and social or charitable work of other kinds, has from the beginning frankly stated that it was the example of Christian Missions (to which it is opposed) that put the conception, and the courage to act, into its head.[1]

Taking all this into account, it has nevertheless to be said that this condition of affairs under the aegis of colonialism (which was in no sense the creation of Missions but simply overtook it) had also its questionable sides. Peoples belonging to societies, to which the whole notion of the separation of Religion and State is alien and the new-fangled Western idea of the relative autonomy of the differentiated fields of culture is opaque and unthinkable, were so to speak by their whole

[1] For years I had close contact with this movement.

habit of mind disposed to see Western colonial Government and Western Missions, run by Westerners (often of the same nationality as the foreign rulers) as somehow having an understanding with each other. The partial integration of the practical, social aspects of missionary activity in the framework of Government policy by means of the grant-in-aid system, could not but substantiate this natural interpretation (natural to these peoples) and strengthen the prevailing conception that Missions were nothing but an aspect of Western colonial rule. Maybe, with some difference and distance from each other; but these were Western subtleties of no relevance to the Asian mind.

This situation was resignedly accepted as the unalterable situation in which one lived, and on that basis an attitude of studied aloofness from Missions or of more or less eager contact were both possible. The studied aloofness could, however, also mean the deep conviction that Missions embodied the subtle, spiritual aspect of foreign political dominance, the mask under which this political dominance hypocritically tried by a spiritual imperialism to bring not only bodies but also souls under its control. This suspicion was the natural reaction of a mind which thinks in a totalitarian way about the manifestation of Western activity, founded in a Western apprehension of life and the world, and which could not but be a closed book to the Eastern mind. The more or less eager contact led either to appreciable influence or to a genuine religious meeting and dialogue, in many cases resulting in accepting Christianity as a personal faith.

The realistic considerations offered in the preceding reflections do not, of course, minimize in the least the great significance of Missions as agent in the cultural and spiritual East-Western contact. These objective changes, however, landed Missions in an ambiguity which obscured their true character. It would be unjust to blame Missions for the situation, as it arose out of a changed world picture. The only blame one can and must lay on Missions, looking back on the whole story, is that only rarely were they adequately aware of the obscuring of their character, and often met a world, steeped in an Eastern atmosphere and invaded by the West, with Western arguments. Arguments which might ease one's own conscience, but were not a real answer to the situation as it was.

The most glaring example of obscuring and obtuseness to it has been the way in which Christian Missions (Roman Catholic and Protestant) slowly penetrated into China in the wake of Western mercantile penetration, surrounded by the clamour of such a shameful war as the Opium and other Wars, in which a proud people like the Chinese was humbled to the dust. The fact in itself of penetrating into China, when it "opened", is plausible; but the lack of scruples and the blindness to the ambiguity and its dangers into which one blundered is the sore spot, which cannot be effaced by the equally undeniable fact that it was done impetuously, from ardent apostolic zeal. Ardent as this zeal was, it was not coupled with wisdom and understanding of what really happened to China from a Chinese point of view.[1]

The proof of this is that the extra-territorial rights and privileges wrung from a reluctant and humiliated Chinese Government, and which in the irregular situation of the first decades of Western penetration into China were unavoidable, were kept and required as a right due to a Westerner by the missionary body as well, instead of repudiating these rights for themselves.

Missionary Boards, the Roman Catholic Church and missionaries themselves were not awake to the ambiguity and the obscuring of the true character of Missions in which they became involved by this identification of themselves with Western political power. No amount of apostolic zeal can excuse or justify this lack of depth in truly Christian spiritual strategy. What could the Chinese at large do in answer to it other than identify Missions with political dominance by the West? It is not only due to China's semi-political dependence that missionaries and Chinese Christians were singled out by the Boxer fury against the "foreign devils" and that in China the term "running dogs of capitalism" was invented for the missionaries in the 1920's.[2] The hesitating attitude of the

---

[1] In Chapter 8 we will treat some other aspects of this matter.

[2] It should, however, in fairness to the missionaries, not be forgotten that the famous Sinologist J. M. de Groot wrote his *Religious Persecution in China* and dedicated it to the missionary body out of just indignation about the self-righteousness of the non-missionary Westerners, who ascribed the horror to the *soi-disant* fanaticism of the West, conveniently ignoring the fact that the Boxer Rising was the desperate last revulsion of China against the entire Western Invasion.

missionary body towards the Taiping Rebellion and the curious form of Christianity it represented had its origin mainly in their strong Western inhibitions.

A CULTURAL AMBIGUITY

The ambiguity which often obscured the true character of Christian Missions manifested itself also in another field than politics and economics, viz. in the field of culture.

The natural and simple fact that the missionaries were Westerners implied also that they were products and expressions of Western culture, with all the apprehensions and norms it stands for as a culture included. In the great process of the Western cultural invasion and the ensuing cultural conflicts and contacts, Missions, as said already, were by their work, example and institutions an important agent. The more important, because missionaries were that class of people amongst the Westerners which as a rule stayed longest and lived in closer contact with the people than most. Inevitably Missions became a great distributor and advocate of Western culture. They had to, because they could not do otherwise, being what they were and caught up in this pluriform Western Invasion. And if they had hesitated, the impatient minority in the Asian countries, thirsting for "Western knowledge and efficiency" with which Missions had so much to do, would have wrenched it from their reluctant hands. Such great upheavals as the meeting of contrasting cultural and spiritual worlds require not only meditation, but decision and action. The more so, because as Westerners the missionaries belonged in this meeting on the side of the "possessors" and "distributors", and the eager minority of the people, amongst whom the missionaries spent their energy and life, were on the side of the "have-not's" and the "receivers".

As a rule the missionaries fulfilled their transmitter-rôle in this cultural and spiritual drama with sincere conviction and enthusiasm. This was as it should be, because it was evident that the progressive West in its collision with a stagnated, tradition-bound, ill-implemented East *could* be a blessing. This conviction impressed itself on every missionary who was concerned about the people for whom he laboured, the more so as in the 19th century nobody could be haunted by the vast problems that were to arise later on and are evident to the present generation, but which could not be foreseen in the first stirrings.

The instrumentality of Missions in transplanting and mediating Western culture is, therefore, speaking in general and keeping in mind the historical context, not a matter for regret but a title of honour.

The difficulty and the ambiguity which I mentioned enter in, however, at another point than the substantial collaboration of Missions in the Westernization of Asia and Africa. It is just this point which has made Western civilization in the East at once a deeply-desired and a deeply-hated thing. This point is the triumphant superiority-complex (humanly speaking inevitable) of the West and of the Westerners, who claim this superiority as an inalienable divine right. This superiority-complex was the driving motive in the whole process of cultural transmission. To be sure, the members of the great Asian civilizations themselves had a superiority-complex of the same magnitude. This made their position of "receivers", "have-not's", resulting from an adverse and inauspicious historical conjunction, all the more bitter, while the overbearing cultural pride of the Western "donors" added, unintentionally, insult to humiliation. The more so because the instruments and knowledge of the West were indispensable for overcoming the state of humiliation in which the course of history had placed them.

Again, generally speaking, Missions and missionaries shared this cultural pride, this feeling of the West's innate superiority. In the 19th century this is not a thing to be amazed or scandalized about. It is arrogance to condemn it out of hand because we happen to live at a time when the West, though secretly guarding its superiority-complex, is passing through a vociferous period of excessive self-depreciation.

Yet missionaries are Christians, who consider it their vocation to carry the Message of Truth in Jesus Christ to the whole world. One cannot be content to judge them exclusively on the basis of a historical situation. As Christians and missionaries they are called to bring all things, actions and motives, into the light of a higher authority and tribunal before which relative historical judgments do not lose all value but find their appropriate, i.e. subordinate, place. Before this tribunal all cultural pride and claims to superiority, Western or Eastern, stand condemned.

Seen from this angle it is undeniable that Missions, broadly speaking, were infected by the common Western virus and so, unintentionally, slid into ambiguity and into compromising and obscuring their true nature. The way in which Christianity was often presented as the religion of the victorious West, and as the real secret of Western pre-eminence, blurred the abiding, fundamental and universal motive of Christian Missions; a motive which transcended all cultural claims and values. It gave occasion to doubt whether the missionary was first and foremost an ambassador of Christ or of Western "Christian" civilization. In some missionary quarters this latent identification of Christianity with the values of Western "Christian" civilization was even clearly rationalized, thereby converting Missions—again unintentionally but none the less actually— from a religious concern, which implies the redemption of all aspects of human life, into a concern of cultural transmission and exchange, the confrontation of religious values being included.

The involvement in this dilemma and ambiguity is an exemplification of what Richard Niebuhr in his *Christ and Culture* has (among the five approaches to the problem of the relation of Christianity and culture which have appeared in Church history) baptized with the name: "Christ in culture". In this another of the five, viz. "Christ against culture", has evaporated. The great merit of Richard Niebuhr's book is that it makes abundantly clear that, looking at the Christianity-culture problem in the light of the significance of Jesus Christ, one is squarely faced with a paradox, in which the "in" and the "against" are an antagonistic, polar unity. It demonstrates the peculiar tension inherent in Christianity in regard to culture.

Speaking from the practical point of view, the ambiguity which manifested itself in the practice and theory of Missions in relation to the cultural invasion of the West (in which Missions were inescapably involved and active) doubtless strengthened the vigorous, instinctively antagonistic reaction of the great Eastern civilizations to Christian Missions. It did this

95

by regarding them preponderantly as a camouflaged aspect of Western invasion and dominance as a whole, and so contributing to the humiliation of the East. Under the ashes of an acute inferiority-complex the fire of superiority-consciousness burned unabatedly in the Eastern soul.

MISSIONS—THE THIRD REDEEMING FACTOR

I have treated to the best of my ability these sailings of Christian Missions on dangerous waters, in order to make clear in essential outline the varieties of Scylla and Charybdis they met and meet on their adventurous course through a changing world; a world which, by its dynamic and revolutionary character, puts forcibly on the agenda the crucial problems of Christianity's paradoxical relation to politics, economics, culture, human fate and destiny. Yet, when all this has been said, it must emphatically be repeated that Christian Missions and their activity, the peculiar vitamin they have injected into the body of Eastern life, can be adequately evaluated only by calling them the third redeeming factor in the colonial era.

Those who in the main find cause only for condemnation and scorn—and there are, to be sure, many sticks available, justifiably or not—are neglecting the simple duty of taking all the facts into account when studying such a colossal phenomenon as the East-West meeting, because they are blinded by an emotional inhibition. Easterners are in this case more excused than Westerners. Moreover, they forget in their blindness that it is only Christian Missions, as emanating from the Christian Churches of the West, which can put on record such an outpouring of consecrated lives for the sake of Christ, and in this are unique amongst all other agencies of the West which have worked in the East. This needs to be stated, because the Western intelligentsia (which treats Missions mainly with contempt), although animated by a sincere love and admiration of Eastern wisdom and culture, would never dream of showing a comparable amount of consecrated "abandon" to the needs of the far-away neighbour.

It is striking to find again a true recognition and evaluation of the significance of Christian Missions to the East in an Eastern author, whom we have quoted once already in spite of the fact that this author does not conceal her inability to appreciate the primary urge of Missions, viz. the proclaiming of the saving Truth for the whole world in Jesus Christ. The passage is to be found in Han Suyin's *A Many Splendoured Thing*,[1] where she describes her impressions of the many missionaries pouring through the Church Guest House in Hongkong after their expulsion from China by the Communist Government.

> In this room were the remains of a hundred years of missionary work in China. A hundred years of devotion, sacrifice and good works. For the glory of their God, in unselfish zeal; men and women of 29 denominations had gone to baptize the heathen, teach their variety of the Only Truth, heal the sick, feed the hungry, fulfil themselves and the will of their God. . . . In this room were the people who had worn down our traditions, broken our selfishness, awakened our social conscience, armed us with ideals, dragged our scholars from their poetic torpor and our peasants' superfluous babies from the cesspits, built our universities, our hospitals and our puritanism. They also had made New China. Although now we cast them out as instruments of foreign aggression, they have also made us. We were part of each other. Sitting with the missionaries, listening to Mary Fairfield with one ear and to the scarlet woman with the other, I thought that I saw what place missionary effort would hold in my country. And I was ashamed of my people. I was not ashamed of getting the missionaries out. Perhaps it was time they went; but I was ashamed of the way it was done.

For a right understanding of Missions and their significance, this fair-minded testimony by a very able Chinese woman may be supplemented by a quotation from an English author who drove military supply trucks on the roads of China during the Second World War, and describes his impressions and experiences. One night he is the guest of amiable, hospitable Swiss missionary sisters, full of fun, in a lonely part of China, and says:[2]

> Their[3] God might have disapproved of tobacco, but He was a living God, not some vague essence of Pure Being, which we

[1] p. 289.   [2] Bernard Llewellyn: *I Left My Roots in China*, 1953, p. 62.

[3] i.e., as Llewellyn says, the God of these women missionaries, of childlike faith, in the interior of S.W. China—a faith undisturbed by Strauss, Renan, Rashdall or Schweitzer, based on eternal promises validated by an infallible Word.

moderns set on the heavenly altar, and, because we cannot worship what we cannot at least in some degree comprehend, find it so often impossible to worship at all.

The three redeeming factors of the colonial era and of the Western Invasion in its creative and destructive aspects form together the new dynamizing and disturbing forces that worked in the 19th century. Yet, in spite of the West's increasing knowledge of and penetration into the East, in spite of the East's inescapable immersion in the stream of the West's disposition and tempo, and in spite of the revolt of the East against Western political dominance, the encounter of cultures remained in an inchoate stage. No longer, indeed, a marginal affair, as in the 17th and 18th centuries. Compared with that it had become a real meeting, but still a meeting, in which feelers were put out and contacts essayed, important and operative. Not yet, notwithstanding the amount of writing about it, a true dialogue.

The main result—and that is the great thing—is the many-sided response of the East and the increasing cultural and spiritual irradiations of the East towards the West. These will be discussed separately in the next four chapters.

Chapter Five

THE CULTURAL RESPONSE OF THE EAST TO THE WESTERN INVASION: THE MUSLIM WORLD

FROM the whole tenor of the two preceding chapters it will be clear that the insistence on the "unbroken" and "broken" epic in the framework of colonialism did not mean a justification of colonialism and imperialism. I simply wanted to point to the mystery which is always hidden in all great historic events, and to the transcendence of the consequences of historical acts and human decisions and aims over the conscious intentions of man in these decisions and aims. Even our indispensable moral judgments are not adequate to what *really* happens. History cannot be fully understood by analysing its causes in the past, but will only be adequately understood at its end. Theologically expressed: the historical process, far from being self-explanatory, requires and itself calls for a transcendent eschatological judgment.

Nor does this insistence on the "unbroken" and "broken" epic mean a disqualification of Missions, but an endeavour to do justice to their inevitable involvement in concrete history, in merit, failure and guilt—the insoluble tension in which the Christian Church ever finds itself. By its message of divine love and redemption and by its calling to show forth "the new creation in Christ", the Christian Church is a body that transcends history and the common level of human existence. It is commissioned to proclaim and to show evidence of this new dimension. It has to do this, not in a vacuum, but in the perplexities and obscurities of concrete history, becoming necessarily involved in them. "The deeper the consciousness of the tension and the urge to take this yoke upon itself are felt, the healthier the Church is. The more oblivious of this tension the Church is, the more well established and at home in this world it feels, the more it is in deadly danger of being the salt that has lost its savour".[1]

GENERALIZING ABOUT "THE EAST" MISLEADING

Turning now to the response of the East to the Western Invasion, one has to begin by stressing the necessity of delimitation of this theme. As well in quality as in quantity this response has been enormous. It constitutes the most important part of modern Eastern history. The literature about it, in the East and in the West, is immense. By their markedly different physiognomy, substance, reaction and response it is imperative to treat the response of the Muslim, the Hindu and the Buddhist world separately. Generalizing about "the East" in this dramatic period of its long history, and only in passing paying some rapid heed to the cultural and religious individualities, is too vague and unsatisfying a procedure. Moreover, the Muslim world has itself different distinct individualities, which show in their response marked characteristics, and, although Buddhism naturally leads us towards China and Japan, it is essential to our subject to pay special attention to Chinese and Japanese civilization as monumental entities in themselves, which gave their response to the challenge of the West.

And last but not least, in all these different religious-cultural areas the response went of course through various stages, which need attention.

The arduous task that has to be performed is not to generalize, but to be succinct and concise and yet, in the qualitative sense of the word, complete. This attempt is therefore presented with deep awareness of its shortcomings.

It is not out of place to repeat a previous observation, viz. that the Western Invasion aimed primarily at political dominance and economic control, leavened by a feeling of moral and cultural superiority. The cultural Westernization as such was never an aim. In spite of the talk about "transmitting the blessings of Western civilization", it was a by-product, planned or unplanned. It was done with the object of making these societies as malleable and manageable as possible for the purposes and benefit of the Western invaders. The "broken

[1] Cf. my *Communication of the Christian Faith*, p. 36.

epic" of the colonial policies in regard to education and other activities had no intention of causing any inner revolution. This proved to be an illusion. The dogma or myth of the "unchangeable East" helped towards living with this illusion. The by-product proved more and more to be an uncontrollable ferment which had often violent effects.

On this background a few general observations are possible and helpful. The Western Invasion has meant, after more than a hundred years of Western infiltration, for the great Eastern civilizations a forced, violent and painful transition from their past of unbroken continuity to a new uncharted course. The ferment and shock have proved so strong that a constant search for new self-interpretation and self-expression is going on, and is far from having arrived at its terminus.

The shock and effect of the Western Invasion in *all* its aspects (not only its cultural ones) has for the first time brought into being a hitherto unknown kind of spatial contact and intellectual awareness of one another, which these great regional civilizations had never experienced in this way before. They are all challenged in regard to their sacralized "centrism". The interesting prehistoric cultural contacts between Asia and Europe (which then was a space and not what is meant by "the West") or the equally interesting cultural contacts between the Roman Empire and the lands of the Eastern civilizations, up to the times of Byzantium, are fascinating and yet remain in their result fascinating curiosities. The colossal influence which India has exercised since the beginning of the Christian era in South-Eastern Asia and the Far East by her religious culture and by the export of Hinduism and Buddhism is a fine example of religious-cultural expansion. Without minimizing this in the least, still, it seems to me, it has to be maintained that the spatial contact and intellectual awareness of one another, remarkable as these were in the great days of Indian religious-cultural, mercantile and political expansion over Asia to the east of her, are of different character and force from what happened in the Western Invasion as the term is used in this book.

The striking difference can perhaps be best expressed in the terms *osmosis* and *shock*.[1] The Indian invasion in South-East

[1] I owe these terms to K. P. Landon: *South-Eastern Asia, Crossroad of Religions*.

and Far-Eastern Asia gave rise to a colossal process of religious-cultural osmosis. The reason is not far to seek. The fundamental presuppositions and apprehensions of all the Asian peoples and civilizations, notwithstanding their marked varieties, belonged to the same spiritual kindred and their technical implementation was largely of the same type. No revolutions or well-nigh unbearable convulsions could occur; what occurred was assimilation and transformation according to one's own type.

The Western Invasion has meant and means a shock, an earthquake, for the obvious reason that now for the first time the Asian civilizations are confronted with a confrère of fundamentally different apprehensions and a totally different technical armour.

This is the reason why on the one hand the present East-West meeting means a qualitative break with the past such as has never before occurred in the East, but on the other hand it is still in the balance whether in the future the East ultimately will revert to its fundamental type of apprehension or will demonstrate a mutation that means a quite new stage in its being.

INVASION OF THE MUSLIM WORLD

Islam and the Muslim world are, particularly from the religious viewpoint but even as to cultural structure and content as well, entirely different from the great East- and South-Asian religions and cultures. Nevertheless, in regard to the Western Invasion and its significance as an irresistible wedge, they are all in the same position. The Western Invasion meant nothing less than the penetration of a rationalist, individualistic, secularized civilization, provided with a great scientific, military and technical superiority, into a world which was living in a timeless, leisurely atmosphere, determined by age-old religions and social traditions. This applied to the Muslim world as strongly as to the religious cultures of Asia.

Islam can only be adequately understood, if one keeps steadfastly to the point that it is a huge religious, social and cultural system. Islam as a religion in the stricter sense of the word is the system's soul and basis, its unifying principle. The system is therefore infused by a total religious motivation and regimentation of life in all its sectors, professing to be based on Revelation as contained in the Koran. The real basis is the core of the whole system, viz. the Divine Law (Ar. *Shari'a*), which has its roots in the Koran, the Tradition (Ar. *ḥadīth* or Sunna) and the Consensus of the Scribes of the formative centuries (Ar. *ijma'*).[1] The system found its definite form in the 11th century, and is therefore a truly mediaeval structure. Ghazzali, the great thinker and theologian, gave it its finishing touch by a mystical interpretation, which meant at the same time the incorporation of Mysticism as a legitimate part of this religion of Revelation in Islam.

Soon after this decisive event the Muslim world, particularly in the East, became theologically and culturally a stagnant world.[2] The main internal cause of this stagnation was the incubus of the finalized mediaeval system itself, which left no room for a truly new, creative beginning, as it was founded on submission to traditional authority as embodied in the system. The main external causes were the appalling destructiveness of the Mongol invasions, culminating in the sack of Baghdad in 1256, the official centre of the then already dissolute Empire, and the elimination of the Muslim world itself from the main stream of world intercourse by the European discoveries of the routes to India and the Far East.[3]

It is essential for the understanding of the effects and reactions of the Western Invasion in the Muslim world, and its interactions, to keep in mind the cardinal significance of the fact that to the old core of the Muslim world (Near and Middle East, North Africa) the "West" has meant always, in a far more stringent sense than for the other Eastern civilizations, the "Christian West", and that it has always regarded and known this "Christian West" as its *enemy*, its opponent. The memory of the Crusades may have faded out in the West; in the Muslim East it has not. Moreover, this Muslim East's experience, through the modern Western Invasion, of the

[1] There is a fourth "root" as theological terminology has it, but that can be neglected for our purpose.

[2] Of course, there have appeared since the 12th century many interesting personalities and movements, but it all happened within the bounds of the normative system.

[3] Excellent pictures of this self-contained, colourful, rich and self-repetitive world as it still was even in the 19th century are to be found in two justly famous books: E. W. Lane: *The Manners and Customs of the Modern Egyptians*, and C. Snouck Hurgronje: *Mekka*, Vol. II. (E.T. *Mekka in the Latter Part of the 19th Century*).

"Christian West" impressed upon its mind the picture of having to do with an organized assault of deceit and exploitation. Here lie some of the deep roots of what is at present called the virulence of Arab Nationalism.[1]

The "Christian" West also must never forget that the Muslim world as a political and religious entity has a special significance for the West, which does not exist in the case of the great Asian religious cultures. The reasons for this special relatedness to one another are (1) that Islam is the only post-Christian world religion, which moreover is one of the greatest facts in world history; (2) because the origin and development of Islam as a world empire and a religious-cultural system have happened in *contact* with and *antagonism* to the "Christian" West. These fundamental facts, like those mentioned before, are by no means memories of the past but living, operative forces of great importance.

Around the year 1800 the drama of the Western Invasion in the Muslim world began. This beginning was dramatic and spectacular. The great actor was Napoleon Bonaparte by his secret expedition to Egypt. He aimed in his wide political scheming at India, but he became by his adventurous exploit the opener-up of the Muslim world.[2] The most interesting aspect of Napoleon's undertaking was that he, the great military conqueror and ambitious political genius, brought on his ships not only soldiers, but a big, carefully selected team of scholars, that during and after Napoleon's presence in Egypt applied itself to the investigation of the land, its resources, needs and history. This first dive into the Muslim world and into the East, in which the combination of the imperialist lust for conquest, the thirst for knowledge and idealism already appears clearly, is a fascinating story and has had incalculable consequences. This is not the place to enlarge on it. Only some bare

[1] H. Kohn: *Western Civilization in the Near East*, 1936, is, it seems to me, quite right in saying that, in spite of its negative, strongly emotional aspects, Nationalism has been and is *the* positive factor, creating for them the possibility of working out their political-economic independence. Properly speaking, economic independence is in my opinion the most coveted one, but political independence is the absolutely indispensable condition for obtaining it.

[2] The richness of literature on this subject, especially in French, is entirely justified. The most exciting book about it is undoubtedly the *Ta'rikh al-Jabarti* (3 vol.), whose writer al-Jabarti was an Egyptian contemporary of the event. It is highly instructive to read his wonder and stupefaction at the astounding capacities of the "Franks".

facts cannot be left unmentioned if we are to see the outlines of the external image of the Western Invasion in the Muslim world.

Napoleon's dash inaugurated the process of Egypt's being drawn first into the orbit of French, and later into that of British civilization and relations. The conquest of Algeria in the thirties of the 19th century meant a new inroad for Western cultural contact in its French form. The political and economic pressure which was increasingly brought to bear on Turkey, the representative but decaying power of Islam, was another example of the meeting of exuberant Western civilization with a world in stagnation. Turkey in its own centre and in its neglected Syrian and Mesopotamian territories began to experience the ferments and vitamins of Western civilization in their stimulating and confusing effects. Christian Missions from their centre in Beirut gave a great impulse to a renaissance of literary activity in Arabic and to the growth of the Press as a new feature of society. Persia, the present-day Iran, also a battlefield of rival Western political powers (England, Russia), was infiltrated by Western cultural influences, which led as in Turkey to stormy political revolutions. The cultural influence was, however, mainly French, because especially in the 19th century the universities of France were the places where Muslims from all these countries sought for a Western education. This accounts for the fact that the *idées mères* (governing ideas) of the French Revolution and its ideology have exercised such a deep influence in all the revolutionary changes in the Muslim East. A stronger explosive in a stagnant and tradition-bound world could not easily have been found.

Indian Islam, in many respects different from the ancient lands of Islam, came to experience the Western Invasion under the aegis of Britain. The gloomy significance of the advent of British rule for the Indian Muslim world was that it was ousted from its rôle of ruler and became, with the Hindu world, merged into the mass of the ruled, subjected to foreign domination. This for the first half of the 19th century made for an attitude of great aloofness on the part of the Indian Muslim world, which made it more impermeable to the Western Invasion than Hindu India. The Mutiny of 1858 was the last great convulsion in this unpreparedness to face a new situation.

After the Mutiny a new trend of gradual opening-up set in. So the Indian Muslim world, which is such an important section of the Muslim world as a whole, met the Western Invasion in the form of British civilization. The ensuing endeavours towards adjustment bear the clear marks of this.[1]

THE CONVICTION OF ISLAM'S SUPERIORITY

The Islamic world in its general attitude to the Western Invasion, compared with the great Asian cultures, gives mostly the impression of suffering and undergoing it as a fate and of being bewildered by the perplexities to which it leads and has led the "House of Islam". I believe this impression holds true, although one is fully prepared to take seriously the movements and responses as manifested in many tendencies, actions and important publications.

Turkey occupies in this regard a special position, because by its radical Westernization, its secularization of the State, of Law and Education, its abolition of the Khalifate, and its repressive attitude towards Islam as a religion, all under the leadership of Kemal Atatürk, it stands unique in the whole non-Western world by its thorough right-about-face. It has adopted consciously for good or for evil the Western way, has broken with the past and has made the Western orientation and attitude, with open eyes and clear determination, its own guiding principle. This does not, however, mean that the Turks regard themselves no longer as Muslims. The other Muslim countries, for more than one reason, have never looked with sympathy, nor with even secret envy, at this amazing leap into a new destiny on the part of the country that has been since the 15th century the leader of the Muslim world. Their attachment to Islam as a culture and a religion, their rootage in it, makes them even in their positive responses more resistant to the Western Invasion; perhaps one might say that they are more yielding to the irresistible corrosive effects of the Western Invasion than resolutely striking out a new way on the basis of a clear programme of response and self-expression.[2]

[1] The literature on the Muslim world and the West is so enormous that it is only feasible to quote from time to time a book that has helped the present writer in supplementing his own study and experience.

[2] W. Cantwell Smith's *Islam in Modern History* gives a penetrating study of the Turkish case.

The striking difference between Turkey and the other Muslim countries is of course due to various political and psychological causes and situations, into which we have no call to enter. But, giving this aspect its due, there is to be found a satisfactory explanation for the general reaction of the Muslim peoples, except Turkey, to the Western Invasion.

There is in the first place the deep-seated conviction of the superiority of Islam and all that it represents, which is a natural part of the make-up of the Muslim mind. Superiority-feeling must not only be understood in this case as the Muslim variety of the universal human tendency to consider one's own spiritual and cultural world the supreme, the superior one. In the Muslim world, where, again as everywhere else in the world, pride in the past "glory of Islam" is a normal pheno-menon, the feeling of superiority has a special quality and acuteness, because its motivation is ultimately purely religious. The feeling of superiority in Islam has this special quality by its mode of self-understanding within the divine dealings with the world.

The self-understanding of Islam consists in the conviction that Islam is the last, the crowning revelation of Allah through the "Seal (or Last) of the Prophets", Muhammad the "Best of the Prophets", the founder of "the best of all Communities". It consists also in the conviction that being according to the will of Allah "the best of all Communities", it is destined to be the supreme ruling world empire. In other words, in Islam the religious and political are indissolubly one. State and Church, to use Western (not really applicable) terms, are one without being really distinct. On this background the victorious, exuberant West, the superiority of which in *all* fields contrasts sharply with the undeniable inferiority and backwardness of the Muslim world in the present world set-up, adds, to the natural feeling of humiliation, the special sting of the inscrut-ability of Allah's ways. Both the superiority of the West in every respect and the inferiority of the Muslim world in every respect are what ought not to be.[1] They are obscure,

[1] One constantly realizes in intercourse with educated Muslims how touchingly happy they are when they get information of the great influence "Arab" and "Muslim" philosophy and science had on the mediaeval West. They easily leap to the conclusion that the modern Western world with its imposing mastery of nature and society is merely the result of "Muslim" mediaeval supremacy in science and that Islam consequently is the Mother of all Progress.

painful mysteries in the divine economy. This constitutes the peculiar Muslim inhibition in regard to the Western Invasion and accounts for the tinge of reluctance in all response.

The second reason that should be mentioned hangs partly together with the first, but is not so much an outcome of Islam's fundamental self-understanding and its psychological consequence in the baffling situation of the last 150 years. It is implied in the structure and spirit of the Muslim system of life as embodied in the Divine Law (Ar. *Shari'a*), this being a divinely authorized system on the basis of explicit Revelation, which orders all levels of life—the moral and ceremonial rules for a God-fearing life, the domain of social life, civil law, politics, etc. even in great detail. It presupposes and reflects a tradition-bound, stable (moreover mediaeval) society. The finalized system, as such, was too rigid to function in its completeness even in the Middle Ages, but still it has the status of being the obligatory ideal of Muslim society if it wants to be—as it should—a community obedient to Allah's will. The rigidity inherent in the system, because it presupposed an unchanging society which does not exist even in cases of extreme social and political stability, in the past accommodated itself to changes and obvious needs, not foreseen in the Divine Law, by letting parts of it quietly lapse.

ISLAM'S UNBEARABLE DILEMMA

But the Western Invasion posed a far more formidable problem. The Western penetration means not only a temporary dynamizing of all fields of life, but a permanent, fundamental one. Continuity with the past, the Muslim conception of Revelation and obedience to Allah are at stake. Justifying in theory the central position of the Divine Law and yet in practice abolishing, ignoring and seeing it abolished and ignored by the imperious impact of the new social dynamic coming through the Western Invasion, this forces the sincere, thinking Muslim into an almost unbearable dilemma. In these circumstances it is not surprising that the conflict between the different types of conservative and the different types of modernist, i.e. the prudent or reactionary traditionalists and the advocates of judicious or bold adjustments, is long-drawn-out and, in spite of many schemes and visions of Reform, is undecided.

In this long-drawn-out struggle real strides towards healthy change are of course made everywhere, often by simply by-passing the unsolved fundamental questions.[1] Yet, it remains for vitality, for inner cohesion and for convincing power in the future a question of life and death for Islam to find a new religious orientation, organically connected with its fundamental idea of ordering society as the theatre of a God-fearing life on the basis of detailed Revelation, contained in the Koran. The peculiar difficulty of Islam, in the storm of the Western Invasion, is that, in contradistinction to the great Asian cultures, its hard-core problem is theological and not philosophical. Moreover, although undermined and ravaged, the mediaeval *corpus Islamicum* holds its sacral position. The theological problem is ultimately how to switch over in a legitimate way from a thoroughly fundamentalist, legalistic apprehension of Revelation to a dynamic one.

This is a problem full of dynamite. It is understandable that, leaving aside some daring individual attempts to face it,[2] it is generally avoided. Very conspicuous is this understandable reluctance in the general refusal to enter on the path of applying historical criticism to the Koran as it has been and is done to the Bible, with all attending upheavals.

It is impossible to portray the many interesting and influential persons who have tried and still try their hand at Muslim self-interpretation, at apologetics or self-assertion. I will confine myself to some observations on the main centres of discussion: Egypt, India, Turkey.

G. E. von Grünebaum gives[3] a very interesting appraisal of the various Muslim writers he analyses. He sees the problem of Islam and the Muslims' self-assessment as strongly determined by despondency about the present state of Islam, the

[1] A good illustration is the silent way in which, e.g. in Egypt, a complete new legislation is being enacted in the field of personal and family law (the only part of the Divine Law which has kept on functioning up to the present day).

[2] e.g. Ali Abd ar-Raziq's *al-Islam wa 'usul al-hukm*, in which, contrary to historical and Koranic evidence, he tries to make the Prophet the founder of a secular community.

[3] Cf. his *Attempts at self-interpretation in contemporary Islam* in the 6th and 10th Symposium of the Conference on Science, Philosophy and Religion, and his study: *Islam, Essay in the nature and growth of a cultural Tradition.*

dominating significance of political considerations, the comforting pride in a great past, the somewhat uncertain conviction of a formative share in the shaping of the world and its civilization. He opines—and for my part I agree—that it is still entirely uncertain whether the hoped-for Islamic revival will have an anti-Western outlook or will represent a blending of Eastern and Western tradition. In a vein akin to what I have said above, Grünebaum explains that the latter possibility is beset by an element of conflict. On the one hand the necessity to adjust to the Western pattern is recognized, and the wish to do so is alive, but on the other hand there is a clinging to the past and its essential assets, which is the natural attitude of every historic self-conscious civilization because it tends to maintain its feeling of self-identity, implying also identity with the past.

The Muslim world like the great Eastern civilizations implicitly faces, without actually realizing it, a possible choice in the future between: continuity maintained by going through some sharp breaks, discontinuity with many deep tinges of the past. These two possibilities are hidden in what is at present called transculturation, to stress the point of view that acculturation of some kind is not the only option in the meeting of cultures, particularly of cultures so contrasting as East and West.

Egypt, India and Turkey naturally were the main centres of reaction and response, because politically as well as intellectually they were important centres of intellectual activity and had an élite-group. It needs, however, to be mentioned that before Napoleon took the initiative in breaking through the "iron curtain" of Muslim isolation, there had emerged in the second half of the 18th century from the deserts of Arabia a movement of radical reform in Islam. Later on, after the Western Invasion began, this was of real significance for some of the most important responses to the Western Invasion, especially in Egypt. It has become known as the Wahhabite Movement.[1]

A REFORM MOVEMENT

This movement is a purely autochthonous Muslim Movement, and in the way it has formulated the problem and

---

[1] It continues to be an important factor in the Muslim and in the world scene, because the present Saudi-Arab Kingdom is a creation of the Wahhabites. This is the first time since Muhammad that Arabia (except on the fringes) has been united into a single political unity.

meaning of Islam, had nothing whatever to do with any response to the Western Invasion. It was a puritan movement and for quite a long time very fanatical. Its inspiration came from an important undercurrent in Muslim life that remained alive for centuries in theological form as a protest against the "syncretistic" universality of the Muslim system, as it had become through Ghazzali's famous reconciliation of opposites on the basis of the consensus of the whole body of Islam (*ijma'*).

The protest was a vigorous one, rejecting the validity of the finalized "orthodox" system and of *ijma'* as the principle of legitimation. Instead it raised as the norm of true, undefiled Islam the religious belief and ideals, the austere moral code of the springtime of Islam, the period of the Prophet and the first four Well-guided Khalifs, the golden age of Islam before it had solidified into a system, combining in itself the four-centuries growth of Islam. "Back to the origins", or, in their own terms: back to the *salaf*, i.e. the ideal, pious founder-generation. Therefore the attack was directed not only against the system as justified by the consensus-principle, but also against basic elements of the hallowed system such as mysticism, saint- and grave-worship, laxity of moral and social behaviour. Theologically, it was a true revival of the austere prophetic proclamation of God's oneness in the Koran, finding its expression in a fierce protest against all *shirk* (polytheism, lit. giving God a companion) in faith, conduct and usage. This really meant a radical self-assertion and re-assertion of Islam's true nature and message.

The Wahhabi Movement—and this is its dynamic historic significance—turned this explosive theological and religious programme into a political and military movement, which did not even shun the sack of the sacred sanctuaries of Mecca, Medina and Kerbela.

It lies outside our scope to describe the repercussions and reverberations it had all over the Muslim world. The point we have to stress is that here was a real revival movement, happening within Islam from internal, purely Muslim reasons, virile, vigorous and genuinely Islamic.[1] It should, however, be noted that its anachronistic reaching back to the "origins", to

---

[1] It practically repeated in full Muhammad's achievement in the 7th century in regard to Arabia.

the great *salaf*, made the movement, in spite of its authentically Islamic theological vigour in principle and fact, a movement of repristination, of re-enacting the Arabia of the 7th century, and not of creative re-interpretation of authentic Islam in a new historical situation. Its determined rejection, however, of the classical orthodox system of Islamic catholicity[1] and its reviving of the original Allah-centric emphasis of Islam, have yielded great help and inspiration to the new movements in Egypt, in which was embodied a response to the situation as becoming changed by the Western Invasion.

THE EGYPTIAN PATTERN

Only mentioning in passing the great 19th-century protagonist of religious and political revival of Islam, Jamal ad-Dīn al-Afghani (d. 1897), we turn immediately to his disciple, Shaikh Muhammad Abduh (d. 1905) because he has imprinted on the Egyptian pattern of response to the Western Invasion the mark of his personality.

By his great gifts and independence of mind, he became the leader of the progressive modernist forces against the strong opposition of the Conservatives. The line he took was that of practical reform in education (*al-Azhar*) and society, and above all of restatement of the Muslim faith in its encounter with Western civilization. His restatement, phrased in exchange with the new knowledge and powers of the modern Western world, was, as well as a restatement, an apology and a vindication of the superiority of Islam over all religions, because of its being the only truly "reasonable" religion.[2] In far greater detail he performed the same double task by writing a Commentary on the Koran (not completed).

Abduh had enthusiastic disciples. One of them, the Syrian Shaikh Rashid Rida (d. 1935), who showed more of the characteristic religious-political spirit of Islam than his master,

---

[1] They are, seen from within Islam, the anti-catholic rebels. More than once Wahhabi's from central Arabia, whom I met, presented themselves to me by saying: We are the Protestants of Islam.

[2] The title of the book is *Risālat at-tawḥīd*, translated into French by B. Michel and Moustapha Abd ar-Raziq.

For Muh. Abduh and for the whole modern movement in Islam in response to the Western Invasion, see H. A. R. Gibb: *Modern Trends in Islam* and his *Mohammedanism*; C. C. Adams: *Modernism in Egypt*; W. Cantwell Smith: *Modern Islam in India*, to mention only a few out of many.

founded the Salafiyya Movement, which has many ramifications in different parts of the Muslim world, disseminating their point of view in a great output of literature and in their journal *al-Manār*. They represent the combination of the anti-catholic inspiration of the Wahhabi's, which affords them the opportunity of repudiating the stifling power of the mediaeval system, and an opening for (as they see and feel it) a basically anti-Western retreat on Koran and Sunna, conceived in a rather fundamentalist way. So they are at once defenders, critics and reformers of Islam, but in the framework of a deep distrust of the West, politically as well as culturally.

To get some idea of what is happening in the field of *cultural* and *spiritual* response (which is our subject) to the Western Invasion, it may be helpful to look at two remarkable personalities, although this selection suffers not only from an unavoidable lack of completeness, but also from a certain personal, arbitrary preference. The two men are: Taha Hussain, one of the outstanding professors of the University of Cairo, and Abd Ali al-Qāsimi.[1]

Taha Hussain has had a long career already as a participant in the great cultural-religious encounter of East and West. He started this career by some very provocative books, which could hardly conceal his disaffection from Islam and evoked strong protest. In later years he has taken a more moderate, mediate position, moving from pugnacity towards a more reflective and considerate attitude.

In the thirties he published a remarkable book on the future of culture in Egypt.[2] In this book he strenuously defends a cultural thesis, recommending it as the basis for the orientation of education. His thesis is: Egypt, including Islam, belongs to the West, not to the East (as India, the Far East). This is a bold and far-reaching idea, particularly so because it is as well in the East as in the West the habit to reckon the Muslim world and Islam to the East. In the Muslim world itself this latter position is, independently of every other argument (and there are, to be sure, strong arguments), the more spontaneously accepted because the whole history of the Muslim world is one

---

[1] Cf. von Grünebaum's excellent surveys in the 10th Symposium of the Conference on Science, Philosophy and Religion.

[2] In Arabic the title is: *Mustaqbal al-thaqāfa fi Misr.*

long-drawn-out antagonism to and struggle with the West. At present the solidarity with all the Eastern peoples, placed together by historical grouping in an inevitable position of antithesis to the West, naturally strengthens this attitude in the Muslim world.[1]

Taha Hussain refuses to accept it, and marshals his arguments from cultural history. The driving power behind his scholarly philosophical position is clearly his desire to orientate his country towards the free, critical spirit of the West. He argues therefore that, from the time of ancient Aegean culture onwards, Egypt has belonged to the West. It belonged to the Mediterranean culture as dominated by Greek rationalism. The Muslim world, Islam itself, entered culturally into the orbit of Hellenistic culture, absorbed it, transmitted it in the Middle Ages[2] to the West with its characteristic key-ideas of Reason (Ar. *'aql*), of Understanding (Ar. *fahm*), of Idea (Ar. *ma'nā*). All these historic reasons in their cumulative effect impel towards orientating on Western civilization in its present manifestation. As to religion, Christianity and Islam are in essence identical, though Islam is superior.

He simplifies the problem very much and even occasionally distorts the historical picture, but his book is evidence of the fact that the Muslim world is undoubtedly torn, in its present predicament, between "Orientalists" and "Occidentalists". The outcome of this conflict is wholly uncertain, but of great importance.

Qāsimi follows a quite different line. His real inspiration is indignant wrath at the backwardness of the Muslim world, caused by its being fettered to a deadening past. He identifies ideal Islam with the Arabs, inveighing against the non-Arab Muslims, whose books, written by mystics like Ghazzali, Sha'rani, Suyūti, Ibn Arabi, or by dogmatists like al-Ash'ari, incorporate a lack of self-reliance which still dominates men's minds. His fiercest attack is on superstition, resignation (*Kismet*), mysticism, dogma, subservience to tradition (*taqlīd*).

[1] The symbolic word for this whole situation is now Bandung Conference, or simply Bandung.

[2] It is well to keep in mind Denis de Rougemont's statements in *Man's Western Quest*, p. 5: "In many respects, indeed, the Middle Ages represented the 'Eastern' period of the West." This quotation is the more apt because of the similarity of outlook and structure between the "Christian" Middle Ages and the Muslim world of that time.

This sides logically with his equally fierce plea for complete secularization, for self-reliance, for belief in Man as a noble being, capable of controlling his own destiny. He is aglow for the modern West, using it as an example to stimulate his co-Muslims towards emulation.

He defines the decisive problem as he sees it in this way. The Muslim's belief in God as the Supreme Cause prevents man from conceiving himself as a causer and so from succeeding in the world. How to combine this kind of belief in God with that in Man as a causer (*sababī*), is the problem. Qāsimi is merely interested in safeguarding his claim for man-wrought evolution. The place God keeps is that of a deistic God. He not only exalts the incredible greatness of man as demonstrated by the self-reliance, vigour and planning of the West, but does not even shy away from saying "the impious only have success", quoting al-Ma'arri's dictum that there are two kinds of people: the one has brains and no religion, the other has religion and no brains. Mankind goes through three stages: no religion, vain religion (an example, he says, is Islam in its traditional form) and true religion. True religion is what he himself advocates, being thus a true Muslim, because purification and rectification of decadent religion was the programme of the Prophet. The obstacle is not religion but the religionists. His indignation and zeal become very outspoken when he says that there is no rescue for the Islamic world, unless it is able to deny adherence to its whole religious and cultural heritage. This unbelief (*kufr*) is imperative. He ends up with the words: "Can this be done? But there is no other way."

Another remarkable document is a report of a fictitious Congress of reformists, said to be held at Mecca in 1897. The title is: *Umm al-Qurā*. The author is Sayyid Abd ar-Rahmān al-Kawākibi, a Syrian. The participants give a detailed account of the decadence of the Muslim world. Its causes are political, economic, psychological, religious. The pride of the learned class of scribes, the enmity against science, the complicated character of Religious Law (*Shari'a*), the slavery to tradition, the ignorance of women are responsible for the down-at-heel religious situation, mainly a result of arid theological hair-splitting and the enervating influence of Sufism. The conclusion is that the princes and the learned scribes, who have neglected their duty, must be called upon to take the lead in reform.

Although Islam in India is divided by various shades of conservatism and liberalist modernism and their often violent controversies, its principal advocates of new ways of adjustment of the Muslim heritage to the Western Invasion never speak in tones so harsh as the iconoclast Qāsimi does. The general tone is more urbane, more in the direction of reasonable self-criticism and self-revision, with greater confidence in the feasibility of synthesis. At the same time, when genuine attachment to Islam and genuine religious sentiment seem nearly or wholly absent, the need to extol Islam as a glorious cultural heritage and a beloved social community is unbroken. On the other hand, brilliantly and eloquently written liberal interpretations of Islam are to be found, presenting Islam as the most progressive movement there ever was and as the anticipator and originator of the creative ideas of the modern Western world. Active rationalist defenders of Islam as the only satisfying religion for the rationalist West launch out in missionary activity from India to various parts of the world under the sponsorship of the Ahmadiyya movement.

This different mood when compared with the Arabic-speaking Muslim world is due, it seems, to a difference of temperament in Indians and Semites, but probably most to a great difference in situation. The fact that Indian Islam has lived for centuries as a big enclave in a mainly Hindu world may possibly account for a subtle, but real, difference of feeling. The former well-known Hindu-Muslim controversies, so bitter that they have resulted in the Partition of India into two States, do not minimize the fact that the great difference between Islam in India and in the ancient Muslim key-lands in the Near and Middle East is that Indian Islam for centuries has lived in co-existence with such a remarkable and outspoken type of spiritual and cultural life as Hindu India, whereas in Egypt the sole reality always was the massive system of Islam. Moreover, Indian Islam is not created on an Arab basis, but is religiously and culturally an offshoot of Persian Islam and culture. The dual effect of such a massive system as Islam in times of great and unmanageable transition is that loyalty and pride in the values for which the system stands, in spite of its having become a problem in principle and practice, coincide with a feeling in the Arabic-speaking part of Islam mounting even to exasperation about its incubus-like character. This, even independently of an existing difference between the Indian and the Semitic temperament, more easily results in a greater shrillness of tone.

Also the fact that India has met and meets the Western Invasion in British disguise, to which it seldom occurs to put intellectual problems in violent forms, and that the Near and Middle East have met it mainly in French disguise, far more radical and antithetical in intellectual formulation, may partly account for the unmistakable difference in mode of response and reaction. One might perhaps venture to say that in the Arabic-speaking Muslim world the theocratic character of Islam is determining the reactions. In India, where the co-existence with Hinduism produces at the same time a softening of temperament and an instinctive group-loyalty, moral and cultural emphases are more prevalent than doctrinal.

After a long period of sullen aloofness, Indian Islam made a first attempt at adjustment to the Western Invasion in the person of Sir Sayyid Ahmad Khan (d. 1898). He was a sincere Muslim, a man of noble mind and far-sightedness, who was convinced that the Western Invasion would stay and was not only a curse, but could also be a blessing.

After the Mutiny he started on the uphill task of giving to a despondent society (as Indian Islam was then) a new orientation, and of building up a group of co-workers and sympathizers. His aim was twofold. First, to throw open the windows of the Muslim mind by a theology, free of the shackles of classical Muslim theology, which vindicated the fundamental concord of Islam and Science. In regard to the other religions of Revelation, to the peoples of a Book (*ahl al-Kitab*), especially Christianity, he broke through the customary exclusiveness of the Muslim attitude, crystallized in the idea that the other books of Revelation (*kitab*) were corrupted, and, dropping this tenet, made a serious study of the Bible.[1] He undertook a

---

[1] He is the only Muslim up till now who ever wrote a Commentary on the Bible, not in Arabic, but in the Muslim lingua franca of India, Urdu.

prudent but determined revision of Muslim social ethics and institutions. Second (and this was his main concern) he established in 1875 the first Muslim college at Aligarh, in which he realized his dream of a place where religion and learning could be harmoniously combined,[1] and which should be the centre of his reformist movement.

The most-widely read apologist of Islam in the West is also an Indian, Sayyid Amir Ali. He was a man of Western training and moreover had thoroughly imbibed it. His apology is entitled: *The Spirit of Islam*. (The original title was: *The Life and Teachings of Mohammed*.)

Sayyid Amir Ali presents Islam wholly in terms of the 19th century and its ethical and social ideals. Islam in fact becomes under his hands the Religion of Progress. He is quite aware of the decadent state of present Islam, but the only thing that interests him is its "philosophical and ethical spirit". The tenor of this appears from the picture he gives of Muhammad, who practically becomes a noble 19th-century idealist, a Unitarian, consecrated to God and humanity.

The book is enthusiastically and brilliantly written, reflecting the taste and aspirations of a cultured Western gentleman. To speak candidly, as well from the standpoint of the Islamic Western scholar as from that of a well-informed Muslim who knows his religion, it is a highly misleading book. The reason that it nevertheless deserves to be mentioned is that it represents a real episode in the Muslim response to the Western Invasion. Not only because it has been (and perhaps is) widely read in the West and taken as a true picture, or absorbed by Western-educated Muslims with avidity as an inspiring heart-warmer in the midst of an uninspired, deadening reality. Such well-meant fancies belong to the whole process of the West-East cultural meeting, especially in regard to Islam, because when compared with Chinese, Indians or Japanese—the other main representatives of great Eastern civilizations—the Muslim, it seems, suffers more under the impact of being considered a despised inferior in the *salon des civilisations mondiales*, the polite society of world civilizations, than the others do, *if* they do. Therefore it is understandable that in all sincerity many a

[1] In 1920 it became the Muslim University of Aligarh. The Sayyid's harmonizing ideal did not become what was hoped of it.

Westernized Muslim in the meeting of East and West recommends such a distorting book as a "standard work" on Islam.

A striking example of the cultural bias in Indian Muslim apologists of Islam is Khuda Buksh in his *Essays, Indian and Islamic*. There is in the make-up of this writer clearly no interest in religion or Islam as a religion, but a strong loyalty and enthusiasm for Islam as a universal, social and cultural community, with which the regional, "provincial" character of Hinduism compares, in his opinion, unfavourably.

A very characteristic figure amongst the collaborators of Sir Sayyid Ahmad Khan was Maulavi Cheragh Ali (d. 1895). He deviates from the general Indian attitude by his direct, clear-sighted theological approach.[1] He belongs to the same category as the Egyptian Ali Abd ar-Raziq, who wrote in 1925 the book: *al-Islam wa 'usul al-hukm*, the most radical treatise produced so far in the Arabic-speaking Muslim world on one of the fundamental problems that the Islamic world has to face in its meeting with Western civilization. Raziq is a pupil of the Western school of historical criticism as applied to Islam. His thesis is that the Prophet never intended to be a political and social law-giver for all times, as is assumed in the total make-up of the classical Islamic system, but only a religious and moral reformer. He advocated on that ground the abolition of the Khalifate (which had happened *in fact* already in Turkey, but was not and is not yet accepted by the Muslim world *de jure*) and the separation of civil affairs from religious Law. The Court of Professors of al-Azhar dismissed him and forbade to him the holding of any religious office.

What Raziq actually did was to try to modernize and adapt the theocratic system of Islam to a secular conception of state and society by eliminating one of its pillars, which is moreover, judged from the standpoint of the nature of Islam and of history, quite rightly one of its pillars. The reaction of the body of Azhar professors was therefore entirely logical, though at the same time an evidence of the refusal to face the problems squarely as inherent in Islam's *present* situation.

[1] Strange to say, in the many books treating modern trends in Islam he is scarcely mentioned or not at all, although he is one of the most clear-sighted Muslim writers of the 19th century.

The amazing thing about Cheragh Ali is that, without the aid of Western historical criticism, right back in the 19th century he opened a far more radical attack on the bases of Islam. Starting from his personal gospel of Islam being the ideal model of "progress" and "adaptability", he demolished the hallowed bases of historic Islam because they motivated and engendered an all-comprehensive order of life, bound and sanctioned by religious tradition. His animus was the same as Raziq's, as appears from the words: "What it (viz. the Koran) teaches is a revelation of certain doctrines of religion and certain general rules of morality." The great pillars of the Islamic system (Koran, Sunna or ḥadīth, ijma') he either, as in the case of the Koran, re-interpreted in the rationalist/moralist spirit of the 19th century, or without any apology brushed them aside. A new Islam, the herald of the contemporary (Western) ideals of the 19th century, has to take its place and finds its justification, Cheragh Ali believes, in the Koran.[1]

Raziq, and particularly Cheragh Ali, are the two men who have formulated in inescapable terms the crucial problem with which Islam as a system is confronted in its meeting with the Western Invasion. The fact that their own vindications of the true Islam are contrary to historical evidence, converting Islam into the exemplary embodiment of the ideals of the Enlightenment, indicates an understandable lack of religious depth and an evasion of the basic question: what to think of the Koran as *the* final and perfect Revelation, and, therefore, the authoritative and only valid basis and guide for human life?

As we have remarked before, many obstacles to living life in modern conditions, which are contained in the System, succumb in many parts of the Muslim world silently under the pressures of exigencies arising in societies in convulsive transition. Yet the theoretical, the fundamental question remains standing in the background, waiting for a solution. How long, and with what results, nobody can tell.

The Western observer cannot, however, remain merely an observer, sympathetic as he may be. He has not even the right to remain an observer, because in the first place it is the Western

---

[1] I have written more extensively about Cheragh Ali in my: "Eenige grepen uit de moderne apologie van den Islam", *Tijdschrift voor Indische Taal, Land en Volkenkunde*, LXXV, 1935. Cf. also my: "Islam in India to-day", *The Muslim World*, April 1931.

Invasion that has thrown the Muslim world into this predicament, and consequently a Westerner, who has a responsible
place in life, must share in it with genuine inner participation.
In the second place, the solution to which the Muslim world
may come, out of inner logic and under the pressure of incalculable external factors, matters not only to herself but to
the whole world. Eventually to part with the divinely sanctioned mediaeval system would mean for Islam not only reform,
but revolution. Hence these huge internal struggles of the
Muslim part of our present world are always also a world
concern, not a mere spectacle for observation but a human-
divine drama for reverent participation.

IQBAL OF PAKISTAN

The best-known Muslim name at present is that of Sir
Muhammad Iqbal (d. 1939), the real founder of Pakistan,
although he never lived to see it. For the present Muslim
intelligentsia of Pakistan he is *the* philosophical light, *the* quasi-
normative thinker about the problem Islam/modern world. He
has given a re-interpretation of Islam and a kind of programme
for realizing a true synthesis of Islam and the secularized world
in his famous book: *The reconstruction of religious thought in Islam*,
(1930).[1]

Iqbal, a famous poet and a scholarly philosopher,[2] differs in
two respects from all other Muslim writers on the subject. He
approaches the predicament of Islam in the way of a philosopher, deeply attached to Islam as a religion and culture: and
he does so on the basis of a sound knowledge of the most recent
European trends in philosophy and science, with a mystic
(Sufi) strain in his thinking, couched in Nietzschean and
Bergsonian terms.

The dynamism of "act" in contradistinction to the static
character of "idea" is one of his key-thoughts, which he finds
expressed in the Koran. In this key of dynamism he synthesizes
the Islamic conception of God and Prophethood with the
modern vision of science. Of course, he faces in this context

[1] Note that the outstanding Muslim writers on the problem Islam/modern world,
in India as well in the Arabic-speaking world, are nearly all laymen and not
theologians.

[2] I have devoted many pages to him, his writings and personality in the study
I have mentioned: "Eenige grepen. . . ."

the rigidity of the classical Islamic system. Unfortunately, in the light of his own approach, he deals with it in a very unsatisfactory way, and is in practice in this one field extremely cautious. Though in the realm of Indian politics he has been the prime mover of violent Muslim self-assertion, he is a typical modern intellectual in the sense that he considers Religion (or mysticism, which amounts for him to the same thing) as another "level of knowledge-yielding experience of ultimate Reality". His dimension of speculative thought[1] lacks real contact with his dimension of practical, concrete problems. His great prestige, especially in Pakistan, will, however, secure him there abiding influence.

TURKEY AND ISLAM

Turkey, as already remarked, has followed a different course, as also in many respects Persia. The main reason is that, belonging to the few truly independent countries of the whole "House of Islam" and being also the foremost Muslim country, it could handle the convulsions caused by the Western Invasion and the Western political encroachment on its life in a way different from the rest of the Muslim world, which was under colonial or semi-colonial tutelage.

Since the thirties of the 19th century, Turkey has reacted with political *pronunciamiento*'s and edicts of reform to the insidious ferment of Western ideas and models. It is significant that these ferments came mainly from France and the principles of the French Revolution, which may be termed one of the great explosives in the non-Western world. The First World War left Turkey as a power and as a country at the abyss of annihilation.[2] The iron determination of one strong-willed man turned the scales. (The same happened in Persia.) This man, Atatürk, knew how to rouse the spirit of national self-respect and self-sacrifice and how to profit by the enormous changes in the political set-up resulting from the appearance of Russian Communism as a world-political factor. A new Turkey arose.

Its national hero, Atatürk, himself a good example of a con-

---

[1] The last chapter of his book bears the title: "Is religion possible?" (that is to say in the light of modern philosophy of science).

[2] Compare the reflections I wrote at greater length in my book: *The Christian Message in a Non-Christian World*, pp. 268-283. They appear to me, though written more than twenty years ago, still to hold good.

vinced French anti-clerical *laïc*, took the amazing step of leading his country resolutely on the road of wholesale Westernization, in state, society; law and "Church". Being a great statesman and an ardent nationalist, he was not plagued with theological or cultural sensitivities. Hence by his drastic determination he shocked not only the outside world but even the most progressive Muslim protagonists of reform. All their carefully and responsibly thought-out programmes for synthesis of Eastern and Western elements, for social and moral reform, for preserving the essential truths and values of Islam, for re-interpretation of Islam in terms of contemporaneous ideals and norms, were swept aside by this cutting of the Gordian knot. From the Muslim point of view Turkey could not but appear to the rest of the Muslim world—though there were everywhere a number of secret sympathizers—an appalling riddle.

The unthinkable thing, the reduction of Islam from the status of a religiously sanctioned cultural, social and political system to the position of a private and unfavoured religious opinion (the very position Islam can never accept as long as it holds to its innate theocratic character), had happened within the course of a few years. From a secular standpoint Atatürk has been splendidly justified. The miserable fragments of the Ottoman Government have been converted into a new Turkey, a strong Mediterranean state. The instruments to achieve it were the combined forces of a determined nationalism and secularism. The problem of Islam and of Turkey's Islamic past was, in the process, not "solved", but forcefully eliminated, by-passed and suppressed. However, it cannot but reappear. For even great statesmen and giants of will-power, though they are able to manufacture radical revolutions and force a people into new ways, are no masters of the dormant needs and forces that are embedded in and undergirded by the religious-cultural-social system of the past. In a later chapter I will have therefore to turn again to Turkey.[1]

ISLAM IN SELF-DEFENCE

The survey of the Muslim response to the Western Invasion, given thus far, has had to be brief. Some summarizing remarks

[1] Cf. for the whole story H. A. R. Gibb and Harold Bowen: *Islamic Society and the West*. Two volumes.

must still be added. The first is that, as in this whole book, we are reflecting on largely contemporaneous happenings. Even the best analysis and shrewdest interpretation cannot ignore the fact that in analysis and interpretation we are groping in the dark because of this contemporaneity. The many facets of the response to an event (viz. the Western Invasion in all its aspects) which cannot be gauged in all its dimensions and effects, give the impression of being still initial responses, initial endeavours to seize and meet the emerging problems, partly evasions of the fundamental problem, partly too much under the suggestive power of Western ideals and ideas, or utilizing its achievements without really understanding them.

It cannot be otherwise. A convulsive time is not propitious to creative, lucid, unerring concentration. One of the paradoxes of history is that so much happens through trial, error and confusion, especially the *confusio hominum*, confusion of men. I for my part therefore read with great reserve Gibb's words about "the profound disservice done to Islam by the modernists".[1] Who knows and divines fully the *true* significance of the conflicts and bickerings of "conservatives", of "reactionaries" and "modernists" of various attire, impressive or ridiculous? Yet this philosophical reflection does not exonerate us from the task of making evaluations and passing judgments. As contemporaneous historical observers of a process in which we look "through a glass darkly", we must allow ourselves a myopia, with stronger or weaker ingredients of perspicacity and divination.

The indispensable requirements that should be demanded as critical salt in an opaque situation are sincerity and respect.

I agree with Gibb[2] when he says that

> there is no stronger proof of the superficiality of the Western impact upon the Muslim peoples than the fact that the immense revolution in historical thought in the West in the 19th century has not yet penetrated into the Muslim world.

Although Gibb does not advocate a mere taking-over of Western historical method as the way of advance for Muslims, he nevertheless seems to see the way for them in their

[1] p. 127 in *Modern Trends in Islam.*   [2] *op. cit.*, p. 127.

predicament in a creative rebuilding on the foundations of their own early historical criticism, with the aid of Western method. It seems to me that the crux of the question lies somewhere else. The Muslim world in responding negatively or positively, constructively or destructively, to the Western Invasion is unavoidably still in the stage of self-defence. That is, for instance, the reason for the strong tendency to reconcile Islamic Orthodoxy, or an Islam contrived by one's own fancy, with modern movements of thought, with social and cultural reforms and with modern science. The West and its dominant ideas and ideals are still setting the pattern for response, by their sheer suggestive weight. The real thing has still to happen, i.e. "the launching into the deep". The time for ways of response which take their terms from the heart and not from the system of Islam itself seems not yet at hand. In this period of inevitable self-defence and self-assessment as dictated by the overwhelming suggestive power of the West, the depth-dimension remains, it seems, out of reach. For only a new creative urge, issuing from the depth of Islam itself and true to its authentic *religious* self, can give a new beginning.

So the ultimate question is: has Islam this depth? Can the old vessels be broken or has it so adequately expressed itself in these old vessels that no new creative start is possible, but only a break? This questioning within the "House of Islam" has still to begin, as far as one can see.

Chapter Six

THE CULTURAL RESPONSE OF THE EAST
TO THE WESTERN INVASION:
HINDU INDIA

THE world of Indian religion and culture is entirely different from the Islamic world. The Hindu Kush is not only a geographical frontier but a spiritual one. Alexander the Great, however much the Mediterranean world to which he belonged reveals many secret channels of similarity, had this feeling of entering a different and alien world when he crossed this small threshold of India. He was right and will remain so, notwithstanding all the present results of comparative and cultural philosophy.

India—and this is true also for Chinese and Japanese civilizations—has developed a pattern of life and a symphony of emphases and orientations that has its unique type of self-identity. It is therefore one of the three great representative patterns of civilization which have grown out of a definite fundamental option—to use a happy expression of Denis de Rougemont's; the other two being the Chinese and the Western. The Islamic and Japanese religio-cultural worlds are of course also crystallized round fundamental options, but not in an equal degree of pristine, inexplicable originality. This is not meant as an option for "East is East and West is West and never the twain shall meet"; but it means remaining aware, in our time in which East and West do and must necessarily meet, of the requirement that the endeavours rightly made to discover our common humanity behind each other's faces should never make us overlook the reality of deep difference, which this irreducible uniqueness of "fundamental option" implies. Historical, psychological, climatological mental explanations can all make it more understandable, but cannot really explain it.[1]

THE MULTIFORM PATTERN OF HINDUISM

Hinduism in its entirety as a religion gives the impression of a huge, impenetrable jungle. Multiform in the extreme, it presents itself as the *sanatadharma*, the everlasting pattern of life, as well by this self-same multiformity as by unchangeable, ever identical essence hidden in all these forms. The famous French Indianist Auguste Barth, writing in 1879,[2] formulated its indefinable character inimitably in the words:

> Nowhere else can one observe, in conditions so favourable, the successive transformation and, as it were, the destiny of a polytheistic conception. Among all the similar conceptions, no other has shown itself so lively and flexible as this one, so gifted at reclothing the most diverse forms, so ingenious at reconciling all extremes from the most refined idealism to the lowest idolatry; none has known so well how to repair its losses; none has possessed to such a high degree the faculty of ceaselessly producing new sects, indeed great religions; and, by a perpetual self-renewal process, of resisting all the agencies of destruction, whether internal attrition or aggression from without.

And in order to show why Hinduism is by nature refractory to any reduction of all its manifestations to a systematic unity, he says:

> They constitute a floating mass of beliefs, opinions, customs, practices, religious and social ideas in which one does discover a certain common basis and a pronounced family likeness, but from which it would be very difficult to extract a real definition. It is in fact almost impossible to state exactly what Hinduism is, where it begins and where it ends.

[1] S. Lévi, *L'Inde et le Monde*, p. 90, is vexed by the enigma and leans to climate as a decisive factor: "The civilization of India, alone, has grown up between the Tropic and the Equator in reaction against a nature which exceeds normal limits."

[2] See *Oeuvres de Auguste Barth*, Vol. I, pp. 11, 140. The only point at which to-day, after nearly a century more of research into religions, Barth shows that he is inevitably situation- and time-conditioned is when he chooses the "polytheistic conception" as the matrix of this multiformity in Hinduism. In this case we are looking, to-day, in a different direction.

On this background it becomes understandable why in Hinduism there is no binding doctrinal unity. Westerners are usually baffled on hearing that in this *religion* one can be an ardent monotheist, a convinced polytheist, a simple idol-worshipper, an atheist, an absolute idealistic philosopher for whom only attribute-less, transcendent Being is the sole Real, and be all this at the same time, and nevertheless be a full-sized Hindu. The freedom in regard to religious notions is entirely unlimited. A more radical "tolerance" is unthinkable. The authority of customs and of social rules of conduct, within the caste group to which one belongs by birth, is however equally unlimited. "Tolerance" has here, in principle and in practice, no place. The polymorphous *sanatadharma* serves the needs of the primitive village religionists, of those who live in the sphere of popular polytheist religion, of the various groups of sectarians (Vishnu, Shiva, etc.); of those who see the many gods as one and who belong to the sincere, fervent Pietists (*bhaktas*); also of the philosophically-minded, whose standard philosophy is mostly (certainly not necessarily) the classic non-duality (*advaita*) monism. There is no real cleavage between the "intellectuals" and the "people" (hoi polloi). In short, it is really all-comprehensive.

Graf Keyserling, who was fascinated by this whole spectacle, has in his well-known *Reisetagebuch eines Philosophen* ("Travel Diary of a Philosopher") found not only striking formulations but also words of enthusiastic praise. He says, e.g. in regard to what, speaking in Hindu terms, is perfectly legitimate crude village-religion: "The simpler and rougher a man is, the coarser and less spiritual must be the pictures held up to attract his attention." "Only the gifted man attains to God through knowledge." Keyserling in a happy term defines Hinduism as a metaphysical pragmatism, on account of which the eventual form and substance (he uses the expression *"Da- und Sosein"*) of one's religion is always good and, consequently, change of religion is always wrong. Every form of religion, he continues, and of devotion, is good in so far as it helps towards realizing oneself. His conclusion is:[1] "India and not Europe has produced the deepest metaphysics and most complete religious system to date."

[1] *Reisetagebuch*, I, p. 358.

This pronouncement certainly renders exactly the deep conviction of India about herself. It touches the all-pervading, elemental apprehension of life, man and the world, which characterizes India and is very important to keep in mind when trying to understand the manifold reaction and response to the Western Invasion in the 19th century. This is, as can be expected from a people so gifted as the Indians and a religious-cultural history of such complexity and longevity, a thrilling story.

INDIA MEETS THE WEST

India met the beginnings of the Western Invasion in the first quarter of the 19th century, at a time when she was in a stage of decadence and stagnation; a tradition-bound society, living in self-isolation and sterile introversion. A static "mediaeval" world, hiding its treasures and secrets. The last truly great religious personality, whose religious epic has become practically a Bible for the people and who exercised a vitalizing influence, especially in the North, was Tulsi Das, who lived and worked in the first half of the 17th century.

It is well to keep this in mind in order to understand the first reactions and responses from the Hindu side, as well as the reactions of prominent Westerners who lived and worked in India, mainly missionaries and gifted agents of the East India Company, which was practically the British Government in India. The Hindus had for centuries been accustomed to living under foreign rule. The British Era meant for them a change of masters, and, all things considered, not a bad change. For the Indian Muslims it had an entirely different meaning. From being the super-class in Indian society they became subject, and equal subjects with the Hindus. As we have seen in the preceding chapter, the reaction of the Muslim to British influence and rule was the sullenness of resentment. The Hindus, already by nature versatile and adaptable, had acquired a great aptitude for adjustment to changing conditions. With characteristic swiftness and subtlety they began, in spite of the wrong-headed conservatism of their social system, to react to the new possibilities, especially to openings in Government service, which involved a certain amount of contact and making acquaintance with Western knowledge, ideas and habits, necessary to fill the posts that became open to them.

The contrasting attitude of the Muslim group strengthened this tendency. The self-willed isolation and exclusion of the Muslims, caused by their political melancholy and religious exclusivism and suspicion, opened the way still more for the Hindus. They did not have the inhibitions of the Muslims through remembrance of lost political glory or through that typically Muslim consciousness of well-defined principles and contrasts. Their innate Protean adaptability helped them, apart from the new economic opportunities in status, to respond eagerly to the educational policy of the British.[1] They showed, in the words of a writer of those days, a great avidity to drink "the wine of the new learning".

Dazzled and intoxicated as they were by this wine, suddenly offered after a period of national decline and stagnation, two things happened. First, new horizons were opened to which many Hindus with their great native intelligence responded warmly. Second, in the light of this "New Learning" and the explosive new ideas it contained, Hindu society looked ugly and there were many courageous men who recognized this with dismay. Christian Missions, with their merciless and often inconsiderate criticism of the degraded religious practices and the blighting power of many religiously sanctioned social customs and institutions, aroused the indignant protest of such great champions of Reform as Ram Mohan Roy, but seen in historical perspective they stimulated the awakening from a dismal cultural and spiritual coma and contributed by their work to the opening up of new horizons.

[1] It is very instructive to compare the attitude of Muslims and Hindus to this policy. In the heated debate between "Occidentalists" and "Orientalists", leading Hindus stood in the fore-front of the "Occidentalists" (the Western orientation of education). Ram Mohan Roy, the most brilliant and determined Hindu leader, maintained even in 1824 the uselessness of Sanskrit and affiliated branches of knowledge. Quite opposite was the Muslim attitude. When Lord Bentinck (1835) decreed the famous Educational Resolution in which the Western orientation in education was definitely adopted, 8,000 Muslim notables of Calcutta presented a petition for the rescinding of the Resolution. They not only felt this decision of the Government quite naturally as a degradation of Eastern learning, but—and this is the most characteristic feature in the petition—they suspected that the Government in choosing this way aimed at the Christianization of India. I have treated this whole story and the rise and growth of the Hindu-Muslim conflict in the 19th and 20th centuries in a study called: "De tegenstelling tusschen Hindoes en Mohammedanen in India", to be found in *Koloniale Studiën*, 18th volume, 1934.

The ugliness of which many sincere and upright Hindus became aware was, in the actual process of events, materialized in some topics of controversy in the field of social-religious reform: *sati* (burning of widows), enforced widowhood, child-marriage, the paria- and caste-problem, purdah (seclusion and veiling of women, customary as well in Hindu as in Muslim circles), prohibition of foreign travel for Brahmins (punished by excommunication from caste, which then meant social death), the institution of temple prostitutes (*devadasi*). This enumeration affords the important lesson that even the initial confrontation with the Western Invasion, with an alien Western Government seeking to apply the particularly cherished principles of "enlightened" rule,[1] acted like a cold douche and forced the best Hindus to question the unquestioned and hallowed social-religious fabric of their community.

The meeting of West and East could hardly have come to Hindu India at a more sensitive historical moment. On the one hand a West, not only full of dynamic vigour, but inebriated by the enthusiastic self-assertion and self-glorification of man for whom the impossible has become possible, by the gospel of the Enlightenment. On the other side a religio-cultural society, in essence great but in the situation of the historical moment a stagnant, dormant, tradition-bound world. A young giant, taken on the face-value of his ideals, met a diseased, seemingly decrepit man. It could not but work like a shock to a band of the moral and intellectual élite of the Hindu Community.[2]

One must realize the implications of this historical contingency, and not less how all-important this point of historical contingency and its dramatic vicissitudes is in the whole process of the meeting of India with the Western Invasion, from the

---

[1] In so far as Westerners in responsible positions had ideals, they were the ideals of the 18th century Enlightenment.

[2] All this happened mainly around Calcutta, for the simple reason that this place was the chief centre of British power. The importance of the historical moment is aptly illustrated by a few (out of many) facts. It was Caste that provided for Hinduism the impregnable shell of defence against the shock of the Muslim invasion. At the historical moment considered here, the Western Invasion by its quite different nature made Caste instead of a *defence*, a moral and social *offence*. In 1930, however, when Katherine Mayo's scrutiny of Hindu society (*Mother India*) discussed the social-religious institutions enumerated above, the great reformer Gandhi reacted by saying, not without justification, that the book was the "report of a drain-inspector".

days of Lord Bentinck, William Carey and Ram Mohan Roy
till the day in 1947 when India gained her independence.

THE REFORM MOVEMENT

The shock released a movement towards reform, led by
Indian initiative. In this light the great personalities Ram
Mohan Roy, Debendranath Tagore, and the emergence of the
Brahmo Samaj acquire their real significance. They embodied
a sincere and devoted attempt to set the Hindu house in order.
By the nature of Hinduism this meant a revaluation and re-
interpretation of the fundamental religious principles of
Hinduism as well as social and religious reform. For what one
might call, reminding oneself of the mediaeval *Corpus Christianum*, the *Corpus Hindicum* is a far more essential element in
Hinduism than the *Corpus Christianum* ever could be. The great
difference in weight of these two mediaeval conceptions,
within their respective structures, is due to the fundamental
religious difference between Christianity and Hinduism.

The characteristic of this first response of a band of Hindu
Reformers towards the Western Invasion is that it was positive,
open, prepared to apply a searching self-criticism, intending to
purify and regenerate Hinduism by refashioning the expression
of its perennial spirit and tenets in the light of Western
rationalist and idealistic thought.[1] Historically speaking India
owes her cultural and religious "renaissance" to the West and
to the noble, sincere response of many of its finest sons.

It is not necessary to enter into detail as regards the Brahmo
Samaj's chequered and often dramatic career. It has suffered
many splits, from the time of its foundation right up to the
present day. Only a few observations are necessary. This
Movement has in all its splits remained a rather select group
of sincere Hindu intellectuals, though in all its stages it has not
only shown a missionary spirit, but used officially some of its
best members as missionaries. The original Brahmo Samaj had
a "Protestant", puritanical complexion, and enunciated as its
fundamental principle a personal theism (presumably the core
of Hinduism) which had even a deistic hue. Its distance from

[1] It is not feasible to mention all the literature, Western and Indian. I refer
to D. S. Sarma: *The Renaissance of Hinduism*; J. N. Farquhar: *Modern Religious Movements in India*; Upendra Nath Ball: *Ramohun Roy*.

the mass of ordinary Hindus has been great from the beginning. Its central pre-occupation, in all its splits and branches, has been the question of religious truth, although social reform was seldom absent from the programme. Its central point of division, within the realm of a personal theism and a stress on the moral life, has been the relation to Christianity and its attitude towards idolatry.

A number of the best members of the Movement were in their formulated opinions practically Christians, but never became confessing members of the Christian Church. An undefinable loyalty to the Hindu heritage, which allowed certain ambiguities to linger on in their strongly Christian affirmations, determined them to avoid that definite choice which is in regard to the Christian faith, where unequivocal choice is so central, of decisive importance. The popular saying often was that Brahmoism was Christianity without Christ.

The most striking personality in this respect was Keshub Chandra Sen (d. 1884), who founded "the Church of the New Dispensation". He was deeply influenced by Christianity and extolled Jesus Christ and His teaching even to the degree of making Him the sole, universal standard of Truth. He electrified India by his lectures: "Jesus Christ, Europe and Asia"; "India asks: Who is Christ?" But he never made a clean break with Hinduism.

Professor Sarma in *The Renaissance of Hinduism* opines that he practically achieved an indigenization of Christianity, which is an interesting angle from which to look at the person and work of Keshub Chandra Sen. It seems to me, however, that a truly indigenized or a truly Indian Christianity (which is badly needed) must have its bases in a firm decision to be Christian and not in an undecided wavering between Hindu and Christian, a half-way house of, religiously speaking, dubious construction. The latter can only produce an artificial, cultural synthesis without pure religious life-blood. Jesus Christ is neither Asian nor European, because He is the Christ *for* both. Sarma may be right in saying[1] that Brahmoism, apart from popularizing social reform and rousing orthodox Hindus to work for a revival of Hinduism, "prevented conversions to Christianity" just by creating a half-way house.

[1] *op. cit.*, p. 116.

SOCIAL REFORM AND NATIONALISM

Another positive response to Western stimulus and influence had its main centre in the Western part of India, Bombay. It applied itself more to social reform. The dominating personality was Justice Ranade, who became the life and soul of the Prarthana Samaj, originating from impulses given by Keshub Chandra Sen and other Brahmo-Samajists and of the Indian Social Conference and Movement.

Ranade was the real type of dedicated social reformer, who clashes with forces in his own society. His reformist career was marked by many conflicts with the strong conservative forces of orthodox Hinduism. This is a good illustration of the fact that the Western impact caused a painful but unavoidable internal upheaval within the Hindu world. To Ranade, social reform was the return to the pattern of a great past by liberating the present fallen state of society from the unhealthy restraints imposed upon an essentially superior religion, law and polity.[1] His orthodox opponents were not merely conservatives, but understood that radical social changes would not so much reform as deform the face of Hinduism. For Hinduism could not be separated into a province of religious belief and a province of social customs, but was a religious-social unity. Courageous and well-intentioned reformers like Ranade could not see, notwithstanding their sincere religious loyalty as Hindus, that the assumption on which they proceeded was as such already a deviation from basic assumptions of Hinduism. Later on, in quite a different historical context, Gokhale, one of Ranade's disciples who had the same temperament as his leader, revived the Prarthana Samaj in the "Servants of India Society". In this society, personal consecration and disinterested service to the ills and sores of the social body found an outlet.

The great change, which affected nearly all movements of religious and social reform and orientated the minds of the Western-educated, was the rising tide of Nationalism in India. Even during the lifetime of Ranade the first rumblings were clearly audible. The way a man like Ranade, who was of course a sincere patriot, came to meet it manifests the quite different quality and calibre of the new nationalism from its old patriotic

[1] *op. cit.*, p. 155.

form. This difference was personified in Bal Ganggadkar Tilak, one of the most remarkable men of modern India.

This highly gifted man, living in the orthodox stronghold Poona, was a staunch orthodox and the great opponent of Ranade's school of reform. His special trait was, however, that nationalism was with him an overpowering passion, a burning fire. The temperament of liberalism and moderation in the social reform movement and Tilak's all-consuming and all-determining nationalism were related to each other like water and fire. Orthodoxy and Nationalism were combined in Tilak. His nationalism, the conviction that the greatest good above all other good (such as social reform) is political freedom, was more uncompromising than his orthodoxy, because he was far too intelligent a man not to see that much needed to be changed in the *Corpus Hindicum*. One of his utterances[1] was: "*Swaraj* (Home Rule) is my birthright and I will have it." He showed himself prepared to suffer everything for it.

His nationalism was different also from the nationalism which since 1884 had found its channel in the Indian National Congress, struggling and clamouring for political and constitutional rights. Tilak lived in a different dimension of nationalism. With him it was more than the natural result of a newly awakened self-consciousness and self-respect, which was part of the normal condition of a people—that is, freedom. With him it was a devouring disease, a permanent fever.

To understand the intricacies of the meeting of East and West, it is helpful to look more closely at Tilak. Although it is not easy to understand this enigmatic figure, yet he may be the clue to some essential aspects of the depths that the Western Invasion in all its implications has stirred. Owing to the violent frenzies Tilak evoked and sanctioned about the year 1905 his reputation with Western writers is very low.[2] Sarma, who sees, it seems to me rightly, that Gandhi is the true successor of Tilak (strange as it may appear to bring together so closely two persons of such opposite character and attitude), leaves the point too much in the air by stating briefly: "He was an embodiment of the newly awakened national spirit, which had not yet learnt its bearings."[3] That is, in Sarma's opinion, Gandhi's

---

[1] Sarma, *op. cit.*, p. 145.   [2] Farquhar's book, pp. 354-365, is an example.
[3] *op. cit.*, p. 143. I refer also to some of Valentine Chirol's books: *India, Old and New*; *Indian Unrest*.

bearings: truth (*satyagraha*) and non-violence (*ahimsa*).

Nationalism, as the most disturbing factor in colonial countries before Independence, has been viewed far too much from an exclusively political angle. Colonial nationalism was, as explained in Chapter 4, an unintentional fruit of Western education and an unintentional gift to the subjected peoples or those that were shaken to their foundations by the Western Invasion. It is, however, an essential factor too in the meeting of East and West. The impact of the Western Invasion set in motion, sub-consciously, new visions of true nationhood, of self-respect, of acute realization of one's own spiritual and cultural authenticity and value, and not only a marriage of Western and Eastern values. Synthesis- and harmony-loving Western idealists dream too exclusively about this last, encouraged by the fact that especially in the 19th century there were a number of outstanding Indians who seemed to be promising embodiments of this measured irenic synthesis.

Nationalism, when it appeared on the scene, formulating its main interest in terms of change of political status and not primarily in terms of cultural and spiritual internal reform, turned against their Western overlords the ideas of dignified nationhood, consisting in liberty and justice, which the nationalists had imbibed from the textbooks of Western education. It is significant how frequently Viceroys installed Commissions to investigate the shortcomings of the educational system, particularly when waves of political unrest were threatening. It is also significant that the findings of these Commissions regularly proposed corrections of the system, which should obviate its too intellectualist character and the sociological impasse it created by over-production of "School Certificate" candidates, who could not be absorbed by the market and so contributed to the growth of an intellectual proletariat, the ideal feeding-ground for discontent and sedition.

Definite as these shortcomings were, it was seldom realized by these Commissions, composed of competent and able men, that at any rate the sociological shortcomings could never be satisfactorily mastered, being an unavoidable result of the meeting and clash of two civilizations. In this clash the superior side for the time being determined the kind of people it wanted for running its own machinery, but doing this primarily to serve the needs of the machinery and only secondarily in the interest of true education for the Indian people, it created involuntarily an artificial situation of "over-production", because absorption was outstripped by the evoked desire for Western education and new economic possibilities.

Nor did they realize that the injection of an entirely different civilization with Western ideals and ideas, once in operation, is uncontrollable in its most significant effects.[1] All education is in some way transmission of cultural values and tradition. Western education, because of the dynamite of its key-ideas (especially in its higher stages), when applied to *subject* peoples puts Western Governments unwittingly and unwillingly in the position of Goethe's "Sorcerer's Apprentice", who could not control the forces he had created.

This little digression on Western Education amongst subject peoples of a different culture is intended merely to stress the incalculable ferments let loose by it in an alien world equally incalculable in its reactions. It does not infallibly create Western cultured gentlemen or half-gentlemen, but in most cases it produces hybrids, split personalities which can in certain unpredictable situations reveal themselves in various guises as "progressives", "reactionaries", or "gangsters".

TILAK'S INFLUENCE

A clear example in India was the violent unrest about the year 1905 in Bengal, in which Tilak played such a considerable rôle. India, always believed to harbour essentially people of a mild, suave, uncombative temper, showed suddenly a face of Medusa-like terror and wildness. The unpredictable situation to which I have alluded was the coincidence of two facts, which triggered off an explosion of immeasurable violence. One was the Partition of Bengal for administrative reasons, which suddenly unleashed a flood of *Swaraj* and *Swadeshi* frenzy as never before. The other was Japan's victory over Russia. The momentous consequences of this on the growing trend of Asian revolt cannot easily be over-estimated. The innate pride of superiority, hidden under the feeling of humiliation, surged up with mighty force and made the feeling of humiliation in the

---

[1] Good books on the educational problems are A. Mayhew's *The Education of India* and *Christians and the Government of India.*

present more acute. The horrible outbreaks of murder and banditry, the exaltation of the bloody cult of Kali, the Mother Goddess, and of Russian nihilistic anarchist methods, were all exalted as deeds done in the name and spirit of Shiva the Destroyer, justified by quotations from the Bhagavad Gita, universally revered as one of the greatest gems of Hinduism at its best. They deserve of course not a word of defence or exoneration. In the face of the firm attitude of the Government they ebbed away as rapidly as they had arisen. It was frenzy, it was madness, but a madness which contained a lesson.

Tilak, who played such a great rôle in this epidemic outburst of religious nationalism, was a brilliant scholar in Hindu lore and at the same time a Western-educated man. To him the Holy Scriptures of current Hinduism, the Shastra's, were the authoritative expression of the *Corpus Hindicum*, the incorporation of the ideal society, whose delineation rested on the unassailable basis of Religious Tradition founded on a metaphysical idea of Revelation from eternity. In other words he was a staunch believer in *sanatadharma*. It was to him the real treasure of India, which neither could nor should be altered, nor undermined by the corrosive influence of the Western Invasion.

He was therefore the equally staunch opponent of social reformers of the type of Ranade and Gokhale, who in his eyes were willing henchmen in this work of alteration and corrosion. This was a quite logical standpoint. The extent to which this event pierced to the very quick of his vital existence as a Hindu, appears first in the vehemence of his polemic, which did not shrink from violating all rules of decency, and second in his elementary, furious nationalism. Tilak leapt at once to the demand for full *Swaraj*, thereby anticipating by several decades the organized, political nationalism of the Indian National Congress, which in 1929 raised for the first time the cry of *Swaraj* (Independence) as its defined aim.[1]

Living in the concrete situation of an India, not existing as an isolated, sacral society but shot through with fermentative and subversive extraneous influences, Tilak in practice of course recognized the inevitability of a certain margin of

[1] It was the first Indian National Congress of which Pandit Nehru was the president.

change. And most certainly he was not slow in using all the new means of expression and organization of Western origin as effective weapons. But this did not affect his deepest inspiration, that is to say to preserve the integrity of the sacral Hindu Society unimpaired. *Swaraj* had to be so absolute and central, because it was the only way possible to allow India to decide *for herself* about her peculiar, hallowed form of life. In the context of the historical moment this meant in fact a monstrous reactionism, as became especially clear in the anarchy of the 1905 period. Yet it is understandable that a man of Tilak's calibre should have protested, as he did[1] in 1908 when condemned to eight years imprisonment, both his innocence and his conviction that he was an instrument of "higher powers" or "Providence".

THE SIGNIFICANCE OF GANDHI

This makes a good place to turn to Gandhi, and his significance for Indian nationalism as one of the noteworthy aspects of the Western Invasion in India. It seems a rather fantastic stride from the violent Tilak to the frail apostle of non-violence. Yet in my opinion Sarma is right in saying[2] that although Gandhi himself always called Gokhale his political *guru*, it was Tilak's mantle and not Gokhale's that fell on Gandhi.

The deep differences, one might almost say the incompatibility, between the personalities of Tilak and Gandhi are as glaring as one might wish. In most respects Gandhi is the greatest imaginable contrast to Tilak. His paramount feeling for justice; his astounding fairness; his fearless[3] independence towards British and Indians alike; his unique type of Hindu spirituality, rooted in Visnuite piety of great sublimity; obedience to an elevated moral ideal of non-violence and sincere love of Truth as he saw it;[4] his ascetic conception of life; his fearless advocacy of the abolition of that blot on Hinduism, the pariahs (whom he characteristically called *Harijan*, children of God); in these and many other assets of his personality he is worlds asunder from Tilak's fierce, bigoted, mystical obsession

[1] Cf. Sarma, p. 145.   [2] *ibid.*, p. 143.

[3] In one of his speeches he says: "God is fearlessness. The way of the Lord is for heroes, not for cowards."

[4] Some of his other characteristic utterances were: "Love to the meanest creatures is the basis of politics"; "God is Truth"; "God is morality".

with absolutist loyalty to the mediaeval social-religious entity of Hinduism.

Their profound difference is equally clear from Gandhi's strong individualistic conception of Truth, demonstrated in the paradoxical combination in one and the same person of the ultimately agnostic seeker after Truth and the man of baffling certitude and unwavering conviction. He is a true Hindu in maintaining that the real thing is to realize the absolute Truth (which he always disclaimed having done); but his deep admiration for the Sermon on the Mount—next to the Bhagavad Gita—and of Ruskin's and Tolstoy's ideas on non-resistance; the absence, in his thinking and speaking, of mysticism, ecstasy, and the authentic Indian metaphysical conception of God as Absolute Being; his stress on morality and utter sincerity; all these clearly indicate his openness to influences other than Indian. Naturally he often used famous Indian expressions such as "self-realization", "attainment of *moksha* (deliverance)", but always with a twist to them of non-Indian origin.

His heart was in the programme of the "spiritual and moral progress of the nation". This spiritual and political dynamism has made him one of the greatest activists of history, just as his unique personality makes him one of the greatest men of our age. He united in himself aspects of St. Francis, Cromwell, Muhammad and, very intriguingly, the subtlety of a lawyer (as a young man he came back from England a barrister-at-law). This frail ascetic, this saintly warrior for whom the *practical* application of "truth" and "non-violence" in *political* life was the real passion, turned Nationalism, the movement for *Swaraj*, formerly a cause of the Western-educated intelligentsia, into the cause of the masses, and so gave it an irresistible impetus. Irresistible, not only through the dynamism of his personality and approach but also because he stamped upon the masses the conviction that voluntary submission to being an unfree, subject people meant injuring one's very soul and human dignity. Irrepressible too, because Gandhi accomplished the unbelievable feat of changing (and that in a noble sense) an individualistic, soteriological, entirely a-political religion into a *religio politica*.

Similarly he turned purely soteriological key-ideas such as

ahimsa and *moksha* into irresistible weapons of political combat. Dormant elements of the Hindu heritage freed from the limitations inherent in their individualistic focus on individual salvation in the Indian sense, became irresistible weapons in the struggle for independence, the more so because they had a peculiar appeal to the Western sensitivity of conscience as represented in the British.

A "SATANIC" VIEW OF THE WEST

Yet, though the similarity between Tilak and Gandhi seems only to concern some external features, that is to say that both were indefatigable fighters, prepared to suffer everything for their cause and wholly intent on *Swaraj*, there are deeper connecting links which justify Sarma's words about Tilak's mantle falling on Gandhi. True as it may be that Gandhi either waived or invoked the "Shastra" so authoritative to Tilak, according to his personal religious interpretation of Truth, Gandhi nevertheless was inspired by a dream of an undefiled Hindu land, "a holy Hindu people in a holy Hindu country".

This most dynamic of "saints in politics" looked, as Tilak did, essentially backward, not forward. From this standpoint he regarded Western civilization and, implicitly, the Western Invasion as "satanic". In spite of his practical rejection of the caste system he explicitly clung to the famous *caturvarna* doctrine (four main castes). His strong leadership in the *Swadeshi* movement, which meant not only the discarding of Western economic methods and the Western industrial-technical type of society, vividly symbolized in the homespun Gandhi cap and the vigorous propaganda for the spinning-wheel (*charka*), but also his rejection of Western ideas, brings him into closer contact with Tilak's idealism. Even in the field of the religious quest and expression of Truth, notwithstanding his love for Ruskin and the Sermon on the Mount, his well-known predilection for certain Christian hymns or his attempts to construct a fundamental basis for Hindu-Muslim unity, he applied the *Swadeshi* principle also to religious Truth. The logic of this position explains his antagonism to Christian Missions and "conversion", not to missionaries as human friends and social workers.

In this important point Gandhi represents an expression of

what Sylvain Lévi has called the "provincial spirit" of Hindu culture and religion (Lévi uses the words "civilization brahmanique" over against the "universalist spirit" of Buddhism) with the important difference that by his action and theories he converted an innate tendency into a propagandist tenet. A hidden affinity between Gandhi's and Tilak's passion for *Swaraj* appears also in a point, mentioned again by Sarma,[1] that in 1907 Tilak predicted already the whole programme of Non-Co-operation, for the elaboration of which (as well in its theory as in its technique) Gandhi has become so renowned.

It is important not to forget that the present "conservative" Movements in India such as the Mahasabha and others, which oppose the Congress policy of a secular democracy for India, can rightly regard both Tilak and Gandhi as their patron saints. They embody in a new historical moment the fundamental "reactionism" and nostalgia of Tilak and the *Swadeshi* doctrine of Gandhi, but in this case without a glimmer of Gandhi's great and incalculable prophetic spirit.[2] Therefore the danger of Tilak's unavoidable bigotry "lieth more at the door" of these movements than the startling dynamic effects of Gandhi's "reactionary" *Swadeshi* doctrine in relation to religious truth.

EFFECTS OF WESTERN EDUCATION

The foregoing discussion of nationalism in the light of the Western Invasion and of the important rôle the Western educational programme of colonial government has played in its genesis, prompts to some additional observations on the effects of Western education, in spite of the shortcomings of the system. This can best be done by recording the conclusions to which Panikkar comes in his oft-quoted book, as they express aptly the things that should be basically said.

Panikkar[3] starts from the link that exists between the production of the "Wogs", the Westernized Oriental gentlemen, by

---

[1] *op. cit.*, p. 143.

[2] I have confined myself, in what I say about Gandhi, strictly to what seems to me essential to the subject of this book. But I want to stress that this is very little compared with what could and should be said in an attempt towards exhaustive interpretation. The more so because Gandhi is not, as he seems at first sight, a simple but a very complex personality, in make-up as well in effects. To enlarge on the many fascinating aspects would require a thorough discussion of the whole life and career of this truly great man, which is impossible to attempt within the framework of this book.

[3] *Asia and Western Dominance*, p. 490.

Western education, and the rise of nationalism. He too calls nationalism "indubitably the most significant development in Asian countries during the last hundred years of European contact". Philosophically speaking it would be very interesting to discuss at length the question whether nationalism and sense of nationality are alien ingredients injected by the West-Eastern contact into the Eastern peoples. In my opinion two remarks can suffice. The first is that it has arisen out of resistance to foreign rule; in this case favoured not only by compulsory study, in the Western schools, of Western ideals and of examples in Western history but also by the telling contemporaneous nationalist happenings in the West. The second is that if this natural reaction certainly has (as it seems to me) no organic link with the fundamental Oriental life-apprehensions nor with the local "patriotisms" the Oriental peoples knew, the *consequences* of this "reactive" nationalism (viz. the acquisition of a dynamic conception of history and historical responsibility and of society as a continuously changing and changeable field of responsible action) are certainly not in tune with the fundamental Oriental apprehensions. They are therefore implanted by Western contact.

The points Panikkar mentions as new abiding Western introductions into the body of Asia, and which are mainly a result of the educational system and of the observation of Western examples, are the following:

"The first and perhaps the most abiding influence is in the sphere of law".[1] In all Asian countries the legal systems have been fundamentally changed and reorganized according to the post-revolutionary (i.e. French Revolution) conceptions of 19th-century Europe. Panikkar pays a sincere tribute by saying: "The imposing and truly magnificent legal structure, under which not only 360 millions of people of India but the millions of Pakistan and Burma have lived during the last 100 years, has changed the basis of society in a manner which few people realize" and he adds a little later "There can be no going back on this—in any case to the old Hindu ideas".[2]

One wonders what face Dubois, the author of *Hindu Manners and Customs*, whose melancholy and pessimism as to the alterability of Hindu society we quoted earlier, would make in

[1] *op. cit.*, p. 497.   [2] p. 498.

reading such sentences, written not by a Westerner but by a Hindu, proud of Hindu culture. Such a comparison helps us to estimate the enormous dynamic of the Western Invasion. Everywhere in the non-Western world, not only in India, one can observe sincere appreciation of Western culture (whether in a British, French or other form) by numberless intellectuals, conscious of the great liberation it has brought as well as its confusing and vexing influences. This applies to the Muslim world as well as to the great Asian cultural areas and begins to apply to Africa south of the Sahara also. This is a fact, although their criticism of Western civilization is as a rule very outspoken and their pride in their own culture and the consciousness of their abiding "otherness" are unbroken.

Moreover, this acquaintance with Western ways of thought and method has engendered a quite new autonomous activity in all these countries in the various fields of modern knowledge and in social action of many kinds. The Eastern world is astir in response to the Western Invasion in an unprecedented degree. This holds especially true for the appreciation and the position of women. "Emancipation of women" in the tradition-bound Oriental world is a far more formidable undertaking than it ever has been in the West. Represented in many stages of emancipation in different parts of the Oriental and African world, the change in status and position of women is more than a formidable undertaking. It is a revolution. It is perhaps the best indicator of the colossal dimensions of culture change and culture transmission taking place in our day.

To return to Panikkar, he candidly says that it is not possible for him to speak with the same certainty (as about the abiding influence of law) regarding the political and social structures brought about as a result of the contact with Europe; but he is confident that urbanization, the great economic shift from a rural to a multiple economy, the rise of the middle class and its consequences will make a reversion to the old political structures impossible.[1] He rightly mentions specifically the great influence of Western ideas and new forms of philosophical and religious thinking, and of art, in the cultural life of the

---

[1] He does not mention the crushing problems caused by these social and economic shifts. Later on I will draw them into consideration, because they belong essentially to the results of the Western Invasion.

East, and points to the beginning process of interpenetration of culture. Apart from Gandhi, men like Tagore, Ghose, Radhakrishnan, etc., (to mention for the moment only Indians) are figures not only of Indian but of world stature.

EARLIER RESPONSES TO THE WEST

Nineteenth-century India is rich in striking personalities. One of them was Swami Dayanand Saraswati (d. 1883), the founder of the Arya Samaj, a religious reform movement of great interest.

Dayanand himself in criticizing the Brahmo Samaj as lacking in true patriotism and showing too great openness to Western and even Christian ideas (he rebukes some of its members especially for having adopted the doctrine of the forgiveness of sins) wanted a movement of reform, but on nationalistic and indigenous lines. This became the Arya Samaj (founded 1875). The spirit and outlook of this movement has been largely determined by the personal religious experience of its founder, who was a profound Sanskrit scholar and a powerful, militant personality. The influence of the West and of Christianity is visible in his new, puritanic orientation on the personality of God, the reality of the world and the distinctness of the soul, with a strong un-Hindu rejection of idolatry, a break with India's *philosophia perennis* and the basing of his "pure Aryan faith" on the sacred Vedas[1] as the authoritative Divine Word. Dayanand in his deep religious sincerity revolted against the type of Hinduism dominant since the Middle Ages: so-called Puranic Hinduism, in which he himself was educated. His final stage was to raise, as the standard version of Hinduism, Vedic Hinduism, which by its purity and simplicity—as he maintained—condemned exuberant, mythological, ritual-ridden Puranic Hinduism, and whose main tenets were a purified conception of God, of Man in his relation to God, and the necessities for salvation. This programme in fact meant nothing less than a declaration of war against dominant Hinduism, in the name of "true" and undiluted Vedic Hinduism. From the standpoint of the cultural observer it is a remarkable blend of

[1] i.e. the four Samhitas proper, not their appendix. This is extremely important, because by this restriction the Upanishads are excluded; also the Bhagavad Gita. This goes contrary to what is now part and parcel of every cultured Hindu's list of religious "classics", i.e. Upanishads and Gita.

new "Protestant" orientation with a strong self-assertion of Indian "selfness".

This appears very clearly from the practical, organizational forms[1] of the Movement, given to it by Dayanand and remaining characteristic of it to the present. The essential militancy becomes conspicuous especially in the fact that the reformatory "theological" orientation points, West-inspired as they were, were used as weapons in the great battle for Indian self-assertion.

These practical forms are: first, a system of national education. The programme of this is the teaching of all new Western knowledge, having become indispensable in this time of change, on the basis of a Hindu classical training (Sanskrit, Vedas, Hindu moral and religious instruction, restoration of Hindu ideals of life such as *brahmacarya*, etc.). It resembles the analogous system of education for Indian Muslims by Sayyid Ahmad Khan.

The second practical form reveals more clearly the militant spirit in the Arya Samaj. It is called *Sangathan* (union) and is a systematic attempt, by publications, by public speeches and debates, to conduct an aggressive campaign on behalf of Hinduism and by attacking, often violently, Islam and Christianity as the "alien", non-Aryan intruders.

The third practical form is properly speaking a practical application of *Sangathan*. Its name is *Shuddhi* (purification). It denotes the organized attempt to bring back all non-Hindu Indians into the Hindu fold by converting them back to Hinduism and admitting them again to allegiance in the Hindu Dharma by a purification-ceremony. This *shuddhi* movement is a continuing concern and has played a great rôle in nationalist politics, especially in the days of the tensions around the Hindu-Muslim unity, pursued by Gandhi but opposed from both quarters often with great violence.

Sarma[2] justly calls the Arya Samaj the church militant in the Hindu fold, living on the short creed: Back to the Vedas. From what has been said above, it follows that the Arya Samaj has originated the principle of *Swadeshi*, which occupied such a

[1] Cf. Sarma *op. cit.*, pp. 164f.; Farquhar, *op. cit.*, pp. 101f., where an account can be found of the diverse movements aiming at defence of the inherited Religion by modern methods.

[2] *op. cit.*, p. 191.

great place in Gandhi's approach to the problem of India and in the vicissitudes of the nationalist movement. It proves that with all the passive and active openness to the influence of the West, as abundantly manifest in India, there is constantly running parallel with it a strong current of self-assertion, often even defiant self-assertion. The Arya Samaj is conspicuous by a degree of virility and combativeness which has long been an absent trait in the image of "Mother India". In many respects it borders now upon being a sect, because Dayanand's *Satyartha-prakasa* has become its canonized Holy Scripture.

The parallel (or diversely mixed) existence of openness and self-assertion, noticeable in most of the numberless Indian movements created in response to the intoxication by the Western Invasion, is entirely natural. It is what should be expected. In the slogan *"Swadeshi"* the urge towards openness and towards retreat into oneself are inextricably mingled, stimulating or restraining one another, but it is impossible to say with any certainty, in critical movements of such importance, in which direction the pendulum will swing.

THE RE-INTERPRETATION OF HINDUISM

The influence of the Theosophical Movement from the West, and especially of Annie Besant's powerful personality, cannot easily be exaggerated. There seldom has been active in India a person who has equalled Mrs. Besant in eloquence and ability such as to make India culturally and religiously self-conscious and proud. This is a fact notwithstanding the other fact that the Western theosophists with their "occultist" preoccupation are not interpreters, but misinterpreters, of what they call "Indian Wisdom".

This symbiosis of openness and self-assertion is exemplified in a far more subtle, urbane, though also virile way, in the world-famous Ramakrishna Movement. It is necessary to look into some phases of its pre-history and its history in order to grasp its true significance for our subject.

The creative personality of this fruitful movement of re-interpretation of Hinduism, significant too in the field of interpenetration of cultures, was Shri Ramakrishna Paramahamsa (1836-86)—to give him his full title. He became creative without knowing or intending it. The founders of the movements already discussed were all Brahmins, men of great knowledge and scholarship in Sanskrit lore, with a Western education and endowed with that natural quality for leadership, which seems to be a fruit of the process of hereditary selection in the leading caste of Hindu society. Gandhi is, as we saw, quite different, belonging as he did to a Vaishya, very religious, middle-class family, without any training in Sanskrit scholarship, but having enjoyed a Western training in law in London.

Ramakrishna is entirely different, and unique. He had no education or scholarship whatever. He was a simple specimen of the Hindu masses. During his whole life he showed no preoccupation whatsoever with response to the Western Invasion. His uniqueness lies in what might be called his religious genius and versatility. He was the very embodiment of the peculiar Hindu genius for religious experience and to an amazing degree a master of experimentation in Hinduism in all its aspects. A quotation from Sarma's book[1] describes it very well:

> His life represents the entire orbit of Hinduism, and not simply a segment of it, such as Theism or Vedism. He was a *jñānī* [gnostic in the highest mystical sense. K.] and a *bhakta* [a religious devotee of a special God. K.]. To him God was both personal and impersonal. He laid equal emphasis on both the householder's life of good works and the *samnyāsin's* life of renunciation and yoga. Like a true Hindu, he gave free scope to the individual variations in the Kingdom of the Spirit. And again, like a true Hindu, he held that all religions were branches of the same tree.

He claimed to have attained realization of the truth and way of Islam and Christianity as specimens of man's possibilities of religious experience, and so was an epitome of the whole cycle of universal religious realization. The term "realization" is to be taken in the sense of traversing all types of religious experience, confirming in them one's personal experience, in a life of secluded exercise, and so to realize the truth behind all religions and their various expressions. He had a vision of Jesus Christ and a realization that He was an incarnation of

[1] *op. cit.*, p. 228.

God.[1] The central, guiding figure in his multiple identification with all the "Gods" and central religious mystical and historical personalities—he not only in his experience *saw* and met them, but *became* them—was "Mother", in his case a coalescence of Kali and Sita.

Dakshinesvar near Calcutta was his place of abode and became a centre of great importance. From 1879 onwards he was the nucleus of an ever-growing number of devoted and admiring disciples, listening to the enthralling account of his spiritual pilgrimages and asking eager questions about how to live the true life of renunciation and consecration.[2]

Ramakrishna is, indeed, an astounding phenomenon. In the midst of an India torn by her groping efforts towards radical change and self-questioning caused by the Western Invasion, and her now obscure, now determined intention to remain herself, he suddenly emerges like a meteor, embodying Protean Hinduism in all its depth and variety. The only adequate way to attempt to describe it is to apply to him in the purely religious sphere the words of Rilke in his *Stundenbuch* about Michelangelo, which characterize however a great *cultural* event. These words, although not at all envisaging a personality like Ramakrishna, express excellently that mysterious concentration of a person on a special world of experience and insight and perhaps give some idea of what his disciples experienced through him. They are:

Das waren Tage Michelangelos, von denen ich in fremden Büchern las. Das war der Mann, der über einem Masz, gigantengrosz, die Unermeszlichkeit vergasz. Das war der Mann, der immer wiederkehrt, wenn eine Zeit noch einmal ihren Wert. . . . zusammenfaszt.[3]

[1] It is important to notice here the little word "an" instead of "the", as it indicates clearly that his realization of Christianity was indeed a genuinely *Hindu* act, an absorption of Christianity *within* the fundamental religious option of Hinduism.

[2] See on him the books already mentioned, and especially the volumes: *Life of Sri Ramakrishna*, compiled from various authentic sources on the initiative of "Advaita-Ashrama", and *l'Enseignement de Ramakrishna*, collected and annotated sayings, Jean Hébert, 1949.

[3] "These were the days of Michelangelo, of which I read in foreign books. This was the man who, measuring in gigantic proportions, was oblivious of immeasureableness. This was the man who always returns, whenever an epoch once again concentrates its value."

The man through whom Ramakrishna not only acquired all-Indian importance but also provided the impetus enabling India to take her place as a spiritual entity in the world arena, was his pupil Narendranath, known as Swami Vivekananda. He was the born leader in the group of Ramakrishna's disciples, who decided after Vivekananda's death to spread his teaching and renounce the world, becoming the nucleus of the future Ramakrishna Mission. Ramakrishna himself had always regarded Vivekananda as destined for a great career.

THE RAMAKRISHNA MISSION

Again it is significant to note that Vivekananda was not a Brahmin, but belonged to the Kshatriya caste (*kayastha*). In good Indian fashion, for more than six years he led a life of wanderings through India from north to south, withdrawing for long periods in isolated meditation and undergoing deep mystical experiences. He definitely belonged to the category of active mystics, which is to be found in all great religions. In other words, although he was a thinker and had unusual religious experiences, he was a man born for action. The two decisive moments which shaped his short-lived career and which made India's spirituality through his instrumentality a world affair, are his resolve at the sacred temple of Kanyakumari at Cape Comorin and his plan to leave India and visit the First Parliament of Religions, held at Chicago in 1893.

At Kanyakumari he decided to consecrate himself to the service of India's starving, oppressed millions, and not merely to wander about and teach metaphysics. By this resolve the Ramakrishna Mission was virtually founded in its two aspects: the service of the masses on the basis of a Vedantism filled with religious fervour and interpreted in a dynamic sense, open to the realities of the world. Seen in a wider context, Vivekananda was the agent for a marriage of Indian spirituality with Western dynamism and sense of responsibility.

The decision to go to Chicago was the beginning of an unintended, but vigorously executed, career of proclaiming in America, England and Europe the glorious universality of Vedanta as the *philosophia perennis*. It led on to the winning of a small group of American, English and European disciples, whom he trained to become world-renouncing *samnyasins*, adopting the title Swami and an Indian name; and to the building up, especially in America, of centres in which these Swamis and their sympathizers started a missionary enterprise for the spread of the modernized Vedantism as conceived by Vivekananda and as embodied in the Ramakrishna Mission. Vivekananda's appearance and presence at the Parliament of Religions constituted its greatest and most exciting event. By one stroke he conquered for Hinduism and Indian spirituality a place of honour and equality among the great religious Traditions of mankind. From this moment dates the beginning of the Indian cultural and spiritual Invasion in the West as a counterpart to the Western Invasion in the East. It was not planned. It happened, and then developed its own course.

Vivekananda's return to India with some of his Western disciples in 1897 became a triumphal procession through the whole of India. Its significance in the context of the East-West meeting through the Western Invasion matched the significance of what had happened in Chicago. It meant that India recovered a renewed consciousness of her individual self and envisaged for the first time a universal calling and mission.

In the same year the Ramakrishna Mission was organized as a band of *samnyasins*. It became and is still the body which carries on, in the spirit of Ramakrishna and Vivekananda, the work of spiritual education and social and philanthropic service in India, and the work of representing and propagating Indian wisdom and spirituality in the West, in encounter with Western intellectual and spiritual trends. At this latter point a genuine dialogue is on a modest scale already a fact.

Belur Math (a monastery near Calcutta) became the permanent headquarters of the Ramakrishna Order. A second Math at Mayavasi near Almora in the Himalayas, called Advaita-Ashrama, was established, and later on a third in Madras. During a visit of inspection to America in 1899 Vivekananda established various Vedanta-centres in California, the chief being the Shanti-Ashrama in the district of Santa Clara. In 1902 Vivekananda died at Belur, a mere 40 years of age.

Sarma[1] rightly remarks: "With Swami Vivekananda the modern Hindu Renaissance becomes self-conscious and

[1] *op. cit.*, p. 294.

adolescent." Vivekananda has himself characterized Vedantism, which was to him the very soul of Hinduism, as possessing the unique combination of universality, impersonalism, rationality, catholicity and optimism. It is extremely interesting to penetrate into this eloquent combination.

The underlying and all-uniting principle inherent in it is expressed in the Rig-Veda: *Ekam Sat, vipra bahudha vadanti* (One is Being (or Truth); the sages speak in many ways about it). All religions, *in their stage*, are good and true. Therefore, people should remain in their own religion, recognizing themselves as relative, secondary and partial expressions of Vedantic impersonal Monism. The spiritual unity that, on account of the ultimate oneness of Being, pervades the whole universe is the basis of the brotherhood of all creatures. The catholicity of Vedanta, rooted in the quoted Rig-Veda saying, reconciles, relativizes and yet consolidates all religions. Peculiar stress was always laid by Vivekananda in his version of Vedanta on its capacity for adamant optimism, self-reliance and self-confidence and strength.

HINDU UNIVERSALISM

This all-too-brief indication of the Vivekanandian Vedanta-Gospel, which one might call the New Vedantic Dispensation, suggests sufficiently how appealing it must be to the Hindu mind and to the mood of numberless Westerners in their own cultural and spiritual crisis. It nourishes the pride and happiness of the Hindu about the sublimity of the Indian heritage and achievement. As such it has been, and is still, the source of the misleading adage: The East is spiritual, the West is materialist. Vivekananda's gospel is the fruitful originator of a Hindu claim for universalism, which had never been raised before in India's long history. For its genius was to be introvert towards the soul, not to be extravert towards the world of ordinary realities. It has been created out of almost nothing by the rude and yet beneficent shock of the West. The affirmation of rationality and catholicity meets the present clamour for the reconciliation of Science and Religion and titillates in the West the many who know spiritual longing but are entirely at sea in the present chaos of competing doctrines and gospels, and not less the very many who in their virtual relativism of indifference are delighted to find such a magnificent justification of contempt for all "narrow dogmatism". Vivekananda's presentation of Vedantism as the herald of genuine American self-reliant optimism is an astounding demonstration of the radical *Umwertung* (revaluation) of Hinduism's authentic orientations under the influence of the West.

We must leave it at these few points, which are purposely made to show that the coming and already existing dialogue as introduced by the Vedanta missions in America will also have to consist in a mutual cross-questioning on new self-interpretations.

In the East-Western religious-cultural contact as set in motion by the Western Invasion, India not only produces personalities of great stature such as Shri Aurobindo Ghose and Radhakrishnan, or able scholars of various types, all taking part in discussions on a global scale or planning for creating a comparative philosophy. She builds also, on her own initiative, organizational channels for cultural fertilization and interpenetration. Among these are, e.g. *The Aryan Path*, organ of the Indian Institute of World Culture, or a place like Tagore's Shantiniketan foundation.

COMPARISON OF THE MUSLIM AND THE INDIAN SITUATION

Involuntarily one is driven to a comparison of the Muslim and the Indian situation, on account of their remarkable contrast in mood and outlook. As we saw in the preceding chapter, the Muslim world in its movements of response to and frustration by the Western Invasion finds, so to speak, its inescapable problem pressed upon it. This is due to the fact that its inherited order, founded on Revelation crystallized in a Book that has been spelled out in a fundamentalist way in a theocratic law for all sectors of life, clashes with the fundamentally untheocratic, de-religionized, secularized West, and tries to come to terms. It is thoroughly understandable that this endeavour to come to terms is accompanied by pain, perplexity and melancholy diffidence. Even when tones of victorious harmonization are sounded, they remain restrained. Yet in the Muslim world of to-day there remains always recognizable in the "discussion" with the Western Invasion, a subdued feeling of virile dignity on account of having to live by a divine Revelation. For it gives by its transcendent quality a sense of security in the face of the difficult task of ordering this rather un-manageable world. At the same time there is the nagging uneasiness, the haunting uncertainty, whether this wholly new type of world with its incalculable dynamism can derive stability from a Revelation that reflects so clearly a bygone age.

As appears in this chapter, the Indian scene offers quite a different spectacle. The Indian world of to-day, in so far as it finds expression in its representative writers and movements, sounds an unbroken note of victorious self-confidence. It is through Vivekananda's Neo-Vedantism, which is in essence a new, dynamic, extraverted interpretation of classic Vedantism, that this self-confidence has been achieved. It is an inoculation applied by the Western Invasion, the virus of which has in proper Indian fashion been absorbed and integrated into India's own spirit.

Whereas in the Muslim world to-day the Koranic Revelation is, in the whole problem of responsible Muslim adjustment, the fixed star and yet also the ground of uneasiness, in India by her Protean, dynamic Neo-Vedantism the centre is nowhere and everywhere. Vivekananda's appearance at the World Parliament of Religions at Chicago is to a high degree symbolic of the way in which India has grown into her way of meeting the challenge of the Western Invasion. Vivekananda when at Chicago responded with great hesitancy to the insistent demand of the chairman that he should speak. As it were stumbling and trembling he came forward,[1] invoking the Hindu Goddess of Speech, Saraswati. Then, suddenly fired by boldness, he poured out with dazzling eloquence a quite unpremeditated witness to the universal, all-comprehensive message of Vedanta and Hinduism as the mother of all religions, the true abode of tolerance, the ultimate oneness of truth in all religions.

By this announcement of Vivekananda's, which was in fact the underlying philosophy of this World Parliament of Religions, India entered the world arena as a natural, born, predestined *leader*, and not, as in the case of Islam, as a *pleader*, who laboriously tries to justify his case before the forum of the world. Hinduism graciously but boldly has since 1896 presented itself to the world at large as the *sanatadharma*, the Eternal Way, not only comprehending the numberless types of *matta*, *dharma*,

1 Sarma, *op. cit.*, p. 270.

154

darçana, *Samaya* and *marga* which India has produced, but of all religions possible under the sun. A vast application of the well-known word (though used in quite a different context and orientation): "In my Father's house are many mansions." All religions not only can but should formulate their meaning and justification within the context of the all-comprehensive Hindu *sanatadharma*, as in so doing lies their only chance of adequate self-understanding.

It is, in my opinion, this confident and bold Neo-Vedantist thesis which enables India's religious and philosophical spokesmen, in and outside India, on the one hand to offer with great assurance the Indian way as the universal way to cure the ills and solve the problems of the world, and on the other hand to be the foremost among all the peoples, vitalized by the Western Invasion, to establish world-cultural contacts.

In closing this chapter it is significant to note that the present Neo-Vedantist tendency shows an important alteration when compared with the first great responses and reactions to the Western Invasion, represented in the Brahmo Samaj and its offshoots, the Arya Samaj and the Prarthana Samaj. These earlier movements evinced a great sensitivity to the Western Invasion and its inherent critique of Hinduism by their stern un-Hindu rejection of idolatry. In Neo-Vedantism the tables are turned entirely in that it unreservedly accepts the validity of idolatry, thereby showing a return to old Hindu apprehensions. Sarma[1] expresses it unequivocally in saying: "Shri Ramakrishna was a standing refutation of all the eloquent diatribes of the Brahmo Samaj against what they called Hindu idolatry." In the same passage he quotes Vivekananda as saying that to call image-worship sinful is like calling childhood sinful, and points to Ramakrishna as the true source of this great *volte-face* in comparison with the former movements. It is indeed Ramakrishna's reversion to the genuinely Indian type of Protean religious philosophy which has engendered this de-Westernizing trait.

[1] *op. cit.*, p. 253.

Chapter Seven

THE CULTURAL RESPONSE OF THE EAST TO THE WESTERN INVASION: THE BUDDHIST WORLD

THE Buddhist world is a different proposition from the Indian and the Islamic worlds. Buddhism as a religion is a product of Indian soil and spirit, and in its essential traits and religious-philosophical expression always betrays this original kinship. It has even become the greatest and most effective organ for spreading Indian culture and thinking as a moulding force through the entire Far East and South-Eastern Asia, making Sanskrit the main classical language for the immense domain, in the same sense as Latin became the classical language of the West.

Whereas Indian religion and culture was (except in very recent times)[1] a provincial and regional affair, though on a vast scale, Buddhism by its very principles has been universal from the beginning. This universalist spirit, outlook and concern is the very reason why it was rejected by the great stream of Indian Tradition and ultimately expelled from the country of its birth, where it has left such magnificent monuments of its spiritual and artistic expression. This fundamental unwillingness on the part of Indian Tradition to acknowledge Buddhism as a legitimate part of itself (a fact which is amazing in the light of its fundamental "tolerance") is nevertheless quite logical. The limits of the elastic Indian "tolerance" were overstepped by the universalist tenets of Buddhism, because these implied either an explicit rejection or a disinterested ignoring of some essential, inviolable bases of the Indian Tradition (e.g. the authority of the Vedas and especially the Upanishads, the caste system and the Brahmanistic theory of society expressed in the term *caturashrama*, which means the canonical Indian life-pattern in four stages).

[1] See the preceding chapter.

From a certain angle Buddhism was but a new specimen of the many ways of salvation (*moksha*) which grew up in India, a new variety of the endless possibilities of soteriological doctrine inherent in the Indian quest, and as such seemingly quite acceptable and innocuous in the Indian "house with many mansions". But Buddhism's universalism, which ignored and dethroned without any elaborate polemic, as a simple matter-of-course, the basic elements of coherence and authority in the Indian Tradition, made this innate Indian spiritual strategy of seemingly endless absorption and recognition inapplicable. In the whole Indian Tradition, Buddhism was an illegitimate child, and in this light its ultimate disappearance from Indian soil and the oblivion into which it fell in India after the Middle Ages are entirely logical.[1]

BUDDHISM'S FORMATIVE POWER

Yet Buddhism, by its missionary expansion throughout Asia, has made Indian religious-philosophical thinking and ideals a Pan-Asian formative power through many centuries. At this point lies Buddhism's special significance as a religious and cultural factor of great magnitude in the Asian world. It penetrated into countries where archaic societies existed, as in South-Eastern Asia, and into the realm of Chinese and Japanese civilization, which were of the same representative calibre as Indian civilization. Buddhism, the rejected daughter of India, has thus become the great mediator in the meeting and blending of the great Asian civilizations or religio-cultural life systems: the Indian, the Chinese and the Japanese.[2]

Buddhism shares with Islam the universal outlook and claim. Yet in each case it works out differently. By its theocratic presuppositions, its identification of political-military and religious subjection and its inherent tendency to build a Muslim Empire over and in the world, Islam has operated quite differently from Buddhism in its political and religious expansion. This, just as in the case of Buddhism, brought many non-Arab

[1] As an effect of the Hindu Renaissance and the resurgence of religion in the East this attitude has radically changed.

[2] The peoples of S.-E. Asia, Indonesia included, have also a very interesting place in this vast cultural process, but a different place, because their peculiar position is that they never created civilizations transcending the archaic stage, and owed their cultural uplift in the past to the civilizations which did, that is to say the Indian and Chinese.

peoples and civilizations under its sway. Buddhism on the contrary has spread through the whole of Asia without any violence, by the mere power of preaching, teaching, translating its sacred scriptures, initiating people into the manifold Buddhist forms of worship, meeting the popular taste with new incantations, relics and ceremonies, particularly for the dead, and so on.

Buddhism is the most radical system of self-salvation and self-deliverance (*Selbsterlösung*, auto-soteriology) that can be imagined. Of its two well-known divisions, Hinayana and Mahayana, the first represents what may be called a monk-soteriology, in which the main aim is the individual striving to become an Arhat, that is to say one who has realized the ultimate goal, Nirvana. The second stands for a lay-soteriology. One might say that it represents the most formidable, passionate form of soteriological ambition, because its ideal is not the restricted, individual quest for Arhat fulfilment, attainable only for monks, but is universal and cosmic. Everybody, lay or monk, can become a Bodhisattva, a candidate for Enlightenment (*bodhi*) and Nirvana, in order to become, compelled by compassion (*maitri* or *metta*), a Saviour to inhabitants of all the worlds, just as every human being has the Buddhahood in himself as a seminal potentiality.[1]

This "salvationist" compassion, which has pervaded Buddhism in both forms though in a characteristically different way, has been one of the most striking contributions of Buddhism to the varied peoples and backgrounds which came under the spell of its message. It has engendered that "sweetness", that *douceur*, that tranquil gaiety, which cannot but strike a foreign observer of Buddhist life in various countries; a quality which seems so incompatible with what one knows about the austere and seemingly deeply pessimistic teachings of original Buddhism on the inescapability of impermanence and suffering as the outstanding marks of life, and on the urgency to seek escape from this predicament. Sylvain Lévi has rightly stressed the point that Buddhism, as a religious and cultural factor, has by the philosophical acumen which it developed, and the elevating discipline which it inculcated, taught many a one in the various

[1] Within Mahayana there is a clear distinction between schools of Salvation by Works (auto-soteriology) or by Faith (hetero-soteriology), but this does not concern us here.

peoples it influenced and moulded a "savoir de vivre spirituelle-ment" (the art of spiritual living). Therefore it deserves, culturally speaking, his judgment that it has become one of the "highest points which dominate human history".

It is no wonder that in the West, already in the 19th century and also now in the 20th, amongst all the non-Western cultures and religions which have become known to the West by study and contact, it is undoubtedly Buddhism which has made the deepest impression because of its *douceur* and *sagesse* and especially by its marvellous artistic achievements. Art, being in our present epoch of religious and philosophical diversity and atrophy the most universal, easily understandable language between men of culture all over the world, and so being practically the substitute religion of to-day,[1] is a great winner of souls. Art, which except in the modern secularized West is always the expression of a religious culture, is therefore an important vehicle of winning over unobtrusively numerous Western minds to absorb fundamental apprehensions of the great non-Christian religions, often almost without noticing.

THE IMPRINT OF BUDDHISM

All countries which are either wholly or partly Buddhist have been of course subdued to the mighty impact of the Western Invasion. With the exception of Thailand, they have all known colonial rule, whether English or French. K. P. Landon[2] is right in observing that these S.-E. Asian Buddhist peoples, in which Buddhism is deeply entrenched by a long history and whose social and cultural habits have a strong Buddhist imprint, have been more deeply affected by the Western Invasion than by any former cultural or religious penetration. Mainly as a result of its dynamic character, calling for the first time into question the bases upon which, from time immemorial, their structure of life and their evaluation of existence had rested.

These countries had continued, practically undisturbed, to live by the apprehensions and patterns of the archaic stage, typical of agrarian societies, that have never produced by their own power a higher, more complex culture. Their main

[1] I refer again to H. de Lubac's book, and will return more concretely to it below.

[2] *South-Eastern Asia, Crossroads of Religions*, passim, especially in the Preface.

features were a tribal or clan organization, in which the collective will as expressed in tradition is the norm and law of conduct; an outlook on life determined by the peculiar apprehension of the mutual correspondence of the cosmos, human society and moral behaviour, including in this metaphysical apprehension of the totality of life the belief in and intercourse with good and evil spirits and a strong ancestor worship.

All these peoples have become either Indianized or Sinicized, or have mostly accepted Buddhism as their official religion. This has enriched, elevated and refined their style of life, but in spite of the great impact of these higher religions, these peoples have never forsaken their fundamental beliefs, attitudes and patterns. Landon certainly goes too far in saying in his Preface that the invading religious cultures such as Buddhism and Hinduism have failed to convert these peoples to new points of view. He accentuates this affirmation by saying that these invading "higher" religious cultures rather have been converted by these peoples to serve the ends of their aboriginal religions, in deriving from them more potent sacral "force" from the tremendous prestige which accompanied these higher concepts and its agents, using it to the benefit of their well-established ancestral worship or their treasury of magical lore.

The thesis as expressed by Landon contains a great deal of truth, as anybody who knows this kind of people of "secondary" civilization will realize, but it is an exaggerated truth. It under-estimates and minimizes the change and refinement in spiritual orientation and the broadening of outlook these "higher" cultures and religions have silently operated. Landon's most important observation is, however, that the earlier invasion of these higher cultures has worked out as a process of *osmosis* with the archaic civilization. The reason for this procedure is quite obvious and both, reason and procedure, can be found everywhere confirmed where Buddhism or Hinduism have met with other types of civilization and amalgamated with them by absorption and adjustment. This obvious reason is the fundamental, naturalistic, syncretistic attitude common to both the archaic and the "higher" Eastern religions and cultures.

Viewed from the angle of this osmosis, which left the ancient

structure wholly intact and therefore had nothing revolutionary, the impact of the modern Western Invasion is indeed
terrific in comparison. Terrific and dynamic, in the sense of
revolutionary and upsetting, not because its impact means a
more radical spiritual appeal to these ancient structures than
the earlier cultural invaders represented, but rather because it
is so utterly alien in spirit and structure, so aggressive in its
ways and for that very reason so uprooting and confusing.
Landon opposes it aptly as shock to osmosis. The collective
thought pattern and the never-challenged idea of authority are
cut by the roots through the individualist neology which pene-
trates into these Buddhized or Sinicized archaic tradition-
bound societies. Modern transport, political innovations,
money economy, dislocation of the village unity, etc., work like
irresistible little bulldozers and have set in motion a confused
process of revaluation.

RESPONSE AND REACTION TO THE WEST

In what form does the response and reaction to the Western
Invasion, which includes the well-known accompaniments of
Western colonial rule such as schools and new administrative
organization, manifest itself? There is as everywhere a top
layer of Westernized individuals, who practically reject the
ancient world from which they come, and become a kind of
Western humanist with a peculiar Eastern flavour. Others,
quite naturally, construct various combinations of the old and
the new, either harmonizing incompatibles or trying to achieve
a reconciliation or synthesis. Others again follow the age-old
method of trying to apprehend the new in the ancient well-
known categories, and so to use the new; a reaction which
seems quite natural, as this is the most obvious way to understand and digest the West within the framework of their own
experience. Of course the shock has also caused an awakening
among loyal Buddhists, making them more keen on discovering
anew the meaning and mission of Buddhism, in many respects
strengthened by the general resurgence of a new self-understanding in many Buddhist lands and by movements in the
West that sympathize with Buddhism.

So Westernization goes on, developing a definitely Westernized minority, an intelligentsia with the features of a situational

élite.[1] In spite of the shock and the undermining of the basic ideas, sentiments and structures of the ancient society by the "Great Society", outwardly the common masses seem still to continue in the traditional practices, but the inexorable truth is that the bottom has fallen out and that, therefore, quite unpredictable developments may happen.[2] It is important to refer here to a passage in D. G. E. Hall's book: *A History of South East Asia*, (1955)[3] about the Japanese invasion in S.-E. Asia during the Second World War. He says:

> The amazing Japanese success and the rapidity with which it was achieved did irreparable harm to Western prestige. "Asia for the Asians" was the general theme of Japanese propaganda, and she sought the complete eradication of Western influence and culture.

This view is also the opinion of L. Abegg (in *Ostasien denkt anders*), who even extends it to the whole of Asia. I think this judgment has to be modified for two reasons.

First, because of the very conspicuous failure of the Japanese to enlist, generally speaking, during the War the nationalist forces in S.-E. Asian countries. Second, because Western civilization, notwithstanding all criticism against the West, represents as well a desire as a fascination for the whole non-Western world. Even the evident resurgence of indigenous cultural and religious heritages does not wipe out this persistent impact and attraction. The nationalists during the War were driven by a revulsion not so much against Western culture as against *all* foreign domination, Japanese included. Their prevailing passion was to take their own destiny into their own hands as the golden occasion offered. Just for the sake of this taking of their own destiny into their own hands in order to regain fully their self-respect and sense of human dignity, they intuitively feel the need for a self-determined, positive relation to Western culture.

The condition of Buddhism in the various countries where it

[1] In this respect one finds the same phenomenon as emerged in the period of Hinduization or Buddhization, when "élites" were also formed especially around the royal Courts.

[2] Landon's expectation that the Westernized class will all become "humanists", either right- or left-wing, looks somewhat too simplified.

[3] p. 688.

occupies a preponderant place was in the 19th century and the first part of the 20th, generally speaking, not very flourishing. A look at these various countries will suffice to substantiate this judgment.

BUDDHISM—IN INDIA AND CEYLON

India, from which Buddhism since the 11th century had disappeared and was forgotten, began to enter again into the picture, although very modestly, because of its belonging to the British Empire and as a result of the work of Western Orientalism and archaeology. The enormous importance of Buddhism as part of the history and ancient glory of India began to dawn thereby upon the minds of Western-educated Indians. Not as Hindus, but as nationalist Hindus, they began to realize Buddhism's significance as a national cultural asset, and consequently dropped the age-old idea about Buddhism as an non-Hindu heresy. Many able Indian philosophers, versed as well in Indian as in Western philosophy, aided by the efforts and results of Western scholarship, did (and do) not only share in the new attitude of spiritual and cultural self-affirmation, but claimed (and claim) the Buddha as a true son of India, trying to give him his place within the wide circle of Indian religio-philosophical thinking and metaphysical mysticism.[1]

Theosophy has also played an important rôle here, which should not be under-estimated. Evidence for this can be found in the creation of the Mahabodhi Society (1891) by Angarika Dharmapala of Ceylon, who was a great traveller and speaker in Europe and America, a delegate at the World Parliament of Religions at Chicago (1893) and who in his work was from time to time associated with Mrs. Besant and Col. Olcott. The object of this society was to develop relations between Buddhist and non-Buddhist countries. In the context of this aim the society showed special interest in Buddhism's birthland, India, by taking upon itself the care for pilgrims from abroad to Buddhist sacred places, by stimulating preaching there on the Dharma, providing for schools, libraries, bookshops and

[1] The best known authors, who have done much to "rehabilitate" Buddha and Buddhism as precious parts of the Indian heritage, are such able thinkers as A. K. Coomaraswamy, S. Dasgupta, R. K. Mookerji, S. Radhakrishnan and others.

temples. Although also a sign of the Resurgence of the Great Asian Religions, which will be discussed separately, the bringing back of the relics of Sariputra and Mogallana, two of Buddha's most famous direct followers, from the Victoria and Albert Museum to the Sanchi Stupa in 1952, in the presence of the Prime Ministers of India and Burma, Nehru and U Thakin Nu, is an act wholly in line with the aims of the Mahabodhi Society.

Ceylon is the oldest Buddhist missionary conquest as a result of the Emperor Asoka's efforts through his son Mahindra (3rd century B.C.). To mention only a few facts, the splendours of Anuradhapura and Polonaruwa remind us of the central place Buddhism held in Ceylonese life as early as the beginning of the Christian Era and in the Middle Ages. In the 19th century and earlier, Buddhism, although the religion of Ceylon, had sunk into decadence and routine, which was especially evident by the low temperature in the life of the monks. Although the monks are indispensable on the many religious and social occasions which accompany popular life, the main instrument that served and serves to capture the hearts of the common Ceylonese for Buddhism and instil the peculiar spirit of Buddhist compassion, is the recital not of the Scriptures (*Tripitaka*) but of the *Jataka* stories, which tell the many deeds of compassion accomplished by the Buddha in his incarnations as Bodhisattva before he became the Buddha.

The presence of the West with its peculiar institutions and ideas, and of Christian Missions, widening the horizon and inviting to comparison, has brought about in Ceylon also a sort of fermentation, which crystallized in the Mahabodhi Society already mentioned. Especially since the First World War a certain revitalization of Buddhism has manifested itself in attacks on Christianity; in the utilizing of Western humanist or atheist writings for demonstrating the compatibility of Buddhism with modern thought, whereas Christianity is patently in disharmony with it; in imitation of Christian activities such as Sunday school, Y.M.C.A., etc.

As to Burma and Thailand, also Theravada- or Hinayana-countries like Ceylon, the first thing that has to be said is that Buddhism as a social-religious fact dominates and colours life completely. This is mainly because of Buddhism's close and ancient alliance with the native *nat* (spirit) worship. Every lay person lives in his youth for a time as a monk in a monastery, which provides the basis for a certain knowledge and attachment. The Burmese love the Buddha, but fear the *nats*. The well-known phrase: scratch the Burmese and you find a Buddhist, must be understood in the sense of the strong hold which a fundamentally Buddhist outlook on life and the world has on the people's mind. The inextricable intertwining of Buddhism as the self-evident fountain of wisdom and insight with the common life is found clearly demonstrated when visiting the Shwe Dagon Pagoda in Rangoon with its relics of the Buddha. It blends with the market-place; it is a centre of pilgrimage, and life in all its boundless variety streams through and around it.

In the colonial era Buddhism continued its ordinary routine in accompanying and moulding the life of the people.[1] The signs of revitalization or orientation to the world abroad were not absent, but neither were they striking. Of course, in fact all these peoples are more and more drawn into the crucible and the shock-treatment of the Western Invasion as characterized above.

IN CHINA

In China, Buddhism was by the 19th century a decaying religion and in the Western Invasion underwent alternate stages of decline and revitalization. Buddhism in China has behind it a long history (the first signs of Buddhist presence in China date from the 1st century A.D.) of great ascendancy or of persecution. For in China it met not only with the universal *religio publica* of the masses, but with a totalitarian system and way of life, based on the moral and social principles of Confucianism (loyalty and *pietas*), and having its apex in the person of the Emperor. He, as bearer of the Mandate of Heaven or Tao, was both mediator and heavenly appointed custodian of the harmony of the cosmic, social and political order.

The Revolution of 1912, China's belated but final decision to recognize the inescapable pressure of the Western Invasion, electrified decaying Buddhism also. A kind of renaissance,

[1] Fielding's formerly well-known work *The Soul of a People* gives a good idea of the charming aspect of the typical atmosphere of "happiness" in Buddhist countries.

especially evident in active lay groups, produced various kinds of renewed self-revision and self-expression. The leading personalities in this movement were Kuang the evangelist and pastor (to use Christian terms), and T'ai Hsu the philosopher, a scholarly Buddhist of great parts.[1] T'ai Hsu tried to harmonize Mahayana Buddhism and Western philosophy. "Mahayana religious philosophy is the sole philosophy which agrees with Science" was one of his theses. He maintained also that the Dharma perfectly agreed with Democracy and that only Buddhism taught and practised universal brotherhood and peace.

Since 1949 all this new effervescence has come to a standstill under the Communist régime. Buddhism, as far as it still exists (and it certainly does amongst numerous lay people) is in chains. It is alternately persecuted, harassed, left in comparative peace, or "organized" for Government purposes, according to the varying winds of Maoist ideological moods and strategies. By the "secularization" of the monasteries Buddhism has been greatly weakened, the more so because by its loose organization it has no rallying point of real significance.

IN JAPAN

Japan is at the present time the real stronghold of Buddhism. 40,000,000 Japanese are counted as Buddhists. In many respects Japanese Buddhism, which historically came from Korea and China, not from India, has remarkable peculiarities.[2] It began as the state religion of Japan, by Imperial Ordinance issued in A.D. 594 by Prince Shotoku. He adopted Buddhism as the state religion of the country with the conviction that this was in his days the world trend of philosophical thought. He sent envoys and students to China to collect the sources of the new religion and study the high culture of China. This has set an important tone as well for the cultural development of Japan in general as for that of Buddhism and its status in Japan. Prince Shotoku's act initiated the great cultural influence which Chinese civilization, also in its Confucianist form, has exercised in Japan. It made Buddhism at the same time the basis of a new Constitution, embodying a way and norm

[1] Much information is to be found in Chan Wing Tsit's *Present Religious Trends in China*. Cf. also my book *The Christian Message in a Non-Christian World*, pp. 229f.

[2] Cf. *The Path of the Buddha*, Buddhism interpreted by Buddhists. Edited by Kenneth W. Morgan, 1956.

of life which would enable the people to live in harmony.

The subsequent development of Buddhism in Japan regularly took its cue from the representative "sects" in Chinese Buddhism and developed them in a characteristically Japanese fashion. Japan has introduced into Buddhism many striking innovations, such as its pronounced form of Zen Buddhism with its variegated influence on the Japanese expression of culture, the Amida religion (the Japanese edition of Chinese "Pure Realm" Buddhism) with its emphasis on *sola fide* in the Shin sect; the right of monks to marry; the notion that women can attain Buddhahood.

Japanese Buddhism has produced a host of remarkable personalities, men of great learning and capacity for vigorous leadership. The faith and practice of Shin and the nationalistic, Japan-centred interpretation of Buddhism by Nichiren find no counterpart in the Buddhist world elsewhere, whereas the many different approaches to Buddhism and its interpretation and application have fertilized Japanese Buddhism. There is, moreover, no country in the Asian world of naturalistic monism, where the figure of the reformer of prophetic temperament is relatively so prominent as in Japan.[1] Also it is in Japan that vast systems have grown up welding Buddhist philosophical principles with Confucian tenets and authentically Japanese Shinto notions. The indigenous gods and goddesses have slowly risen to the status of being incarnations of Buddhas and Bodhisattvas.

Buddhism played also a very active rôle in the many periods of political unrest in Japan. Monasteries as fortresses and doughty warrior-monks equal, even often surpass, in the time of the Middle Ages, the great bishop-warrior-statesmen of mediaeval Europe.

This intense activity and productivity within Japanese Buddhism took place up to the end of the so-called Kamakura era (14th century). The net result of this long development has been that in Japan as well as in China the general attitude is "to use" all cults.

Nowadays the common people do not distinguish between Buddhistic divine beings and Shinto gods. In the past in Japan

[1] Cf. my *Christian Message in a Non-Christian World.*

167

there were very few shrines that did not have Shrine-temples built in their confines where Buddhist priests performed the morning and evening practices of reciting Sutras and served the Shrine gods and goddesses together with Shinto priests. The majority of the Japanese pray before the Shinto shrines and at the same time pay homage at the Buddhist temples without being conscious of any contradiction.[1]

This attitude, innate as well as fostered, must always be kept in mind when in the meeting with the West one notices the strong tendency, prevalent in Buddhist countries and also in India, to leap as it were to synthesis and harmonization. This is not primarily an intellectual, philosophical urge; it is a spontaneous act.

From 1606 to 1868 the Tokugawa[2] military dictatorship (*shogunate*) led the destiny of Japan and isolated it (since 1638) systematically from any contact with the outside world. Buddhism thus enjoyed little State favour. Confucianism, interpreted one-sidedly in the sense of unquestioned obedience to authority, was in fact the State philosophy. It meant a conditioning of thought to a degree which might even arouse the envy of the powers that be in present-day Communist China.

THE ABANDONMENT OF JAPANESE ISOLATION

The great resolve of Japan in 1868 to abandon its isolation and to start the uncertain experiment of keeping intact its spiritual and cultural personality, and yet to launch forth into the hazardous undertaking of Westernizing its political and economic life, led country and people into the turbulent, confused, but—from the standpoint of prestige and power amidst the world of nations—victorious Meji era. The partly formulated, partly unformulated ideology which governed this process centred in the worship of the Divine Emperor, who remained in the whole new structure of representative government the fixed pole of absolute autocracy.

This colossal, self-piloted change in Japan[3] meant a great

[1] Cf. *The Path of the Buddha*, p. 370.

[2] In Chapter 8 this period is treated in more detail.

[3] Cf. G. B. Sansom: *The Western World and Japan* (1950), which treats the subject up to 1894. One can find there good bibliographies of the voluminous literature on the subject.

deal for Buddhism. Under the new régime of constitutional liberty of religion (1889) it did not get any favoured position. It became in a certain sense more State-controlled, but on the other hand it was able to determine its course in a new world. The newness of this world consisted mainly in the removal of the complete isolation in which Japan had lived for more than two centuries. This removal meant her being taken up into the Western Invasion with its two main consequences.

The first consequence was the contact with Western philosophical and religious literature, acquaintance with the political and economic thinking of the West, and confrontation with the message and activities of Christian Missions. This induced comparison, self-examination and new forms of self-assertion.

The second consequence was that the revolutionary change of Japanese economic structure and its many, often incalculable, repercussions on individual and social life called for new forms of social service. This situation revived memories of the past, when Buddhism, inspired by its altruistic, humanistic ethics, deployed in various periods of Japanese history a great activity in the field of what is now called social service (hospitals, roads, orphanages, schools). This was in Mahayana Buddhism a domain of great lay activity, from which there accrued to the laity enormous religious merit on the way to salvation. Moreover the vigorous example of Christian Missions in this respect stimulated the desire for new social expression in a new age, in which self-help and self-reliance became invigorating principles urging a refined, tradition-bound culture like the Japanese in a new direction.

In brief, the natural response in various quarters of Japanese Buddhism consisted in attempts at revitalization. In many respects a vast social, educational and religious activity has grown up, using often forms and methods learnt from Christian Missions. Very significant is the fact that Japan is undoubtedly, amongst the Buddhist countries, the centre of Buddhist scholarship. Many of the leading scholars in Buddhism, especially Mahayana, are Japanese, well versed in the methods and results of Western scholarship in Buddhism as in those of indigenous scholarship. The names of Anesaki, Suzuki, Takakusu, Bunyian Nanjio, for example, are known all over the world. Japan takes part in the growing international Buddhist attempts towards Buddhist co-operation, but one always feels a certain detachment because of Japan's peculiar assimilation of Buddhism. In 1952 the Second World Buddhist Conference took place in Tokyo and led to the formation of the Japan Charter of the World Federation of Buddhists, the All-Japan Young Buddhist Federation and the Japan Buddhist Women's Association. The professors and research scholars of Japan are banded together in the Nippon Buddhist Research Association and the Japanese Association of Indian and Buddhist Studies.[1]

Japan is unique in this respect, not because of Buddhism's fairly strong and established position in that country, but because of its Mahayanist character. This, especially when compared with the Hinayanan countries, implies a peculiar stress on the significance and necessity of lay activity.

The various parts of the Buddhist world have become aware of one another and of the need for mutual acquaintance and co-operation. One of the results is that, whereas in the past the two great "Churches" (Hinayana or Theravada, and Mahayana) ignored each other, signs now begin to appear of "ecumenical" discussion and rapprochement.[2]

DIFFERENCES IN THE BUDDHIST AND HINDU RESPONSE TO THE WEST

When surveying the Buddhist world's response and reaction to the Western Invasion, one is struck by a certain difference from the Indian religions and cultural world in regard to the same point. The impression the Buddhist world makes is that it is more placid in comparison with the Hindu world. Involuntarily the question arises: Why?

One reason, to be sure, is the obvious difference between the sincere, gifted Hindu and the peoples who inhabit the Buddhist lands. There is, generally speaking, a superior human substance in India. This has made her the mother of a great culture and religion of a luxurious growth and variety. The peoples of the Far East, who are in spiritual endowment the equals of the

---

[1] Cf. *The Path of the Buddha*, pp. 362, 363.

[2] See the interesting 8th chapter of *The Path of the Buddha* on "Unity and Diversity in Buddhism", in which H. Nakamura, Professor of Indian Philosophy at Tokyo University, surveys the agreements and disagreements in "theology", faith and practice of Hina- and Maha-yana.

Indians and therefore have similarly become creators of imposing systems of culture, differ in a peculiar way from the Indians precisely in the measure of religious and metaphysical seriousness. It is after all a notable fact that the fountain-heads of the profoundest and keenest philosophical thinking in Mahayana, which found its main abode in China and Japan, are Indians such as Nagarjuna.

This is not of course meant to imply that, broadly speaking, Chinese and Japanese Buddhists do not evince metaphysical and religious seriousness. They do have it, and many fine examples could be mentioned, especially in Japan. Yet this seriousness is of a different quality and texture. The Chinese and Japanese mind has, in contradistinction to the Indian mind, an innate streak of urbane scepticism and relativism, and a strong aptitude for social and political duty without deep religious sentiment, which is not so conspicuous in the Indian mind. They are practically-minded rather than speculative.

Another reason which might account for the difference is perhaps this: that Buddhism's serene subtlety, flexibility and evasiveness have hitherto protected it against the feeling of being in danger of dislodgment by the Western hurricane, as the Hindu world has sometimes felt.

The phrase in which the effect of the Western Invasion and the response to it can be summarized is that it is a complex event of simultaneous corrosion, adjustment to new conditions, and remaining true to type. Necessarily the situation is unstable, because these peoples—and this applies to the peoples of all the great non-Christian civilizations—are in a very stringent sense living "between the times", in violent transition. Leaving their ancient, well-built life structures, plucked at by the roots in the storm of the Western Invasion yet voluntarily and involuntarily holding to them, they are plunging none the less into a new world of huge unfamiliar patterns, at once inexorably compelled and freely desiring to do so. In what way the objective and subjective (psychological) pressures will mingle, and mould the decisions, nobody can foresee. One can make intelligent guesses informed by critical knowledge, or work with a kind of divining rod; but one cannot calculate, measure and know.

Chapter Eight

THE CULTURAL RESPONSE OF THE EAST TO THE WESTERN INVASION: CHINA AND JAPAN

I. CHINA

CHINESE civilization stands equal in significance and originality to the other great Asian civilization, viz. the Indian. Japan, culturally and religiously, has been thoroughly influenced and moulded by these two fertile "mothers" of culture, but shows her own originality, not only by the very peculiar way in which she has digested the rich Indian and Chinese nutrition, but as much by her characteristic endowment.

Both, China and Japan, although like India having reared magnificent civilizations which are (as I have shown in my book *The Christian Message in a Non-Christian World*)[1] mighty and exuberant elaborations of the "naturalistic monism" fundamental to all archaic life systems, are nevertheless deeply different from India by the worldly "secular" bent they manifest, in spite of their unmistakable religious foundation and flavour.

By way of introduction to the reaction and response the Chinese cultural-religious giant has shown to its meeting with the West, I apologize for amplifying the foregoing sentences by a long quotation from *The Christian Message in a Non-Christian World*,[2] as I feel unable to improve on it. This summary background delineation is given, notwithstanding the fact that by

[1] Published 1938.

[2] pp. 182-186. The literature on China and Japan and their meeting with the West is, as everyone knows, enormous. Out of many I refer here only to E. R. Hughes: *The Invasion of China by the Western World*, 1937; Hu Shih: *The Chinese Renaissance*, The Haskell Lectures, 1933; G. B. Sansom: *Japan, a Short Cultural History*, 1931; G. B. Sansom: *The Western World and Japan*, 1950; R. Benedict: *The Chrysanthemum and the Sword*, 1946.

Communist domination and indoctrination the typical Chinese fact of cultural creation seems definitely to have been wiped out. The writer believes, however, that, decisive as the turn may be which China has taken since 1949, in order to understand the last 150 years of Chinese history—including Communism's seemingly ruthless iconoclasm in regard to the past—China's historic record of cultural achievement and the underlying regulative *idées mères* (governing ideas) remain relevant. Clean slates on which to write a new code of life do not exist.

The quotation from my former book is as follows.

China, through Buddhism, has been deeply influenced and moulded by Indian thought and religion. The amount of enrichment in philosophical thinking, in religious quest, in psychological penetration, in art, that this great culture has derived from its being impregnated by Buddhism and the cardinal Indian motives of life, is simply incalculable. Without this Indian impact the civilization of China would probably never have known to such a high degree real metaphysical thinking, acute logical analysis, the lofty heights of radical mystical gnosis, the deep mellow tones of the longing piety of faith, and the great development of rigorous ethical systems of discipline which have become its possession. In short, the many sided cultural stimulus that has gone out from India influencing this civilization is enormous, and demonstrates convincingly that the Indian type of apprehension of existence is one of the most cardinal and representative of the existing types in the world.

The civilization that is China's original creation, however, is also one of the truly remarkable expressions of the human mind. In its own very characteristic way, which is the outcome of aptitudes and geographical and historical circumstances different from those of India, it is an expression of the primitive apprehension of the totality of existence. Confucianism and Taoism, the typically Chinese spiritual creations, are so emphatically an expression of this apprehension that the comprehensive endeavour by the great Sinologist, J. M. de Groot, to evaluate Chinese culture as a whole has caused the enormous elasticity and fertility of the primitive apprehension of existence to become more widely understood. He has given it the name of *Universismus*.

In the preceding chapter[1] we indicated that the two outstanding tendencies—following from the primitive apprehension of

[1] I.e. of my book, *The Christian Message*. . . .

173

existence—of the tribal religions and of the great religious civilizations of Asia are that they are strongly naturalist and strongly social in conception and outlook. China affords a very vivid illustration of these two inseparable strands in Eastern religion.

The French scholar, M. Granet, whose works testify to great knowledge and great originality, has characterized Taoism as a *naturisme magico-mystique* and Confucianism as a *sociocentrisme* with ethical ends. This formulates the Chinese situation tersely, but aptly. The naturalist and social apprehension of religion have in China acquired an exceptionally high degree of interdependent unity, which in its turn has produced an adjustment and attunement to the universe that from the standpoint of cultural history must be called marvellous and unsurpassed. This exquisite spirit of harmony is China's characteristic and outstanding achievement; and in it lies the explanation of the fact that this so-called practical people has manifested such extraordinary artistic ability and taste.

The interdependent unity of the naturalist and social apprehension of religion has been so peculiarly strong in China because in Confucianism the notion of religion as Dharma, as a divinely-sanctioned social order to which everyone necessarily has to conform, was not linked as in India with the fissiparous conception of caste. Nor was it confined to the family and the clan—although in this respect also Confucianism is the classic expression of religion as a social notion—but it contracted a very intimate relation with the State and its symbol, the Emperor. Thus the grand idea of the interdependence of the primordial cosmic order and the social and political order is made the creative impulse of that aristocratic life-conception which we call by the name of Confucianism.

This is also the reason why Chinese civilization has become the classic embodiment of conservatism with its vivifying and petrifying possibilities. The Chinese mind, because it served as the vehicle of the primitive, naturalist apprehension of existence, can be as exuberant and grotesque in its fantasies as India. But this strong concentration on man as a social and political being, and on the discipline needed to make him function harmoniously in the totality, gives Chinese civilization that aspect of common sense and aristocratic reserve and restraint which is lacking in India. There, social thinking has remained caught in the concept of caste and the religiously-established superiority of one priestly caste, the Brahmans.

The enormous sweep and width which this amalgamation of the

naturalist concept of the universe and its majestic order with the social concept of the Empire and its august prestige has instilled into the Chinese view of life is the background for its remarkable creation of officialdom, open to everyone from the highest to the lowest strata of society, so radically in contrast to caste-ridden India. One could go on drawing outlines, for the study of Chinese civilization as a cultural achievement is a fascinating theme, but it would carry us too far.

The highest category of the Chinese apprehension of the world and of life is Totality, or the Primeval and Eternal Order (*Tao*), which is the moulding principle of the universe. It manifests itself in a process of antithetic but complementary rhythms, such as Yang and Yin, macrocosm and microcosm, which correspond with and counterbalance each other. To preserve the harmony of this primeval rhythm is the meaning of the natural and the human world. The law of nature and the law of human social life, namely morality, are essentially one. Man and the cosmos are one undivided unity of life. Primeval Totality or Order (*Tao*) realizes itself in the ordered life of man, and the reverse. Therefore the first commandment of all Chinese ethics is to live in harmony with Tao, and the second, which is like it, is that traditional rules and etiquettes through which society and state function reflect— or ought to—the behaviour of the cosmos.

To keep this harmony intact and to find herein the true life is the foundation of both Confucianism and Taoism. *Tao* and *Li* are the appropriate terms to express these two cardinal aspects of the Chinese apprehension of life and world. It is a symbol of the Chinese apprehension that Chu Hsih, the great systematizer of Neo-Confucianism under the Sung dynasty, knows in his system only cosmology and ethics.

Confucianism and Taoism have each elaborated this naturalistic monism and this cosmic-human monism in their characteristic way, virtually becoming radical contrasts, but essentially spring-ing from the same life-impulses. Both coincide in the imman-entist, anthropocentric and relativistic key-note which pervades the background of all their attitudes. Here again not the problem of truth but of realization of spiritual values is the guiding principle. The hyper-individualistic ethics of Taoist *wu-wei* and the aristocratic social ethics of Confucian conformity and etiquette, in which self-mastery is the way to world-mastery, are both thoroughly immanentist and anthropocentric. Not the Will of God, but the ideal of the "Perfect, Holy Man" whose inner being is one with *Tao*, and that of the "Noble Gentleman", is the norm of ethical striving and aspiration.

A transcendent norm of ethics is impossible in this naturalistic apprehension. The command of Heaven is to be found in the heart. All ethics are a form of human wisdom, never the expression of a personal divine Will which is the Measure and Judge of all life and action. The whole spirit of Chinese civilization is that of humanism; it is one of mankind's classic achievements in humanism. In this idealism of harmony good and evil are, of course, no real contrasts. Everything or every condition that breathes harmony is *eo ipso* good, for instance universal welfare. The same subtle or coarse eudaemonism, that is everywhere the child of a naturalistic-monistic apprehension of existence, permeates all Chinese ethics, for within this *harmonia praestabilita* of the natural order of the universe and the moral order of human life it is impossible to see the irreparable rent of sin that runs through it.

The much-debated Chinese aversion to a personal conception of God has its deep roots in this same naturalistic monism. In its sphere the conception of transcendence and of so-called pure spirituality of God is, properly speaking, absurd. The conception of the Divine as something wholly independent of nature or man is simply impossible, for nature and man are *aspects* of Totality, while Totality expresses itself in man and nature. A real difference in substance or essence is unthinkable. The Chinese mind has therefore always abhorred the idea of a transcendent God-Creator, who again and again takes the initiative and acts in history. In religious speculation the Chinese mind turns naturally and inevitably to the conception of an impersonal, *super-divine* entity. We intentionally use the word super-divine, because the divine belongs to the sphere of the world, of nature and man. The ultimate is super-divine, ineffable, indefinable, immutable Essence, outside all activity. In other words, naturalistic monism leads always to some kind of ontological conception of the Divine or Ultimate Reality.

Though there had been cultural and religious contacts between China and the Western world in the times of the Roman Empire and of the Middle Ages, the year 1514 marks the beginning of what would three centuries later appear in China's long history as the irresistible Western Invasion. It was in this year 1514 that the Portuguese made their first appearance at Canton. The ardently-sought way to Cathay had been found.

This first appearance remained for a long time symbolic, as well for China's attitude towards this unexpected, inaudible knocking at the door by the impetuous West, as for a great many (not all) of the appearances of Europeans. Hughes formulates it in this way: "If Chinese ports did not welcome the visitors, or trade was not to their liking, they had no scruples about the use of violence. Thus to the Chinese they appeared as nothing but marauding pirates".[1] The name "redheaded barbarians" was not only an expression of the xenophobic self-isolation of the Ming period, it was founded in substantial fact.

However, the arrival of the Jesuits in Peking in 1601 in the person of the great Ricci, after many unsuccessful attempts, marks the beginning of the modern period when cultural influences as well as trade began to find their way.[2] The Jesuits were determined to conquer the Chinese world of culture, life structure and religion for the Church. Their main instrument in their long-drawn-out siege was, symptomatic enough, culture and science. Symptomatic because in so doing they demonstrated that they had a right appreciation of the Chinese world, namely that it was primarily a truly character-istic culture. Symptomatic also, because they could bring with them evidences of Western sciences (mechanics, astronomy, physics) that were superior to what China had, and they did so precisely at a time when there was a new stirring of interest and desire to know in China's leading circles, ready to show that important turn of mind, curiosity.

As the Calendar is the most concrete expression of the "universist" basis and background of Chinese life and culture, and just then happened to need correcting, the Jesuits by their superior astronomic knowledge could leap immediately into the heart of Chinese culture, so becoming (in the view of the Chinese concerned) valuable collaborators and servants in setting the huge system right. Europe, which in the 17th century was experiencing one of its grandest creative periods, seemed through the instrumentality of the indomitable Jesuits to graft itself on to the great civilization of China. As well in science as in religion, if one takes into account that two outstanding

---

[1] E. R. Hughes: *The Invasion of China by the Western World*, p. 9. Hughes says on the same page that Portuguese and Spaniards showed a ruthless combination of religious zeal and lust for money. When the Spaniards established themselves on the Philippine Islands, and found there too capable competitors in trade in the great number of resident Chinese, the Spanish Government summarily cleared them out in a wholesale massacre.

[2] Cf. Hughes, *op. cit.*, p. 3.

M

scholar-officials, Li Chi-tao and Hsii Kuangchi, became sincere converts to Christianity.

This smooth prelude to a meeting and dialogue between the rising modern West and the giant China ended abruptly in a dismal and dissonant finale by the inner conflicts between different Orders (the Jesuits on one side and the Dominicans with the Franciscans on the other) about the methods of "conversion", resulting in the blind interference of the Vatican which hurt the Chinese apprehension of the world and China's place in it to the very quick, and brought about the Chinese return to orthodox isolationist Confucianism.

TRADE FORCES THE DOORS

The only way left to force the closed doors of the self-satisfied, self-sufficient Chinese Empire, the entrance to which was so strongly coveted by the dynamic West, was trade. As the impetuous demand for trade met with stubborn unwillingness, born from a haughty cultural pride and sublime, wilful ignorance of the Western world in its imperialistic 19th century outburst, trade engendered armed conflict. Isolation was gradually battered down by violence. It is out of place in this book to enter into more detail and adduce the extremely enlightening examples of China's persistence in declining, in proud serenity, the embassies of the "barbarians" for relations on equal terms, or the many sordid and shameful aspects of this blind meeting of two giants, especially sordid and shameful on the Western side. In this setting of a dynamic, technically superior West and a self-contained static Chinese bloc, the human confusion, which is so typical for many historical situations when there is on both sides blindness to oneself and also to the other, could not but work out in violence and force such as violated all rules of decency, in spite of the fact that both sides invoked august principles.

Such crucial periods of human confusion make all participants, particularly the victorious ones, unconscious hypocrites, and point to the inadequacy of even our most refined methods and rules of historical scientific interpretation. The outward symbol of this enigmatic element in the violence which seems so easily explicable by psychological and economic reasons, was in this case the forced opening of the five harbours for foreign trade by the Treaty of Nanking of 1842. The Western Invasion began.

The word "invasion" is cruelly true in the case of China, precisely when we take it in the first place in the cultural and religious sense. De Kat Angelino[1] aptly comments that China had always been by its superior power and quality an absorber of foreign cultures; it had always in its history "changed the barbarians into Chinese". In its encounter with the West, however, it came into contact with a cultural conviction as strong as its own, and this strong Western conviction had, at the stage of dynamism in which the West found itself, the greater force of penetration and expansion.

Before the Revolution of 1912 there was a long period, beginning with 1839, of tough resistance to adjustment, resistance which much resembles an ostrich hiding its head in the sand. It was the natural resistance of an old civilization with deep-rooted principles, which was drawn impotently against its will into close contact with Western civilization, coming in the disguise of ruthless economic and political exploitation. There is a redeeming touch in Gladstone's plea during the Opium War (1840) in Parliament when he stated that the Chinese, the pagans and semi-civilized barbarians had justice on their side, whereas the enlightened and civilized Christians were pursuing objects at variance both with justice and with religion. The same thought echoes in the note Lord Elgin, the British Envoy to execute Palmerston's imperialist policy, put in his diary: "I thought bitterly of those who for the most selfish object are trampling underfoot this ancient civilization."[2] Also in figures like Sir Robert Hart, the organizer of China's revenue system and postal service, or like the missionary Timothy Richard, who wanted to serve China by helping it to reform itself.[3]

THE SLOW ADJUSTMENT OF CHINA

The slow adjustment of China to this unprecedented predicament was full of dramatic episodes and the suffering of great humiliations. The centre of unyielding resistance and blind refusal to recognize the new situation was the Manchu Court,

[1] *Staatkundig beleid en Bestuurszorg in Nederlandsch-Indië*, Vol. I, 1 (1929), pp. 520, 521.

[2] Hughes, *op. cit.*, pp. 25, 26.

[3] More examples could be mentioned of disinterested service, sincere devotion and vision, but to list a few is sufficient.

led by the strong-willed, wily "Old Buddha", the Empress Tzu Hsi, and the class of conservative literati. The Taiping Rebellion (1849-65), an extraordinarily important event from the political and religious point of view, was a colossal endeavour to get rid of the Manchu Dynasty, which certainly according to the Chinese way of thinking had forfeited the Mandate of Heaven, and to found a new dynasty.

It held great promise for a quite different adjustment by its openness to better, spiritual goods from the West, as was evident in many of its best leaders. It built its new dispensation of the Chinese Empire on a remarkable combination of Chinese and Christian regulative ideas, as the whole movement had its origin in a vision vouchsafed to its founder, Hung Hsiu-chi'uan, which led him to study Christianity, seek contact with some missionaries and ask for baptism. The content of his vision was that he was called by God to overthrow the Manchu Dynasty and establish a new State, called the Great Peace Heavenly State (*Tai Ping T'ien Kuo*).

After an amazing success, the Taiping Rebellion tasted defeat through the military co-operation of the European Powers with the tottering Manchu Dynasty; a co-operation mostly instigated by mercantile greed and the political calculation that a dissolving state under a decaying government is a more favourable object of political and economic exploitation than a reviving one. To some extent also a suspicious aversion to this rather incomprehensible Taiping phenomenon, on which all expert interpreters of the Chinese mind disagreed, contributed to the decision to deny support to it. With few exceptions the missionaries too found the Taiping people wanting when measuring this imperfect, but highly interesting Chinese version of Christianity with their too naïvely Western dogmatic yard-sticks.

It is useless to speculate upon a cause that was definitely lost, but it is wrong to treat the Taiping Movement for this reason as irrelevant.[1] It held great possibilities, cultural as well as

[1] This historically speaking "irrelevant" episode cost 20 million lives. The West has a great share in the responsibility for this horrible thing, because one of the consequences of the Western invaders' economic and political rivalries at the expense of the living body of China was that the Chinese people could not (as they tried to do in the Taiping Rebellion) apply their traditional method of displacing rotten dynasties which had lost the Heavenly Mandate by helping a new one to get the Mandate. The Western Invasion and its complications frustrated China's habitual political surgery in times of crisis and made the crisis a festering disease.

religious. It could have meant an encounter of China with the West of quite different quality and less painful development. Everything in this respect has naturally to be said in the conditional, but on the other hand to treat the unsuccessful and abortive in history as irrelevant or no longer worthy of serious reflection, indicates the essential superficiality of much of our famed "historical thinking", which labours under the illusive dogma that history is one-dimensional.

One of the curious results of the Taiping Rebellion was that it forced upon the leading officials and generals of the Manchu régime the necessity to study the Western craft of ship-building and manufacturing arms. One such was Tseng Kuo-fan, the Manchu general who defeated the Taipings. Another was the well-known diplomat Li Hung-chang. This caused a going abroad of Chinese to Europe and America for purposes of study, first of a technical and military kind[1] but increasingly also of other kinds of Western knowledge. A still stronger incitement to take, on their own initiative, serious notice of Western knowledge and achievement was the Sino-Japanese War in 1894. The easy victory of Japan revealed China's weakness and backwardness and engendered a strong national mood in China. The facts spoke loudly and demanded change, not unwilling but willing.

The religion of the West, Christianity, entered China also (through the activity of Missions) under the inevitable aegis of the expansion of Western political and economic interests and rivalries. This expansion was the inescapable framework in which all penetration, including the cultural and the religious, had to take place. Necessarily this whole framework has stamped Missions with an indelible ambiguity. Once they had got a footing, they developed into a vast enterprise of cultural, religious and social penetration and have done enormous service. They have been one of the great agencies in making Western civilization, its spirit and achievements, accessible to the Chinese. At the same time this inevitable function of mediating Western culture has increased the ambiguous position of Missions, since their cultural services and religious

[1] This priority of technical and military science in the pursuit of Western knowledge, as positive response to the unrequested contact with the West, is to be explained by the fact that the humiliating superiority of power on the Western side was at first sight interpreted as meaning that the secret of the West lay in its technical and military skill.

purpose could never be separated by reason of the historical situation, and could rarely be distinguished in a way satisfactory for a clear and sound understanding of their primary motivation.

Hu Shih in his Haskell Lectures[1] poses the question why China's response to the Western Invasion has been so different from Japan's. In regard to Japan, he says, one can speak of a seemingly speedy success of its adjustment. In the case of China this is absent. In Japan there was, in the great transition from centuries-old isolation to openness, effective leadership and a consolidating centre, especially around the inviolable sacredness of the Emperor as the supporting pivot in the cyclonic change. This centre of stability and at the same time symbolization of the trustworthiness of the new course was entirely lacking in China. Therefore, the contact with the West had to happen in involved confusions and humiliations, in a continuous and tortuous up and down. He calls Japan's method of adjustment "centralized control", in which much of the mediaeval structure and ideals was protected by a shell of militant modernity. China, on the contrary, had to go the way of "diffused penetration and assimilation". Consequently its reaction and response were spasmodic, wasteful and discontinuous, as there was no political stability.

CULTURAL ADJUSTMENT

This is perfectly true. On the other hand, however, China produced in the 19th and also in the 20th century a striking number of brilliant men, wrestling with the fate of their country and the challenge of Western civilization to their ancient cultural heritage. They began to see that the real secret of the West was not technics, but something behind it.

K'ang Yu Wei has become in recent decades the revered initiator of many disciples into the deeper meaning of Western culture. Liang Ch'i Ch'ao, his most famous pupil, to whom we will return, is in his life and literary output the mirror of the agonies through which these brilliant men went. The advocates of reform saw in science, in education, and in the manifestation of civic morality, the great liberators. In so doing they acted in truly Chinese character. The pre-eminence they gave to science,

[1] *The Chinese Renaissance.*

education and civic morality was not in the first place an expression of what struck them in coming to know the West by living there, although it was that too, but because they were moulded by a Confucian culture and thence derived their fundamental Chinese apprehensions and predilections.

It is illuminating, in comparing the Indian and the Chinese response to the Western Invasion, to see that in India most responses were a kind of *religious* reorientation and self-interpretation. In China, however, quite in character with its civilization, being a great culture suffused and supported by a cosmic religious apprehension, the responses move in the *cultural* dimension. The reformist and also the more conservative thinkers such as Ku Hung Ming,[1] who formulated the problem and the dilemma in this awesome meeting of two grand, mutually alien worlds of the spirit, did it always in *cultural* terms; one might say, in terms of "comparative culture", hardly mentioning the religious aspect although there is latently a religious aspect implied.

The spasmodic character of China's adjustment is vividly illustrated by the famous "Hundred Days of Reform" in 1898, when K'ang Yu Wei and his devoted disciples planned with the young Emperor Huang Hsii a radical reform of the whole orientation and government of the country, and the overthrow of the "Old Buddha" and her supporters of a doomed world. The attempt failed; the old system survived under the Empress; K'ang Yu Wei and Liang Ch'i Ch'ao made a narrow escape to Japan, which became not only till 1912 the reformist centre for China, but also a refuge where great numbers of Chinese students sought acquaintance with Western science and thinking.

Still more spasmodic was the Boxer Rising (*I Ho Tuan* = justice harmony society) in 1900 and 1901. This Rising was a movement which brought to a head all the excitement and agitation about the Old and the New, which had convulsed China for so long and was not diminished but rather augmented by the Empress's dexterous overthrow of the Reformists. As is

[1] One of China's most remarkable modern thinkers, who lived through all the revolutions till the days of Chiang Kai Shek's starting of the Kuo Mintang Government. He understood the West in its sincerity and deepest impulse perfectly well and respected it for that, but remained himself a noble defender of classic Chinese culture without compromise. Cf. his book *The Spirit of the Chinese People*.

natural in such movements harbouring the most conflicting ideas and emotions, it virtually held the possibility of striking out for the New as well as for the Old. In fact, it became a tool in the hands of the reactionary Empress party and suddenly burst out in an anti-foreign movement of extreme violence.

The international repercussions and the military intervention of the combined Western Powers led to the occupation of Peking and a peace treaty in 1901, which meant China's radical humiliation. The country was dictated to in regard to her innermost affairs; a crushing indemnity was laid on her, and yet none the less, entirely contrary to all truly Chinese notions, the Manchu Dynasty (long since ripe for removal, to Chinese notions in the first place) had to be maintained by Western authority. The only redeeming feature in this whole dismal story of Chinese humiliation and Western arrogance was the decision of the United States of America to use their part of the indemnity for enabling Chinese students to study in the West, and supporting organizations for research and furtherance of Chinese culture.

China's adjustment to the great fact of the Western Invasion is an inextricable tangle of political and economic interests and clashes with the vulture-like Western Powers and Japan; of cultural reform and readjustment, and consequent radical alterations in the inherited cultural implementation of China. This is particularly evident after the dictated Peace of Peking in 1901. It lies outside the scope of this book to discuss any but a few of these political facts. In the first place: in 1905 the age-old State examination for all literati officials of old bureaucratic China was abolished. It was a political act, because in this case the Manchu Dynasty did, forced into it by its position of political servitude, what the Reformers had always demanded. But, independent of this political motivation, it was also a cultural event of enormous importance; the disappearance of one of the stoutest pillars of the ancient Chinese cultural-political structure. A Ministry of Education came in its place. Although it happened without conviction or vision under the existing unnatural government, which was in fact a corpse, nevertheless it was a step on the way to adjustment, a belated response to the Western Invasion and therefore a clearing of the road towards a new historical period.

THE UPHEAVAL OF REVOLUTION

Sun Yat Sen saw the only road to radical reform and adjustment in transformation by political and social revolution. He probably had even fewer inhibitions than the other convinced revolutionaries, because he was a Christian, had lived for a long time in Western countries, and was imbued with Western democratic ideas. He succeeded where the Taiping failed, namely in the overthrow of the Manchu Dynasty. He could succeed because the patent fact that the Dynasty, symbol and fortress of the Old China that refused to yield, had outlived itself together with the old dispensation, became irrefutably clear to all parties concerned, Chinese and foreign, by the death of the Emperor Kuang Hsü and the "Old Buddha". Only a baby emperor was left. The country disintegrated into virtually independent provinces. The revolutionary leaders, who had planned for a long time in exile, particularly in Japan, proclaimed the Republic of China and Sun Yat Sen as its first president.[1]

This Revolution, the unavoidable necessity of which was revealed in the scanty disturbance and the enthusiasm by which it was accompanied, was, however, in fact a colossal change, bearing immense upheaval and confusion in its womb. Natural as the downfall of the Dynasty and the programmatic establishment of a "democratic" China might be by force of circumstances, it meant on the one hand the definite collapse of the Confucianist world order, and on the other hand the adventure of building up, and not merely of proclaiming, a totally new "democratic" order without any roots except the enthusiasm of the revolutionaries.

The adventure was bound to have a dramatic, chaotic career. Soon civil war broke out and the period of the "War Lords" began. It appeared a superhuman task to create a tolerably functioning New China. There is no country and no people in the world which has bought its transition from its ancient structure and spirit to an entirely new one, set in motion by the Western Invasion, so dearly as China. It is possible to make sententious remarks about the impossibility

[1] We are silent on all the political implications of this momentous step, as for instance that Sun Yat Sen resigned in favour of Yuan Shi Kai and all that this entailed.

inherent in such a cataclysmic switch towards a purely Western
secular parliamentary democracy, especially in the case of the
old, huge, bureaucratic China, borne by a static religious
culture founded on a naturalist cosmic apprehension of man,
society and world. This reasonable wisdom is in the face of the
facts an arrogant naïveté on the part of the outside observer.
Events had drifted in such a direction that no other "solution"
was at hand. Cataclysmic changes in the spiritual and political
realm usually leave little scope for benevolent, sweet reasonableness. They happen like nature-catastrophes and not like
laboratory-projects.

The noble, perspicacious and idealist programme, conceived
by K'ang Yu Wei, of a constitutional monarchy built on a
specific philosophy, seemed to represent a better synthesis of
China and the West. But it would have been frustrated by
colossal unforeseen problems and by its too theoretical China-
centredness in spite of its openness to Western values. The
blindness of the Manchu made it impossible, and the only
appeal that gained support, because of its radicalism, was Sun
Yat Sen's.

The republican way was the way of freedom, prosperity,
progress and reform. As always in such situations, there was a
belief in the mechanical magic inherent in new forms and
institutions. His Kuo Mintang (Nationalist Party) after
China's many tribulations during and following the First World
War, with the help of Communist Russia[1] finally achieved
ascendancy and also a somewhat precarious reunification of the
country under Chiang Kai Shek, who suppressed the menace
of the Communist wing in the Nationalist Party. The slogans
under which the Nationalist Army marched were: "Down with
Imperialism" and "Down with the War Lords". In 1929 the
Nationalist Government established itself in Nanking as its
capital. It seemed that an era of reconstruction could begin.

Ever since 1912, when China set out on the long road to
political stabilization, the working out of her cultural and
religious salvation has been a tremendous up and down of
vehement fluctuations, in which the constantly shifting evaluations of Western civilization and the West fulfilled an important
rôle. There was a pressing need not only for guidance by a

[1] England refused help.

fundamental view of life embodied in persons, but above all for a new spiritual foundation, namely the collectivity, as the substitute for the ancient foundation which had carried China for so many ages. A new culture and a new philosophy of culture was imperative, but could by the necessity of the case, China being in political and social convulsion, only be born in a laborious, painful process.

CONFUCIANISM IN THE WHIRLPOOL

It is interesting to glance for a short while at the place of China's old rationale, Confucianism, in this chaotic whirlpool. By the Revolution it was officially disestablished and has remained so. Naturally, however, it continued to work as a ferment, transfusing the make-up of the Chinese mind and outlook. Immediately after the abolition of the famous examination system (one of the pillars of the old Confucian world order) in 1905, the search began for a way of maintaining the Confucian life-view as a philosophical and ethical system.[1] What had never happened in all the years when Confucius was the Great Sage of China, happened now. In 1906 Confucius was accorded the status of deity, and the sacrifices due to Heaven and Earth were prescribed as his prerogatives. His words were declared divine revelation. In fact it was an abortive, un-Chinese, imitation-Western endeavour to bolster up a decaying world. The Revolution of 1912 swept this empty gesture aside and radically disestablished Confucianism as the symbol of the rejected past. In 1916 efforts were made to declare Confucianism, in the Constitution, the religion of the State. But this pathetic attempt to construct at least formal continuity with the spiritual history of the past broke down on the resistance of the progressives.

Yet in various modernizing interpretations and movements, in which Confucianism often figured as the true expression of modern ideals in moral terms, it remained alive as a habit and apprehension of the mind. It is very evident also in the "New Life" Movement, inaugurated by Chiang Kai Shek in 1934. This was in fact the endeavour of a Government to give to the people in "the national crisis" (the current term for expressing the existential nature of the situation) a new "religion" or

[1] Cf. my *Christian Message in a Non-Christian World*, pp. 250f.

"pseudo-religion", a moral basis for its new situation. The moral and spiritual chaos could not engender that sense of direction and meaning and that discipline, without which no people can attain cohesion nor a Government that stability which is indispensable for real growth.

National regeneration and healthy social morality were the aims. Democracy as the new standard pattern and the good management of a modern Government as the omnipresent factor of initiative and control should receive moral and spiritual bases. The prestige and persistence of the old Confucian heritage shone through in the "New Life" Movement in the four ancient Chinese virtues, which were its proclaimed foundations: *li* (regulated attitude), *i* (right conduct), *lien* (clear discrimination and honesty), *chih* (true self-consciousness).

This "New Life" Movement was one of the many symptoms of a China in all-round transition and ferment, trying to find new ground for its spiritual feet. It was also a symptom of rationalized social and moral engineering, so symptomatic for our time of world-wide, turbulent transition. It was inevitable and yet essentially impotent, because the true inspiration from the depth and from on high cannot be engineered, but is an incalculable creation. In the case of China (it has to be repeated again and again) the stress lay always on the moral and the cultural aspect. The religious aspect remained at best marginal, although irrepressible.

RELIGION—A MARGINAL FACTOR

This can be discovered in the "ideology" of the Nationalist Party (Kuo Mintang) as formulated by Sun Yat Sen. The great new thing which broke the ancient order of hallowed custom and ritual was the conception of a purely secular State, from which every trace of cosmic liturgy and theocracy as the soul of the ancient structure had vanished. Sun Yat Sen's teachers in new political theory were the great heralds of the Enlightenment and their later interpreters in America and Europe. For the first time in their history, having always been ruled jointly by family and clan, welded into unity by the overarching bureaucracy of the Emperor, the mediator between Heaven and Earth, the Guarantor of harmony and stability, the Chinese were seized by the "love of country" (*ai kuo*), patriotism and nationalism in one. Sun Yat Sen, who had failed in his first Revolution of 1912, succeeded after his death. He died in March 1925 in Peking, while trying to reunite the South and the North and heal the disintegration into which the country had fallen after 1912. "His Will and his writings became the Bible of the Movement."[1] In addition to a Bible the Movement got in the dead leader a saint and sage, more powerful after his death than during his life.

The greater part of this "Bible" was his book: *San Min Chu I* (the Three Principles of Democracy). These three principles are: people or nation, self-government or democracy, and the livelihood of the people. The way in which they are developed shows that the First World War, and the dealings of the Western Powers with China before and after the War, had caused in Sun Yat Sen an attitude of critical and disillusioned distance towards the West, especially in regard to safeguarding the true interests of the people. Nevertheless the book, which became in the Nationalist China of Chiang Kai Shek the prescribed textbook in all schools, codified the programme and philosophy of the modern all-provider, the State.

The religious tinge appeared in the cult that grew up around the Saint-Leader. It was just this fact of his being the sainted Leader by his death, which made that religious tinge possible. It manifested itself in the ruling that the text of the *San Min Chu I* was unalterable; in the institution of specially trained teachers, one might say instructors in "nationalist ethics", used for inculcating the truth,[2] and in weekly memorial services accompanied by a salute to the portrait of the dead Leader. So some numinosity of a religious quality hovered around the new secular doctrine of national homogeneity in a world of rapid, incessant change.

LEARNING—CIVILIZATION'S ROOT

In all the new independent countries Education is one of the crucial issues, because the necessity of adaptation to a new future and a new place in the world puts Education in the

[1] Hughes, *op. cit.*, p. 146.

[2] Mainly a condemnation of Imperialism and extolling the necessity of becoming a strong, self-reliant people. On the background of the Chinese experience with the West, this is thoroughly understandable.

centre of interest. It is the most important instrument for achieving the metamorphosis implied in adaptation. In regard to China this is still more valid, because an educational attitude belonged to the backbone of Chinese civilization. This civilization is marked in a unique way by the conviction that learning is civilization's root. That conviction, materialized in the examination system which aimed at a thorough training in the sources and fundamental ideas of Chinese culture, thereby pursuing the formation of true men in the moral sense of the word, had given China in the past a temper at once democratic (the road to all talents was open) and aristocratic (the rulers were men of erudition). This conviction and this system have always induced the Chinese, even when deeply impressed by Western civilization and learning, to entertain the idea that Western civilization was characterized by a repulsive element of barbarism.

Christian Missions were the forerunners in the field of "Western" education, and till the advent of Communist domination remained an important factor. The Reform party in the 19th and the beginning of the 20th century saw the necessity of creating a new educational system in which Western fields of learning and knowledge got their due place. K'ang Yu Wei and his disciples have been the prophets of this new Education. A vast labour of translation was coupled with this plea, opening access to the great writers of the West on science, politics, philosophy, moral and social science, history, etc.

It is not necessary to delineate here the modern history of Education in China, since it began its real career in 1905 after the abolition of the examination system. It is, of course, a chequered career full of currents and counter-currents. A matter of great moment, however, is the big place America has played in this mighty endeavour to absorb Western knowledge, learning and know-how, as a consequence of the decision of the United States Government to use its share of the Boxer Indemnity Funds for the education of Chinese in America. Thousands of Chinese went to the United States and, especially in relation to the specific field of Education, Teachers' College in Columbia University became the great beacon-light.

After the Revolution of 1912, in spite of the embroiled state of the country, some universities in particular became, by the leadership of brilliant young men, centres seething with life and interest. A great struggle for a new critical self-interpretation of China began; a new creative understanding of history, tradition and religion burst forth. In this whole fascinating story the striking thing to note is the great natural endowment, the brilliancy and determination which characterize the Chinese. Enthusiastically received as fertilizers of the mind were John Dewey and Paul Monroe from Columbia University, and Bertrand Russell, in 1919 and 1920. They were invited by the Ministry of Education and exercised an enormous influence on the development of higher and mass-education. These three men constituted a Western Invasion that was *called for*, not suffered or obstructed as in the past. It is significant to accentuate the fact that these three great representatives of Western secularism in its most radical philosophical formulation, the advocates of complete freedom of thought versus tradition, proved to be to China the welcome apostles at this stage of its emancipation from the past and heading for the future. It led even the Ministry of Education to great reforms in 1922.

The latent problem behind Education in China is this: as everywhere in the world to-day, as much by the necessity of the new requirements of modern dynamic society as by its rôle to be the instrument for absorbing the new knowledge, Education gets an overbearing pragmatic, even utilitarian, tendency. It is in great danger of proving unable to transmit real culture.

The deepest reason is not sufficiently expressed in the two causes just mentioned. This deeper reason is the radically secular basis and outlook, which prevents a fuller and truly universal motivation. Men like the great trio mentioned could afford to be radical secularists and even combine with it idealist philosophies of life, society and the universe; but they could do so because they were, as to the urge to give true meaning to life, still feeding on heritages of the Western past. Chinese youth was in a quite different position. The ebulliency which characterized the Prometheus Unbound of China's youth élite manifested itself in one of the most revolutionary things that could happen on the background of classical Chinese culture. This is the *Pai Hua* or Plain Language Movement.

This was an aspect of the total ebulliency which was labelled, after *c.* 1919, the New Tide, the New Culture or New Thought Movement, and was one of the symptoms of the indomitable will to achieve complete emancipation from the bondage of the past. Another name for this *Pai Hua* Movement was "Renaissance".[1] Students at Peking University established a monthly magazine in 1918 and called it *The Renaissance*. The promoters of this magazine were mature students, trained in the old cultural tradition, but wanting to study it with the new methods of historical criticism and research. The magazine was intended to be the organ of the New Tide and so was deliberately named *The Renaissance*, that is to say, the renaissance not of a glorious venerated past but of a new China.[2]

In Hu Shih's opinion, the strength of this Renaissance lay in its being a conscious and studied movement. It *wanted* desperately a new language, a new literature, a new outlook on life, a new scholarship. It conceived this aim consciously as a mission. This consciousness was a result of the contact with Western civilization. "Without the benefit of an intimate contact with the civilization of the West, there could not be the Chinese Renaissance," says Hu Shih. This dictum is remarkable for its honest concern for truth, in this sense: that Hu Shih shows a deep awareness of the crushing incubus of Tradition, and of the impossibility that China would ever have been able to strike out for a radical self-revision by its own force alone. It could not happen without a dynamic power from outside, provided in this case by the Western Invasion with all its glorious and hideous concomitants.

The New Language and Literacy Movement (*Pai Hua*) was born, according to Hu Shih who was the originator and guiding spirit, in American universities and colleges (Cornell, Vassar, etc.) amongst the Chinese students.

They felt deeply, having drunk the wine of Western knowledge, that the bottles of the ancient classical world could not

[1] See the whole story in Hu Shih's *The Chinese Renaissance*. Hu Shih has been himself the creative and driving spirit in it.

[2] Hu Shih, *op. cit.*, analyses in a very interesting way three former Renaissances in the sense of new creative stages in Chinese Culture in the T'ang and the Sung dynasty and under the Ming. They played a vital rôle, in his opinion, but had one defect: the absence of a *conscious* recognition of their historical mission. This absence made them unable to achieve a revolution. The fourth Renaissance is this one of 1918.

contain it; that a freer, less conventional mode of expression was necessary to convey a new universe of ideas and aspirations. They turned to the colloquial literature of plays and novels and demonstrated its great resources as against the over-stylization of classical Chinese.[1] For some years there raged a fiery battle between the conservatives and the young pioneers. The latter won in an amazingly short time, partly aided by the student revolt against the Versailles Peace Conference, which rejected China's claims on Shantung, lost by Germany. The northern colloquial language, *Kuan hwa*, became the national written language through the Board of Education.

This whole battle was, in fact, an episode in the long-drawn-out struggle between New and Old China, fought out in this case on the essential point of language as the vehicle of the mind and the great thought forms of the human mind. The new thought forms could not be expressed in the language of the Old China. Consequently a new language-instrument was imperative. The living language of the people proved malleable. Hu Shih formulates the whole background of the New Tide in saying that it was a protest against many institutions of traditional culture and an emancipation of individual men and women from Tradition. It meant reason versus reaction, freedom versus authority, glorification of life and man versus their suppression.[2]

In reading this sketch of a decisive but passing stage in the revolutionary transition period for China, one can imagine that the voice of Bertrand Russell, who was in China at that time, came like a heavenly melody. The spirit of China's youth found itself just at that period in a mood of new adventurous leaping towards liberation. Liberation from past institutions, from past assumptions and dogmas, from past binding customs. Therefore this New Tide generated not only a quite new activity in science and history, and not only plunged the leading minds into a critical questioning of the authoritative assumptions of the ancient Chinese view of life and the world, and of the authenticity of the Classical Scriptures, but it generated a new idea of man and his destiny and consequently a rich literature.

[1] Cf. in Hughes' book the interesting Chapter 6: "The New Literature".

[2] After finishing the proof-reading I found the recently published, very important book by Chow Tse Tung: *The May Fourth Movement (1919). Intellectual Revolution in Modern China* (486 pp., Harvard Univ. Press). This book is probably the best and most exhaustive treatment of the crucial significance of May 4, 1919 for China's modern history.

WESTERN SCIENCE—NOT RELIGION

This magnificent spiritual battle China went through is, in comparison with other parts of Asia and Africa jolted by the Western Invasion into a new direction, unique by its brilliance and passion. A striking feature in it is the differences in appreciation of Western civilization and in defining the mode of synthesis between the West and China as characteristic spiritual and *cultural* entities. China with its relativist, pragmatic conception ("the three religions are one", Religion is a way of "using gods") never conceived its meeting with the West in religious terms. The prominent leaders of China's modernization were agnostics or atheists. All the Chinese who experienced the meeting of East and West and expressed themselves about it were educated as well in Chinese as in Western culture, and were unanimous in finding the spiritual power and significance of the West in science and not in religion.

Yet there are significant nuances in sympathy and reserves. These nuances often became sharpened by the repercussions of events in the West on their appreciation, which was reflected in the waves of pro- and anti-foreignness (particularly after 1922) in reaction to Western "imperialism".[1] In the first decades of this century Western civilization was, generally speaking, extolled by its Chinese protagonists for its brilliance, especially Europe as offspring of the Renaissance. In the West, however, the process of self-criticism was at that time in full swing. Reverberations of this Western self-questioning and self-rejection blew over to China and caused confusion and "new doubt", as Hu Shih says. Moreover, the First World War and the treatment the Powers meted out to a weak China brought to many a deep disappointment. It caused the West to lose prestige, bred a tone of aloof criticism of the idolized West, and engendered a more acute consciousness of the incorruptible value of basic elements in Chinese culture. The current juxtaposition of the materialistic West and the spiritual East seemed to be vindicated again by the bloody World War. In the case of the Chinese interpreters "materialistic" had moreover the

---

[1] This virulent anti-imperialism after 1922 was partly a first symptom of Russian influence, which tried to draw China also into the communistic programme of world revolution.

undertone of "barbaric", and "spiritual" that of "cultural refinement".

SOME PERSONALITIES

By way of illustration only, a few figures of importance will be briefly reviewed. Chiang Mou Lin is a contemporary Confucianist, formerly Vice-Chancellor of Peking University and at present living and working in Formosa.[1] He affords in his book *Tides from the West* a useful insight into the deep difference of context, orientation and purpose between the Confucian world view with its strong moral, even moralistic, bias and its aptitude for creating an attitude of merging with nature in everybody, and the West as after his Confucianist youth he came to know it. That is to say the West meant to him the "all-piercing intellect" and the fundamental concept of subject and object. Chiang's appreciation of the West is sincere, but he wants to retain the Confucian all-embracing attitude of immediacy to the universe without rejecting the Western way of rationalizing abstraction. He is convinced that the attempt after the Revolution of 1912 and up to the advent of Communist rule to modernize and Westernize China in all respects, has been a failure; mainly because it has not taken into account sufficiently the truth that civilizations are built around different systems of the universe, and as long as this is ignored Asian resurgence and Western ways will not merge. Chiang Mou Lin's opinion carries great weight because it comes from a very refined and sympathetic mind.

Hu Shih, at present an exile from Communist China and in a certain sense also from Nationalist China, is a very marked figure. He gives an account of his attitude in *The Chinese Renaissance*. Amongst the great heralds of modern China, he is perhaps the most determined Westernizer. Being educated in his youth in the traditional Chinese way and having later on acquired access to Western knowledge, it seems that this acquaintance with the West has meant for him more than a sincere admiration and partial absorption of Western apprehensions and methods, as in most other cases. It seems to have meant a kind of intellectual "conversion", fundamentally an

[1] Cf. F. S. C. Northrop: *The Taming of the Nations*, passim, and Chiang Mou Lin's *Tides from the West*, Yale Univ. Press, 1947.

adieu to the peculiar Confucianist Chinese "system of the universe",[1] without ceasing to be Chinese in temper and outlook.

According to Hu Shih's own words, the surface difference between East and West is, especially in this era of technics and industrialization, "a difference of tools". The basic difference as he sees it lies in that of mode of intellectual pursuit and endeavour. India developed great religious systems, when China worked out its moral and political philosophies and the Greeks created their intelligible world. The Greeks, however, developed an interest in nature of a kind that led to its subjugation and to reducing it to all-encompassing formulas, quite different from the Chinese contemplative attitude towards nature, with which one had to live in harmony. In other words, Hu Shih states: the truly scientific interest was alien to the East, which made "humanists", not researchers. The West, he continues, brought to China both: true science and research and an independent critical spirit in all fields of life. For China the most important of these was the field of history, since China was built on a history in which certain structures won absolute authority. It is science alone and not religion that can make mankind better and more moral. Man must feel completely at home in the world. Such is Hu Shih's credo.

Hu Shih clearly rejoices that K'ang Yu Wei, who was the first interpreter of the spiritual background of the West to his pupils, failed in making Confucianism the religion of the Republic. Only the political revolution of 1912, which included the abolition of the Confucian political theory, made the intellectual and social changes possible. Hu Shih's authentic Chinese temper reveals itself, however, in his emphasis on the *humanist* nature of Chinese life apprehension. He even calls the ascendancy of Buddhism, "that dazzling religion", a defeat of humanist China by religious India, and conceives of Zen Buddhism, based solely on meditation and the awakening of the understanding of one's true self, as a re-assertion of the Chinese humanist spirit.

The most dramatic personality of modern China is Liang Ch'i Ch'ao.[2] A brilliant man; a real scholar in the Chinese

---

[1] The words "it seems" are used to indicate that this interpretation is tentative.
[2] Cf. J. R. Levenson: *Liang Ch'i Ch'ao and the Mind of Modern China*, 1956.

cultural heritage; a devoted pupil of K'ang Yu Wei; a writer of enormous range: at the same time enthusiastic interpreter of Western culture and defender of the abiding, superior worth of Chinese culture. Yet he knew periods in which he discarded the total Chinese Tradition and eulogized Western civilization as the only road to liberation and happiness.[1] He became in the decisive days of the Revolution of 1912, after having helped to prepare it in Japan, a dissident from his venerated master K'ang Yu Wei, because he followed Sun Yat Sen's road. In his writings it is evident that he ultimately always felt unable to replace Chinese "spirituality" wholly by allegiance to Western "spirituality". Even when rationally vanquished by the West, he remained emotionally bound to Chinese "spirituality". The First World War meant also for him an enormous loss of prestige by the West. He even spoke of the West's *débâcle* and joined in the choir that chanted the slogan of the materialist West and the spiritual East.

Liang is typical of the many who went through the experience of the encounter of East and West as two cultural entities *in themselves*. He was trained in both, suffered agonies, and attempted patterns of selective syntheses. Intermittently he showed signs of reverting to type, naturally concerned to save his self-identity in the turmoil. In all these dramatic metamorphoses a man like Liang is also an exemplification of the still initial and provisional character of the encounter between East and West.[2]

COMMUNISM—A RADICALIZATION OF THE WEST

This, it seems to me, applies also to Communist China, radical and definite as the break with China's past may appear in the light of Lenin-Marxist dogmatism. It is difficult to formulate an unambiguous opinion without the possibility of patient research and self-criticism. The following points,

[1] It is significant to note that the object of his eulogies was always the modern West since the 18th century Enlightenment.

[2] It must be kept in mind that the drama, inherent in the Western Invasion in Eastern countries, is by the nature of the case far more dramatic in non-colonial countries (e.g. China and Turkey) than in colonial (e.g. India, Indonesia). Colonial Governments, notwithstanding the revolutionary forces they almost unconsciously set in motion, had by their foreignness and "neutrality" to be cautious. An indigenous Government, as long as it is resolute at times of crisis, has far wider scope for initiative and need not have many scruples.

however, should not be left out of sight. Marxism and concrete Communism are violent and heretical embodiments of Western idealism. Seen from this angle the Communist indoctrination applied to China is a radicalization of the Western Invasion, a new wave of the same thing, specified by its compulsory methods and narrow dogmatism. Therefore it is not only a radicalization of the Western Invasion, but also culturally speaking an intensification concentrated on a reduced focus. Indoctrination China had already known for centuries. She knew it also in the days of the Kuo Mintang, but never in this methodical intensity. The Communist slogan against the West as embodying "imperialist cultural aggression" has an ironic ring in face of the fact that Communism itself is a vehement form of Western cultural invasion, the most vehement China has yet known, because the element of liberty and criticism is absent and the richness of variety Western culture represents is arbitrarily and drastically reduced. Under these circumstances, it is by no means a certainty that the drive for adherence to the infallible truth of Marxism has great chances of eradicating the grand cosmic, moral and political Chinese conception of nature, man and history. Just as there is by no means a certainty that in Russia the pseudo-religious *Weltanschauung* (world outlook) of Communism will eradicate the Orthodox spirituality of Mother Russia.

Although such investigations on a small basis of material are interesting reconnoitrings rather than reliable knowledge, nevertheless D. S. Nivison's article in *The Journal of Asiatic Studies*[1] is noteworthy. The article bears the title "Communist Ethics and Chinese Tradition". The author tries to show that, consciously or unconsciously, there is visible in the indoctrination process a grafting of Marxist ideology on Confucian principles. In the process the latter are unmistakably distorted, as it were exploited, and given an un-Confucian orientation; but somehow Marxism and Confucianism, being both moralistic and idealistic, have some affinity. From this angle the writer discusses the great rôle played by purely Confucian principles in the process of gradual indoctrination or brainwashing; such principles as self-criticism, sincerity, nonsubjective understanding, self-watchfulness. The distortion

[1] Vol. XVI, No. 1. Nov. 1956.

comes from the utter difference in aim of all these virtues, in Confucianism and Communism. In Confucianism they aim at the true independence of the "superman", in Communism at the ideal man, who is loyal to the party-line without reserve and utterly dependent.

In this sketch of China and the West it has become abundantly clear that China, as a civilization, considers its confrontation with the West predominantly a *cultural* one. This is in striking difference from India and the Islamic world, which each in its own way, behind and above the cultural, sense the *religious* confrontation. What is commonly called the Hebrew-Christian strain or component in Western culture is entirely ignored by the spokesmen of China. They acknowledge the Greek component only.

II. JAPAN[1]

When the "Western Invasion" began, it met in Japan, as it did in China, an independent country with a fierce will to preserve her independence and autonomy, and a very refined culture.

In regard to the West, Japan had adopted in the 17th century under Shogun Ieyasu, as China had done under the Ming Dynasty, a policy of complete seclusion and isolation, even more radical than Communism and the present Iron and Bamboo Curtains. Like China, Japan gradually realized in the 19th century that a dynamic West was knocking at her doors. Unlike China, after a short period of unrest and fermentation Japan took upon herself the leadership in the reversal of this seclusion policy, which had lasted more than two centuries; because, unlike China who kept her eyes fixed on the past, Japan was above all concerned about her future.

Before penetrating further, however, into the motives which led to this astounding somersault, executed with such dexterity, it is indispensable to evoke briefly the peculiar individuality of Japan as a culture and way of life.

[1] In Chapter 7, in regard to China and Japan, observations have been offered concerning the present resurgence of Buddhism (at least in Japan), but in this chapter Buddhism has to be dealt with again in relation to its position in the making of Old and New Japan. As to China, Buddhism has had a manifold significance but has never played such an important rôle in the making of China as it has in that of Japan.

199

Although to a great extent it is true to say that Japan, in contradistinction to India and China, does not represent in the full sense of the phrase an autochthonous civilization, born out of her own resources and creativity, she has in fact produced a peculiar, impressive type of culture. Her culture is so characteristically itself that it deserves to be regarded as another representative type of Eastern civilization with a very outspoken individuality. It is important to restate this with some emphasis, because the frequent habit of calling the Japanese marvellous imitators, in recognition of the fact that Japan does not represent an autochthonous civilization in the strict sense of the term, fails to hit the mark. To be sure, without the fructifying contributions and stimulus provided by the two genuinely creative civilizations, China and India, Japan would probably not have developed that type of cultural expression, from her own primitive basis, which she has developed. But it should not be forgotten that she has shown a special genius in giving a highly characteristic and original dress to the cultural synthesis which resulted from the coalescence of the foreign import with the fundamental, authentic Japanese temper and apprehension.

To call this imitation as distinct from originality is misleading and wrong. Study of the Japanese people in their genesis and development leads to the unavoidable conclusion that they are a people with a highly distinctive character. This character, in spite of the fact that their composite culture is *formally* speaking a loan culture, has developed a cultural style so unique that *materially* speaking it may claim to have its own status and rank.

It is part of this distinctive character that Japan, unlike India and China as cultures, never has, up till now, culturally proliferated outside her borders, and that of all the Eastern peoples the Japanese seem to the Westerner the most enigmatic.[1] At the present time especially we need to be fully aware of the highly distinctive character of Japan and the Japanese. For in a time like ours, when the inter-existence and interdependence of different worlds is so crucial for everyone in the world, the Japanese people with their unique capacity for single-mindedness (for good or for evil) occupy an important

[1] Cf. Ruth Benedict: *The Chrysanthemum and the Sword,* an excellent analysis of Japan's distinctive character.

place. The label "imitative" simply perpetuates misunderstanding.

We will try to illustrate the preceding paragraphs by a glance at history.

JAPAN—A SECTOR OF THE CHINESE REGION

Japan, then, is a country with an extremely interesting cultural and religious history.[1] It is difficult to over-estimate the significance that China, and through China Confucianism and Buddhism, have had in the formation of Japan. One could call her to a great extent a sector of the Chinese region of civilization. A good illustration is the fact that the capitals of the Nara period (719-793) and the Heian period were laid out on the plan of the Chinese capitals of the time.

Sansom[2] states rightly that for a proper understanding of the growth even of early Japan some knowledge of the leading facts of Chinese history "is essential". His remark is related to some centuries B.C., the time of the Han Dynasty. Korea was the link in the establishment of these relations. The adoption of the Chinese script in the 5th century A.D. was, as Sansom says,[3] a "landmark in Japanese history, and shaped the subsequent development of nearly every Japanese institution". It furthered, through the intermediary services of the Koreans, the gradual absorption of Chinese learning, political and moral philosophy. On this, the first occasion we know of when Japan made contact with a superior culture, the Japanese manifested as they did ever afterwards that they were by nature eager pupils, not even deterred by the enormous difficulties of the Chinese script. This was utterly unsuited to their own polysyllabic language, so greatly different in structure and morphology from Chinese, whose pictographic script matched admirably with its monosyllabic character.

Confucianism, which meant Chinese civilization, was brought in from the 1st century B.C. on, first in trickling infiltrations, in the later centuries (till the 18th) broadening into a wide stream. By its cosmic range it effected a deepening and multiplying of the Japanese naturalist apprehension, and an

---

[1] Cf. my *Christian Message in a Non-Christian World*, pp. 191f. and 256, etc. Also G. B. Sansom: *Japan, a Short Cultural History*, 1931.

[2] p. 13.   [3] p. 43. The Japanese had then no script of their own.

enormous enrichment of political-ethical thinking and practice. The strongest impulse, however, came through the entrance of Buddhism, again from China via Korea. Buddhism was to Japan a new religion and a culture. It meant to semi-primitive Japan a special process of Sinification, and gradually became an inoculation with Indian religious metaphysics. It has been for Japan of far greater significance than for China. As B. H. Chamberlain[1] has justly remarked, during many ages "Buddhism was the paramount moulding influence in Japanese life in the fields of philosophy, religion, medical science and care, education, art, etc."[2]

The first step in the introduction of Buddhism in Japan, with its vast consequences, was the initiative of the King of Paikchè in Korea in sending to the Emperor of Japan[3] an image of the Buddha and a number of sutras (Buddhist Holy Scriptures). In his message the King recommended[4] the adoption of the new religion, because, though hard to understand, it was of all doctrines the most excellent and "brought the realization of all desires". Throughout Japanese history the men in power often lauded Buddhism as "excellent for protecting the State". This argument sounds queer as a recommendation of the Buddhist Dharma, which teaches the extinction of the fatal "Thirst" of Desire, including thirst for worldly power, but it was an excellent example of adaptational presentation.

Some decades of trial and indecision followed. The definite step was taken by Prince Shotoku, the Regent (not the *de facto* ruler) of Japan from 593-621. The Prince was a student both of Buddhism and of the learning of the Confucian classics. He propagated the moral, intellectual and material benefits of Buddhism and furthered the building of temples and monasteries, peopled mainly by priests, scholars and monks from Korea, who became the teachers of Japan. The most revered legacy of Shotoku is his 17 "Injunctions to Governors and Governed", in which he gives in the form of moral exhortation a sort of religious-philosophical theory of government, a compound of Confucian, Buddhist and genuinely Japanese principles. This is, as well in its composition as in its main stress, a revealing document, because it recommended

[1] *Things Japanese.*   [2] *The Christian Message in a Non-Christian World*, p. 196.
[3] In 552. The exact date is under debate.   [4] Sansom, *op. cit.*, p. 65.

Buddhism, which in Japan was welcomed as another means of acquiring material benefit and warding off calamities, as a means to strengthen loyalty to the Emperor and the State.

Shortly after Shotoku's death, when in China the T'ang Dynasty (618-906) inaugurated the most brilliant flowering of Chinese culture in the history of the country, a constant stream of keen Japanese began to flow directly to China. "Politically China was at this moment perhaps the most powerful, the most advanced and the best administered country in the world. Certainly in every material aspect of the life of a state she was overwhelmingly superior to Japan."[1] China was by right the Great Teacher. Every impulse towards a new development in Japanese Buddhism had till the 13th century its primary source in China. But it was immediately Japanized or nationalized.

THE ACCEPTANCE OF BUDDHISM

For our purpose we can dispense with giving a survey of the marvellous but chequered career of Buddhism in Japan, with its ups and downs. Nor is it necessary to enter into any detail about the deep influence of China as exemplar and pattern. In the beginning, considerations of State and Government were paramount in adopting and using it. There is abundant testimony that the Japanese, particularly the rulers, were attracted by the "magical advantages of Buddhism and the occult science of the Chinese" (geomancy, divination). This remained the case through all the centuries and determined the ups and downs, the fortunes and misfortunes of Buddhism. A few remarks, however, need to be made.

In the first place this wholesale acceptance of a thoroughly foreign religion with all its paraphernalia, in the garb of an exceedingly difficult foreign language, is an astounding pheno-menon. When one seeks an explanation, it is to be found not in religious ardour but in a different category—that of strength-ening the country, or rather the realm. The Japanese have never been by inclination isolationists; only by compulsion. By nature they are open to every possibility of acquiring new knowledge; they are keen learners. Sansom[2] may, therefore, be right when he speaks of "the business-like procedure", in time

[1] Sansom, *op. cit.*, p. 81.   [2] *op. cit.*, p. 66.

of trial and indecision, of the *de facto* ruler of the country, Umako, who favoured Buddhism. Umako "made up his mind that the new religion was a necessary feature in an up-to-date country, which had already imported other advantages of civilization such as literature and geomancy".

In the second place, the Chinese fecundation caused an amazing deployment of the innate artistic sense and ability of the Japanese. In religious and secular art they have produced an exquisite variety and finesse, and not less in the artistic expression and decoration of the forms of home and social life. In artistic respect in general, in delight with the sensual world and its expression in art, they certainly equal their former masters. A natural proclivity and sensitivity, as well as the stimulus of refined Buddhist thinking and psychological penetration, have contributed to this result.

Yet having pondered all this about the great significance of Chinese culture and Buddhism, and what the Japanese made of it for their upbuilding into a people of impressive stature, we would nevertheless have a very imperfect picture of that elusive thing, Japanese culture. To get a less imperfect one, due attention must be paid to their primordial being and basis, that essential core of religious and ethical notions which is so important, though under the surface, in their make up.

From this angle one might even say that, great as the moulding power of Confucianism and Buddhism may have been, the Japanese have never been really *changed* by them nor been affected in their authentic being. Confucianism and Buddhism sit lightly on them. Neither ancestor worship in the true Confucian sense, nor ideas of transmigration, *samsara* and Nirvana in the true Buddhist sense, have ever penetrated Japanese thought, and Japan is the only Buddhist country which knows married priest-monks and has never really learnt to appreciate asceticism.[1] We ought therefore to glance at this indigenous ground-structure which has always remained, latent or manifest, one of the essential strains if not the essential strain of their peculiar being and behaviour.

---

[1] Keyserling, *op. cit.*, p. 583, says significantly: "The Japanese have none of the Chinese depth and gravity", and p. 612: "As to the life of the Japanese common people, the Buddhist church in so far as it is really Buddhist signifies merely an artistic frame and nothing more."

NATIONAL SHINTOISM

The national, genuinely Japanese religion, inherited from the pre-Confucian and pre-Buddhist past, goes under the name of Shinto (the Way of the Gods). As to classification it belongs to the "primitive" tribal and clan religions. "It was a religion founded upon a conception, a vague and unformulated conception, of the universe as composed of a myriad sentient beings."[1] This is a general definition which needs amplification. In Shintoism were expressed a rich naturalist mythology, a deep sensitivity to nature in its many manifestations (which is to this day one of the main sources of the beauty and grace of authentic Japanese life and art), and a profound attachment to and veneration for the immediate ancestors as far as living memory goes. The Japanese scholar, Anesaki, characterizes this innate naturalistic tendency in Japan's own religiosity by saying that the question of monotheism or polytheism in Japanese religious life is quite irrelevant, because one virtually worships in many forms the omni-present and ever-active life, manifesting itself equally in nature, men and gods, one and at the same time many.[2]

Shintoism thus constituted a variety of beliefs and a ceremonial cult centring around shrines. The central significance of the notion of ritual purity, in which there is no distinction between ceremonial impurity and moral guilt, points to a bedrock of truly archaic religion.[3] Very significant is it that in this nature-religion the historical destinies of the nation have been incorporated; because the Emperor was in the first place the sacral Head of the ceremonial cult, "the Manifest God" as is said often in "Imperial Rescripts", and at the same time the Head of the political community. This finds one of its clearest expressions in the Japanese word for government, *matsurigoto*, which means religious observances and which testifies to the archaic idea of ceremonial religion and of the sacral chief of

[1] Sansom *op. cit.*, p. 45.

[2] See my *Christian Message in a Non-Christian World*, p. 193.

[3] Sansom, *op. cit.*, p. 52, ventures the important reflection that the conception of sin as distinct from pollution is wanting and rudimentary, and that throughout their history the Japanese seem to have retained in some measure the incapacity to discern or the reluctance to grapple with the problem of Evil. He even goes on to say that much that is baffling in their ancient and modern history becomes clearer when one remembers that they have not been tortured by the sense of sin. When we come to the present time, we shall have to return to this remark of Sansom's.

the Tribe as the means to secure civic well-being and happiness.

When coming to closer consideration of the Meji Era, with which in 1868 the determinate Westernization of Japan began, it will be necessary to take up this aspect again and marvel at the stabilizing power of this archaic conception in a tremendous crisis. The Japanese idea of the Emperor as the central figure in national life, in the background or in the foreground (mostly the former) expresses the unbroken perpetuation of the sacral Chief-figure, which we know especially in Polynesian tribal structure. Its mythological justification was the divine descent of the Emperor from the Sun-Goddess Amaterasu, whose worship became centralized in the national shrine in Ise (c. 6th century B.C.). So this cult, in which the Emperor by his position of Sacral Chief was the centre, became established as the State religion, and acquired political and religious significance till in A.D. 604, through Shotoku, Buddhism displaced it; which really meant—pushed it into the background.

Even in this far-away past this did not signify that the Emperor (here also true to the Polynesian pattern) was not necessarily the paramount political power in actual fact. Whether this was the case or not, the Emperor always depended, though supreme and inviolable in theory, on the support of the mightiest of the great clans competing for the wielding of actual political authority. The Chief of the most powerful clan often usurped the political paramountcy, theoretically belonging to the Emperor, thereby reducing him to his position of the Sacral Inviolable Chief. The whole image of Japan, appearing to Western eyes in the 19th century in the form of a shadowy Emperor and a ruling military dictator, the Shogun, is therefore deeply embedded in ancient Japanese history. Or, as Sansom[1] puts it, through all Japanese history till recent times the persistence of de jure sovereignty, even reduced to mere external forms, and de facto government by someone else, has been a characteristic phenomenon.[2]

[1] op. cit., p. 74.
[2] Yorimoto of the Minamoto clan was the first Shogun, who in the 12th century established his own political/administrative centre (bakufu=literally, military encampment) at Kamakura in East Japan. Since his time the supreme family in power, who held the Shogunate, had (till 1868) its own centre, apart from the court-town of the Shadow Emperor, who kept the right of investiture.

The main point, however, is that this archaic religious idea of the Sacral Chief, in whom the well-being of people and country is condensed, has resulted in Japan in the conception that the people of Japan and her *salus* (welfare) are incarnated (or at least enshrined) in the Emperor, in the periods of shadowy political existence. Emperor worship is, therefore, as Keyserling says,[1] for the Japanese "the deepest profundity", "metaphysically the uttermost", and[2] "Patriotism is the profoundest quality of the Japanese man. His relationship to his country, its greatness, its continued glory, means to him what the Indian's relationship to Brahman, the Chinese membership in the universe, mean to them."

Shintoism therefore, though when looked at from outside it is an ordinary instance of so-called "primitive" religion without any particular depth, has become and is, by the peculiar history and the no less peculiar character of the Japanese, the standard expression of Japanese national consciousness of self and destiny, a first-rate motive power, an elementary reality in Japanese life. Through Shintoism, an immeasurable indebtedness to the Emperor and to country and people is *the* Japanese ultimate.[3] Patriotism, which everywhere readily acquires some pseudo-religious undertones, is through Shintoism in Japan radically religious, if "religious" means unconditional, absolute surrender and allegiance to an ultimate,[4] which can only be defined as a metaphysical unity of country, people, state, nation, family and sovereign,[5] or as the Japanese say: *Yamato damashii.*

Shintoism is, therefore, a unique phenomenon. It is the only "primitive" religion that in a highly modernized state maintains an independent and institutional existence. And, most important of all, this "primitive" religion has been the true elixir of life for Japan, in spite of the commanding presence of Buddhism which is a world-religion, and of Confucianism which meant a vastly superior civilization. It is so still, notwithstanding the destructive acids of

---

[1] *op. cit.*, p. 657.   [2] p. 600.

[3] Here lies the source of the compact singlemindedness already referred to.

[4] The word "patriotism" is therefore very unsuitable, because far too weak, as it evokes only our Western affective associations.

[5] Cf. Keyserling, p. 600.

modernity.[1] It is so, because it is the expression of Japan's deepest self.

Even in the times of Buddhism's *political* primacy in Japanese life, Shintoism always lived on persistently, either in the garbled form of the syncretistic Ryobu-Shinto, which theoretically and practically was a deliberate attempt at amalgamating and harmonizing the two religions, or under a Buddhist guise without any definite theory. The unconscious syncretistic bent of Shintoism and the conscious philosophical syncretist theory of Buddhism met spontaneously when the situation invited this procedure.

"WAY OF THE *SAMURAI*"

There is, however, still another aspect, which throws light on the characteristic moral code of Japan. The modern term gained currency through Dr. I. Nitobe's book entitled *Bushido, the Soul of Japan*, and means "the Way of the *Samurai*", i.e. the virtues implied in knightly loyalty according to Japanese ideas. But it is in fact misleadingly one-sided, and a distortion of a far more comprehensive code which is one of the great patterns of Japanese culture. Its keyword is "debt" or "indebtedness", which has already been used above.

Ruth Benedict, by her eminent ability in analysing cultural patterns and bringing Comparative Culturology to life, has made a new and great contribution to the understanding of the Japanese mind in her book which we have mentioned previously, *The Chrysanthemum and the Sword*. This book is the report of her assignment by the Office of War Information to provide, by her training as a cultural anthropologist, a dispassionate picture of the habits and values of America's most important enemy, Japan.[2] The results of Ruth Benedict's labours are extremely illuminating. No better book is available to show the diametrical opposition between the Japanese and the American moral code and attitude, and, it may be added, the Western, notwithstanding the fact that the common humanity is quite

[1] Keyserling, *op. cit.*, p. 657, tells the remarkable story that in the days of his visit to Tokyo a Shinto shrine was consecrated for Robert Koch. He adds that probably most professors and students who participated were agnostics, but to all of them the erection of a temple and the institution of a cult according to Shinto ritual appeared to be the most adequate expression of veneration of the great scholar.

[2] It came under the "Foreign Morale Analysis Division".

evident. The gist of her analysis is to detect the crucial place of hierarchical order and the taking of "one's proper place" in the hierarchy of stations and values. The basic word in all stages of human inter-relations and proprieties is *on*. This is, of course, extremely difficult to translate, because it is a specifically Japanese category. It is paraphrased[1] in the following words:

> *On* is in all its uses a load, an indebtedness, a burden which one carries as best one may. A man receives *on* from a superior and the act of accepting an *on* from any man not definitely one's superior or at least one's equal gives one an uncomfortable sense of inferiority.

The Japanese speak of "wearing an *on* to someone". This basic concept of *on* is particularized and rubricated in many categories, which comprise all human relations. Ruth Benedict puts it in tabular form,[2] from which it appears that the "debts" one wears ask in various ways for reciprocal repayment; payment of obligation and duty to the Emperor (implying the Law and Japan), to parents and ancestors, to one's work, which all fall in the category *gimu*, and are always valid; then the repayment of *on* (indebtedness) to the world in which categories of persons are of less consequence than those who require *gimu*. This is called *giri*, in which a special category, *giri-to-one's-name*, is extremely important for understanding the niceties of Japanese behaviour such as their respectful attitude, the curbing of all display of emotion even in the most provocative circumstances, the conception of insult and shame (*haji*),[3] the duty of revenge, etc.

This scheme is elaborated in a lucid manner and shows incidentally that not only Western or American but even Chinese concepts of ethics differ from it totally, although—and this is truly significant—some central words of the Japanese code such as *chu* and *ko*, i.e. unconditional duty to Emperor and parents, are Chinese words, whose connotation has been entirely changed. These indications are sufficient for our purpose. Only two other points, immediately related to our

---

[1] *op. cit.*, p. 99.   [2] p. 116.
[3] This reminds us again of traits in Polynesian and Indonesian anthropology.

subject and necessary for comprehending Japan's Westernization, need to be stressed.

One's Imperial *on* is the first and greatest indebtedness a
Japanese has; a debt of limitless, unconditional devotion. This
indebtedness, moreover, one should receive with unfathomable
gratitude. It is in the light of this basic conception of indebtedness (*on*) and obligatory repayment that the famous Japanese
conceptions of loyalty and filial piety have to be placed, and
also the "metaphysical" (Keyserling) place of Emperor, country,
nation and family. It is also only in the light of this basic conception that the paradoxical behaviour, baffling to Westerners
(in the first place to the Americans as the occupying force)
becomes transparent; behaviour which the Japanese people
manifested during the War and in and after their defeat. Their
chu to the Emperor made them prepared to persevere to the
most desperate extremes of resistance. The moment, however,
that the Emperor ordered surrender, they obeyed immediately,
acknowledged their "error" (note, not their guilt) in having
pursued the wrong course, and received the victors with
amazing kindness and grace.

Social anthropologists sometimes use as a means of classification in cultural anthropology the distinction between cultures
that emphasize guilt and those emphasizing shame, because of
their great difference in moral orientation. Japan very clearly
belongs to the category of accentuating "shame", which largely
accounts for Sansom's observation already quoted about the
Japanese rudimentary conception of sin and reluctance to
grapple with the problem of Evil.

In Ruth Benedict's delineation of the Japanese moral code
that works behind the immeasurable variety of conduct, the
linking circuit between the world we delineated in our previous
discussion of Shintoism and the world of this code is closed.
In both one encounters the bedrock of native Japanese being
and self-affirmation (even in self-annihilation), which has never
been changed, either by Confucianism or by Buddhism, and
asserts itself to-day in the midst of Japan's complex cultural and
religious situation. Its only deadly opponent is an incalculable,
soulless, nihilistic cosmopolitan secularism. This, all over the
world, eats at the vitals of real culture.

THE SUPPRESSION OF EARLY CHRISTIANITY

In order to get a proper understanding of the Westernization of Japan and the unique purposefulness through which it happened, the Tokugawa Shogunate (1615-1868) needs some closer consideration. The Tokugawa régime became the stabilizing power after more than a century of civil warfare, in which the vigorous character of the Japanese became manifest. The great men of this period of warfare were Nobunaga, Hideyoshi, one of his generals, and his ally Ieyasu, who became the first Tokugawa Shogun and the unifier of Japan. The colossal ambition and vigour of these architects of a unified Japan appears from the daring ruthlessness by which Nobunaga broke the political power of mighty Buddhist sects and monastic centres, and Hideyoshi's bold expeditions to conquer China and Japan, which ended only with his death in 1598. These illustrations are mentioned here as a clear indication that even then, shortly before its enforced seclusion from the outside world, Japan harboured not a small island-people but a people of remarkable strength and cultural ability, a strong sense of destiny and a resolute will to play a great part in the world.

Another important indication they contain is the breaking of the power of Buddhism, which was the basis for the peculiar ideological policy of the Tokugawa. Under Nobunaga the first contact with the West occurred in the appearance of Portuguese traders (c. 1542) and somewhat later of Jesuit missionaries.[1] The chequered career of this missionary enterprise, the great number of converts, even from the ranks of powerful nobles (daimyo), the comparative tolerance with which they were treated by Nobunaga and Hideyoshi, the increasing suspicion of the Missions beginning with Hideyoshi's proscription of Christianity and a rather restrained persecution, the increased fury of this persecution on the basis of ever severer Edicts, the great number of martyrs and of converts even in times of persecution, are a fascinating story. Its main significance, however, in relation to the purpose of this book, is that it was of decisive importance to the birth of Japan's resolute policy of seclusion.

[1] Cf. G. B. Sansom: *Japan, a Short Cultural History*, pp. 406ff., and his *The Western World and Japan*, pp. 167ff.

Japan, although always open to foreign intercourse and hospitable to foreign cultural influence, as demonstrated by the cordial welcome to Buddhism and Chinese civilization, had always, by her insular position, lived and digested foreign influences in comparative seclusion. The real animus behind the expulsion of missionaries and the suppression of Christianity was, in conformity with what has been said about the Japanese people's fundamental being, political. Political, however, not only in the current sense of power conflict, but far deeper, connected with the peculiar religious-moral being of Japan and culminating in the desire to remain one's own independent self.[1]

The competition of the various Western trading nations (Portuguese, Spaniards, Dutch, etc.) appearing in Japan's harbours; their mutual accusations, within the hearing of Japanese ruling circles, of fostering military and political designs against Japan; the great prestige the Western missionaries enjoyed with the Japanese converts; all these combined to arouse deep suspicion in a newly-established régime like the Tokugawa with its hard-won hegemony over Japan. This suspicion had two facets. The one was the fear of a secret alliance of the Catholic Church with one or other of the two great Catholic powers, Spain and Portugal, to interfere in Japan's domestic affairs; a thing that never had occurred and an idea that was a horror to entertain. The other way to express the aversion, to Christianity particularly, was the attempt at refutation of Christianity: to become a Christian was to deny the national deities by this form of "dangerous thought", and so to imperil the State. An argument universally used against any undesired introduction of new fundamental ideas.

The many anti-Christian Edicts from 1598 till 1637, which, taken as a whole, resulted in a repression policy rarely equalled for ferocity (in the form of torture to death or lifelong expulsion), were yet surrounded by many hesitations out of the desire to keep trade relations open. In 1637 the third Tokugawa Shogun, Iemitsu, with an internal Japanese revolt on his hands, evidently made up his mind that if he wanted to remain the undisputed master, all dangerous outside interference, a constant threat of conspiracy, had to stop. The only radical way

---

[1] The Great Transition from Seclusion to Opening in 1868 had, as we will see, this same dominant motive.

was the definite expulsion of all Portuguese, traders and missionaries alike, and the closing of the door to all other Europeans;[1] the prohibition of foreign travel to all Japanese under death penalty to anyone who attempted to leave the country or to return to it after having left.

TWO HUNDRED YEARS OF SECLUSION

This unconditional and drastically maintained cutting-off of all communication with the world is one of the most amazing acts in history. The more so if one takes into account that it lasted more than 200 years. It is not our duty to enter the debate of the historians who proffer different reasons for this exclusion- and seclusion-policy of the Tokugawa. Although it is mere speculation, one would be inclined to express the suspicion that Japan acted in this drastic way from an intuitive premonition of the tremendous consequences the contact with this active, dynamic West would have, and, for the time being, out of sheer desire for stability, retired behind the wall of seclusion.

The main points to notice for our purpose in this long period of seclusion are on the one hand that, culturally speaking, Japan experienced then a delicate and exquisite flowering of learning and the arts, and on the economic side slowly underwent a revolution which did much in preparing the setting for the Great Change in the 19th century. Both developments were possible through one of the consequences of seclusion: a state of undisturbed peace. No people of historical significance has ever made such a protracted experiment of this rare phenomenon. Undisturbed peace for more than two centuries, and that by a people of warlike qualities and feudal knightly tradition.

As security of its position and power had been for the Tokugawa military dictatorship one of the chief reasons for deciding upon the policy of seclusion, its maintenance naturally became a great concern. This dictated automatically a policy of "no change", and, in order to ensure that, a minute regimentation of conduct and behaviour. All classes had to be kept in their bounds and under control, the military class (*daimyo* and various grades of *samurai*), the city people (merchants and

[1] The only exception was the tiny Dutch settlement on the little island Deshima.

artisans) and the peasants. A minute legislation and also a spy- and very strict passport-system between the provinces were indispensable to achieve this end.[1]

This centralized, autocratic kind of government was applied to a society which was at the moment of seclusion a feudal society in full maturity. It was the guiding principle of the Tokugawa to preserve this feudal system unchanged. In order to achieve this illusion of unchangeable stability and order, the "ideology" needed to give a moral basis to this rigid regimentation was Confucian philosophy, interpreted (at least by the rulers) as a social ethic with a very rigorous and absolutist conception of obedience and loyalty. Buddhism, under Nobunaga and his successors, having collapsed as a religious-political power, remained eclipsed as a religious or cultural entity of importance during the Tokugawa period.

The social ethics of the Tokugawa's "state philosophy" were purely secular. This dictator-bigotry was necessarily narrow-minded, and the strangling of values higher than obedience and authority was its consequence. There is therefore real wisdom in Sansom's observations:[2]

> Enforced as they [i.e. the prescribed standards of conduct] were by severe penalties, they inculcated in the whole nation habits of discipline and obedience, which eased the task of the government and enabled Japan to pass through two hundred years of unbroken peace with but little disturbance of the social order. Consequently when in the nineteenth century the course of events made it necessary for Japan to enter the modern world and change many of her ancient habits, the most sweeping transformations were accomplished with relative ease because the mass of the people was schooled in respect for authority.

JAPANESE FEUDALISM

If ever the idea of an unchanging and unchangeable society, even when aided by the unnatural artifice of complete seclusion, proved an illusion, the demonstration is to be found in Tokugawa Japan. The irony of the case is that the regulations aimed at implementing and sustaining the "no-change" policy turned out to be one of the most effective means of producing

---

[1] Cf. Sansom, *The Western World and Japan*, pp. 182ff.   [2] p. 185.

social and economic shifts, which gradually dissolved the Japanese feudal society into one in which a money economy with all its attendant vagaries became a decisive factor.[1]

It meant the advent of the townspeople or *chanin* to an unprecedented place of influence in the social system of Japan. In a feudal society such as Japan was and had been, they had always kept a low rank, the dominant class naturally being the warrior nobles (*samurai*) with their enormous pride of "race". The artificially maintained stagnation of a feudal-military society in a time of unending peace caused the domestication of an unemployed warrior class and the ascendancy of significant towns, whose *chanin* (merchants, money-lenders, brokers) had to provide for the needs of the, economically speaking, parasite nobility. The growing money economy made possible town populations of culture and affluence. The greatest irony of this irresistible development, created by the minute social regulations of a "no-change" dream, is that culturally speaking, the towns (Yedo the capital, Kyoto the town of the Shadow-Emperor's court, the provincial capitals) became centres of refined aesthetic culture. In the field of theatre and painting or drawing especially it was in no wise inferior to European 18th century culture, and with a strong tendency towards gaiety and licentiousness.

This gradually led to the breakdown of feudal government, and so fostered a mood sensitive to the unnaturalness of seclusion and open for a resumption of intercourse with foreign countries. Tokugawa Japan is a monumental example of the truth that even the most rigorous system of thought- and behaviour-control, all the more under such favourable conditions as in this case (seclusion, peace) is bound to defeat its aim of no-change and necessarily becomes its own grave-digger. Its effort for immutability involuntarily creates a different social configuration and the longing for adventure, the risk of which was proscribed by the system.

The unquenchability of the movings of the human spirit are clearly demonstrated in the cultural scene of the Tokugawa period. At the same time it testifies to the great qualities of the

[1] We confine ourselves to this bare indication of a well-known fact. For those interested in a more detailed description, hosts of books written by competent Japanese and Western authors are available.

Japanese mind. The governmental Confucian orthodoxy could not prevent, but rather created, an intense pre-occupation with the possibilities inherent in Confucian moral philosophy. Especially, though by no means exclusively, in the Neo-Confucianist version of Chu-Hi (1130-1200), the Chinese thinker who re-conceived Confucian moral and political thought in terms borrowed from Buddhism; or the very different Shingaku or Heart Learning derived from the intuitionist philosophy of the 15th century Chinese thinker Wang Yang Ming (called in Japan O-Yomei). Many writers of great distinction (Kaibara Ekken for instance) had a wide reading public.

A striking feature is the inquisitive leanings of the Japanese in the pursuit of learning, which they manifested in their secluded condition. These were partly induced by the possibilities of contact with the outside world, particularly the Western world, through the Dutch factory on Deshima.

FOREIGN RELIGIOUS INFLUENCES

Before coming to the breakdown of Seclusion and the opening of the New Era, two points need attention, because they mean much for the present face of Japan as a cultural and religious entity.

Bushido (already mentioned), usually somewhat misleadingly translated as "Way of the Warrior", became during the Tokugawa régime, when the old military virtues declined under the conditions of enforced peace, a more precisely formulated doctrine. Right up to the present time it has preserved some of the magnificent qualities of the Japanese. Alongside many other influences, Zen Buddhism has played and still plays, as an upper-class cult for expertness in self-discipline (*muga*), a great rôle as inspiring source of this doctrine. It acquired its great vogue in the Tokugawa period, although it had for centuries held a place amongst the Buddhist "sects" in Japan.

The way Zen Buddhism is used and understood in Japan is a clear testimony to the strong aptitude of the Japanese for incorporating foreign religious influences outright into their own moral system of obligation. Zen Buddhism represents originally a radically mystical "sect" of Buddhism, originated in China. Its essence was that neither sacred scriptures nor creeds nor philosophies, but only studied contemplation and intuition, leads to Buddhahood or Nirvana, the realization of Truth. In Japan, and particularly through the Bushido code, it has received a quite different orientation and context. It is the Japanese version of Yoga, but in principle and practice totally secularized.[1] A "religious" goal of self-discipline is only one of many others, which are all mundane. Every trace of real mysticism has disappeared. Even the special expertness in self-discipline of religious persons, in which it yields the moment of "enlightenment" (*bodhi*, *satori*) which is equivalent with Nirvana, is emptied of genuinely religious significance.

Terms like the "interfering self" or the "observing self" as hindrances or obstructing screens to the realization of the goal of expertness in self-discipline have their original roots in Buddhist religious psychology but are now purely psychological terms. The Yoga practices, still largely used, are completely de-religionized and have become psychological techniques. The many mundane goals (in art, in politics, in fighting or fencing, in the art of the tea ceremony, in public speaking, etc., etc.) find in this technique for self-discipline their adequate way towards totally effortless, ego-less, "one-pointed" action, in which mind and act are inseparably one.

The Zen Buddhism of Japan is usually misrepresented as to its real functioning and meaning because it is usually described as the most remarkable "sect" of Japanese Buddhist mysticism. This is utterly misleading, because in fact it is a secular cult of mental training with no trace of mystical sense or aspiration left. Only its origin lies in mysticism, and some of its techniques are reminders of this origin. It has, however, become totally divorced from its origin and has developed a structure of its own. It is now not only one of the most acclaimed techniques of mental training for numberless purposes in Japan, but seems to be making a bid for the same popularity in the West. Looking at it from the standpoint of its Buddhist origin, one might venture to say that it is the radically secularized metamorphosis of *ji-riki*, of "self-help", that is to say Buddhism's original auto-soteriological quality. Above,[2] when discussing resurgent Buddhism, it was said that

---

[1] Cf. Ruth Benedict, *op. cit.*, pp. 235ff.　　[2] Chapter 7.

WORLD CULTURES AND WORLD RELIGIONS

original Buddhism is the most colossal and systematic expression of self-release (*Selbsterlösung*) in the field of religion. The present Japanese Zen cult is its inverse representative in mundane mental hygiene.

The second point is the fortunes of Shinto during the Tokugawa period, which need mention because of the rôle it occupied in the beginning and in the progress of the New Era since 1868.

There are writers who explain this rôle on the assumption that it can only be attributed to deliberate political motives. In the light of what has been said above about the lasting significance of "Shintoism", whether in disguise or undisguised form in the Japanese make-up, this opinion seems erroneous. The great Shinto shrines of Ise and Idzumo, and many besides, have stood through the ages. Although Confucianism was a kind of established "religion" or state ideology in Tokugawa Japan, Buddhism being "disestablished", Shintoism never was moribund. In the 15th century[1] there were already efforts towards Shinto recovery through Kanetomo's attempt to purify Shinto from Buddhist influences. In the 18th century a centre was founded for the study of ancient Japanese history and mythology. This led to the restoration of what was called Fukko-Shinto (Pure Shinto). Its three great expounders were Kamo Mabuchi (1697-1769), Motoöri Norinaga (1730-1801) and Hirata Atsutane in the first half of the 19th century.

So the theocratic idea of ancient Japanese history and mythology became alive again and its flame was nourished by the growing discontent with the Government, which in its feudal infatuation could not meet the economic and social shifts and their attendant ills. This discontent turned men's eyes to the Imperial Court, which in all its miserable decay nevertheless continued to represent the living symbol of Japan's soul, uncontaminated by foreign influences; that is to say the Shadow-Emperor. Thus many eyes turned to Shintoism and the Emperor. Atsutane expressed this dynastic tendency in aggressive tones, which were simply a symptom of increasing displeasure with the Government and the state of the country.

[1] Cf. my *Christian Message in a Non-Christian World*, p. 259.

THE RISE OF THE IMPERIAL IDEA

In the 19th century the stage became set for a big change in Japan. American and Russian ships visited Japan in 1791-92. They were sent away. The first gentle knock on the door was faintly heard. Decrees against foreign shipping were re-issued. 1797: another American ship appears. The treatment was a bit more friendly, but—an important symptom—relaxations alternated with reinforcements of the Seclusion Edicts of old. 1846: American warships invited Japan to sanction foreign trade. A brusque refusal. 1853: Commander Perry of an American squadron repeats the invitation and significantly adds that he will return next year for an answer. 1854: Perry does return and a treaty between Japan and the U.S.A. (followed by treaties with other Western Powers) is concluded. The long period of seclusion is at last officially ended. Japan enters a new, unknown future.

These bare dates cover a course of long-drawn-out drama of agony, doubt, confusion, conflict at the Shogun and Imperial Court and amongst the people. After the conclusion of the Treaty there was enacted a second drama of conflict between the desire to slam the door again and to keep it open, complicated by the competition between the declining star of the Tokugawa and the rising star of the Emperor. It still took fourteen years (1854-68) till the decisive moment of the fall of the Shogunate and the Restoration of the Emperor broke. Dual rule was finished.

It requires an enormous amount of imagination to realize the unbelievable confusion in which New Japan embarked on its great adventure and entered an unknown world after a long period of isolation. The name "Restoration", given to the so-called Meji reform, itself serves to illustrate the confusion. The supporters of the Emperor's "restoration" to the central position of power and leadership in the country really meant restoration of the ancient ways of Japan. They did not mean the reform of the country in view of its task of partnership in intercourse with the wider world. The battle about expulsion or admission of the foreigners, notwithstanding the concluded treaties, raged in 1868 as fiercely as ever. The Court of the Emperor was strongly anti-foreign. The battle-cry of the

Restoration was: "Restore the Emperor and expel the Barbarians."

It was emphatically "restoration", not "revolution". Revolution is a thoroughly un-Japanese concept. Everything, the mood of the opponents of the Shogunate, the mood in the country, the mood of the Court, seemed to point to a return to isolation, broken by the persistent intrusion of the outside world, with the only difference of living one's own life undisturbed under the divinely-sanctioned Monarchy instead of under the Shogunate. And yet the amazing fact is that the new régime did exactly the opposite. It issued a whole series of unpopular reform measures. It deliberately chose the plunge into the unknown and uncharted. No wonder that Japan in the first decade went through great convulsions, the more so because this resolute step of facing the challenge of an unknown destiny followed a centuries-long term of isolation and introversion.

Why and how could this happen? Why and how was it possible that Japan took the Western Invasion in its political, economic and cultural offensive into her own hands, and moulded, out of this unbelievable confusion of conflicting emotions and ideas, a planned, centrally controlled assimilation and adaptation—and yet remained herself? One of the leaders in the Reform, Katsu Awa,[1] rightly said: "It is impossible to measure or to estimate the great difficulties which await us." The men who constituted the first Meji Government and did the job, came from the ranks of the lower *samurai* and the merchant class, which had become in Tokugawa times a new class of great importance, containing clear-headed, able job-doers. On the one hand they saw the impossibility of Japan retracing her steps to the past which was irrevocably past. On the other hand they seized on the crucial importance of keeping the management of the new dispensation, which the "Western Invasion" threw upon Japan, in their own hands.

It seems that deep-rooted convictions, belonging to the real soul of Japan, guided them. First, the fierce will to independence and to preserving integrity and self-identity, which according to the record of history is a very conspicuous characteristic

---

[1] Cf. G. B. Sansom: *The Western World and Japan*, p. 291.

of the Japanese nation. Second, the latent feeling of "mission", another conspicuous Japanese characteristic, which from the beginning focused their ambition on the goal of becoming a decisive and respected world factor in the realm of world relations, and by so doing helping Japan to her "proper" status in the proper Japanese sense of the words.[1] This demanded conscious, planned adjustment to the new situation.

Third, the centre around which this whole new structure could be built was the sacral, inviolable person of the Emperor. So Japan was able to achieve a gigantic feat of adjustments and of integration into the network of international relationships (political, economic, cultural) without any real denial of her past, nor any real addiction to new Western ideologies such as democracy and the like. Instead of denial and rejection of the past (like China in 1912), what really happened was the use of genuinely Japanese ground-assumptions, structures, emotional values and long-acquired habits of obedience to authority as the cement for a modern empire with imperialist ambitions. A careful scrutiny of Western institutions and ideals was undertaken, but although in many respects they were copied, they got a different context and orientation. But the job was done with methodical thoroughness, as can be seen in the organization of a formidable conscript army,[2] of the school system which in a few decades nearly annihilated illiteracy, and in the establishment of Parliament in 1890, to mention a few instances.

Of course these immense transformations did not happen like a mechanical device, automatically. They were necessarily accompanied by deep emotional upheavals and antagonistic views, and demanded supreme statesmanship. But in all these storms the great asset was the fact that at critical moments the sacred, inviolable Emperor gave his sanction to the vast transformations. Therefore, his "Rescripts" have always the elevated, unctuous tone of paternal and moral exhortation. The Japanese *on* conception is the moral pivot and basis for the astounding *volte-face* of Westernization. The normative and directive place

[1] Compare our explanations above.
[2] One must measure this undertaking on the background of 230 years of peace and devaluation of military virtues.

of Imperial Rescripts appears from the fact that, as Ruth Benedict rightly says, the Rescript to Soldiers and Sailors and that on Education are the true Holy Writ of Japan. The main virtue that is inculcated in these Rescripts is *makoto*, translated usually by sincerity, but perhaps better rendered by single-mindedness. The reading of them is a sacred ritual, and the whole act of reading and listening a sacred ceremony, the attributes of which fully suggest a deeply solemn religious performance.

These are some of the basic reasons for the story of Japan's Westernization being no less thrilling than that of China, but less dramatic, more continuous, less passionate.

GOVERNMENT AND RELIGION

Lastly, the relation of Government and Religion in modern Japan requires special consideration. In the administrative organization[1] of the first Meji Government, as brought about (significantly!) by a movement called "Return to Antiquity", there was placed above the six Ministries a Department of Religion. Its president ranked next to the chancellor of the realm. The Emperor, in taking his Charter Oath, swore to the national deities (not to his subjects) in imitation of an ancient ritual. This Department, which was amongst other things an expression of the desire in certain quarters for restoring Shintoism as State Religion, did not last long. Nor did the enmity shown towards Buddhism.

The Government saw that it had to deal in the new state of affairs with a far more complicated situation. First, because a modern country ought to honour religious liberty, even freedom of thought in general.[2] Second, because the problem of freely teaching Christianity in Japan needed careful handling. It was not till 1873 that the Edicts against Christianity as an "evil sect"[3] vanished from the public notice boards. Christianity's position did not acquire a legally unassailable status till the Constitution of 1889

[1] G. B. Sansom, *op. cit.*, pp. 387f.

[2] With the penetration of the great Western writers on politics, philosophy, religion, etc., into Japan, a new fermentation of the spirit set in, which made freedom of thought no imaginary thing.

[3] So Christianity had been labelled since the expulsion edict of 1637.

included in Article 18 the freedom of religion for all subjects.

Did this mean that the Government adopted also the formal attitude of Western Governments, that is to say of neutrality in religious matters? It did not and could not, because this is a concept entirely alien to Japanese thinking. This is not to deny that there were bizarre waverings in the minds of leading statesmen in the 1870's, quite understandable in the turmoil of ideas that came flooding in from the West. A remarkable example is the stirring in the minds of the members of the Iwakura Embassy to America and Europe. They were struck by the great place Christianity held in Western life. With impetuous and thought-compelling logic some leaped to the conclusion that the adoption of Western civilization required the adoption of Christianity, not only as a religion, but even as the State religion.[1] This would have been a repetition of what was done to and with Buddhism in the 7th century. There was in this idea some unconscious profundity and a great deal of the truly Japanese pragmatic evaluation of Religion. In the rush of the national evolution, however, it was a passing vagary of the mind.

The dilemma in regard to the relation of Government and Religion, nevertheless, demanded a solution. A solution which would reconcile the desire to use *Kodo* (the Way of the Emperor) as the means for cohesion and stabilization of the nation on the basis of inviolable authority, with the principle of religious liberty and freedom of thought. The *Kodo*, as appears from Shinto publications and from the text of Imperial Rescripts, has as its basic principles: reverence for the national deities and love of country; the Law of Heaven and the Way of Man; loyalty to the throne and obedience to the authorities.

The way out which the Government found was a semi- or pseudo-neutrality by introducing a State Shinto (Jinja-Shinto) as the area of national jurisdiction, defined as an act of patriotic allegiance, a patriotic cult of reverence for the principles mentioned and the Throne, who is in the Rescript on Education (the reading of which is one of the rituals of State Shinto) "coeval with Heaven and Earth". To accentuate this special "no-religion" position the so-called purely religious Shinto

---

[1] G. B. Sansom, *op. cit.*, p. 471.

(Kyoha-Shinto) appearing in Japanese life in great variety and abundance of expression, was rubricated in the category of "free churches", on the same footing as Buddhism and Christianity, on the basis of the article of the Constitution on religious liberty.

The exceptional place of State Shinto is therefore emphasized as well by its belonging to the domain of governmental jurisdiction as by its being placed outside the article on religious liberty, which applies only to religions, and not to "no religion" as State Shinto is alleged to be. With scrupulous care this exceptional position was elaborated. It is State-supported and State-regulated. Its financial and administrative organization is separate from the dealings with the "religions". It has thousands and thousands of shrines, with the Shrine of the Sun Goddess in Ise at the top, and also numberless priests, who are considered civil servants and not priests. Their only function is to perform ceremonies *for* the people, not conducting worship *with* the people. As State Shinto is "no religion" (a thesis always maintained with solemn seriousness) these priest-civil-servants were forbidden to teach any dogma or to conduct any "worship". State Shinto has its official festival days. The Emperor then observes the rites for the people in the Shrine of Ise.

The Government defended staunchly (till 1945) this huge administrative apparatus as necessary for fostering "national morality" (*kokumin dotoku*) against all those who protested that this "no religion" label was a fake and a camouflaged religion. They had ample reason to question the Government, as they brought proofs that the ritual of the State Shinto shrines was full of old nature mythology; that amulets were sold, sacrifices and prayers offered; that the people at any rate treated the shrines not as places of patriotic respect but of religious worship and took part in it with religious emotion. The Government answered always with bland persistence, without explanation, repeating that it was a non-religious institution for developing true patriotism through honouring the Emperor and *Kokutai* (ideal of State).

LEARNING THE DEMOCRATIC WAY

After the American Occupation, when Japan had to start afresh with a clean slate and learn the "democratic way", under American pressure the Emperor disavowed his "divinity" and State Shinto was abolished. It would, however, be all too naïve to think that the Emperor by this disavowal before the radio had altered anything in the hearts of the Japanese as to his real pivotal position in the Japanese "hierarchical way". He remains the sacred Inviolable Chief, exempt from all criticism. It would also be nothing less than astonishing and *un*-natural (seen from inside Japan) if State Shinto or something equivalent did not creep in again. In fact it is already doing so, although still only surreptitiously.

We have dwelt rather long on this point of Japan's religious policy since she entered the period of Westernization, because of its significance for the interpretation of this Westernization. This pantomime of ambiguity or seeming duplicity is not, as the words "ambiguity" and "duplicity" seem to suggest, hypocritical. It is the acrobatics of a Government that must, before the forum of the modern international world, play the rôle of State neutrality in religious matters, and does so with true Japanese methodical thoroughness. Yet in its axiomatic assumptions of life, regarding the world and the hierarchy of relations and status, and in its spontaneous emotional evaluation of Emperor and Country, it has not changed in the least, because it is Japanese first and foremost. Therefore the pantomime has been enacted with grim and solemn seriousness.

Hence this ambiguous civil-servant-priest position of the celebrants and of the Emperor in this State cult. It defended the soul of Japan in the midst of the modern deluge caused by the West and (important to note) this defence was achieved not by using its rich Buddhist and Chinese-Confucian cultural and spiritual heritage, but by going straight back to the bedrock of Japan's uncontaminated nature, which is embodied in Shintoism.

Seen from the outside it was an awkward performance, but its significance is that Japan, though changed in form and function by the marriage with Western civilization, did not and does not propose to change her essence. No real concession was made. A State or a Government without a doctrine of the place of Government and of its subjects within the framework of the "eternal laws" of nature and cosmos is, to Japanese feelings, unthinkable. It does not matter very much whether one calls it, on the evidence of its specific wording, religious, ethical or even secular[1] (or better: worldly-minded); on closer investigation it always appears that there is a more or less latent or more or less manifest underground of religious Ultimateness.

In the case of Japanese State Shinto it has become abundantly clear that this seemingly placid cult of so-called patriotic nature hid the most virulent Japanese self-assertion. Hid, too, its belief in its world mission to determine the true hierarchy of the world and achieve Japan's "proper station", which was to create universal peace by drawing all men and all peoples into the *Kodo*, the "Way of the Emperor". Shinto was the mythological and metaphysical basis of this fervent "patriotic" religion. No wonder Katsuhiko, one of its dogmaticians, calls this "primitive" religion a world religion. It lay behind all the "fascist" movements which in the 1930's were such a characteristic of Japanese life. They found their common centre in the conception of "sacred" Japan. During the War it became abundantly clear that, behind this seemingly benevolent, paternal scheme of "moral education", the fire of intolerant, determined compulsion towards submission to a prescribed Ultimate and Absolute was blazing.

JAPAN'S SPIRITUAL CORE UNCHANGED

The defeat of Japan in 1945, the Emperor's command to accept it and acknowledge the "error" of the whole inspiration of Japan's participation in the War, have changed the situation. For correctness' sake one has to write as we have done, in the past tense, about it. Yet it will be wise to reckon with the fact that Japan's spiritual core has not changed, that her adjustment to and symbiosis with Western civilization is a process only just beginning and that the future developments, though unknown, are a tale written not on a clean slate (as the "democratization" of Japan under American leadership seemed to assume) but on a palimpsest, remarkable for its age

[1] Provided one does not read into this word any connotation of the modern concept of secularism.

and its specific, ineffaceable configuration.[1] Shinto will continue to enshrine the real soul of Japan.

[1] The State Shinto question is not a specifically Japanese affair; particularly not in relation to its basic artificial distinctions. "Religious liberty" has an honourable place in democratic and Communist Constitutions, and as a consequence of this fact "the separation of Church and State" has become a jealously guarded area of modern State management. This being so, phenomena crop up—even in Western democratic and Communist countries which have the virus of secularism in the modern sense, a Western creation, far stronger in their veins than Japan can possibly have—which show unmistakable similarity and affinity to cult services with a pseudo-religious or religious quality and atmosphere. Take for example the United States and their ceremonies in school around the Flag and the recital of central tenets of the Declaration of Independence and the Constitution, which hold an almost sacrosanct place in American life; Communist countries with their services of homage and veneration for the pictures of great Founder Fathers of the Communist State, and Expounders of the infallible faith; East Germany's staging of the *Jugendweihe* (youth dedication), etc., etc. It is, in essence, the same pantomime of ambiguity and duplicity, arising out of the need for an unassailable foundation of unquestioning allegiance to the State, in a world of ideological confusion and disunity and one in which "religion" has a specified and confined place. Hence the protestations that these ceremonious "cults" are non-religious, although this is, essentially speaking, self-deception. The interesting thing is that the way in which the non-religious character of these "cults" is defined is by using categories akin to the theological distinction of *douleia* and *latreia* in the controversies and justifications of saint worship.

The irony of our modern age is that our de-religionized, a-religious or (think of the immense Communist area) anti-religious world is bristling with clumsily camouflaged idolatry, revolving around two centres: the idolatry of the Inner, personal Self and that of the Collective Self. In both cases God is an annoying or infuriating nuisance, or even too contemptible to take any notice of.

Chapter Nine

THE WESTERN RESPONSE TO EASTERN
CULTURES AND RELIGIONS

I T is not only in the East that there has been, and still is, an "Invasion" with its ensuing reactions and responses, full of disturbance and renewed vigour. There is also an Eastern Invasion in the West, more hidden and less spectacular than the Western Invasion, but truly significant. It requires a special investigation, because although the fact is often acknowledged, this acknowledgment remains too general and uncritical.

The attempt made in several of the preceding chapters to give a studied account of the Western Invasion in the East leaves as the dominant impression the unmistakable toughness these great civilizations evince. In the past, Easterners and Westerners have often expressed opinions voicing the impression of the tempestuousness of Western influence and the great fermentation and dislocation following in its wake; opinions such as Lord Cromer's: "Reformed Islam is Islam no longer." It can indeed be taken for granted that the Western Invasion is the most revolutionary experience the East has ever tasted in its long history and that it constitutes a definite break and irrevocable turning point in its spiritual and cultural continuity. But we are nowadays after longer experience and reflection more deeply convinced than evolutionary thinking of the 19th century was inclined to be, of the toughness which is, by the nature of the case, inherent in spiritual and cultural types with deep historical roots.

On the other hand, the participants in the opposing choir of those who sang the song of the "unchanging East" have been many, because they felt deeply (and certainly were right in doing so) the utter alienness of the Eastern world, so magnificently described for instance in Kipling's *Kim*, and the no less utter alienness of the Western world to the East. What we have

seen in the last 125 years or so through all the deep fermentation
and dislocation, the convulsing and uprooting effects, the many
fluctuations, is a stubborn determination to remain true to type,
to assimilate without being dislodged or capitulating.

All four (the Islamic World, India, China, Japan) each in
its particular way gives evidence of this fact. Of course, it should
not be forgotten that the process of change as well as of re-
assertion is far from closed. Nor have we so far entered specifically into the crisis in which these great civilizations are caught
up under the impact of the world-wide phenomenon of
secularization, just as Western civilization and Christianity are
caught up in it. But at this moment at any rate it looks as if
(to use an expression of the well-known Swedish writer
R. Kjellèn) despite all Westernization, Western civilization is
mainly used as a new "coat of armour" to preserve one's own
spiritual type. Capitulation, especially in the field of religion
(here in regard to Christianity), is out of the question, nor can
it be read between the lines of the dominant tendencies.

THE EAST'S NEGATIVE EFFECT ON THE WEST

It is rather that a *subjective* mood of capitulation to the East
is noticeable in the West. Not in the sense of capitulation to an
Eastern Invasion, but in that of negativism to itself. This
surprisingly subjective mood, in a civilization which from the
objective point of view seems so victorious, is due to the highly
different background on which the West experiences the
Eastern Invasion.

The self-questioning which has been going on for a long time
in the West, particularly in Europe, in many cases leading to
the negativism alluded to, and the inner crisis which arises
from this self-questioning (leaving aside many other big factors)
is in the West a purely autochthonous matter. It is born from
within, from the West's own specific spiritual type and its
inherent dynamism; also from its own specific historical course
of life, full of incisive new starts in exploring the mystery of
Man and the Universe, and new experiments in political forms
of collective life. Just as unbroken continuity in depth, despite
sometimes great changes on the surface, is characteristic of the
great Eastern civilizations, so for Western civilization, despite
much persistent underground continuity, the characteristic

quality is revolution.[1] Not in the sense of feverish seeking for change (man, in all climes and times, fears change, even though beneath the threshold of his conscious life he may also long for it), but as a law built into the fibre of its nature.

The self-questioning and inner crisis in the great Eastern civilizations of to-day is not a self-born product. It is thrown upon them like a bomb from the outside. If they had been left to themselves, in spite of modifications occurring in the course of their history, essentially speaking they would have repeated themselves. This is the deepest reason why the undeniable Eastern Invasion in the West is quite a different thing from the Western Invasion in the East. It has a different physiognomy, a different significance. It fulfils a different function in the critical self-questioning West and in this self-questioning itself. It is as it were an aspect and instrument of the West's self-questioning. It helps to make the West's self-questioning more acute, above all because by its presence and operation it leads the self-questioning process outside the confines of a severe introvert inspection of the West's own resources in truth and values, opening up new horizons, new possibilities of choice. All this accounts for the striking fact that, properly speaking, to a great extent the Eastern Invasion is rather a Western contrivance than an Eastern initiative.

The negativism mentioned above was and is essentially a wistful dissatisfaction with the mood, the content and particularly the drift of Western culture (as one feels it). Above all it has been characterized by a dissatisfaction or even disgust with Christianity. Both, this cultural and religious dissatisfaction, in a rich gamut of tonality, have since the 18th century gone through various periods in which different motivations constituted the dominant note. We should have to write a cultural and spiritual history of the West from the 18th century to the present time to do justice to these motivations and their sources.[2] Revolt against the allegedly rationalist character of Western culture and the allegedly dogmatic narrowness of

[1] See the magnificent work *Europäische Revolutionen* by E. Rosenstock-Huessi.

[2] There is, of course, a vast literature on this wide subject. German writers are particularly conspicuous, for example R. Eucken, L. Ziegler, F. Nietzsche, R. von Hartmann, J. Burckhart, although writers such as Kierkegaard and Comte should not be forgotten. The few names mentioned in this footnote are intended less as representatives of this negativism than as analysers.

Christianity; spiritual cosmopolitism; cultural and religious snobbery and a chase after the exotic, were some of the main aspects of this conspicuous self-negation *in* the West *towards* the West as a cultural and spiritual type.

The intensified contact with the Eastern world, as a result of Western oriental research or of the Western expansion over the globe, fulfilled a significant rôle in the formulation of this self-negation and of the discovery of more satisfying nourishment for suppressed longings. The great contrast of the dynamic but restless West with the seemingly serene and self-assured East offered new vistas and possibilities of interpreting the meaning of human life. The more so, because the Eastern world revealed modes and elaborations of mystical metaphysical or occult "knowledge" (gnosis) and avenues of psychological self-knowledge, which indeed never had occupied that preponderant place in Western culture. At best they had led only a marginal, never a central, existence in it. Moreover, this latter fact was particularly evident in the dominating trends in Western civilization of the 19th and 20th centuries, when science and technics made such enormous strides.

The Eastern Invasion began its career modestly by the way in which the more accurate (but still extremely inadequate) knowledge of Islam and of Chinese civilization (through the instrumentality of the eagerly read *Relations* of the Jesuit Fathers) fertilized discussions on political and religious principles, especially in France, contributing in this way unwittingly to the emergence of that world-historical event, the French Revolution (*la Grande Révolution*).[1] The methodical beginning of investigation of the Indian and the Persian-Muslim world, led by truly great English, French and German Orientalists and linguists, quickly won wide interest, and in the first decades of the 19th century had remarkable reverberations in the field of poetry and religious metaphysical thinking, especially in Germany. One of the most conspicuous examples is Goethe's *West-östlicher Divan*, which testifies to his cosmic sensitiveness and openness,[2] recruiting everything as grist to his mill.

[1] "The influence of China on the 'enlightened despotism' was in one aspect, we might even say in many, a Jesuit influence." H. de Lubac, *op. cit.*, p. 104.

[2] The famous lines: "Gottes ist der Orient! Gottes ist der Okzident! Nord und südliches Gelände, Ruht im Frieden seiner Hände", are eloquent testimony. ("The East is God's! The West is God's! Regions of north and south rest in the peace of His hands.")

THE EAST THROUGH WESTERN SCHOLARSHIP

For the sake of clarity we propose to follow two lines. First, the Eastern Invasion as happening to Western people, stirred by the voices from the East, which became audible to them mainly through Western scholarship or through their own exertions. Second, the Eastern Invasion as embodied in personalities or movements, which regarded and regard it as a kind of mission to represent and recommend Eastern culture and religion in the West.

In both cases it is preponderantly the Indian and the Islamic world which represent the Eastern Invasion, with special emphasis on *Buddhism* which, interestingly, has always been taken since the 19th century as Indian, though it had disappeared from India eight centuries before. Chinese civilization plays, comparatively speaking, a modest rôle in the Eastern Invasion, mostly confined to the great interest shown in higher, mystical Taoism. Similarly Japanese civilization has in both cases occupied a small place in the Eastern Invasion in the cultural and religious sense (in the political and economic sense Japan grew within fifty years from an "Iron Curtain" country into a world power). Only fairly recently has Japanese Buddhism, especially Zen Buddhism, become a real element of the Eastern Invasion.

The self-evoked Eastern Invasion and the hospitality to Eastern and Western advocates of Eastern culture or religion are therefore part of the crisis in which the West has found itself, since it began to undertake the adventure of discovering what man and the world would be like when God was virtually dethroned and Man took the centre—thereby aiming at the "Ausgang aus seiner selbstverschuldeten Unmündigkeit" of Kant (emergence from an immaturity due to his own fault). H. de Lubac justly remarks[1] that the adventure of the modern West's reaction and response to Buddhism (as an outstanding example) "is one of the lines which mark the face of this Europe" (and let us add: America) "where we live; one of the components which, in explaining it, help to explain us to ourselves. *Far from being complete, it has we believe just entered upon its essential phase*".[2]

[1] *op. cit.,* cf. *Avant-Propos.*   [2] Italics mine.

When in the first quarter of the 19th century "Oriental" or "Asiatic" Societies and Chairs for Sanskrit had been founded in the main intellectual capitals of Continental Europe and England, and H. T. Colebrooke, making in India a magnificent collection of Sanskrit manuscripts, had published his painstaking *Essays on the Philosophy of the Hindus* (1827),[1] the plunge into Eastern, particularly Indian, philosophy and religion could be made. Despite the gratuitous and fantastic opinions of many writers, who knew more by hearsay and desultory, avid reading than by proper study, Schopenhauer, who has contributed so much by his utterances and sympathies to the rise of the "Indian vogue" in Europe, sensed the atmosphere when he prophesied that the influence of Sanskrit on our time would be no less profound than the Renaissance of classical languages in the 15th century. In these first decades of the 19th century many highly gifted men of various Western nationalities deployed a feverish activity and curiosity, gripped by the mysterious, fascinating nature of a still largely unknown country. The exhilarating breeze of thrilling adventure inspired their undertakings, often combined with great hardships. There was a real feeling of a new "springtime", of crossing a threshold into a new and wider mansion of humanity. Among many other men of great stature, it is undoubtedly, in regard to the exploration of Buddhism, the towering figure of Eugène Burnouf (d. 1852) that must be mentioned as the greatest pioneer explorer, by his mastery of Sanskrit and Pali and by his achievement as a lone pathfinder through the "hopeless labyrinth" of Buddhist literature.

It lies, however, outside the scope of this chapter to give a survey of the scientific discovery of the Eastern cultures and religions from their own sources. Our purpose is to focus on the reaction and responses of the West to the new worlds of thought and feeling they met along the avenues opened up by the scholars or by some other means.[2]

[1] In these Essays was also included one on the "heretical sects" (Jainism, Buddhism) described by Colebrooke on the pattern of the refutations by Hindu philosophers.

[2] The literature on the influence and attraction Buddhism has exercised on the West is very vast. Except in some cases, expressly indicated, we refer as a rule to H. de Lubac's book (1955); H. W. Schomerus' short study, which is undeservedly forgotten, entitled: *Buddha und Christus*, 1931; and Christmas Humphreys' Pelican Book on Buddhism, 1954. All three, rich in information, confine themselves mainly to the literature published in their own languages.

BUDDHISM IN THE WEST

Our first glance, as to influence and reaction to Buddhism in the West, is directed towards philosophers and writers and the first apologetical reactions. Some examples are given only for the sake of suggesting the kind of fermentation the increasing acquaintance with Buddhism brought about. These philosophers and writers, being the intellectual élite which moulded irresistibly the minds of the reading public, either drew on the works of the great Orientalists, or on the contributions of non-scholarly enthusiasts. Both categories had by their effort put Buddhism on the spiritual map of the West. About the middle of the 19th century, it began to exercise on many representatives of the intellectual class a kind of fascination, though emphatic reactions of rejection were, to be sure, not absent. An authority like Burnouf[1] always declined to draw any moral, social or religious conclusion from his discoveries, but most people who came in contact with information on Buddhism could not afford such a suspension of judgment.

It cannot be said that, in this first period of amazed discovery and encounter, this new knowledge of Buddhism was already a real element of the decline of faith in regard to Christianity, which has become in an ever accelerated pace such a characteristic feature of the European scene in the last hundred years. Buddhism no doubt later became so, but at first not so much in itself as part of the influence of the growing knowledge of and contact with the non-Christian religions.

The initial impress of the confrontation with Buddhism was the feeling of having met with a great and unexpected rival of Christianity. The reactions, of course, were diverse. Positive, sensing in it a different edition of Christianity in its essence. Negative, rejecting it disdainfully, interpreting it as a glorification of Nothingness or annihilation (on account of the concept of Nirvana, which has always been a bone of contention both among scholars and among amateurs in the science of religion in Europe). Or curious and puzzled by many analogies to be found in the stories of Buddha and Christ, and the similarity in hierarchical and liturgical structure which one seemed to discover between Tibetan Buddhism and Roman Catholicism,

[1] H. de Lubac, *op. cit.*, p. 153.

which all contributed latently to the slowly rising tide of relativism. Later on, especially when Buddhist art in its Chinese and Japanese forms and derivations became widely known, the quality of supermundane, sovereign "quietness" and the mysterious identity of artist and nature conveyed the conviction that one met in Buddhism a truly great world of cultural and spiritual achievement, permeated and animated by an awe-inspiring philosophy.

Schopenhauer, though mainly influenced and impressed by his discovery of the Upanishads, became, through his *Die Welt als Wille und Vorstellung*[1] and others of his works, a great factor in creating interest in Buddhism by the deep appreciation he evinced for it. His stress on the fateful "will to live", on "compassion" and "suffering" undoubtedly has a different bias and tonality in his system than that in Indian and Buddhist thinking, but it is as undoubtedly true that his way of thinking owed much to the deep emotive experience he gained through his constant "communion" with Buddhist works and with the Upanishads, even in the imperfect Latin translation of Anquetil Duperron. It is of particular significance that he several times suggested the superiority of Buddhism over Christianity. He noted many similarities between the two, although their dress was different, but he took it as an occasion to emphasize that it evidently did not matter very much whether a religion was theist or atheist, both being able to produce saintliness of the first order.

"THE WEAK POINT OF CHRISTIANITY"

The most pertinent thing, however, in his many remarks, is that he is the leading pioneer in an opinion which up to the present time has increasingly conquered a great number of people in the West, that is to say the opinion that the weak point of Christianity is its being based on a single historical fact. He lauds Buddhism as showing a deeper and higher wisdom by its freedom from such unphilosophical encumbrance. He is quite aware that in Buddhism historical aspects are not absent, but they are, as he rightly observes, irrelevant, not integral to the real doctrine and message.

[1] E. T., *The World as Will and Idea*, Haldane and Kemp, 1883.

Here he hit on a crucial point in regard to the relations of Christianity to the great Eastern religions. Thus he is not only one of the important initiators of the West into Eastern thinking, but is also in the very first stage of encounter of East and West a representative interpreter of the secret suspicion, alive in the intellectual Western élite, of Christianity's irrefutably inferior quality in philosophical depth and liberty when compared with the great Eastern religions.

This point deserves emphasis, because this widely rampant conviction (with some) or suspicion (with others) constitutes in itself an Eastern Invasion of real magnitude in the West. One might even go further and say, that for a great number of the Western intellectual class, though many are too insufficiently informed to make a case for it, the superiority in depth and outlook of Eastern religious philosophical thought is already a foregone conclusion, which determines their spontaneous attitude of having definitely closed their accounts with Christianity. By formulating this matter clearly Schopenhauer has won a great place in modern Western culture, which cannot be gainsaid by the constantly recurring discussions of professional Orientalists as to whether he knew much or little on Buddhism; whether he garbled and misrepresented it or not. Such discussions miss the real point: that Schopenhauer has with great clarity defined a crucial issue to which the learned are often strangely blind.[1]

Several influential writers were profoundly struck by the many similarities between Buddhist and Christian characteristics. Sometimes they admitted a genuine perplexity and confusion. Luminaries like Taine or Renan remained in their observations impenitent sons of the 19th century, but the attention they paid to it contributed to the prestige of Buddhism. Comte, who did not yet suspect the positivist spirit which is one of Buddhism's characteristics, nevertheless accorded Buddha a place in his universalist *Calendrier positive*. Great

[1] H. de Lubac, *op. cit.*, p. 162, rightly reminds us of Schopenhauer's influence on Wagner's music. The point again is here, not whether Wagner interpreted Indian modes of thinking rightly (he most assuredly did not), but that great and famous artists were sensitive to these influences and so became agents in the silent process of permeation of the East into Western culture. From Wagner's papers and projects, found after his death, it appears that he was deeply interested in the legend of the Buddha. His *Parsifal* shows traces of it. Cf. M. Winternitz: *Geschichte der indischen Literatur*, Vol. II, Part I, pp. 224, 288. (E.T. *History of Indian Literature*.)

writers like Flaubert[1] and Amiel are clearly impressed by it and see its point of challenge to Christianity.

As in all chapters of this book, it is not our object to be exhaustive, as that would require a series of big volumes. Therefore only one other philosopher (who has been mentioned before) will get special notice. This is Hermann Keyserling, both for his Protean personality and for the wide influence his *Das Reisetagebuch eines Philosophen* has exercised and probably still exercises.[2]

Keyserling published his two volumes with the motto: "The shortest way to one's self leads all round the world." He travelled as a philosopher, desirous to understand and interpret Eastern philosophy and religion in a way adequate to its own intentions. He has succeeded in this enterprise, a formidable one in regard to such a many-sided phenomenon, in a degree rarely achieved by any Westerner. He could do so because he was a man with a strong metaphysical bent and therefore had a great natural affinity especially with the Indian world. Further, he possessed enormous philosophical and religious erudition (both Western and Eastern), and lastly he was endowed in a very high measure with the gift of *Einfühlung* (empathy). The reason why he could respond to the Eastern world of apprehension without falling into the trap of idolizing it—he rejects emphatically all "Indomania"—was that his real aim, in responding and assimilating, was to increase his own spiritual growth as a European who was spiritually a cosmopolitan and yet a clear-cut character. For all these reasons he is an almost ideal representative of Western response to the East.[3]

Keyserling, who admires greatly the metaphysical profundity of India, considers Buddha inferior in this respect to the

[1] Cf. his famous *Tentation de Saint-Antoine*. Cf. Lubac, *op. cit.*, p. 171.

[2] *The Travel Diary of a Philosopher*. When we come to the Western response to India's philosophy and religion, Keyserling will have to be referred to again as one of the most important witnesses. Schomerus (see *op. cit.*, Vol. III, pp. 86-102) gives a fair and very valuable appreciation of Keyserling's book.

[3] Schomerus expresses rightly his amazement that a man of such versatility in understanding shows in his *Reisetagebuch* so little ability to interpret Christianity adequately and condemns the Christian missionaries without taking the trouble to acquaint himself with Missions. In my book *Religion and the Christian Faith* I have repeatedly remarked on this same phenomenon in many philosophers of Religion, who evidenced an appreciable understanding of the great non-Christian religions, and I have indicated that this strange inability poses a question of great importance.

Brahman philosophers.[1] Southern Buddhism he calls "die ideale Religion der mediocritas".[2] It is a religion only possible to inhabitants of the tropics. In the context of his apt and profound remark that Hinduism (especially in its exuberant mythology) is a vegetative[3] phenomenon, he says about Buddha that his phenomenology of the forms of existence is the most exact theory of vegetation ever propounded.[4] He adds the significant remark that Buddha is of one spirit with the empirical systems of the West (psychology of Mack, James, Comte, Spencer, Ostwald, Bergson). Buddha's religion is in his opinion, philosophically speaking, a phenomenological relativism.

<h2 style="text-align:center">AFFINITIES WITH CHRISTIANITY</h2>

About Mahayanism he uses nearly—not wholly—the same enthusiastic tone as about India's metaphysical achievement. He is struck by the great affinity of spirit between Christianity and Mahayana. He sees a proof for this assertion in what he calls the astounding convergence of both in dogmatic development. He refuses, however, to speak about "Gleichheit beider Religionen" (identity of the two religions), for the confessional embodiment is for Buddhism not an ultimate, as, in his opinion, it is for Christianity. He considers Mahayana, however, as the representation of Christianity as it would have developed itself amongst Indian sages. In philosophical respect Mahayana far excels Christianity, but in efficaciousness it cannot be compared with the Christian religion. Buddhism is, in regard to doctrine, nearest to the seekers for a new religion in the West, because of its undogmatic character.

This is a very important observation, as in making it Keyserling certainly is a spokesman for a wider constituency in the West. In his appreciations of the relation of Buddhism and Christianity, Keyserling contradicts himself more than once, and even constructs, though only by suggestion, a sort of *Wunschreligion* (wish-religion), in which features of Buddhism's undogmatic temper and Christian vigour are combined, calling it "perhaps an ideal for the future".[5]

---

[1] Keyserling, *op. cit.*, I, p. 53.   [2] p. 63.

[3] Keyserling states that, in the tropics, to vegetate is a maximum and not a minimum attainment.

[4] *op. cit.*, I, p. 41.   [5] *ibid.*, II, pp. 68of.

These various illustrations are not adduced with the idea of suggesting that Buddhism became quickly a matter of wide public interest or influence. The Christian apologetic responses in regard to Buddhism were not very numerous, nor (judged by the present-day standard of knowledge on Buddhism) very impressive. They lacked, for very good reasons, adequate knowledge. Both needed time. Yet, in these apologetic labours as well as in the illustrations of the attention Buddhism received from philosophers and literary men, it is evident that Buddhism intrigued many able minds and created a kind of feeling that in Buddhism Western culture and Christianity were confronted with hitherto unsurmised, fundamental questions. This is demonstrated also by the various attempts, either by cocksure *dilettanti* or by professional scholars, to provide the many striking parallels between symbols, institutions or famous tales in Christianity and Buddhism with a historical basis.

One of the earliest attempts to "prove" the Buddhistic origins of primitive Christianity is N. A. Notovick's: *Vie inconnue de Jésus-Christ* (1834) which on the basis of a professedly Indian document asserted that Jesus had been initiated into his career by a sixteen years' stay with Brahmans and Buddhist monks.[1] It is interesting to note that the Essenes, who to-day through the Dead Sea Scrolls are enjoying special attention again regarding their significance for the rise of Christianity, were in 1867 presented by a German scholar, Hilgenfeld, as Buddhists. Hilgenfeld by interpreting Jesus as an Essene in this indirect way made Christianity dependent on Buddhism. Scholars from different countries combined in trying to dig out parallels and cases of Christian dependence from Buddhism. It is sufficient to mention a few: Rudolf Seydel: *Das Evangelium Jesu in seinem Verhältniss zu Buddha-sage und Buddha-Lehre*, 1882, and *Die Buddha-legende und das Leben Jesu nach den Evangelien*, 1884; A. J. Edmunds: *Buddhist and Christian Gospels now first compared*, 1902; G. A. van den Bergh van Eysinga: *Indische Einflüsse auf evangelische Erzählungen*, 1909; Richard Garbe: *Indien und das Christentum*, 1914, etc.[2]

This brief, selective enumeration gives but a faint idea of the

[1] *op. cit.*, p. 205.

[2] *op. cit.*, pp. 205-208 and M. Winternitz: *Geschichte der indischen Literatur*, Vol. I, Part I, on *Die buddhistische Literatur*, esp. pp. 277-288 on *Die buddhistische Literatur und die Weltliteratur*.

great interest the matter of parallels and dependences had, and, it must be added, has till the present time. Rare indeed was the sobriety of the famous Dutch scholar A. Kuenen, who wrote in 1882[1] that, without fearing to deceive himself, he could confidently say that it would be wise to abstain from all endeavours to attribute to Buddhism any influence on the origins of Christianity. This truly sagacious sobriety has rarely become the rule; neither, as things go, with the unavoidable "fantastics", nor with the scholars, although the West has become increasingly critical and prudent on this matter.

It is worth while to pause a moment and try to analyse this complex phenomenon in 19th and 20th century Western culture.[2] Complex, because there is clearly more behind it than learned curiosity or interest in the tracing of cultural dependency. There are various strains in this complexity, in which learned search for and wonder about vast emerging fields of new knowledge, combined with emotive impulses towards unveiling mysteries hitherto veiled, and also often unconscious, fundamental positions taken in regard to Christianity and Western culture, mingle with each other.

GROWTH OF "COMPARATIVE" RELIGION

The first thing to be taken into account is the simple fact of the growth of "Comparative Religion", which has been, and often still is, the favourite name for what should be properly called "the Science of Religion". It opened the eyes of the scholars concerned for wider horizons of historical contacts and of similarities in the modes of religious expression in different spiritual worlds. In such research, proved historical evidence always combines with hypothesis and intuitive suspicions, for which efforts are made to procure evidence and proof. This urge of the "Science of Religion" is in itself quite legitimate. It should therefore freely go on, in trial, truth and error, and there is no reason whatever to oppose this legitimate course of research and hypothetical procedure, provided it is done in a spirit of untiring, vigilant self-criticism and readiness for self-revision. That is the Golden Rule of true scientific work

[1] In his *National Religions and Universal Religions*, p. 251, quoted by de Lubac, p. 207.

[2] It applies not only to Buddhism but to India in general.

which looks after its own recovery to health and equilibrium.

This is not to say that such hypotheses and intuitive suspicions acquire automatically the status of "scientific truth", because they are enunciated by competent scholars or amateurs with original minds. At this point the confusion enters, or can enter, which indicates that the result of scholarly research in the "Science of Religion" is not at all exclusive scholarly territory. Religion and politics are the two outstanding domains of life in regard to which, led by a true instinct, the general public reacts—whether it has the knowledge to do so or not—to the enunciations of scholarly (expert) opinion, because it rightly feels: *tua res agitur* (the speaker is on his own ground). It is for this reason that what from the scholarly point of view are hypotheses and intuitive suspicions acquire immediately the status of "scientific truth" and, as such, influence public discussion.

The case with the ineradicable race of "fantastics" is different. They constitute, especially in a time like ours of unprecedented culture contacts and discoveries of past cultures, a type of people by nature both mystery-mongering and hungry for revealing them, possessing an enormous appetite for all kinds of spiritual food and suffering from a no less enormous lack of discernment. They therefore cook up, often in complete honesty, so-called results of "scientific research" and fantastic assertions into revelatory myths, not even stopping at the assertion that Jesus is Buddha, but turning the Old Testament prophets, from Samuel on, into Buddhists.[1] It is not seldom that even professional scholars have such a streak in their nature, as for instance Rudolf Seydel who did not hesitate to invent the existence of a non-existent Indian apocalypse, known in Palestine and Egypt in the 1st century and which inspired the apostles to invent Christianity. Taking into account the bewildering complexity of modern culture and the unwieldly mass of historical information on which speculative minds can exercise their unrestrained powers of imagination, it must be said that one simply has to suffer such fools, though very seldom gladly.[2]

[1] de Lubac, *op. cit.*, p. 208.

[2] de Lubac (p. 207) rightly says: "But there exists a family of adventurous spirits, whom the weightiest refutations and even the display of the evidence will never keep from talking nonsense."

There is, however, still another reason for this never-ceasing effort to derive Christianity wholly from Buddhism. The dazzling effect of the discovery of India's fecundity in religiosis and the many contacts with this country of mystery which, formerly unsuspected, came to light, is certainly a factor which should not be neglected. But in many cases, in scholars, writers, philosophers as well as in fantastic adventurers,[1] a secret animosity towards Christianity, deriving from many causes which need not be detailed here, inspired the urge to make Christianity a dependent of Buddhism and so rob it of its originality. Buddhism was a powerful help in the internal Western debate about its own foundation and credentials. The alleged demonstration of Christianity's dependence on Buddhism was (and is) a roundabout attack on the resented claim of the exclusive truth of Christianity by undermining confidence in its originality.[2] This is an important element in the spiritual tumult, unleashed by the self-invoked Eastern Invasion in the West, and manifest in the Western responses to it. It contributed substantially to the ever-increasing religious relativism which pervades the modern West.

BUDDHIST PROPAGANDA

So far we have been looking only at what I have termed the self-invoked Eastern Invasion as operated by purely Western endeavour. There is, however, in regard to Buddhism, another side of the medal; that is to say, Buddhist propaganda and the growth of the Neo-Buddhist Movement. It is again remarkable that this aspect of the Eastern Invasion remains, to a great extent, work carried out by Westerners, and only to a minor, mainly auxiliary, degree by born Buddhists from the East.

Propaganda and Neo-Buddhism mean mainly the consideration of the significance of Sir Edwin Arnold's famous poem:

---

[1] Of course, in very different doses.

[2] The writer, being in the U.S.A. in 1956/57, when the general public was immensely interested in the Dead Sea Scrolls, clearly noticed that this interest was chiefly caused by anxiety lest the comfortable belief in Christianity's originality (and consequently in its truth) should be exposed as a fraud on account of the broadcast opinions of "scholars" that these Scrolls made Essenism responsible for the rise of Christianity.

The Light of Asia, and of the contribution of the Theosophical Movement, although some factors of minor significance have a place of their own.

The universal appeal of the Buddha legend is a patent fact. It has stimulated several Western poets and writers[1] to reconceive it. *The Light of Asia* by Edwin Arnold, published in 1879, is justly considered the most famous attempt. This poem, based on the Lalitavistara, sung the life and actions of Prince Siddharta, the Lord Buddha and Saviour, in such a fascinating way that it began a victorious course through the world. The figures for the number of its editions differ, but it can safely be said that 30 years ago it had gone in America through 100 editions and in England through a number between 50 and 100. For hundreds of thousands of people all over the world, Indians included, this poem, truly beautiful as to form and content, has been *the* evangelist of the Buddha by its irresistible charm. It certainly has been and still is the best instrument for creating an attitude of respect and reverence towards Buddhism.

Edwin Arnold in later years had relations with some activities of the Theosophical Society, founded in 1875 by Mrs. H. P. Blavatsky, H. S. Olcott and W. Q. Judge in New York. This Movement, whose significance in the Eastern Invasion and the Western response to it will be considered somewhat more closely in relation to the influence of Indian thought and spirituality in the West, cannot be passed over in silence in a consideration of the reception Buddhism has found in the Western world.

It is from the Theosophical Movement, with its distinction between exoteric and esoteric membership of the Movement and exoteric and esoteric insight into the primeval, absolute Truth (basic to all religions and philosophies except the materialistic), that well-known books have come forth with such titles as *Esoteric Buddhism* by A. P. Sinnett (1883) and *Esoteric Christianity* by A. Besant. It is not necessary to enter into the contents of these books. They pretend to unveil the mysteries of eternal Truth, hidden to the blind eyes of the West but guarded since immemorial times in a secret region in Tibet, where the great guardians, the Mahatmas, were accessible only

[1] M. Winternitz, *op. cit.,* pp. 287, 288.

to adepts and initiates.[1] The real core of the Mysteries and Truth of which they were custodians is the hidden fund of all religions, although the Brahmanic Tradition in fact has a pre-eminent place. The significance of Mr. Sinnett's widely-read book does not consist in its contributing anything to a real understanding of Buddhism. As such it is only misleading. It lies in his using so-called esoteric Buddhism as the vehicle for enunciating the "secret esoteric science" and the explanation of man and the cosmos, of which the Theosophical Society, especially through the intermediary agency of its prominent leaders, has since its foundation behaved as the unveiler. The all-embracing, all-harmonizing and eclectic syncretism of the Theosophical Movement used its alleged esoteric interpretation of Buddhism (which had little to do with Buddhism in its essence and its empirical embodiments) and a similar one on Christianity or "Isis unveiled" (H. P. Blavatsky) to preach its "Secret Doctrine".

So there has been in certain representatives of the Theosophical Society a special interest in and emphasis on Buddhism, creating a kind of theosophically inspired Neo-Buddhism, which had and has branches in America and various countries of Europe. It is *one* of the ways in which Buddhism, although distortingly administered, wins the admiration and devotion of a great number of mainly "upper-class" (France) or "middle-class" people (Great Britain).

Much could be said about the ambiguity of the spiritual "policy" of theosophical leaders and about the flimsy bases of their knowledge of Buddhism, but that is not a matter of special importance for our investigation into the development of the Eastern Invasion in the West and the responses to it. The authorities for theosophical writers on Buddhism were either the unreachable, uncontrollable Mahatmas or the top people in the theosophical hierarchy, who are all by definition above criticism, but not the rich authentic sources made available by brilliant scholarship. It is nevertheless a fact that Theosophy, in its many branches of and schisms from the first Theosophical

[1] According to Mr. Sinnett and much theosophic teaching, these Mahatmas, the source of all true wisdom, have been better organized for their task of dispensing the hidden Mysteries at their due time and place all over the world by the great Tibetan reformer of Tibetan Buddhism, Tsong-Ka-Pa, in the 14th century A.D.

Society, has by its typical Western zest for organization and propaganda done a great deal to turn many minds to the strange world of Buddhist thinking and ideals. Looked at from a different angle, it is one of the most striking manifestations of the colossal confusion into which the West, culturally and spiritually already in a crisis issuing from its own depths, has been thrown since the 19th century by its increasing acquaintance with the East through the scientific study of its religions and thinking, and the sincere or snobbish quest for a new universal truth.

OLCOTT'S CATECHISM

Instead of trying to mention as many important or queer examples as possible, I will confine myself to a brief consideration of one well-known Theosophist and his way of occupying himself with Buddhism, that is to say the American H. S. Olcott.

Olcott is one of the most conspicuous Theosophists in relation to Buddhism in the West, and even in the East. In a theosophical publication[1] he is aptly called a "commis-voyageur (commercial traveller) of Buddhism". In 1881 he published a Buddhist Catechism. It was announced as a short compendium of the doctrine "according to the Canon of the Southern Church" (Theravada). This Catechism numbers many editions in various languages. Olcott claimed the honour of formulating in his Catechism the fundamental teachings of Buddhism, purified from all its later mythological corruptions, and so to have made accessible the ancient esoteric doctrine, the key to which (here the theosophical authority of all secret doctrine appears) had been provided by one of the mysterious Mahatmas.

Not the content of this Catechism but much else connected with it is interesting. First, Olcott's laudatory recommendation of the ancient esoteric doctrine of Buddhism. According to him, it was not a religion; it was a system teaching the highest goodness without confessing a God; the continuity of existence without accepting the existence of a soul; happiness without a belief in a heaven; a way of salvation without a saviour; salvation by one's own endeavour, without rites, prayers, etc.

[1] de Lubac, op. cit., p. 209, note 24.

The striking point here is that it is one of the clear instances of the polyvalent attitude and strategy of the Theosophical Movement, which enables it to have serious-looking flirtations with sundry objects of love: esoteric Buddhism, esoteric Christianity, esoteric Brahmanism, in short all the "esoterisms" of human history; the absolute Truth basic and common to all religions; the claim to respect all the religions and unveil their true esoteric "teachings", etc. In this recommendation of Olcott's it looks as if the clientèle of modern god-less, soul-less, dogma-less, rite-less freethinkerish irreligion is being sought under cover of the mystery-unveiling Mahatmas.[1]

Another notable thing is that after the headquarters of the Theosophical Society had been moved from New York to Adyar near Madras, Olcott's Catechism was approved and recommended for use in Buddhist schools by H. Sumangala, "High Priest" of Ceylonese Buddhism and Principal of Widyodaya Parivena, a Buddhist theological Seminary at Colombo.[2]

The important thing here is not so much the attempt to convey the impression that Olcott's ambitious enterprise to restore Buddhism to its original purity had the active support of the Southern Buddhist Church, for that was a fiction;[3] but that an American Theosophist bluntly proposed and intended to reform Buddhism and be the architect of restoring Buddhism into one ecumenical "Church", founded on its original Creed. This pretentious impetuosity, this behaving, though an outsider, as the standard-bearer of *Propaganda Fidei* and of Reunion is typically Western. Olcott's perseverance and dynamism in this respect appeared once more in 1891 when he drafted as appendix to his Catechism the *Fourteen Articles*, containing the "Fundamental Buddhistic Beliefs". They show again a strong Hinayana (Southern Church) bias, combined with the flatness of a Western rationalist.[4] The closing sentence is:

[1] There are also various utterances of the prominent Theosophists (Blavatsky, etc.) that have a clearly anti-Christian tone.

[2] de Lubac, *op. cit.*, p. 209, note 25; R. Guénon: *Le Théosophisme*, p. 104.

[3] The Buddhist Schools mentioned were schools founded by Western Theosophists.

[4] The Fourteen "Fundamental Beliefs" are to be found in Christmas Humphreys' *Buddhism* (Pelican Book), pp. 71-73. Humphreys relates interesting details about the success of Olcott's endeavours in Buddhist circles. One should read these particulars with a critical mind, as these "Buddhist circles" evidently are under Theosophical Protectorate.

He [Buddha] taught that no one should believe what is spoken by any sage, written in any book, or affirmed by tradition, unless it accord with reason.

The Theosophical Society has since remained active in reform and propaganda of Buddhism, or rather *its* Buddhism. Especially in trying to create a common platform for all Buddhist "sects" and "schools", particularly Hinayana and Mahayana. In a former chapter we alluded to some stirrings of Buddhist "ecumenicity", mainly by the Mahabodhi Society founded in 1891 by Anagarika Dharmapala, which had zealous supporters also in America and Europe; but these Western theosophical efforts are far more determined. The latest attempt has been made at the suggestion of the British Buddhist Society by its President, Mr. Christmas Humphreys. He is an ex-member of the Theosophical Society and composed in 1945 a brief summary of Buddhism, meant as its common, "ecumenical" basis. This leaflet is entitled: *Twelve Principles of Buddhism*. This document is also heavily pro-Hinayana (Theravada), expressed in a typically Western reasoning style, and is a piece of genuine propaganda. The last sentence reads:

It [Buddhism] appeals to the West because it has no dogmas, satisfies the reason and the heart alike, insists on self-reliance coupled with tolerance for other points of view, embraces science, religion, philosophy, psychology, ethics and art, and points to man alone as the creator of his present life and sole designer of his destiny.[1]

From this phrase alone it is clear that Buddhism is confidently presented in terms that pander to the desirables asked for on the Western list for spiritual consumption.

Though Rudolf Steiner separated in 1913 from the Theosophical Society and founded his own system of Anthroposophy and his own school of adherents, he may still be

---

[1] See Humphreys, *op. cit.*, pp. 73-76, and his *Via Tokyo*. The observations made by Humphreys, pp. 73, 74, on his successful experiences with the Buddhists, especially in Japan, who belong to Mahayana, should be read with the greatest reserve. The easy victory Humphreys won for his arch-Western-conceived document is probably due more to Oriental politeness and practice of "tolerance" than to the fact that they consider it, as he does, an important step to "World Buddhism in simple terms", p. 74. Humphreys clearly hopes that his Twelve Propositions may become the handbook for the Navayana (New Way), synthesizing the different ways of Theravada, Mahayana and Zen; *op. cit.*, p. 230.

reckoned, on account of his works and numberless lectures, as belonging to the promoters of a theosophical Neo-Buddhism. However, there are forms of Neo-Buddhism which are no offspring of the Theosophical Movement, although the promoters have in common with the Theosophists the fascination by "esoteric wisdom" from the East and a predilection for the East combined with a patent aversion towards Christianity. All this drives them towards a kind of differently-graded desertion of the particular truths and values of the West.[1]

The many persons and writings which bear evidence to this tendency in various countries are doing this each in their own way. There are the scholars who foster a deep sympathy for Buddhism, like Mr. and Mrs. Rhys Davids, who have done monumental work in editing the Pali sources of Buddhism, and Mrs. Alexandra David-Neel, scholar, reporter and propagandist: or men like Paul Carus, a talented controversialist; or Paul Dahlke, who founded in Frohnau, a beautiful Berlin suburb, a little *vihara* (Buddhist monastery) with a temple, a library, and a publishing department, which published amongst other items a Neo-Buddhist Catechism.[2] A very, very small number of Westerners (Englishmen, Germans) have actually joined the Buddhist *Sangha* by becoming monks and serving in that capacity as "evangelists".

What has been said so far is sufficient to show without fear of contradiction that in the last hundred years something amazing has happened with Buddhism. More *with*, in a certain sense, than *in* Buddhism.[3] It has become a world fact instead of a geographically confined reality. It is discovered to be a "universal humanism", as Sylvain Lévi has defined it, creative in all fields of life. The "story" of the Buddha rivals in impressiveness the "story" of Jesus Christ. Without exercising or attempting any noteworthy effect of conversion, it has permeated many minds in the West, so that there is noticeable in many Western thinkers *une attitude bouddhisante* (e.g. Huxley, Scheler, Hackin, L. Ziegler in his earlier stage). Aldous Huxley sees it as a specimen of the *philosophia perennis*, because

[1] Rudolf Steiner has a special position amongst the "esoterists".

[2] It was closed during Hitler's régime. Only the library is now left; de Lubac, *op. cit.*, p. 241.

[3] Chapter 7 has described what happened in Buddhism in reaction and response to the Western "Invasion".

of its immense psychology, its gigantic cosmology and its deep dialectical philosophical insight. In the West, all over the place, groups of people are more deeply interested in the future of Buddhism than in that of Christianity or Western culture, and are affected by the sweetness and serenity it radiates.

A RECOGNITION OF BUDDHISM'S CALIBRE

The evaluation of Buddhism's calibre and value has in all quarters, missionary circles included, acquired a positive tone of appreciation and respect. Buddhism, long ignored in India, is now enthusiastically acknowledged as part of the great Indian heritage. Gandhi spoke with reverence about it. Coomaraswamy and Radhakrishnan incorporate Buddha's doctrine of salvation without reservation in the corpus of Indian thought. The meeting of the West with Buddhism is already in many respects a fact; it works as a real ferment in the West. It would be easy to continue this kind of statement. The most amazing thing about this event, which stretches over more than a century, is that it is again almost exclusively the effect of Western curiosity and labour. Missionary action in the proper sense of the word, issuing from Buddhist countries (Burma, Ceylon, Japan), is still very small, though not absent. Most "propaganda" at present (without direct missionary intention) is made possible by the West inviting Buddhist scholars, especially from Japan, to universities in America and Europe. America is the most eager country in this respect. All this is illustrated by the interesting facts collected by Christmas Humphreys in the last chapter of his book, *Buddhism*, under the title: "Buddhism to-day".[1]

There is some humour in the fact that in England the first preaching of Buddhism (of course by an English practising Buddhist) was from a soap-box in Hyde Park. The man who did it (R. J. Jackson) founded in 1906 with another Englishman, who had become a monk, the Buddhist Society of England. This became in 1908 the Buddhist Society of Great Britain and Ireland, under the presidency of the famous scholar in Buddhism, Rhys Davids. Their lecturing activity on the Dharma, extending over years, exercised a wide influence. The

---

[1] *op. cit.*, pp. 220f.

Buddhist Lodge founded as a part of the Theosophical Society,[1] which became independent after a few years and at present goes by the name of "The Buddhist Society, London" with affiliations all over the world, became a kind of mission centre working closely with some monks from Burma and Ceylon. In 1948 a *Vihara* Society was founded in England to set up *viharas* there. The English Buddhists belong both to the Theravada and the Mahayana School. The Buddhist Society adheres to no one school and tries to teach, study and apply the whole of Buddhism.

Mr. Humphreys, himself a devoted propagandist with wide international contacts in East and West, makes some very significant remarks on "Buddhist Influence in the West". He says that this influence on Western thought is difficult to measure or define, because, although there are every year hundreds of enquiries and thousands of books, Buddhism does not lend itself to gregarious activities. It is mainly an individual affair. Buddhist influence, therefore, will always be out of proportion to the number of its declared adherents. He even goes to the length of saying that the West will never be "Buddhist". It might be (this is clearly Mr. Humphreys' fond desire) that the Western Buddhists succeed in producing the synthesis of all the great diverging tendencies of Buddhism into one "vehicle" of Salvation. It may be that Buddhist principles will be built into the temple of Western thought as the awakening mind of the West has need of them. To put it in other words: conversion may be possible but is very improbable; permeation, however, is sure and irrepressible.[2]

THE WEST AND THE WISDOM OF INDIA

The Eastern Invasion in the West as embodied in the *Indian* world of religion and metaphysical thought happened mainly, as in the case of Buddhism, through the labours of Western

[1] Humphreys, himself an ex-member of the Society, says *op. cit.*, p. 225 that the interest in Buddhism has been furthered by the interest shown by English Theosophists for many years before any direct Buddhist activity took place. They had prepared the English mind, to an extent which English Buddhists are slow to acknowledge, for the Buddha Dharma.

[2] We are inclined to forget that America, alongside its many purely American Buddhist Societies, has a Japanese immigrant population in the west, who, though loyal Americans, are Buddhists or Shintoists. The most represented types of Buddhism amongst them are Zen and the Shin or Pure Land School.

Oriental scholarship since the beginning of the 19th century, and the many neo-spiritualist and other movements called into existence by men and women whose minds were stirred by the mysterious ancient Wisdom of India or its many cultural splendours. An ever-expanding stream of writing, scholarly, popularizing or distorting, has brought this vast world of Indian spirituality and cultural achievement within the horizon of the West and made it, apart from the growing possibilities of direct contact in our planetary world of to-day, an important element in the welter of opinion and orientation in the modern West, which lived and lives through the critical period of searching for a basis of spiritual unification, which it has lost. For the last 60 years or so India herself has gradually acquired a sense of "mission" to the West and attempts in different ways to present the "hidden, true India" to the Western world, finding a willing audience amongst those who are driven either by curiosity or by sincere interest.

This is what we mean by the "Eastern Invasion", as represented by India, and the reactions and responses to it in the West. Our object is, as in the case of Buddhism, mainly to characterize the growth of this process.

William Jones, the English civil servant who became one of the first famous Indianists, published in 1789 his English translation of Kalidasa's celebrated drama: *Shakuntala*. In 1791 the German translation of Jones' work appeared and immediately evoked Herder's and Goethe's enthusiastic admiration.[1] Herder proclaimed India the miraculous country where the ideal of true *humanitas* was realized. Many of the leading Germans of his time agreed with him.

Another sign of spontaneous openness and enthusiasm can be derived from the fact that Jones' English translation of Manu's Book of Law (done in 1794) had its German translation already in 1797. The expectation of *Ex Oriente Lux*, Light out of the East, dominated the geniuses of Romanticism. The German poet Friedrich Schlegel expressed the opinion that just as one had to go to Italy in order to learn what art is, so India was the ideal place to learn what religion is. In 1808 he

[1] M. Winternitz: *Geschichte der Indischen Literatur*, Vol. I, pp. 11f., for this and the following facts. Also G. Mayer: *Die Begegnung des Christentums mit den asiatischen Religionen im Werk Hermann Hesses*, pp. 9-37, 1956.

wrote a book (provided with translations from Sanskrit) on *Ueber die Sprache und Weisheit der Inder*. It exercised a great influence but represented already a stage of his more temperate enthusiasm, because in the same year he became a convert to the Roman Catholic Church.

His brother, August Wilhelm von Schlegel, the first professor of Sanskrit in Germany, published (1823) the Bhagavad Gita in the Sanskrit text, adding a Latin translation. The great Wilhelm von Humbolt said about it: "It is probably the profoundest and the loftiest thing that the world has to show," and in his turn found it the expression of sublime *humanitas*. This spontaneous enthusiasm, in Germany, in France, in England, hangs of course together with the Romantic wave in Europe, but it is not only that. The mood in Europe was marked by a longing openness to the totality of the world and its wonders. Anquetil Duperron's Latin translation (made from a Persian one by the Mogul Prince Dara Shikoh) of the Upanishads appeared in two volumes under the title: *Oupnek'hat* (1802), and had already its German translation in 1808. Despite the clumsy double translation process, it laid hold of Schopenhauer and not only accompanied him till his death, but influenced his thinking. He declared it "the product of the highest human wisdom".

It lies outside our scope to survey the triumphant course of Indianist studies accomplished by great scholars of different Western nations. These studies have made accessible to the West and the world at large an amazing amount of original Sanskrit works from all branches of Indian literature, through translations in various languages, and have served as a basis for hosts of writings for information of the general public. These few illustrations of the initial receptivity and zeal in the West are sufficient to give some inkling of the massive thirst for knowledge and for penetration into an alien spiritual world (in many cases not only for the sake of knowledge) that was behind this magnificent enterprise. Paul Deussen (d. 1919), the famous German Indianist, specializing particularly in the Vedanta philosophy,[1] was by no means the only scholar who was at the same time an advocate of India's *philosophia perennis*. His personal concern was the ambitious undertaking to

[1] *Das System des Vedanta*, 1906. (E.T. *The Vedanta System of Philosophy*.)

demonstrate the essential religious identity of the Vedanta, the Platonic Ideas, the Bible, Kant and Schopenhauer.

It should be noted moreover that, to take a few examples only, India herself revealed her ethical-political potentialities in a man like Gandhi, who was undoubtedly one of the greatest men of our time, and her no less grand potentialities in the field of letters in Rabindranath Tagore, who is acknowledged as one of the modern world's greatest writers.[1] Men of this stature are not regarded any more as voices of India, but as voices to the world at large, especially to the West. They are figures of world dimension. This in itself indicates that the West has left behind its former provincial dimensions, and is by its approaching symbiosis with the East (which the West itself set in motion by shaking the East out of its introvert slumber), entering a new cultural dimension of more universalist quality. In Tagore's case it has recognized this by according him the Nobel Prize.

THE INFLUENCE OF TAGORE

As Gandhi has been considered in an earlier chapter, this seems the place for some remarks on Tagore's profile in world perspective.[2]

D. S. Sarma[3] aptly remarks: "If the writings of Rabindranath Tagore are a modern commentary on the Upanishads, the life of Mahatma Gandhi is the best modern commentary on the Bhagavad Gita." Tagore was a poet, a thinker and an educator. But he was foremost a poet who sang about Nature, Man and God. The inspiration he drew from a close intercourse with the Upanishads he expressed in all poetical freedom, and also when he put it in more reasoned form in his *Sadhana*. He philosophized as a poet of extraordinary sensitivity, especially for Nature, with a deep mystical tinge. He had himself a strong feeling that New India did not belong to this race or that race,

[1] In the last decades, though his fame lasts, the interest in his works has much declined.

[2] Another Indian author of world fame is the philosopher Radhakrishnan. As to literature on Tagore, we refer to: Schomerus, *op. cit.*, III, pp. 103-118; S. Estborn: *The Religion of Tagore* (1949); S. Ch. Mitter: *La Pensée de Rabindranath Tagore* (1930); D. S. Sarma: *The Renaissance of Hinduism*, pp. 341-402. Sarma reminds us quite rightly that most of Tagore's poetical output is inaccessible to us (and to most Indians), as it has only been to a very small extent translated from Bengali into English.

[3] *op. cit.*, p. 403.

this religion or that religion, but to humanity. As an educator in his centre, Shantiniketan, he gradually reached the view that the university in Shantiniketan should be a place of genuine international understanding and co-operation.

He insisted often that the way most satisfying to himself to express his religious view of the universe and man was "The Religion of Man". Notwithstanding his lively consciousness of the presence of God behind all things in the world and behind all experiences in man, he often stressed that the humanity of God or the divinity of Man, the Eternal, was his real concern. From his positive, active attitude towards life and the world it is easy to construe his thinking as a synthetic blend of Indian and Western apprehension. In his strong aversion to all that savoured of dogma or formulated creed he expressed a genuinely Indian habit of mind, but at the same time fell in with a powerful strand in the make-up of the modern Western intellectual.

Although he is, fundamentally speaking, in his ultimate views undoubtedly a genuine Indian in modern poetical fashion, he moves in his many productions in such a wide range of feelings and intuitive ideas, that the language he speaks finds outside India as much understanding as in India. Perhaps even more. It is marked by a sincerity which by its beauty of poetical expression and its ultimate vagueness in fundamentals has a wide appeal all over the world. To put it in Western categories, Tagore belongs to the cosmopolitan fraternity of great humanists, who are in our present stage of culture considered as the accredited spokesmen. In 1941, when Tagore died, the Syndicate of the University of Calcutta gave a correct appraisal in the statement:[1]

Through him India has given her message to mankind, and his unique achievements in the fields of literature, philosophy, education and art have won imperishable fame for himself and have raised the status of India in the estimation of the world.

THE THEOSOPHICAL MOVEMENT

Although when discussing Buddhism I pointed out the significance of the Theosophical Movement for its estimate in the

[1] *op. cit.*, p. 341.

West, it is impossible to pass over in silence the great significance Theosophy in general, and the Theosophical Society and Anthroposophical Movement of Steiner in particular, have had for putting India on the spiritual map of numberless people in Western countries. The history especially of the Theosophical Society proves that the Indian world in the proper sense of the word occupied a warmer place in the heart of its leaders than Buddhism. India is considered to be the most authentic guardian of the Great Tradition of secret wisdom, of esoteric science, the most understanding interpreter of the transcendent unity of all religions, which goes back to the Primitive, Primeval Tradition as it is called.

Amongst the many peculiarities of the Western Theosophical Movement, the main one is in this respect its claim to have, in its outstanding leaders, the guarantee that they have free access to the Upper Custodians, Interpreters and Directing Masters of the Primeval Tradition, that is to say the Mahatmas. Steiner has, for himself and his Anthroposophical Movement, abandoned obedience to the hierarchy of the Theosophical Society and its particular Mahatma myth, by concentrating on the science of acquiring supra-sensory knowledge of the cosmos and of the occult faculties of man, and in giving Christianity a greater place in his system by his emphasis on the central significance of Calvary. Yet the basic tenet of the Primeval Mystery Tradition with its naturalistic monism, and the important place of India's special way of guarding it, remained also his. For our purpose this is the heart of the matter in regard to the question of the influence of India in the West.[1]

It is not our purpose to offer an estimation of the intrinsic worth and truth of the Theosophical Movement. This is a matter of controversy, outside and inside the Movement, in the West and in India, especially in regard to the Theosophical Society as founded by H. P. Blavatsky. The many schisms and the numerous secessions of many prominent members furnish clear evidence. The most slashing criticism has been formulated by René Guénon, the well-known leader of the most puritan

---

[1] Since 1922 there has existed in Germany a very active *Christengemeinschaft*, which is a new "denomination". It is in principle fully anthroposophic, but with special application of an occult interpretation of Christianity and of Christ-Helios. It expresses itself in a rich liturgy and symbolism as a means of furthering the cosmic-divine process of world evolution.

school of the advocates of the Great Saving Tradition, which is concerned with pure metaphysical Truth only.[1] It is, however, written out of such bitter enmity and scorn that in spite of its rich documentation the interpretation evokes mistrust. D. S. Sarma's[2] sympathetic estimation of Theosophy's and especially Mrs. Besant's significance for India is a welcome antidote, although it does not make a really objective impression.

But whether one condemns the Theosophical Movement as an unhealthy, deleterious phenomenon or hails it as a worthy occupant of a "high place in the Kingdom of the Spirit" (Sarma), or takes a more judicious position, it is an indubitable and important fact that it has orientated many minds all over the world towards India as the land of spiritual promise. This fact is our main interest in determining reactions and responses of the West to the Eastern Invasion (in this case the Indian Invasion). Its strength is not even diminished by the argument —with which the writer fully agrees—that Western Theosophy which uses so dexterously and copiously Indian key terms (Karma, etc.) is in a high degree a Westernized distortion of the Indian system and therefore a misleading falsification, contrary to the intention "to disseminate a knowledge of the sublime teachings of that pure esoteric system of the archaic period" as it is stated in *The Golden Book of the Theosophical Society*. Keyserling's discussion[3] of this matter is fair and illuminating. He epitomizes it in the opening statement of his discussion in the words: "One can take up whatever attitude one likes to Theosophy; its service in the unlocking of the wisdom of the East is undeniable. It brings this about, though, in a form that takes from the wisdom of the East a good part of its peculiar character."

KEYSERLING AND THE INDIAN WAY

Keyserling himself is one of the clearest examples of a Western philosopher who, provided with a solid erudition in

[1] See his: *Le Théosophisme. Histoire d'une pseudo-religion*, 1921. Mark the pejorative "théosophisme"!

[2] *op. cit.*, pp. 193-227. Sarma's opinion is that India has ample reason to be grateful to Theosophy. This is entirely different from the picture Guénon gives of its position in India. He describes it mainly as being there an object of hate and mistrust.

[3] *op. cit.*, I, pp. 127-191.

Eastern philosophies and religions, and therefore often remarkably balanced in his judgments on different cultures (Western culture included), finds himself fully at home in the genuinely Indian way of apprehension of life and its ultimate questions. The first volume of his *Reisetagebuch* contains numberless eloquent pages in praise of India's exceptional power of spiritual creation. In this case he shows not only his remarkable faculties of empathy, but a distinct inner affinity and congeniality of spirit, although he remains fully conscious of being a European and therefore historically conditioned in a way different from the Indian. His book is certainly one of the best phenomenological estimates of Hinduism that has ever been produced.

Most of the time, however, he speaks as a philosopher, as a metaphysician who sees the meaning of life for himself in attaining to a self-realization adequate to his own peculiar individuality. Hinduism at its best and profoundest has, in his opinion, spoken the only relevant truth about the way to self-realization in the full sense of the word. India's version of gnosis[1] (*jñāna*): "Self-realization is God-realization", "Gnosis *is* (not brings) salvation", is its eternal Gospel. "None but the gnostic [in the Indian sense] can afford to look down on all prejudices" (I, p. 125). The wisdom of the Hindus is that from the metaphysical point of view one should not take any phenomenal form seriously, but at the same time one should consider all these forms as having empirically speaking a right of existence. This metaphysical pragmatism of India's best thinkers and saints is Keyserling's delight. Western and Indian philosophy cannot be put in comparison. They are utterly different in intention. The Western art of thinking consists in induction, deduction, differentiating, integrating. Indian thinking aims at something quite different, that is to say to transcend to concrete stages of consciousness. As a philosopher he concludes that India, not Europe, has produced the profoundest metaphysic and the most perfect religious system there are, as yet. On this background it is understandable that he says (*op. cit.*, I, 200, after his very appreciative appraisal of Buddha and Buddhism) in comparing it with the classic Indian way of

---

[1] Indian "gnosis" should not be understood in the sense which the word has in Church history. Gnosticism and Gnosis must be kept apart.

Gnosis: Buddhism is a degeneration; in Buddhism the most philosophical people on earth has abnegated philosophy.[1]

As a man of the dynamic West he says that the unique profundity of Indian Gnosis has done harm to the Indians as a people, because their too-profound insight has paralysed their zest for action.[2]

During the period after the First World War Keyserling's books attracted great interest, especially in Germany. The *Schule der Weisheit* in Darmstadt became his forum and channelled Indian wisdom into the stream of cultural life. It has not lasted very long. Apart from Theosophy and Anthroposophy, which naturally had also their ups and downs but have lasted since they appeared on the scene, many movements or personalities that have mediated Eastern influence have been like waves, rising from and subsiding into the sea of general life. This phenomenon should not, however, mislead us into taking this in the first place as a sign of their ephemeral character, dependent on shifting psychological situations. They do leave their sediments in the ceaselessly moving cultural "conscious" and "sub-conscious" of the West. In this lies the significance of men like Keyserling and others, who act, even though they maintain their own physiognomy, as conducting-wires of the Eastern "current".

UNIVERSAL RELIGION

Planned and sustained action, issuing from India itself, actually started after Vivekananda's appearance at the World Parliament of Religion in Chicago (1893). The bulk of this action is, as to its organizational form, still modest. The Ramakrishna Mission (see above) is its chief organ. This modern Hindu monastic fraternity combines advocacy of the a-cosmic idealist Vedantic position with an attitude of activity and responsibility in this phenomenal world. The Swamis, who represent the Ramakrishna Mission, have a preference for cosmopolitan urban centres. They are conspicuous, especially in America, moving in the society of the recognized intelligentsia and raising their voice in the ongoing debates. Again, the modest bulk of their activity should not deceive us into thinking that their influence is negligible. Their irradiation reaches far

[1] *op. cit.*, I, p. 358.   [2] p. 353.

more people, of very different descriptions, than one is inclined to imagine.[1]

In spoken and literary form the Swamis in America freely join in the discussions on the so-called burning spiritual issues of the day. It strikes one immediately when listening to them or reading them that they have great ability in adapting themselves to the current cultural idiom used in such discussions and consultations, the groundswell nevertheless remaining truly Indian. As a whole, however, it looks like a lofty kind of religious Humanism. E.g. the symposia of the conferences on science, philosophy and religion, which give so to speak a yearly exhibition of the chaotic multiformity of the concerns of America's intelligentsia, in search for more unity and sense of direction, yield interesting examples of the tone of the Swamis' participation. Swami Nikhilanda for instance has in the 10th Symposion a contribution on: "The need for a spiritual revival." The gist of this contribution is that the human situation to-day calls for an intense spiritual revival on a broad humanistic, ethical and rational basis.[2]

The transcendental experience of religion, says Nikhilanda, must breathe a new life and vision into the political, economic and social affairs of a weary and distracted humanity.[3] Religion is to be understood in the sense of Universal Religion, which cannot be an eclectic faith compounded of all the beautiful elements in every religion. For it need not be created; it is the core of all religion.[4] The salvation of the Christians, the Hindus, the Muslims, the Jews and the Buddhists lies through their respective faiths.[5] A genuine religious preacher should try to deepen people's faith in their respective religious traditions, of which the Universal Religion is the essence. Ritual and mythology are a necessary part of all religions, but only for the beginners. The formula for the relative relevance of the various religions and their essential oneness in the Universal Religion is: variety in unity.

[1] This is undoubtedly so in America. One can easily verify it by moving in these cosmopolitan circles.

[2] This is good American language.

[3] One can recognize here Radhakrishnan's "message" to the West, found in many of his books.

[4] This is the specific thesis of Neo-Hinduism and Neo-Vedantism.

[5] This represents also Hindu theory of Religion.

In the 10th Symposion he approaches the present predicament from a somewhat different but fundamentally similar angle. He offers there his view on the soul and says that our present predicament asks for the wisdom that lies hidden in the soul of man to overcome it; and starts from that to explain the philosophy of *tat tvam asi*. Man is the builder of his own destiny and the captain of his own soul. The one goal of the many paths is the realization of God-consciousness. The practical rule for the realization of a Universal Religion is not to organize a new sect, but to have positive reverence for the ideas of other religions and attain the goal along one's own path. It is the *democratic* way of religion. (Italics mine).

This "live and let live" approach to the problem of religion and of the different religions has certainly a great appeal to hosts of people to-day. Well considered, it takes the crux out of the problem by making the whole problem problemless and it can serve as an ideal example for a similar problemless solution of the question of *cultural* pluralism, with which so many parts of the world are confronted. Moreover, as an annotator on Nikhilanda's contribution puts it in an unconsciously self-revelatory way, this problemless solution of cultural and religious plurality excludes the "demand for a choice as a violation of one's integrity".

These quotations from Swami Nikhilanda make a fitting close to an estimate of the Eastern Invasion in its Indian form in the West. For this ongoing Indian influence is undoubtedly one of the main factors (there are other factors too) that have caused in so many Western minds a well-nigh spontaneous affirmation of the idea that all religions *are* essentially one and *have* the same goal, and that consequently the relativistic "live and let live" thesis is the only sensible and irrefutable wisdom. Moreover, it looks like the easiest and cheapest solution of the problem of the plurality of religions. One by-passes painlessly the deeper challenge hidden in this plurality.

ISLAM IN THE WEST

The Eastern Invasion in the West under the form of the presence of Islam in the Western world differs in most respects from what has had to be said about Buddhism and Hinduism. Outwardly the contact of the Islamic with the Western world has moved and moves along the same two main lines. That is to say, the study of Western Orientalist scholarship has enabled us to get a real grasp of the Muslim world in its historical development and its inner meaning. The concrete contact with the Muslim world has steadily grown since the beginning of the 19th century, and the output of a vast literature, of graded quality, has made knowledge of Islam as a religion and culture accessible to everyone who is eager to know. Numberless series of lectures on Islam in the past and the present by competent scholars, published as books, satisfy the needs for knowledge and insight.

Since the beginning of the 20th century especially "Muslim Missions" have appeared on the scene in Europe and America; or Movements having their origins in the Muslim world contribute to the chequered picture of Western spiritual life, drawing Western people into acceptance of Muhammad's Revelation, or, in many cases, away from definite allegiance to the Christian Faith.

When we probe somewhat deeper, however, a great difference from the impact of Hindu and Buddhist ways of thinking in the West becomes apparent. A difference the more striking because in comparison with the Indian and Buddhist world, Europe particularly had, by contacts, study and publication acquired since the 17th century a fair amount of knowledge and appreciation of the Muslim world as a result of its expansionist dynamism in the stagnant Mediterranean section of that world. This expansionist dynamism manifested itself cautiously in the 17th and 18th centuries, but became very determined in the 19th by its political and economic penetration in the Muslim world.

The first spate of self-achieved acquaintance with the faith and institutions of Islam seemed to augur a response to Islam at least as expectant as India and Buddhism met in the 19th century. It is a well-known fact that in 18th century France, bearing a revolution in her womb and going through the glorious experience of the New Age of Man inaugurated by the "Enlightenment", the figure of the Prophet Muhammad as a political hero and the pre-supposed rationality of purely monotheistic Islam were welcomed with enthusiastic acclaim. In comparison with this, Christianity was discounted. In the heyday of Romanticism Muslim mysticism, especially as exquisitely voiced in the great Persian Sufi poets, found a congenial appeal above all in Germany and a magnificent interpreter in the orientalist poet H. Rückert. A leading theologian of the day (F. A. G. Tholuck) published the first valuable treatise on Muslim mysticism under the title: *Sufismus sive Theosophia Persarum pantheistica* (1821). Goethe, super-sensitive as ever, derived inspiration in his *West-östlicher Divan* from many first-fruits of Persian poetry.

Yet the difference in impact and appeal between the Indian and Buddhist world on one side and Islam on the other must be maintained. Generally speaking, it has to be stated that Islam and what it represents, although in some respects arousing deserved admiration (particularly in regard to its artistic achievements) did not become a *ferment* in the Western mind. It remained chiefly an object of knowledge, curiosity and some-times admiration without commitment. It seems not to exercise that mysterious attraction which issues from the region of great Asian cultures and religions.

France, which in the history of the last centuries has entered into closer relations with the Muslim world than any other Western country, adopts sometimes a warmer tone of sympathy and manifests a concern for the mutual understanding of the Islamic and Western worlds which deserves wider participation. One example is *L'Islam et l'Occident* (1947).[1] It shows this concern and sympathy, but nevertheless the highest point to which it attains is that Islam may deliver a contribution to the new Humanism, which is the hope for the future of a multi-cultural existence of the world as the contributors envisage it.

APPRECIATION OF ISLAM

What is the reason for this quite different response to the Islamic world in comparison with the other components of the Eastern Invasion? This question is the more intriguing because in geographical and historical respect the Islamic and the Western "Christian" worlds are far nearer to one another than the West and the great Asian cultures and religions. They are not only near, they are neighbours. Since its appearance as a factor in world history, Islam has lived in constant contact of

[1] *Cahiers du Sud.*

attraction and repulsion with the Western world. We have analysed the great significance of the Islamic world in the cultural development of Europe, and duly emphasized that Islam has developed on the basis of the same Hellenistic cultural background as the West, whereas the great Asian cultures and religions are not only alien to this heritage, but have completely different roots and developments from both, the West and Islam. Everything seems to speak in favour of a more spontaneous openness to the Islamic world than in any other case of Eastern Invasion. But the facts clearly contradict this (in itself) plausible presupposition. This amazing conclusion demonstrates the danger of emptiness, so often appearing in theoretical cultural speculations, because the splendour of their seemingly profound statements leaves too much out of account the concreteness, often the harsh concreteness, of historical reality.

The answer to the query as to the reason for the different response to the Islamic world in comparison with the other components of the Eastern Invasion, lies exactly in that same geographical, historical and cultural-spiritual propinquity and neighbour-ship.

Islam as a religion is in its origin unthinkable without the existence and example of Judaism and Christianity. Its original inspiration is even prophetic in a sense also inherent in Judaism and Christianity. In its Divine Law Islam has a specially defined relation to both, based on elements in the Koran. To make a long complicated story, which can be reconstructed from the Koran, very brief, Islam as the only "post-Christian" world religion has from the outset a dual attitude towards Christianity, the "religion" of the West. It knows about its spiritual relatedness to it,[1] but at the same time it stands to it in an attitude of militant distance because of Christianity's allegedly idolatrous conception of God and its being bound to a corrupted Book of Revelation.

The geographical propinquity animated by the antagonistic affinity just indicated has led to a common history around the Mediterranean, full of contact but still fuller of conflict. Conflicts which have left bitter memories, still living or dormant

[1] One of the sincerest examples is the great stress in Islam on its deep reverence for Jesus as one of the major prophets.

to-day in the Muslim world. The victorious rise of the West to world-hegemony, which is now in rapid decline, has in the West effaced these memories of conflict and dread. They are described in the history books and so do not fall into complete oblivion.

When the West acquired by its own initiative, through its great scholars in Arabic and Islam, a solid knowledge of the Islamic world and its constitutive forces and principles, the Islamic world was greatly debilitated and, contrary to its position in the Middle Ages, underwent new experiences of humiliation by the West, deepening the bitterness and resentment already accumulated from the past. At the same time it had to sustain the shock of the Western Invasion and struggle for the right adjustment, about which we have written above. In brief, the relation Islam-Western world[1] is one of the most thorny questions of the present time and needs far more studious and sympathetic attention than the little it gets.

These facts, although already treated at their due place in this book, have to be recalled summarily[2] in order to come to the point under consideration, that is to say: why in the West this far more reserved reaction and response to Islam and what it represents, than to the alien worlds of India and the Far East?

In the opinion of the writer, the greater knowledge of and the many contacts with the Islamic world have fortunately dispelled much ignorance and prejudice in regard to Islam and what it means. They have opened the way for many to deeper and sincerer appreciation of Islam as a spiritual and cultural entity, and of its important rôle in history. But, though rarely formulated or consciously meant, Islam as a world of spiritual truth and value is not felt to be of the same rank and calibre as the other great representative cultures and religions of the

---

[1] This is not in the first place meant in the political sense of the West and the Arab world. To succeed in arranging Round Tables of Muslims and Christians, where the discussion of no subject is banned and candidness can get free play, is still a rare occurrence. Hence the significance of such endeavours as "Bahamdun", "Toumliline" and the experiments in contact by "Cimade".

[2] An attempt at an exhaustive treatment of determining factors is not intended here. To do that one would have to write a book on the different phases of appreciation of Islam amongst the several generations of Orientalists; on the complicated political and cultural relations of the West and the Islamic world in the 19th and 20th centuries, and their consequences. It has led to a real, baffling tangle.

world. Notwithstanding various expressions of striking originality in some points of religion and art, its message and what is attached to it in various ways appeal by passionateness of expression but not by depth or originality of content. Therefore it does not arouse that mood of expectancy of new spiritual adventure, which rightly or wrongly lures thousands towards the quest for the experience of the mystery of self-realization or God-realization as promised in the great Asian religions. The West has certainly become conscious of the debt of gratitude it owes to the great cultural service the Islamic world has rendered it at a certain stage of its history, but it knows also that this service was, properly speaking, providing the West with the missing link to connect it with its own mother-culture, and not the transmission of deeper religious truth. Nor does it seem to hear a tone of deeper religious truth in Islam to-day.

This explains why one cannot really speak of any worthwhile action of *Western* people, who are gripped in such a way by Islam that they become active and organized interpreters and advocates of it as has been described in relation to Buddhism and the Indian world. Islam's uncompromising exclusiveness over against Buddhist and Indian harmonizing inclusiveness is definitely alien to the temper of the modern mind.

There are, to be sure, many books, mainly written in French or English by Muslim authors on Islam, but as H. A. R. Gibbs observes rightly[1] they are almost all apologetic works, composed "with the object of defending Islam and demonstrating its conformity with what their writers believe to be present-day thought". They present Islam, in all sincerity, as the original fountain and the sole fulfilment of current dominant ideas and ideals of the West or what they consider to be such. The effect of these books is not great and rarely creates converts. It consists mainly in the fact that a certain number of Western intellectuals derive from such books a more sympathetic view of Islam, hitherto unsuspected. That may be in itself a good thing, but the wrong effect is that they conceive a distorted idea of Islam's real content and problems. If such Western intellectuals belong to the category of writers on the general cultural situation of the world, they often use these distorted ideas in regard to the function and contribution of the

[1] In Preface (p. ix) to his *Modern Trends in Islam*, 1947.

Islamic world in this situation without realizing that they are indulging in wishful thinking.

The apologetic aim of these books by Muslim writers is quite understandable, because they are deeply hurt by the prejudice and misunderstanding about Islam reigning in the Western world. They want to remove the stain of inferiority from Islam, which manifests itself in that prejudice and misunderstanding, and demonstrate its right to equality, if not superiority, amongst the religions of the world by its "progressiveness". In a certain sense these are literary "missionary" endeavours, although such views represent only those of small groups in the Muslim world. Yet their activity is by no means looked upon with disfavour by their co-religionists, because they regard with favour every act that can contribute to the "honour of Islam".

Looking at the authentic Muslim world as a whole, it must be said, however, that (again different from what we observed about the Buddhist and Indian world) it does not entertain any conscious missionary activity in the West. Islam at the present day is spreading rapidly in Africa south of the Sahara. This needs to be said, in order to obviate any wrong impression that Islam is not a missionary religion. It is even at present one of the most active and successful missionary religions in the world, particularly in Africa, but also in some other parts. But in the Western world "orthodox" Islam does not perform any missionary action.

ISLAM'S MISSIONARY MOVEMENT

Yet there are Muslim missionary activities in the West, but strangely enough by groups that are excluded from or only half-heartedly included in the fold of "orthodox" Islam. These missionary activities are enthusiastically carried on by the Ahmadiyya movement. The Ahmadiyya (since 1890 officially called in the Indian Census a "Muslim sect") is a new movement which had its origin in the Punjab (India). Its founder was Mirza Ghulam Ahmad (d. 1908), who proclaimed himself a new Prophet, the Mahdi or Expected Messiah of Islam, an incarnation (*avatar*) of Jesus[1] and of Krishna and therefore the

---

[1] A special doctrinal variation of the Ahmadiyya is that Jesus, not having died on the Cross, wandered to Kashmir to preach the Gospel. At the age of 120 years He died there. His grave is to be found in the vicinity of Srinagar and has been falsely called after a prophet Juz Asaf.

final universal Prophet, the Unifier of Islam, Christianity and Hinduism. His second doctrinal deviation from Islam was that he emphatically asserted that the Muslim doctrine of the Holy War (*jihad*) has to be conceived in a pacific and not a military way. For the rest the Ahmadi conception of Islam follows the traditional view. He aroused much opposition by his heretical breach with Muhammad's final Prophethood, which is one of the main pillars of historic Islam. His energetic personality and his dynamism in propagandistic activity gained him a considerable following, foremost in India (Punjab), but also in Afghanistan, Persia, etc. They are, however, *in* the Muslim world itself an entirely separate community with its own mosques, courts and doctrinal authority (at present the son of the founder, the second Khalifa or Vicar of his father the Prophet founder, is the doctrinal authority). They are not recognized by orthodox Islam as part of the *umma*, the Muslim Community of all ages. They are considered heterodox, which makes their existence, especially in Pakistan, sometimes difficult.[1]

The spirit of their tenets and the militant vigour of their founder have made the Ahmadiyya naturally a group with strong missionary and reforming zeal, both inside the lands of Islam where they are represented and outside. They constitute almost exclusively the "Muslim Missions" in Western countries and elsewhere, about which one so often reads in the Western press. They devote themselves with sincere enthusiasm to the task of proclaiming Islam to the world in a rationalist, often combative way, and try in Muslim lands to purify and reform the dominant type of popular Islam.

The Ahmadiyya have split into two groups, each with its own centre. One of these groups, more concerned about solidarity and unity with historic Islam, though holding "advanced" views, broke away after the founder's death and established its headquarters in Lahore under the leadership of Khwaja Kamal ad-Din and Maulvi Muhammad Ali. They repudiated the founder's claim to prophethood and recognized him as a Renovator or Reformer (*mujaddid*) only. By this stand

[1] See W. Cantwell Smith, *Islam in Modern History*, on this matter, and the important 1953 Commission's Report on the disturbances that broke out in Pakistan against the Ahmadiyya.

they consequently rejected the authority of the founder's Khalifa, and embarked on their own strategy of proclaiming Islam to the world in a fashion which combines militancy and a liberalized interpretation of Islam, directed towards the West as they understand it. They have shed all traces of Ahmadiyya doctrinal peculiarities. Maulvi Muhammad Ali's translation of the Koran (entitled *The Holy Quran*) is by its interpretative way of translation and its exegesis, as well as its introduction on "The Religion of Islam", very helpful for understanding their spirit and their specific brand of Islam.

Their name, "Ahmadiyya Anjuman i Isha 'at al-Islam" (the Ahmadiyya Association for the Propagation of Islam) reveals their missionary aim and ardour. They deploy an energetic activity, particularly by literary propaganda, by translation work and by building mosques in great urban centres. These Lahori Ahmadis, as they are called, work mostly outside their place of origin, India. They work in England, continental Europe (especially Germany and Holland), America, and South, East, and West Africa.

The other group, who are called Qadiani after their centre Qadian[1] in the Punjab, have remained faithful to the peculiar Ahmadiyya doctrines, especially in regard to the founder. They are as arduously missionary as the Lahori, in England, America and continental Europe, though not so widespread, but are more active within the Muslim world than their schismatic brethren.

Both groups give, to put it mildly, a misleading picture of Islam. They stress its rationality and humanism. This stress appeals to a certain type of Westerner who is weary of the "complexity" of Christianity. In their activities in the West, both groups zealously seek contact with non-Muslims of all classes, love debate, and are not without results although these so far have been modest. A noteworthy thing in regard to both, as with the Muslim writers we referred to above, is that many orthodox Muslims, although mistrusting and repudiating them as heretics *within the fold*, appreciate them as protagonists of Islam in the Western world. Heretics though they may be, they contribute in this way to the honour and glory of Islam and that, in itself, is meritorious.

---

[1] It was the centre and headquarters established by the founder. At present the centre is Rabwa.

BAHA'ISM AND SUFI

Before closing this chapter we ought to touch lightly upon two influences working in the Western world, viz. Baha'ism and the Sufi Movement of Shaikh Inayat Khan.

The former has its main centre of activity in the United States (e.g. the beautiful House of Worship at Wilmette, Illinois, near Evanston), but there are Baha'i to be found all over the world. Baha'ism originally hailed from a revival movement in Shi'ite Islam in Iran, about 1850, a kind of mystical Messianism with political overtones. This had its roots in ancient developments in Shi'ite Islam, in which Neo-platonism entered into a strange marriage with Muslim allegorism. The movement in Iran (called the Babi Movement) of c. 1850 turned into Baha'ism, and had a tortuous history leading to what it has become to-day.

This modern development goes back to 1908, which means that what now goes by the name of Baha'ism has nothing whatever to do with Islam, nor claims a special relation to it. In that respect it differs from the Ahmadiyya. No genuine Muslim would dream of claiming Baha'ism as Islamic. Its adherents call it "the Baha'i World Faith" and proclaim it as the universal religion in which all religions can meet, being all founded on teachings of great men who were the "Manifesta-tions" of the one God. On account of this basic unity of all religions, unfolding God in progressive stages, the Baha'i Faith proclaims the one God, the one world and the one world order of justice and brotherhood.

Baha'ism, though entirely emancipated from Islam and by its propagation not in the least representing a Muslim endeavour in the Western world, deserves nevertheless to be mentioned in the context of this chapter. For it is, in the last instance, an unrecognizable offshoot of a variety in Islam which had an esoteric, mystical character. Therefore Baha'ism's claim to universality, and the religious-philosophical theory by which it is motivated, are entirely alien to genuine Islam but of the same stuff as the esoteric wisdom from India and the Far East. This accounts for the fact that Baha'ism is not laboriously propa-gated by Oriental advocates, but its pushing power in organiza-tion and propaganda comes from Americans and Europeans, that is to say Westerners, just as in the case of Buddhism and Indian spirituality.

The same observations have to be made in regard to the Sufi Movement, which finds followers everywhere in the Western world. Remotely of course this movement reaches back to that powerful mystical stream in Islam called Sufism, which after long hesitation was accepted, within certain limits, as part of orthodox Islam. Despite the origin of its first leader, Inayat Khan, from India, the Sufi Movement is in no respect whatever a Muslim missionary outreach. By its mystic tone and solemnity, however, it appeals to many people in the West who are seeking for a spiritual dimension in their lives and cannot find it within the orbit of ecclesiastical Christianity. It is a sign of the spiritual indigence of Western culture and of the Christian Church, or perhaps one should rather say of the failure of Western culture and the Christian Church to manifest their true, inner resources, that so many caravans from the East such as this Sufi Movement or the Krishnamurti Movement, etc., supply the required goods in the desert of modern life.

The reader will possibly have noticed that in the present contact between the Islamic and the Western worlds all propagandist religious activity, in so far as it has its origin or background in Islam, comes from *Indian* Islam, not *Arab* Islam. This leads to a concluding remark of great importance.

Not only have we the right, but the facts simply compel us, to speak of an "Eastern Invasion" in the West. It does not matter that it has been brought about by the activity and eagerness of the West itself. The fact remains that the peculiar spirit, the dynamic, the motive forces and the achievements of the great Eastern cultures, religions and philosophies occupy a place, play a rôle, co-determine the chaotic multilogue in which the Western world finds itself, groping in the dark towards an undefined and indefinable new unity of life. Nobody can tell exactly how far this occupying a place, this playing a rôle, goes. We have no methods or instruments for measuring it. But the fact is there.

In regard to Islam, however, a restrictive modification is needed. The term "invasion" (by the Islamic world, culturally and spiritually, in the West) must to a great extent be modified towards "acquisition of a more solid and understanding knowledge of the Muslim world". The reasons for this modification have been given above. Islam as a culture and as a religion has not, as the Indian and Far Eastern cultures and religions have done in a way still indefinable, put its leaven into the "lump" of amorphous modern world culture. In that respect the Islamic world is still an isolated monolith.

Nevertheless, in a quite different and very serious sense, the Western world is really *invaded* by the Muslim world. The present Western world, as a result of all that has happened on Western initiative to the Muslim world, is invaded by the Muslim world in this sense: that this awakened giant, un-chained by our own efforts,[1] has on account of its geographical and historical propinquity and its world-central significance a special call on the West's responsible concern. The Muslim world, especially the Arab Muslim world, *invades* the Western world by its sheer position[2] with a claim for an attitude of greater moral responsibility. This is an "invasion" of a different order, but an inescapable one, as inescapable as the ongoing meeting of East and West. Therefore it should also occupy a place, play a rôle and co-determine the chaotic multilogue of the West.

[1] It does not matter whether these efforts intended this unchaining or not.

[2] Again, it does not matter whether the Muslim world *makes* this claim. Made or unmade, it arises out of the world-historical situation, *and is there.*

Chapter Ten

THE SIGNIFICANCE OF THE POLITICAL REVOLUTION IN ASIA SINCE WORLD WAR II AND OF THE RESURGENCE OF THE NON-CHRISTIAN RELIGIONS

THE cataclysmic close of the "colonial era", the defeat of Japan in its gigantic effort to become in the name of Asia the dominant world power, the accession of the colossus China to the Communist realm, the feverish endeavours of the new independent peoples to become coherent nations and reasonably durable States and recognized members of the political world "community", are events of the greatest import for the cultural and religious development of Asia and for the relations and dialogue between East and West. Everything in this field has acquired an accelerated rhythm and emphasis, a greater acerbity and possibility for explosive conflict, but simultaneously a wider range of positive possibility and actualization of potentialities. Therefore in the title of this chapter this political revolution and its significance has been combined with the religio-cultural resurgence, not—this should be said emphatically—because this resurgence will be presented as a mere aspect of the political, but to indicate the vast field in and through which this political revolution works itself out.

It is, therefore, necessary first to devote special consideration to this political revolution.[1]

We are living at present through a world situation, of which it cannot be said too often that it is unprecedented, however monotonous this repetitious assertion may sound. This fact gets the more weight because we are only beginning to become aware of it, disturbed, shocked and bewildered as we may be

[1] The following pages contain part of a contribution I gave in a Colloquium on Inter-religious Relationships (May 23-25, 1957) but with various alterations and additions. This contribution has appeared in *Civilisations* Vol. VII (1957), No. 4, pp. 557-570.

by the endless political unrest in the world. The amount of imagination, even more than knowledge, which is needed to absorb, digest and disentangle this fact, is simply staggering. Yet somehow we must produce it, because this unprecedented situation undoubtedly will develop in an increasing way its foreseeable inherent consequences, and so be the matrix for the future in which we have to shape and express our attitudes and decisions in the realm of global inter-relationships and mutual responsibility. It must be said that a new ethics of world responsibility is due.

ASIA'S POLITICAL REVOLUTION

Immediately after the Second World War the map of the world underwent changes to an unbelievable degree. So did the interplay of powers and interests in the world, to express it very mildly. The main points to be kept in mind here are the following. They concern Asia, Africa and the dimensions of the ideological and power conflict between the Communist and the so-called "free" Western world.

The lightning-like change of a great part of Asia from the status of being colonies of Western powers to the status of political independence and sovereignty is a fact of incalculable importance. These important parts of Asia, including the Near and Middle East which had already, as a result of the First World War, reached officially the stage of emancipation from colonial or semi-independent status, have suddenly become a crucial factor in the development of world affairs and world events. Although this is common knowledge, it is only partly realized how startling this fact is. Till the Second World War, Asia (with the exception of Japan and its pan-Asian aspirations, and to a limited extent of China) was in world politics, in spite of the difficulties the "colonial" powers had in the countries under their control, an appendix of the Western powers and nothing more. It had no power, influence or voice in its own right. The decisions for the direction or mis-direction of world affairs lay with the West, with London, Paris, The Hague. The Asian countries mainly constituted pieces in the game of Western politics.

Since the great landslide towards independence broke loose in 1947 with the independence of India, this fantastic situation has radically altered. There is ample support for the thesis that suddenly the world in this respect has become, instead of Europe-centred, Asia- and Africa-centred. If not always completely, at any rate virtually so. Notwithstanding the undeniably central place of the U.S.A. in world affairs, it is possible to defend the thesis that the world has shifted from Europe-centredness not to America-centredness but to Asia- and Africa-centredness. The Bandung Conference is one of the most conspicuous signs of this new situation. Asia and Africa have "come of age". There may be a difference of opinion whether this is really so, but the truth is that they not only behave as if they have come of age, but it is a political fact that they are being and have to be treated as such.

It is pertinent to this colossal change to recall the fact that in 1945, even amongst the most "progressive" experts on Eastern matters, hardly anybody foresaw this abrupt change from colonial or semi-colonial status to independence and world-shaking significance. Most of these experts talked and thought in terms of progressive, gradually speeded-up programmes of constitutional schemes, heading for a nearby terminal of independence and continuing relationship between the erstwhile dominant power and the new emerging independent countries. There was little awareness of the elemental, subterranean powers that operated and continue to operate in the Asian and African world; a new, irresistible *élan vital*, which is the fundamental source of the sudden reshaping of the pattern of world forces and of the no less sudden shift in their respective quantity of weight and emphasis in the total balance of world relations.

ASIA AND AFRICA—THE WORLD CENTRE

The startling character of this Asia- and Africa-centredness is not weakened but rather strengthened by the fact that the sudden importance of Asia and Africa looks very incongruous in the light of the other undeniable fact, that neither Asia nor Africa can derive this prominence from their inherent power, as e.g. America and Russia derive therefrom naturally their first-rank place in world affairs. On the contrary. Viewed from this angle of inherent power, they ought rather to have a *secondary* significance. All the newly emerged States, the one more, the other less, are struggling hard to become politically and economically viable propositions, and represent little power in the realistic sense this word has in world affairs. This "weakness", which sets them mostly in the category bearing the resented name of "under-developed or backward countries", demonstrates paradoxically the point that has to be stressed in the interest of a fearless and realistic estimate of the global situation. That is to say that the revolutionary plasticity, first of Asia, but also of Africa, and the stirring of the elemental, solution-demanding aspirations of these awakened and awakening giants, is the hidden, determining factor in the development of world events of our day. The whole world is in the same boat, and it is in Asia and Africa that the future of Europe and America is decided.

The spectacle gets a truly awesome quality when we recognize two facts. The first is that these elemental forces are still ambiguous, in the sense that they can prove to be either creative or destructive. Nobody can tell. The second is that, humanly speaking, their largely creative or destructive or mixed effect will mainly depend on the wisdom, understanding or folly of the Western white world in handling the situation. In having to handle it, *together with* Asia and Africa, not for and on behalf of them but *with* them, the Western world is simply faced with the outcome of its own handiwork. For the stormy penetration of the West, with its quite different patterns of political, economic, social and cultural behaviour and organization, into the worlds of Asia and Africa is the biggest cause of the great and turbulent awakening.

However, another aspect needs special mention in order to see in its full range the global situation in which the issue of inter-religious, inter-cultural relationships has to function. South-East Asia, the Middle and Near East, Africa, form the huge area where the stubborn struggle of Communism to become the world power will be decided. A special discussion of the ideological and political magnetism exerted, especially on the peoples of Asia and Africa, by Russian and Chinese Communism is for our purpose superfluous. But the fact must be emphasized as being of paramount importance. There are no direct dealings with Communist China in the same way as with the rest of Asia and with Africa. But the reality of China, in process of modernization, looms large in the whole situation. Already it is clear, and it will become increasingly clearer in the future, that China is destined to be one of the great world powers.

For the time being, however, this fact "Communism" is one of the main contributors to the Asia- and Africa-centredness of the whole world. Here is the main battlefield between the powers and aspirations of the Communist and the so-called "free" world. Apart from all other considerations, to which we have alluded, it is the deathless competition between the Communist and Western world for the soul of Asia and Africa that makes these continents and the destinies of their countries so pivotal in world politics, in spite of their relative weakness and youthful instability. As everybody understands, it is due to this set-up that a man like Pandit Nehru, with his outstanding qualities, is a world statesman; that the concept of "neutralism" is so agonizingly discussed; and that the Arab world—in itself such a fragile and febrile structure—is so persistently wooed.

The great fact of the Western penetration in Asia and Africa has had revolutionary spiritual consequences. In the preceding chapters we have tried to give a summary view of its magnitude and consequences in the field of culture and religion. If ever there was an opportunity to learn the crucial importance of political and economic factors and ideas for the cultural and religious areas of life, it is now. After what has been said in preceding chapters, it is superfluous to enter into the notable fact that the Western Invasion in its colonial guise meant not only a political and economic conquest, but also a spiritual conquest by the work of Western orientalist research. This brought about not only a discovery by the West of new spiritual worlds and dimensions, but rather unexpectedly a reawakening and new self-discovery of the Eastern cultures and religions.

THE QUEST FOR STABILITY

Keeping in mind what has been said in preceding chapters about the three "epics", it must be added that the revolutionary turn in Asia's rôle and significance in the whole content of world affairs immediately after the Second World War has furnished the entire cultural and religious situation in Asia with quite new traits. Independence meant and means the great quest for stable nationhood and statehood; the peoples of Asia and Africa are taking their destiny as nations and states, which was for such a long time in alien hands, into their own hands. This naturally impelled and impels towards a no less feverish quest for bases, for foundations to build the new structures upon. Or, to put it in a different way, in the face of widely different grades of educational and spiritual background—in many of the countries concerned this is the usual case—one seeks for a cement of inner cohesiveness. A cement that can hold together the various layers of upper-class and middle-class people and the masses of the poor and illiterate, giving them a common aspiration, inspiration and goal.

Again, this quest led and leads naturally back to the ancient spiritual and cultural heritages. And the quest is now wholly their own quest, undertaken on their own responsibility. This, in brief, is responsible for what during recent years has been analysed and discussed as the resurgence of the great non-Christian religions. One can also say that this quite understandable development, just because it is intertwined with political and national reasons and aspirations, especially the aspiration to become fully equal partners in the "community" of nations, tends to put the religions and cultures in the non-Christian world into the rôle of an ideology.

This resurgence is, for life's sake, seeking renewed rootage in the common great religio-cultural tradition, and responding to the imperative need of strongly affirmative self-identification. This implies re-interpretation and new self-expression, which stresses, in a way more fresh and vigorous than has long been seen in the world, the claim of universality, of equality with the other great cultures and religions; or, by preference, superiority. Hence the many evidences of a newly awakened sense of cultural and religious mission. Formerly the instances of cultural and religious mission from the East were, to be sure, not unknown to Europe and America. To-day, however, it may be said that it becomes more a conscious and even provocative programme. In the present world of religious pluralism and of growing secularism in East and West, we see the unprecedented spectacle of the *real meeting and encounter of the great religions and cultures* of the East and of the West—not only in books or conferences and retreat centres, but as an inescapable coming to grips with each other as a result of the no less inescapable interpenetration we begin to discern.

This cultural and religious resurgence is by the nature of the case, and by the circumstances in which it emerges, often rather strongly self-assertive and militant. To make this self-assertive and militant tone understandable, one need only remind one-self that it follows upon a long period of a deeply felt and resented sense of humiliation in the face of the proud over-bearing West and all it represented.

CONTINUITY AS WELL AS RESURGENCE

After these first general comments on Resurgence, it is necessary to enter into greater detail. Some preliminary remarks, how-ever, are needed. First, the way in which at present it is often spoken and written about sounds too much as if it is a sudden upsurge and something quite new. The new element in it will come in for consideration, but, while giving this all the stress due to it, the line of continuity should not be forgotten.

The analysis which has been presented thus far in the pre-ceding chapters has demonstrated sufficiently that during the era of colonial or semi-colonial dependence much has happened in India, China, Japan, the Islamic world that can justly be called a renaissance or recapture of indigenous belief and pride in one's own religious and cultural heritage. The intellectual élite in particular, whether conservative or pro-gressive, has never shown readiness to yield its pride in its all-embracing apprehension of life and the world. C. F. Andrews wrote a book on "The Renaissance of India" as early as the beginning of this century. The Arya Samaj and Tilak's activity, Gandhi's *Swadeshi* emphasis, also in religion and culture, would certainly deserve the name of "Resurgence". The pre-Com-munist Buddhist lay activity in China, the many evidences of Buddhist awakening in Japan, a movement like Muhammadiya in Indonesia and the numerous movements through the Islamic world for the reform or defence of Islam as a religion and culture, should not only be seen as signs of defence or response to the Western Invasion, but have also a right to be put under the rubric of Resurgence and new self-assertion of deeply-rooted religious and cultural ways.

If ever there has been a monumental manifestation of

REVOLUTION AND RESURGENCE IN ASIA

Resurgence before there was any talk about Resurgence, it is the determined attempt by the pre-war Japanese Government to create through State Shinto an emotional, patriotic and ideological rallying-point around the worship of the divine Emperor. Artificial as the undertaking might seem from the standpoint of genuine religion, and especially the assertion that this act of "worship" was not a religious act at all[1] but an act of patriotic loyalty, nevertheless it harked back to deep-seated convictions and sentiments in the make-up of the Japanese people. They coalesced in Shinto as the mythological and cultural expression of the typical religious nationalism of Japan, which is her real religion. Its main tenets through all the centuries, latently or manifestly, have been the belief of the Japanese people in itself, its manifest destiny for a sacred mission and its messianic significance for the world. This religious self-exaltation as a nation was not an extremist reaction to Westernization, but before the Meji Era, that is before the eventful break with the policy of self-imposed seclusion from the outside world, there was (as I have pointed out earlier) a genuine Japanese movement under the Tokugawa régime. This movement strove after a Pure Shinto (Fukko-Shinto) and found its spokesmen in the 18th and 19th centuries. Even at that time it often assumed a very aggressive tone and culminated in the tenet that the divine Caesar embodied the soul and meaning of the Japanese people.

Apart from this secret drama of the Japanese soul around *Kodo* or Jinja-Shinto (State Shinto), the striking fecundity of Kyoha or Sectarian Shinto, which stood apart from State Shinto as the domesticated and canalized form of Pure Shinto, has also a right to be mentioned as an example of what may be called, when adjusting oneself to present terminology, pre-resurgent evidences of Resurgence.

All these things have to be taken into account, when trying to get a basic view of this phenomenon "Resurgence" and to avoid the mistake of treating it (as most publications on this

---

[1] The Government, mainly concerned about a monolithic patriotic cohesion, had to use this vicious and ambiguous reasoning because as a Westernized Government it found itself caught between the conflicting claims of an ineradicable Japanese urge, for the moment crystallized in *Kodo*, or State Shinto, and the constitutional but undigested principle of religious liberty, an alien Western idea. The term "patriotic" served to hide the issues.

exciting theme tend to do) as an entirely new post-war phenomenon, which has suddenly arisen like Athena in full panoply
from the head of Zeus.

In an endeavour to get at its true significance and its proper
peculiarity, it may be of some help to remind ourselves of the
fact that long before the War there was, particularly in the field
of thought, a true, full-sized "Resurgence" afoot. Sarma, in the
book we have several times quoted,[1] written *during* the Second
World War, summarized in his concluding chapter his view
of the state of India in the world scene.[2] In an irenic but firm
tone he confidently states that Hinduism has been re-interpreted in the light of modern scientific thought and not been
found wanting and that "India is now able to meet any of the
world-religions on equal terms as their friend and ally in a
common cause". In Buddhist quarters this same cheerful note
about the easily-achieved harmony of modern science and
Buddhism's world view was often sounded, and, just as in
India, expression given to the conviction that the Eastern type
of tolerance, which declares all religions as true within their
limits, is destined to become the universal conviction in the
near future. Radhakrishnan as the brilliant ambassador of
India has elaborated this theme of the East's growing and
future leadership of the world in the ultimate religio-philosophical questions, not to speak of the prestige in East and
West enjoyed by a man like the late Ananda Coomaraswamy.
Chinese such as Chan Wing Tsit and Fung Yu Lan[3] or the
Japanese Inone Tetsujiro (who founded in 1934 the International Buddhist Society) show this same confident self-
recapture. It is justifiable to put all this in the perspective of
"Resurgence".

"RESURGENCE"—A NEW QUALITY

Why, then, for a number of years has this word "Resurgence",
standing for all that manifested itself in the field of religion and
culture after the War in the wake of the political revolution,
become so prominent in writings of Easterners or Westerners?
Wherein lies the quantitative and qualitative difference of this
signalized post-war "Resurgence"? It seems undeniable that

[1] *The Renaissance of Hinduism.*   [2] See above, Chapter 6.

[3] His dissertation on "A comparative study of Life Ideals" dates from as far
back as 1927.

somehow the cataclysmic political revolution, and the re-direction of thinking, have had much to do with this difference of quality and meaning of the two kinds of "Resurgence"; a difference easy to be felt but difficult to define.

It seems that, before venturing upon any formulation and speculation, the most natural way is to turn first to the facts which are usually adduced in various quarters. In doing so the writer has to proceed in a selective way and will not escape a certain bias, for to give a full picture of the many evidences would require a substantial book. In accomplishing this brief *tour d'horizon*, the writer proposes to dwell on the Islamic, the Indian and the Buddhist worlds. Of these three, the last two have attracted most attention in the literature in this field (almost exclusively articles and notices in magazines and newspapers or in publications about some section of the vast subject, as e.g. those of the Harvard, Princeton and Chicago Summer Schools).[1]

RESURGENCE IN THE ISLAMIC WORLD

The general observation one can make about the Islamic world at the present day is that on the one hand the bulk of the population is keeping loyally to Islam for ethical and spiritual directives. On the other hand the process of corrosion is relentlessly going on: by the constantly changing structure of society, by preoccupation with new political and economic problems and adjustments, by education which in spite of keeping the teaching of Islam and Islamics in the timetable has to give a prominent place to subjects required in modern society. This happens of course in various countries in various degrees, commensurate with the amount of Western penetration and involvement in world affairs and the type of men who have the political leadership of the country concerned or who constitute the reigning bureaucracy and administration.

Morocco is a striking example of a country whose people has lived for ages under the mediaeval discipline of Islam, but which, since in 1956 it acquired its independence, has been abruptly plunged into a storm of social revolution and religious bewilder-ment, such as cannot easily be fathomed. It suddenly faces the

[1] It should be noted that, notwithstanding some excellent scientific journals in Europe such as *Oriente Moderno, Zeitschrift für Religion und Geisteswissenschaft, Revue des Etudes Islamiques*, etc., America exercises this profession of pulse-feeling far more systematically in Symposia and Colloquia than Europe.

problem of adjusting its old Islamic structure to new, entirely
opaque situations, determined to keep its loyalty to Islam and
at the same time harassed by the necessity to make over-hasty
adjustments in every sphere of life to new conditions, which
disrupt the tradition-bound patterns and ideas inherited from
the past. In this case one cannot really speak of a resurgence of
Islam; rather of an ordeal of confrontation with "the Great
Society", in which the future of Islam, whether in the sense of
weakening or of reassertion, is wholly in the balance. An article
in *The Muslim World*[1] on the "The Karawinine at Fez" gives
an instructive example of the innumerable reforms which
Morocco faces. It describes the modernization of the most
ancient university-mosque in the Muslim world (older than the
Azhar), taken in hand by the Government, the Istiqlal Party
and the Trade Unions over the heads of the listless '*ulama*' or
professors.

Tunis, Morocco's neighbour, manifests a longer experience
of Westernization through France, having thereby a greater
number of well-educated Muslims at her disposal. These, in
spite of their determined nationalist stand as well for independence as for rapid modernization, unite loyalty to Islam
and to Western culture as their socio-religious and cultural
abodes. A remarkable thing was the rapidity with which Tunis
attacked a problem so crucial for Islam as the position of
women, by abolishing the legality of polygamy.

Egypt, being the country with the longest exposure to the
West as a cultural and semi-colonial agency, and with the
longest struggle for complete independence, culminating in
the nationalization of the Suez Canal and Egypt's central
position in the Arab world, is already in a further stage.
According to the previous Constitution Islam is the religion of the
State.[2] Muslim religious instruction is compulsory in all schools.
The Christian minorities, although their rights are safeguarded,
are contrary to the Constitution not equal but second-rate
citizens, especially in social and economic respect.[3] In spirit and

[1] April 1958.

[2] The provisional Constitution of the U.A.R. (1958) has dropped this article.

[3] In spite of religious liberty and the right to change one's religion, according
to the Constitution, Muslims (i.e. the overwhelming majority of the people) have
no right to change their religious allegiance. In practice the apostate (*murtadd*)
is socially ostracized.

intention it is a true Muslim country, in which of course various grades of conservative and "liberal" trends continue their struggle. The Government of what one might term "suspended democracy" steers the course of adaptation to its rôle of being a focal point in world politics and is resolutely bent on modernization within the theoretical framework of broad Islamic principles. It is therefore difficult to estimate the strength of the officially forbidden Brotherhood of the *Ikhwan*, which represents a form of reactionary and anti-Western thinking as well as of idealism. One hesitates to call it a sign of Islamic resurgence, but in a certain sense it is, not, however, to the benefit of Islam as an uplifting directive for thinking and action.

The spiritual confusion through which peoples in such transitional stages have to do their scouting and pathfinding appears for instance in a booklet that appeared in 1950 in Cairo, under the title: *Min huna nabda* (From here we start), written by a teacher named Khalid M. Khalid. Its publication was more than once forbidden through the influence of reactionary religious and social forces. At last it was definitely released for publication by a District Court of Cairo on the grounds of freedom of thought and expression. It is a small but veritable example of the unending warfare between Old and New.

The book appears to be written by an ardent, good-hearted nationalist, who calls for social justice, recognition of women's rights, true religion as opposed to "priesthood" and "religious government". It discusses the poverty and ignorance of the masses, the greed of the "capitalists", and pleads for a rapprochement of proletariat and capitalism and for national rule over against "religious government". As usual, Koran and *hadīth* are profusely quoted. Moreover, many Western writers, especially H. G. Wells and his *Outline of History*, are often quoted too. That is the author's source for his denunciation of the "priesthood" and his recommendation of the attitude and activity of the Churches in the West (especially America) which serve the spiritual needs of their members but leave them free in their social life.

Such a booklet, which is rather adolescent in tone and tenor, and repeats in regard to every subject: begin *now* to reform (*min huna nabda*), is very illuminating for a grasp of the average mood and situation. The world *must* change, but Islam has to remain the self-evident presupposition of life. And yet at the same time the corrosion goes on, even in the most essential segments of the Islamic system.

A striking example in this respect is the silent but effective dethronement of the *Shari'a* or Divine Law, which is the real core and basis of the Islamic system. Atatürk, the founder of modern Turkey, in his drastic secular nationalism did not hesitate to establish defiantly a laicized state, sweeping Islam and its *Shari'a* aside. In Egypt, although there too every reformatory step is inspired by ardent nationalism, nobody would dream of doing such a thing. The very thought of it would not cross the threshold of the mind, either on account of an inner attachment to Islam or on considerations of social prudence out of fear of being accused of subverting the theoretically unassailable sacred order. But what has happened in Egypt is the practical dethronement of the *Shari'a*, supplanting it by "national Law".[1] It is a silent revolution, in which was accomplished the argument of Ali Abd ar-Raziq's book: *Islam and the Principles of Government*. In this book he defends the thesis that the Prophet had meant to deliver a purely religious revelation and message only, leaving legislation on all fields of life entirely to human insight. As this meant the summary abolition of theocracy, the core-idea of Islam, Abd ar-Raziq suffered in the twenties of this century stern official and popular condemnation. The revolution recently accomplished was so silent that even the guardians of the *Shari'a* and the faith let it pass unnoticed, without any protest.[2]

The decisive points in this new law, which became effective on January 1st, 1956, are that according to the opening memorandum "the rules of public law require *that the sovereignty of the state* (italics mine) be complete and absolute in the interior" and that its necessity is motivated by the explicit opposition between "the rules of public law" concerning sovereignty and

[1] "National Law" is from a purely theocratic Islamic standpoint an unthinkable idea.

[2] An excellent description of the implications of this piece of modern Egyptian legislation on the background of Islam is to be found in two articles in *The Muslim World* (January and April 1958) on: "Abolition of the *Shar'i* Courts in Egypt" by Nadav Safran. See also W. Cantwell Smith's *Islam in Modern History*, and J. Brugman: *De betekenis van het Mohammedaanse Recht in het hedendaagse Egypte*, 1960.

the inherited traditions of Egypt. This in effect means the unequivocal, summary abolition of the hallowed Islamic theocratic order of life, stated in cold blood. No word is breathed
about Allah and His sovereignty. Egypt, the bulwark of Muslim
orthodoxy, is, as we shall see, more matter-of-fact secular than
Pakistan, which breathes in so many respects a freer atmosphere. The writer of the articles (note 2, p. 284) is probably
right in ascribing the blindness of the guardians of the faith
('*ulama*') to a lack of awareness of the great difference between
a dynastic and a national State, a change-over which took place
at least in the public eye with the rapidity of a blitz, and also
to their inability to realize that the well-known terms used in
the new law (*siyāda* = sovereignty, *mulk* = sovereign rights;
umma = nation; *qanūn* = legislated law; *i'tiqād* = conscience) were
entirely denuded of their Islamic meaning and conceived in
the sense of Western jurisprudence. The factual situation is
that the *Shari'a* has the modest status of a marginal exception,
the greater part of actual law in all fields of life being Western
law, borrowed from Swiss, French, German (etc.) legislation.
This means that the profoundly un-Islamic idea of the separation of "religion" and "secular world" has become the rule. It
does *not* mean that the Islamic consciousness of Egypt has
digested this revolution, nor that the *Shari'a* as a problem is
definitely eliminated.

THE RAPID CORROSION OF ISLAM

The truly important thing, however, it seems to me, is that
in all its aspects (its formulation, its avowed object, the blindness of the "theologians", the acquiescence of public opinion
in the press and outside it) this legislative event proves the
extent of the relentless corrosion by which the theological bases
and the traditional life-patterns of Islam are ravaged. Moreover, the pace of events seems to be so rapid that in the struggle
for life and for adjustment to the terrific mechanical dynamism
of the modern world, no time is left to remain aware of what is
really happening. It is indeed a far cry from the indignant
commotion around the often far more modest pleas for reform
or more enlightened ideas of men like Muhammad Abduh,
Amin Kasim, Taha Hussain, Mansur Fahmi, Ali Abd ar-Raziq
to the unconscious resignation of to-day. It proves also that one

should not look on nationalism mainly as a political phenomenon. It is far more, and deeper, than that. It is the will to a
new form and dimension of existence, in which all backwardness and inferiority are extinguished and one can participate on
equal terms in the one world of to-day, experiencing one's
dignity in the manifestation of one's own personality and of its
innate abilities and cultural-spiritual acquisition. It is the will
to universally recognized adulthood and maturity, and it will
not come to rest until this aim has been achieved.

This will has, as always with man, dual potentialities, for
good and for evil; and this applies naturally also to the part
played in it by religion, in this case Islam. If one sees nationalism
in this context (and thus, it seems to me, it has to be seen in all
Asian countries) it appears somewhat artificial that so many
writers on Resurgence deprecate it, speaking about it so easily
as a manifestation of Nationalism. They take nationalism too
exclusively as a political phenomenon, forgetting that it has
strong pseudo-religious qualities, just as Communism has.

Turkey, which of all Muslim lands has set its course on a
complete secularization, and where Islam seemed to vegetate
as a dwindling remnant of the past, has since the War aroused
the attention of many observers, because signs of Islamic
resurgence have seemed to appear again on the surface of
Turkish life. The writer in his *Christian Message in a Non-
Christian World* (1938),[1] after having analysed the startling
experiment of Turkey aiming at rebuilding a nation on a
purely humanist irreligious, a-religious basis[2] (in this respect
Turkey is paralleled only by its arch-enemy Russia), advocated
there, nevertheless, the need for caution; because a policy of
starvation and underground existence of Islam applied to a
people so thoroughly nourished by a long tradition of Islamic
belief and customs, which with its peculiar Turkish ethnic
stamp constituted its real culture, had to reckon with a kind
of resurgence.

A NEW "RELIGIOUS" CAREER FOR ISLAM?

The unwieldly theocratic *Corpus Islamicum* is undoubtedly
annihilated and will never return, but, as the writer observed
at that time, this annihilation contained the possibility of an

[1] pp. 273-280.   [2] Nothing less was Atatürk's aim.

experiment Islam would or could never dream of in the days of the *Corpus Islamicum*; namely, to start its career as a religion pure and simple.[1]

As far as the post-war literature on phenomena of reversion to Islam goes, this possibility has since 1924 in no sense become actualized.[2] The judgments and evaluations of various Turkish and non-Turkish observers tend to be rather divergent. There are some who think that the more conspicuous signs of Islamic expression mean a definite reversion from the secular religion, "Kemalism", back to Islam. Some even speak of a full-scale religious reaction, threatening the ruin of Atatürk's great creation. The Turkish press often devotes sensational attention to various symptoms. One of the most sober commentators is Professor L. V. Thomas (see note 2 below). He sees all the symptoms together as on the one hand a result of the relaxation of the iron grip of systematic laicization, which has naturally lost some of its vigour by the death of Atatürk and the wear of time, and on the other hand as an equally natural come-back of observance of cherished customs, all called Islamic, of discussions and publications on religious subjects, of re-appearance of Dervish orders, of endeavours for the training of an educated Turkish Muslim clergy (Ankara University houses now a new Faculty of Theology), of the repair and building of mosques, etc.

One is inclined to think that religion certainly will not vanish from Turkey, kept alive by sympathy for cherished traditions, or out of irrepressible religious longings, vaguer or stronger. It is even possible that here and there a hidden revulsion against the new era as embodied in Kemalism may express itself under a reactionary Islamic banner. But in this country which has set

---

[1] Cantwell Smith in his book is perfectly right in stating that the Turks have chosen secularism without rejecting Islam as a religion. The Arab Muslim world wrongly thinks that the Turks have renounced Islam. It seems to me, however, that he over-simplifies Turkey's religious-cultural problem when he says that the Turks have made religion what it should be, a personal matter, a thing of the conscience, an affair of private faith. The still unsolved problem is rather whether this is possible with Islam. Cantwell Smith's "should" is a crypto-Christian version of religion.

[2] Cf. B. Lewis on "Turkey, Westernization" in *Unity and Variety in Muslim Civilization*; B. Lewis: "Islamic Revival in Turkey" (*International Affairs*, 1952); L. V. Thomas: "Recent Developments in Turkish Islam" (*Middle East Journal*, 1952); John A. T. Kingsbury: "Character Studies in contemporary Turkish Islam" in *The Muslim World*, January 1958. The writer himself, having never had the privilege of first-hand acquaintance with Turkey and knowing Turkish Islam only by book-study, necessarily does not permit himself a definite opinion.

its face towards becoming a secular democratic State and so inevitably draws the whole population, not only the "educated", into this secularizing stream, it seems very unlikely that Islam will ever become more than a side-issue of no real relevance to the whole national existence. Unless there should occur a religious revival of elemental strength, a real resurrection from the dead.

Pakistan has a prominent and particular place in the Islamic world of to-day, and will keep this place, it seems, for a good long time. Pakistan's Islam was originally a part of Indian Islam with its characteristically different physiognomy from the Islam of Arabic-speaking countries and Persia. Pakistan's prominence and particularity derives from the fact that by the Partition of India in 1947 she has deliberately chosen Islam as the motivating reason for her emergence and existence as an independent State. For this reason mainly, and not only for the geographical reason that she lies between the Muslim Near and Middle East and the South-East Asian part of the Muslim world, she occupies a pivotal position in modern Islam.

This explains why the Pakistani Government tries to make itself a centre for common Muslim deliberation such as (there are many more examples) the Islamic Colloquium, held at the beginning of 1958 at Lahore. As the urge for her foundation as an independent State has been the desire to create the possibility of existing as an authentic cultural-Islamic body, she is bound to occupy herself studiously with how to realize this emphatic allegiance to Islam as a religion and a culture in the wear and tear of building a new, stable state and nation in modern world conditions and relationships. From this angle Pakistan can rightly be mentioned as the most outspoken example of the Resurgence of Islam.[1]

It is quite natural, notwithstanding the colossal corrosion

[1] Another clear example is the missionary activity, or rather influence, Islam deploys in Africa and in the West. We only mention it as a sign of Resurgence because Islam's missionary expansion and influence is already of long date. The missionary activity in the West takes place (and has done for decades) as explained earlier, through the Ahmadiyya group, which is repudiated by official Islam. But since the end of the War the missionary outreach of Islam has undoubtedly been intensified, were it only because the heated political and social climate, especially through the race problem and the clamour for Independence, favours the position of Islam, which is free from race- and colour-bars and represented by people e.g. from N. Africa and Egypt who are themselves in revolt against white "Christian" superiority. President Nasser even announced once a strong organized missionary bid for Africa, which was clearly a political move in the competition for the allegiance of Africa.

that takes place there, as was shown above by the example of Egypt, that the Arabic-speaking countries of the Near and Middle East and Persia have in their Constitutions declared Islam as the State religion. This is in no sense a matter of Resurgence. It was for them the natural thing to do, and did not call for long deliberation. How this decision to be Muslim States, without giving serious reflection to becoming secular States, will work out in the future in regard to their interpretation of their world relationships, to the real and not only theoretical status of religious minorities within their borders, and to the scope left for "spiritual free-trade", especially in religious respect, is hard to foretell.

Pakistan, however, for quite a different reason, had no choice. It could not but become a pronounced Muslim State because it was unthinkable for its founders to choose the way of India, which established a secular State, as in that case their whole contention for a marked Islamic destiny would have become an outright absurdity. And yet, the spirit and atmosphere of Pakistan, in a certain sense more emphatically a Muslim State than the Arabic-speaking Muslim countries, is freer and more relaxed than in these oldest Muslim lands. The comparative[1] fairness with which the religious minorities are treated (Hindus and Christians) compares favourably with the Arabic-speaking Muslim countries. The tendency in Pakistan to stress the cultural and spiritual norms and predilections, which Islam by its cultural and religious past undoubtedly has in common with Western and not with Asian culture, is striking. The more so if one compares it with the rather lonely fighting position of Taha Hussain in Egypt, who defends the same thesis of Islam's belonging culturally to the West and not to Asia. This is of course strengthened by the fact that Pakistan's whole origin is rooted in a fierce repudiation of the typically Hindu, i.e. Asian, way of life.

PAKISTAN—ISLAMIC AND DEMOCRATIC

The freer and more relaxed spirit of Pakistan and her present leaders is also visible in their sincere endeavour to have a State

[1] The word "comparative" needs great stress, because in fact Pakistan often blunders in its treatment of its considerable Hindu minority. The secular State, India, keeps better to the rules of democracy in regard to its big Muslim minority (not so much in regard to the Christian minority).

which is simultaneously truly Islamic and truly democratic in the Western sense of the word. So Pakistan goes her own way, different from her Arabic-speaking sister-countries, different from India's experiment with an avowedly secular democracy (for Hinduism, the religion of the overwhelming majority, has, unlike Islam, no clear principles in regard to the meaning, function and place of the State); different also from Turkey and its *état laïc*, ignoring entirely Turkey's Muslim past. The only other big Muslim country which has some similarity with Pakistan in this important question of choosing between Islamic-democratic and secular-democratic is Indonesia. Muslim political leaders from Indonesia therefore have frequent contacts with Pakistan. The similarity consists mainly in the fact that Indonesia, since its independence in 1949, has not yet definitely decided as to its political course along the Islamic-democratic or secular-democratic line. Officially it has lived so far as a secular Welfare State with an eclectic doctrine called *Pantjasila* (i.e. five rules), of which nationalism is the soul and the belief in Allah and in Democracy is the twofold expression of an inchoate synthesis of East and West. A Constitution is, however, in slow process of being formed, and it remains still an undecided point whether it will establish Islam as the religion of the State or not.

The peculiar atmosphere and attitude of Pakistan is manifest also in the way in which, differently e.g. from Egypt, the Islamic-democratic State and Islam and its culture should be conceived. Here again it is unmistakable that the leading men, who face this problem, belong to the different spiritual Indian climate and not to the more concentrated Islamic climate of the Near and Middle East. Moreover, their upbringing in the typical British version of Western education shines clearly through. Their guiding authority is not the *Salaf*, the great ancestors of the "Golden Age" of Islam in the 7th and 8th centuries, as in Egypt, but a contemporary philosophical and cultural interpreter of Islam in broad perspective, the brilliant Muhammad Iqbal (d. 1939), who is at the same time both the real founder and ideologist and also the great cultural hero of Pakistan.

In 1956 Pakistan promulgated her Constitution,[1] which was intended to be a synthesis of Islamic and Western political

---

[1] At present temporarily abrogated.

thinking. Liaqat Khan, the first Prime Minister of Pakistan, pointed out in 1949 that the preamble to the Constitution made it clear that Pakistan, wanting to be a democratic Welfare State, plainly declared that this is meant to be done "under God" in the sense that all state-power and statecraft find their only justification in the service of God Almighty. This, as it were, religious confession is the more striking if one compares the structure and spirit of the Pakistani Constitution of 1956 with the (revised) Constitution of Egypt, also of 1956. Egypt's Constitution begins by stating in Western fashion that sovereignty lies with the people. This in the Egyptian situation leans very heavily in the direction of sovereignty of the State, which in practice *may* mean that the democratic idea of the People's sovereignty evaporates. Pakistan, however, opens her Constitution by saying that the sovereignty over the whole universe belongs exclusively to Allah and that He has delegated His rights of sovereignty to the people of Pakistan for the ruling of their own country. This ruling is considered to be a mandate, to be fulfilled within the limits prescribed by Allah as a sacred obligation. Even the innate tendency of Islam to consider itself as an international body finds due recognition in the stipulation that Pakistan should be ready to further the solidarity of the Muslim peoples of the world, whereas the Egyptian Constitution stresses the more limited and nationalistic view that the Egyptian people is part of the Arab nation.[1]

It should certainly not be forgotten that such Constitutions are still mainly verbal pronouncements, which only gradually get their real content and directing power from unpredictable future developments. Yet it is significant to note how differently things are set in two such representative Muslim countries as Egypt and Pakistan. Egypt, which is more weighed down by its Muslim past than Pakistan, ignores or rather placidly by-passes the whole problem of bringing together theocratic Islam (to which the Western conception of democracy is intrinsically alien)[2] and Western democracy by borrowing

[1] Cf. Dr. J. Hans: *Dynamik und Dogma im Islam*, pp. 10, 11, 37f.

[2] This is a much-debated and controversial subject, which would require more extensive treatment. One of the best scholarly treatments of the subject, based especially on the famous book of the lonely Muslim "sociologist" in the past, the *Muqaddima* of Ibn Chaldūn, is to be found in J. H. Kramers: *Analecta Orientalia*, Vol. II, under the title: "L'Islam et la Démocratie".

totally secularized legal Western terms. Even in her Constitution, which naturally stresses *principles* and directives, she pays no attention whatever to the international religious fraternity of Islam, as its general framework, but makes a temporary phase of nationalist politics (Arab Unity) her pseudo-international community. In other words, every sign of truly Islamic thinking and orientation is absent.

Pakistan, however, which is culturally more open and free in her peculiar circumstances of owing her very existence to her desire to be a self-determining Muslim State, has seriously sought in the formulation of her Constitution to achieve a synthesis of theocratic Islam and Western democracy. She has, therefore, consciously adopted the name "Islamic Republic". The future development of Pakistan will present an exceedingly interesting test-case. In accordance with her orientation, in religious and cultural problems, towards recent great Muslim reformists and not towards the mediaeval *Shari'a*, Article 198 of the Constitution circumscribes the Islamic basis of the State of Pakistan in the more comprehensive terms that no law can come into force which contradicts the prescriptions of Islam as to be found in the Koran and the Sunna, and that existing law must be brought into harmony with the aforesaid prescriptions.

This sentence, perhaps, also written down somewhat placidly, reveals the vulnerability and possible ambiguity of the projected synthesis. A struggle between liberal or modernist and conservative interpretation of Koran and Sunna is bound to come, and will undoubtedly mercilessly bring to light how far the synthesis as basic political principle is only verbal and how far it is feasible. In the writer's opinion Dr. Hans, whose book was quoted above, is too optimistic in his evaluation of the situation and in his belief that at least Islamic doctrine and modern dynamism are beginning to find each other.[1] The struggle will be far more difficult than many who are easily inclined towards harmonization are prepared to believe.[2]

[1] The reason for my divergence from Dr. Hans' estimate is that he minimizes the strength and peculiar religious nature of Islam and the logic of its doctrine, and over-estimates the power exerted by the partially Western cultural heritage of Islam in the consciousness of the Muslim world.

[2] Good illustration can be found in Freeland K. Abbott's article in *The Muslim World* (January 1958) on: "Maulana, Maudidi and Quranic Interpretation" and Muhammad Daud Rahbar's contribution in the same number, containing a deeply interesting review of Kenneth Cragg's *The Call of the Minaret*.

This same sentence has too, however, a very noteworthy consequence; that is to say that the normative position given to the Koran, the Sunna and to Islam as a culture and a peculiar way of life, engenders in Pakistan a studious pre-occupation with the Islamizing of life in our modern age. This urge, and the seriousness of intention with which it is pursued, finds a striking illustration in the fact that a special Commission has been instituted, which has the difficult and very problematic task of achieving the constitutionally prescribed harmony of modern, positive State Law in Pakistan with Koran and Sunna. The definite "re-Islamizing" of the Law will from 1962 on become the duty of the National Assembly.

ISLAM'S GRAND DESIGN

In this light it has to be said emphatically for the second time that Pakistan is the place where one can speak of a Resurgence of Islam in grand design. It is, therefore, curious to note that in a very recent report of a well-informed missionary observer it is stated that in Pakistan there is no evidence of the much-discussed Resurgence, for there is no sign whatever of a quickened religious life; it goes on in its ordinary routine. There is no reason to doubt the accuracy of the observation, but nevertheless the writer maintains that on a long range view, taking Islam not in the typically Western strict religious sense but in the broad sense of a system of principles for religion, individual and social ethics and culture, Pakistan is the out-standing example of Resurgence of Islam.

The 1958 Colloquium[1] of Lahore deserves some treatment because it yields an opportunity to sense something of the inner stresses and tensions through which the Muslim world (in so far as it gives reasoned account of them) goes in its pathfinding between self-assertion and adjustment to the irresistible impact of the modern world structure and dynamics. The official interest shown by the Government in this Colloquium, attended by 169 persons of note,[2] was naturally great in a country ruled by a President to whose constitutional duties it belongs to establish an Institute for Higher Studies and Research in

[1] Cf. the excellent report of it in *The Muslim World* (July 1958) by Bayard Dodge.

[2] Thirty-three were scholars from Western countries, of whom four came from Soviet Russia, and the rest competent Muslims from many countries, five of whom were representatives of the Muslims in China.

Islam in order to build a Muslim society on genuinely Islamic bases.[1]

The subjects which were treated indicate the wide range of new situations and problems by which Islam, like all religions to-day, is confronted. In the case of Islam, however, the problems and issues are often sharpened and coloured in a specific way because Islam is in a very outspoken manner a politico-social-cultural-religious body with a markedly theological and doctrinal character. The subjects were: Islamic Culture, and what do we mean by it; the Islamic concept of the State; the challenge of modern ideas and the social values of Muslim society; the rôle of *ijtihād* and the scope of legislation in Islam; the attitude of Islam towards science; Islam's influence on Western history and culture;[2] economics in the social structure of Islam; landed property and land tenure; Islam's attitude towards, and relations with, other Faiths; Islam's potential contribution to World Peace.

It must be kept in mind that in this Colloquium an international group of leading Muslims (the Western participants naturally fulfilled a modest rôle) spoke their minds on all these subjects, which press themselves on the attention of the Muslim world. Occasionally there were outbursts against opinions which were considered unorthodox and dangerously advanced. In some cases this led either to the watering down of a contribution or even to its withdrawal from presentation or discussion. This is important as an indication that the prevailing attitude in the Muslim world is still to follow the line of how to *adjust* positions and principles, considered as themselves undebatable and unassailable, to and in a totally changed world. The way, evidently trodden by a minority, to face and to *confront* oneself with even the most critical questions as to the validity of Islam, its claims and authority, is, it seems, still forbidden. It deserves note that some Pakistanis in particular were conspicuous in entering this way, declared closed by the majority. They tried to give a new, more creative interpretation to some of the main Islamic key-ideas in regard to man, the inter-human relations, society and state, conceiving as the salutary way for modern Islam (as one of them formulated it) that Islam should

[1] Article 197 of the Constitution. See Hans, *op. cit.*, p. 38.
[2] Cf. Chapter 2 of this book.

cut away all unhealthy undergrowth and should recapture and revive its fundamental principles and ideals.[1] Muhammad Daud Rahbar, Professor of the Theological Faculty at Ankara, who made an able attempt to treat Islam's problems with great honesty, provoked protest because, though sincerely keeping to faith in the Koran as God's final revelation, he clearly showed his openness to historical criticism of Koran and *ḥadīth*.

The reporter in *The Muslim World* observes that the papers on "Modern Ideas and Social Values of Muslim Society" were theoretical rather than practical, suggesting no concrete solution of social problems confronting Islam.

> Questions connected with family life, the status of women, improvement of rural conditions, social security and similar issues were not discussed. This is the more significant because all modern Western conceptions of "socialist" flavour as embodied in the Welfare State, were theoretically recognized as principles of the Islamic Theory of Economics, and as proving that the present-day practices in Western countries were confirmations of the Prophet's sagacity.

He reports the same theoretical tendency in the treatment of Islam's attitude to science. To the living problem that many Muslim university students question the inerrancy of the Koran and become agnostics, no reference was made.

It cannot escape notice, when surveying the full scope of the Colloquium, that only a small place was accorded to what Westerners call "personal religion". The main part of the attention was diverted to social, political and moral principles and ideals. This was even the case with the subject: Islam's attitude towards, and relations with, other Faiths. It is significant that according to the report all stress was laid on what might be called the irenic verses of the Koran in this respect, which when taken by themselves open a real avenue towards tolerance and good inter-religious relationships, especially between Islam and Christianity. One contributor did strike a

---

[1] A characteristic example of the legal and social bias of Islamic religious thinking is the suggestion which was made that the basic theological notions of *ijtihād* (independent judgment) and *ijma'* (consensus of the Community or Umma) should in our time be restored to renewed operation by vesting their application in a Muslim Legislative Assembly.

deeper, more personal note when he said that personally he felt profoundly sorry that "such a beautiful expression of human tragedy" as the Crucifixion "is not reflected in the Holy Koran", and made a moving plea for a sincere endeavour for mutual understanding and positive approach of Islam and Christianity to one another.

The Colloquium as a whole and the material give much cause for pondering the present situation of Islam. Evidently the Islamic world is torn in various directions. Its adjustment to the world of to-day and its attempts at new self-understanding happen on different levels, which have little or no real communication with each other. The basic fact in the total situation seems to be the erosive influence of modern science and of the social and economic upheaval, which works in often untraceable ways on men's minds and traditional life-patterns. On the other hand, as to the compatibility of Islam with the modern age, various attempts are made to find new ways of vindicating the validity, even superiority, of Islam by different attempts at re-interpretation of what its mouthpieces call the fundamental principles and ideals of Islam. Involuntarily the re-interpretation has a drift towards rationalistic, moralistic and idealist abstractions, and away from the springs of living religion in which emotion, will and personal religious experience have a full place. This re-interpretation often gives a quite new content and twist to many Islamic key-ideas, which do not find full justification in the original meaning of Koran, Sunna or the classical system, and are strong evidence of the great influence of Western humanistic and "Christian" notions. Granted that this is true, it does not, however, decide the matter and should restrain us from taking a too expectant attitude towards such endeavours for a re-conception of Islam. It is the Muslims' own business to find out and say (if this is, historically speaking, so) whether the mutation of Islam they create is an adulteration of Islam as to its real intent and content or a legitimate re-interpretation. It is not in the first place our business.

This is especially the case in the field of religious and cultural inter-relationships of Islam and Christianity. Again, the exclusive stressing of the irenic, purely-religious tones of the Koran in regard to other Faiths cannot satisfy an historically trained mind as giving the full picture of the Islamic system versus other Faiths, and providing an adequate answer to the problems this other side of the medal raises for Islam itself and for the non-Muslim world. But, again, this should not prevent anyone from rejoicing in this irenic emphasis and meeting it positively, patiently waiting for the day when even the most touchy and critical spots in Islam as well as in Christianity can be dealt with in open-mindedness. The most remarkable and fascinating example of the moving depth and breadth a Muslim mind can attain in endeavouring to enter, on the background of the Crucifixion, into all contemporary human problems and express them in Koranic religious categories is Dr. Kamil Hussain's *Qaryah Zalīma*. As far as the writer knows, in no part of the non-Christian world can one find its equal in sensitivity and humble sense of human solidarity between all the children of Man.[1]

THE POTENTIAL STRENGTH OF CONSERVATISM

The incoherent picture of the situation which has been given in the preceding paragraphs is incoherent simply because it lacks one important feature. In all our meditations on the "modern trends of Islam" we should never forget that the strongest but least palpable force in Islam is everywhere the most conservative wing, which refuses to come to terms with the modern world. From that side unexpected explosions and developments are always possible. Right as one may be in opining that the march of subversive secular ideas and forces will reveal its foolish blindness and pathetic impotence, it seems wise not to under-estimate its potential strength.[2] The Colloquium itself bore evidence to this incalculable factor. Whereas the speech of the President of Pakistan was a forceful plea for a new, dynamic interpretation of Islam's "unchanging principles", and an equally forceful attack on the obscurantism of the Mullahs and their influence, the participants received by mail a remarkable letter. It came from a group of "Muslim

[1] The book is translated into English by Kenneth Cragg, under the title: *The City of Wrong.*

[2] Maulana Maududi, who is the only one who tries to give a systematic answer to the ambiguous politico-religious situation of Pakistan, heads an organized movement, *Jamā'at al-Islām*, whereas the intellectuals in Pakistan, generally speaking, are sad examples of *trahison des clercs*. The arch-conservatives are un-organized but easily sway the masses nonetheless, if so required.

citizens of Lahore" (so they signed), in which evidently the conservative Mullah-group, though keeping aloof from the Colloquium, wanted to manifest their presence. A few sentences from this letter are illuminating: "You are already aware that this is an Islamic country and our Constitution is based on the Holy Koran and Sunna." The Western Orientalists in particular are requested in the letter not to injure Muslim feelings by speaking against Islam, its history, culture and law. "We do not like modernism and Westernism because it has miserably failed in the West."

It is indispensable to look very briefly at Islam in the area of Communist rule. Indispensable, as it should be realized that Soviet Russia comprises a number of Muslim Republics in its system and that the Islamic world has been for centuries one of the domains of Russia's imperialist ambitions. A brief look, because it is very difficult to get a trustworthy picture of the Muslims' lot and of their way of life under Communist authority. Soviet Russia and Communist China number respectively 20 million and 10-20 million Muslim subjects.

Put in the terms of our subject—the effects of the Western Invasion and the Eastern response or reaction to it in religious and cultural respect—the Muslims within the Soviet system and within the Chinese Communist sphere are exposed to a form of "Western" Invasion of extreme severity, if we keep in mind first that Communism and the Marxist-Leninist doctrine of salvation are a gigantic offshoot of Western idealism and second that it belongs to Communist Messianism to indoctrinate and inculcate its view and way of life with an unprecedented systematic determination. In principle Islam, being a religion, is in Communist eyes undoubtedly one of the various brands of "opium of the people", and as a socio-religious system is feudal and a tool for reactionaries. What can be said with certainty is that the Muslims have to submit to the pressure exercised ideologically and practically on them. What cannot be known with certainty is how the policy of pressure or relaxation, according to the shift of tactics and expediency which the Communist lords follow, takes its devious course. Nor do we know with certainty how, to what extent, on what matters the Muslim populations defend and assert their Muslim identity. This whole Muslim bloc in Communist territory is entirely isolated and has no possibility of contact with the Muslim international family outside the borders.[1]

SIGNS OF RESURGENCE IN BUDDHISM

Resurgence in the Buddhist world is unmistakable, even emphatically so. The scene, however, and the ways in which it manifests itself, are utterly different from the Islamic world. The basic reasons are twofold.

First, Buddhism, like all the great religions and cultures of S.-E. Asia and the Far East (India and Hinduism, China and Confucianism, Japan), is worlds apart from Islam. Spiritually they are nearly as alien to each other as the West to the East. Second, the great geographical and geophysical difference between them. The Islamic world, having since the 16th century lost its central political and economic place, has regained it gradually since the First World War because of its rise from impotent colonial and semi-colonial status to independence, and because of the new world-strategic importance which fell into its lap by its richness in oil and its crucial place in modern world traffic. The Buddhist world (Chinese Buddhism having lapsed) has only partly known colonial rule (Burma, Ceylon, Indo-China); elsewhere it comprises countries that have remained free (Thailand, Japan). It has never known a theologically motivated, clear-cut political and social system, like Islam, as Buddhism is essentially an a-political religion. It is therefore very noteworthy that the lands which have known colonial rule (Burma, Ceylon), are mainly the parts where Buddhist Resurgence is most evident. Of course, in the other parts a somewhat heightened activity is noticeable in the organization of religious celebrations and big meetings, stimulated by the present atmosphere of turbulent transition from an Old to a New World, with all its anguish and expectation; but it does not deserve the special name of

[1] In spite of the difficulty of entering these Muslim Republics, the literature is profuse, produced by journalists or visitors who have managed to travel there, or by scholars, who have collected material where possible. I mention only two books, in which one finds extensive bibliographies. The first is by Ivar Spector: *The Soviet Union and the Muslim World*, 1917-56, a well-written account, founded on sources in many languages. Mainly political, written with the aim of providing American, anti-Communist Muslim policy with a good guide. The second is: *Revue des Etudes Islamiques*, 1952, 1953. The first contains many important Communist Manifestos to the Muslim peoples, but little information on what goes on in the Soviet Muslim Republics. For the latter purpose the French studies yield more.

Resurgence as a distinct post-war factor. Burma and Ceylon, however, do, and require in this respect special consideration. Yet it may be of interest to preface this record about Burma and Ceylon by some remarks on Buddhism in present-day India.

For many centuries (since the 11th century), Buddhism, Nepal excepted, was non-existent in India. At another place in this book I have already noted that by the *Pax Britannica* of the colonial era and by the new interest awakened in Buddhism amongst India's intelligentsia through the work of Western orientalists and archaeologists, Buddhism returned after long absence into the Indian perspective. Since the last decade of the 19th century new endeavours have even been made, issuing especially from Ceylon and leading Western theosophists, to introduce Buddhism anew in its homeland. Great expectations were roused when the official leader of India's Outcastes, Ambedkar, in 1950 at the First Buddhist World Congress declared himself a Buddhist. So far this step has not resulted in any effect on the huge mass of "Outcastes" in India. The really important thing is the fact that modern Indian thinking has again incorporated and readopted Buddhism as a legitimate and splendid part of India's cultural and spiritual heritage. In this fact lie hidden potentialities as to Buddhism's influence in India in the future, but the writer naturally refrains from any forecast.

BURMA'S LEADERSHIP

The prominence of Burma in regard to Buddhist Resurgence is mainly due to the energetic initiative of the Prime Minister U Thakin Nu, who is a devoted, sincere lay-Buddhist.[1] A vision seen in sleep instigated him in 1948 to build the World Peace Pagoda (*Kaba Aya*) to further peace in Burma[2] and in the world. It was built and finished (1952) at State expense and is situated five miles from the famous Shwe Dagon Pagoda. U Nu acquired part of the Buddha relics, which had returned to Sanchi in India, for the Pagoda, in order to justify the claim that this World Peace Pagoda, through the effect and irradiation of

[1] Christmas Humphreys' *Buddhism* (1951) contains much useful information. Prof. U Hla Bu's article: "The Christian Encounter with Buddhism in Burma" (*International Review of Missions*, April 1958) is an excellent and truly sagacious contribution, written on the assumption that "revival of non-Christian religions" is "to-day a world-wide phenomenon".

[2] The political instability of the country, particularly through the organized resistance of Communist "pockets", makes this very real.

these relics of the great preacher of peace and harmony, is a strong means to influence the growth of World Peace.

This act of U Nu's has more than one motivation. It is not simply the act of a sincere individual, who happens to be in a commanding position of power. It is an act of religious-cultural policy; that is to say, it expresses the determination of the *secular* Welfare State, Burma, to use Buddhism as the cohesive ideology for its building a new new nation and state. This cannot but win the spontaneous approval of the Buddhist Burmese, as Buddhism is so interwoven with the cultural and social life of Burma that such an undertaking finds naturally positive response. The country is, however, in spite of the dominant position of Buddhism, a multi-religious country, as in the big pagan parts Christianity is either established or making progress. Paganism is still strong in the northern parts of the country, and there is a minority of Muslims, practically all from outside. The question how this multi-religious composition of Burma will work out in the framework of Buddhism as the uniting ideology for a secular Welfare State, and what this will mean for the relation of Buddhism and Christianity in their efforts either to absorb pagan tribes gradually in the religious-cultural body of Buddhism[1] or to convert them to Christianity, is a matter for the future.

U Nu's act is, however, also a demonstration in the field of world politics, and at the same time a missionary claim that Buddhism can give and guarantee the real solution of the problem of World Peace. The name "World Peace Pagoda" is a religious-political programme.

U Thakin Nu received also in a dream the commission to call together the sixth Buddhist Council in commemoration of the 2,500th year since the death of the Buddha. It took place from May 1954 till May 1956 and was attended by monks from various Buddhist countries, though the main body came from S.-E. Asian countries. To make possible this great meeting, which was mainly a colossal, constantly changing team of

[1] Buddhism, exactly like Hinduism in India, in countries where it is strongly established follows as a rule in regard to pagan populations the way of absorption, not of conversion. U Hla Bu (*op. cit.*, pp. 172f.) gives a lucid description of the great advantages of the "absorption" way and of the pragmatic way in which Buddhists experiment in proving the efficiency of authentic and cultural Buddhism to adapt itself to modern needs and assumptions.

scholarly co-operation, many buildings were planned and completed. A big air-conditioned meeting hall (*Chatta Sangayana Mahapasanguha*), an artificial cave-building near the World Peace Pagoda, which provided room for 5,000 monks and 10,000 laymen, was built. Also a library and hospices and an International Institute for Advanced Buddhist Studies, provided at State expense.[1] The main work that was done in those two years (and in fact continues in various forms) is the editing of a universally recognized text of the Buddhist Holy Scriptures in Pali (the *Tripitaka*) in 54 volumes. This is an immense undertaking, to which is added the plan to edit abbreviated additions of the *Tripitaka* in Pali, Hindi, Burmese and English. Significantly these abbreviations are announced as editions in which the miraculous, the legendary and the rhetorical are left out. It is also significant that the programme-title under which the Council meets is: World Peace and the Evangelization (i.e. the Buddhizing) of the World.

Although certainly this whole immense work of textual criticism or popularization of the Buddhist Scriptures can be seen as an internal concern of the Buddhist world, yet there is also a missionary interest visible in it. The tenor of the entire programme, of the spirit of the Council, of the publicity created around it, indicates that the Buddhist world is consciously claiming the whole world, and particularly the West, as its mission field. This is a fact which should be noted; for even if the acts will perhaps for quite a long time not measure up to the intentions and aspirations, Buddhism will increasingly present itself as a missionary force, as the sole guarantee for the world's salvation and as a great asset to the world-political situation, particularly in its feverish search for realizing World Peace.

It is important to take notice of U Hla Bu's remark that this Resurgence in Burma, of which the writer has described the most conspicuous expressions, is not a mass movement. He specifies that by stating that it is "neither widespread nor deep-rooted" and that it has (up till now) not led to a re-awakening among the masses, nor caught the imagination of

[1] The Burmese Government got for the International Buddhist University a substantial grant from the Ford Foundation on the ground that it is a venture for inter-cultural relations between the countries of S.E. Asia, and between East and West. It is chiefly meant as a place where scholars from all over the world can study Buddhism, thus making Burma a central place in the Buddhist world of to-day.

youth. The masses still move on the roads of conventional and traditional religion, whereas youth is stirred not by the ancient faith, but rather by the new social and political ideology. The main dynamic force is the religious ardour and the political prestige of U Nu, who in his initiative has been supported by his Government.[1]

It seems, taking the facts into account, that the Resurgence in Burma cannot be understood as a religious revival, at least in the sense in which this expression is generally interpreted in Western Christian usage. Many factors contribute to it: political, nationalist, cultural and spiritual, and it is very difficult to estimate the amount of weight that respectively belongs to each of these factors. Every judgment necessarily is a compound of weighing the factual evidence and of subjective intuitive perception, and therefore always open to contradiction. As to the writer's estimate, it would tend towards stressing very strongly the dynamic political, social and ideological atmosphere and its repercussions, the realization of a new vindication of Buddhism's spiritual and cultural significance and greatness, and the need for an ideological common basis for the new political and social reality in which one lives. Religious impulses in the genuine sense of "religious" are, if they are there, difficult to detect. If they were there in a Buddhist country it ought to become manifest in many persons wandering out of deep spiritual urges *in die Heimatlosigkeit* (into a state of homelessness). It seems—and taking into consideration the kind of world people live in, quite understandably— that rather the contrary is the case. This seeming absence of a really potent, truly "religious" ingredient does not imply, however, that therefore the Religious Resurgence has no religious significance at all. It means at any rate for the Buddhist world a stronger consciousness of Buddhism's religio-cultural identity and a greater self-assertion as a body that claims to have a Message of Salvation to the whole world.

BUDDHIST NATIONALISM IN CEYLON

Ceylon shows this same multi-coloured picture of causes, expressions, motivations and claims in tortured vehemence. Like Burma, she aspires to pose as a centre of modern Buddhism.

[1] *op. cit.*, p. 171.

She is one of the oldest Buddhist countries. One must realize that since the 3rd century before Christ this country has been moulded religiously and culturally by Buddhism. Being a Buddhist is inseparable from being a Ceylonese. It is the *national* religion and the *national* culture. Before the Western Invasion, beginning with Portuguese domination in the 16th century, it was the religion of the State. The period of Western dominance, the British period included, meant largely speaking a decline and frustration of Buddhism, because it meant a frustration of Ceylon's distinctive kind of national life.

One must grasp the significance of these few essential facts in order to understand the present situation and the shock the acquisition of political independence in 1948 has produced. It was as if an incubus of long standing was suddenly removed. The era of independence was indeed a new era which loosened deep-seated questions that had been suppressed for four centuries. Even before Independence, under the stimulus of Western civilization and through increasing contacts with other Buddhist lands, a certain revitalization of Buddhism had been in progress. This became evident after the First World War. We have already mentioned the Mahabodhi Society as a Ceylonese creation, active in taking responsibility for Buddhist concerns in India, in publishing literature and planning Buddhist "Missions" to "pagan" Europe. As in Japan, the Y.M.C.A. and the Sunday school were adopted as patterns for educating or attracting people in a more modern way towards Buddhistic thinking and behaviour. Attacks on Christianity appeared in the new literature, and attempts were made at adjustment of Buddhist assumptions to dominant modern ideas. In many cases it was rather the demonstration of the harmony between Buddhist key-ideas and dominant modern ideas, with the implication that Buddhism has been ahead of the Western world for some millennia. To prove this, atheistic and humanist writers of various sorts from the West were ransacked. Since 1950 Ceylonese Buddhism, which in the Mahabodhi Society possessed already an organization concerned about missionary outreach to the West and "ecumenical" contact with other parts of the Buddhist world, has been the centre of the World Fellowship of Buddhists, founded by the professor in Pali, Dr. G. P. Malalasekera, one of the ablest Buddhist leaders.

This whole process, led by monks, can also be characterized as a sign of Resurgence, of reviving self-confidence. The Resurgence, on which in recent years so much has been spoken and written, is on the one hand an accelerated continuation of the pre-Independence process, but on the other hand something comparatively new, because of the shock at a deep level which Independence signified. Therefore not only are the signs of revitalization, mentioned above, quickened and enormously intensified, but—and this is the real point—everything has entered a new setting, and acquired a new dimension of purposiveness and intensity. The old glories of Buddhism, as visible for instance in Anuradhapura and Polonnaruwa, thanks to the excavations and restorations in the colonial era, have now acquired new glamour and inspiration. Naturally in Ceylon Buddhism, being felt as the national culture and the national religion, is also considered the ideology for building a new nation and State of one's own design. The huge problems this implies in the stress of modern life and conditions are to some extent recognized, but in practice shelved for the time being. The urge for Buddhist self-assertion after a long period of self-suppression overrides all these problems with elemental force. A strong anti-Western spirit is the inevitable consequence.

This powerful current of thought and feeling, directed towards the recovering of Buddhism's supreme pre-colonial position as the State religion, exerts enormous pressure on the Government to recognize Buddhism constitutionally as the national religion and to introduce compulsory religious (Buddhist) instruction in the schools. The existing Constitution contains the article that the State shall not discriminate in matters of religion, but the support and patronage of Buddhism in its religious and cultural activities has already emptied this article of most of its content. The Government tries to uphold its formal respect for the secular democratic principle of non-discrimination in religious matters by assuring all religious bodies that the Government is ready to extend support to other religions, but this assertion is of even less than theoretical value. The monks have become fierce, implacable political agitators and there is no politician who dares to ignore and forego their support, as the last elections for a new Government have plainly shown.

The thinking on the relation of the Dhamma with a world-denying monastic religion, which Buddhism is, especially in social and political matters, is still very confused. This confusion, however, does not put any brake on the emotional vehemence by which the demand for absolute Buddhist supremacy is proferred, or on Buddhist self-assurance in its encounter with Christianity or Western philosophy.

The recent colonial past, when the educational and social work of Christian Missions was supported by governmental grants-in-aid (a fixed item in all colonial policy), lends impetus to the demand for support, as appears in the constantly recurring argument disarming by its plausibility: "If Christianity received State support, why should not Buddhism?" This explosive determinate drive for Buddhist supremacy in all sectors of life engenders not only an anti-Western but above all an anti-Christian spirit. Christianity is hated as the concomitant of the colonial era. It is the more hated and combated because the Christian Churches, though a small minority of the population, are the greatest obstacle in the way to achieving a Buddhist State. By propaganda and by proposals to curtail or even to crush the possibility of existence of the Christian Churches, determined attempts are being made to achieve the wiping of Christianity from the map of Ceylon, and to make Buddhism the sole religion. This fierce drive for autarchy affects one as the Gandhian *Swadeshi* principle in religion and culture, run mad. The Buddha Jayanthi, that is to say the commemoration of the 2,500th anniversary of the death of the Buddha, has also given an enormous impetus to this Buddhist upsurge, because for the two years (May 1954-May 1956) of this commemoration a programme to intensify all Buddhist activities was operative.

In the midst of the religious and political agitation there were also trends which manifested messianic hopes for the appearance, in May 1956, of the Righteous Ruler who should set the world right. Also a Buddhist "ecumenical" breeze was blowing, as expressed in the pleas for overcoming the cleavage between Hinayana and Mahayana and replacing the "confessional" duality by agreeing on a harmonized creed, called Ekayana (One Way) or Navayana (New Way). The awakened consciousness of Buddhism reveals itself, as in Burma, in missionary ventures too, such as materialized in the first contingent of missionary monks sailing from Colombo to Germany in 1957.

This unbridled thrust for Buddhist supremacy, aggravated by the manipulation of the mechanics of the Western demo-cratic machine introduced in their formal governmental structure, clashes, however, with realities in the Ceylonese situation of the 20th century. The Ceylon of to-day is quite different from the Ceylon of the 18th century, when the Buddhist Kings gave all patronage to Buddhism and in so doing simply expressed the existing reality that the national religion and culture were Buddhist. Nowadays the population, which totals about eight million, is made up of five million Buddhists, practically all Sinhalese; 1,600,000 Tamil Hindus (mainly but by no means exclusively in the northern part of the island); 500,000 Muslims; about 750,000 Christians. In regard to such a demographic situation in religious respect, the constitutional rule of non-discrimination in religious matters seems to fit better than the imperious demand for Buddhist supremacy. In times of revolutionary transition, such as the time after Independence undoubtedly is, emotion and deep-rooted assumptions play, however, a far greater rôle in politics than any commendable reasonableness.

The numbers as to religious demography do not, however, give the full and real picture. There are more, very important, factors which necessarily force the tempestuous Buddhist drive into an insoluble clash with present reality. The Western pene-tration in all walks of life cannot be eliminated, in spite of all anti-Western sentiment. It is an irremovable political, economic, cultural and even spiritual force with moulding power. The Buddhist majority is in fact identical with the Sinhalese part of the population. The claim for Buddhist supremacy is there-fore identical with the claim for Sinhalese supremacy. In this light the claim for Buddhism as the national and paramount culture and religion must seem to the other groups outrageous and an insult to their peculiar "national" feeling. Moreover, the strong minority of Hindu Tamils are in economic respect better endowed, and therefore more progressive, than the Sinhalese. They still have strong ties with the 35 million Tamils in South India. The Christians count Tamils as well as Sinhalese amongst their numbers.

BUDDHIST PARADOXES IN ACTION

These observations reveal the inextricable tangle of religious, cultural, political and economic passions which are let loose by what is called the Resurgence of Buddhism in Ceylon, and which, on the political plane, focuses on the issue of *swabasha*. The duality of Ceylon in "national" respect (Sinhalese-Tamil) requires a parity of the two great languages for instruction and other purposes of literary expression, formulated in the word *swabasha* (each his own language, and the other's language as the second language). The Buddhist monk-politicians, in their wrathful zeal for the Buddhist cause, have voiced the demand for Sinhalese as the sole legally allowed language for all inhabitants of Ceylon: the exact counterpart to the justly famous Swiss solution of Switzerland's linguistic problem. As a result, an imbroglio of passionate economic, national and cultural-religious antagonisms has developed, which inevitably engenders the dangerous riots happening at the moment of writing this.

One can get some idea of the emotional and political situation in which Ceylon has now been caught up from the following quotation:[1]

Extremist and nationalist groups in Ceylon have launched a violent campaign against Europeans and against Christian, Hindu and Muslim minorities following the recent outbreak of violence between Tamil and Sinhalese speaking groups in Ceylon. The 7,000 Europeans, predominantly British, are being told that they must leave the country by the end of the year or face possible death. Thousands of leaflets and letters are also being distributed to members of Christian, Hindu and Muslim minorities. . . . One of the pamphlets reads: "Ceylon is only for the Buddhists. You are the people who brought these foreign religions to Ceylon and we orthodox Buddhists feel that unless and until we liquidate you we will not be able to stop the spread of Christianity and Islam to Ceylon."[2]

This analysis of the post-war resurgence of Buddhism calls

[1] Taken from the Ecumenical Press Service of the World Council of Churches; July 4th, 1958, p. 196.

[2] In the riots of the summer of 1958 about 20,000 persons were made homeless and about 300 killed (*loc. cit.*).

for a few further remarks. Involuntarily, in face of this explosive, dangerous situation, the question arises: What does this all mean? It is easy to condemn and bewail, and it is clear without any need for further exposition on what points one should condemn and bewail. It is, however, difficult, without minimizing condemnation and bewailment, to understand. It is clear that such a dangerous situation as has developed in Ceylon cannot last long without becoming suicide. Yet it is patently dominated by emotional frenzy that eventually must subside from sheer exhaustion and from the inherent impossibility of the demands. The destructive demonism which is inherent in it will, however, keep Ceylon, it seems, for a long time in the situation of a camp where different groups of people are living with one another at daggers drawn.

The focal question, however, is: how to explain that in this very country where the monks had for quite a long time a greater reputation for sloth than for learning, they are now the leaders of a fantastically desperate extremism? Moreover, an extremism which flouts all the glories of Buddhism as the paragon of tolerance, sweet reasonableness, peace, and harmony, substituting for them a demonic totalitarianism.[1] And this is happening while Buddhism in Ceylon is at the same time absorbed in the task of rethinking its place in the world, in its encounter with an adjustment to the thinking of the West. The way in which for instance attempts are made to rationalize the rabid political activity of the monks on Buddhist lines, is an indication of this struggle. On the one hand one feels the tension between ancient world-denying assumptions and modern demands of existence when one reads articles condemning the monks for taking part as propagandists in the governmental campaign under the slogan: "Grow more food". On the other hand the participation and training of monks in works of social service and in politics is commended as being

[1] In regard to the renaissance of Buddhism there is both co-operation and rivalry between Ceylon and Burma. They compete for leadership in the Buddhist world. A curious contrast between the situations in Burma and in Ceylon concerns this point of totalitarianism. In Ceylon it is blatant; in Burma it is subdued. In Ceylon the liquidation of all non-Buddhists is demanded, resulting in fierce anti-Western, and anti-Christian, anti-Muslim attitudes. In Burma the claim for religious and cultural Buddhist totalitarianism is pressed along many channels, but, as U Hla Bu states, the atmosphere contains that peaceable element to which we pointed above in regard to men like Sarma in India, and the tendency is to regard all religions as allies rather than as enemies.

an expression of truly Buddhist disinterestedness in the sense that, in doing so, one burns oneself out in movements which have nothing to do with one's own salvation.

The explanation of this paradoxical phenomenon of a hyper-violent, hyper-intolerant Buddhism at a time when it presents itself to the world as the acme of tolerance and the only hope for world peace, is perhaps in this case of Ceylon that it is a violent reaction against what has been undergone as a forcible Westernization (politically, economically, culturally, religiously), which was lorded over them (so it is felt) by the sheer inescapable power of the West. Although it has found its formulation in a programme of outright Buddhization of the country, it has ultimately little to do with Buddhism as such. Probably it can better be explained as another example of convulsive, rebellious reaction to the West, such as has manifested itself in Indonesia in its treatment of the Dutch, and in the Mau Mau troubles in Central Africa. And finally it should not be forgotten that the election of 1956, which meant the fall of Sir John Kotelawala and the rise of Mr. Bandaranaike, was at the same time an indication that the determining political power lay with the votes of the semi-literate villagers and factory-workers, to whom Mr. Bandaranaike's programme of socialism and rehabilitation of Buddhism appealed. The small group of Western-educated intelligentsia and Westernized well-to-do people ("the old gang"), which after Independence naturally assumed leadership, lost its prominent position and was replaced by a new class from the common ranks, which have not been exposed systematically to Western cultural orientation. This shift of the centre of power to other social classes is in all the Asian countries which achieved independence a fact of great importance, whether it is happening more below or more above the surface.

RESURGENCE IN INDIA

Much has been said in this book already on the Resurgence of Hinduism and its vicissitudes. The Neo-Vedantist version of Hinduism, whether it is that of Radhakrishnan, Aurobindo Ghose or others, clearly expresses the new self-consciousness of Hinduism as a universal and not as an ethnic philosophy of religion and way of life, and nourishes all the diverse attempts to restore the prestige of Hindu culture and religious renaissance. This point of the presentation of Hinduism as the most valid answer to the problem of man, world and life, and therefore with a claim for universality, deserves special emphasis.

The legal abolition of caste is in this context an important fact, with far-reaching possibilities for the future development of Hindu self-understanding and self-interpretation as to its place and claims in the world of to-day. Being a member of a caste has always been the indispensable condition for being a Hindu. Consequently conversion to Hinduism never belonged to the way of Hinduism, as one could be a Hindu by birth only. With the legal abolition of caste the emphasis of Hinduism has to fall more and more on its credal core or basic tenets, in so far as that has not happened already by the meeting with Western habits of mind. It means, however, also that, at least theoretically, it is not birth but conviction which decides whether a man has the right to call himself a Hindu or is rightly called so by others. For instance, it need not happen now as it happened to Mrs. Besant, who was by conviction an ardent Hindu, but who, when the plans for the Hindu University demanded the creation of an official governing body, could not be a member of it, because she was not Hindu in the technical sense. Mrs. Besant accepted this verdict loyally, though she had been one of the main dynamic forces in achieving the establishment of this University. Although the Hindu world as a result of its age-old "provincial" inhibition is not speaking in the same clear tones as modern Buddhism of its missionary nature and aims, yet in principle, by its bid for universality, it has become missionary. In practice this is already a fact in the activity of the Ramakrishna Mission Swamis in the West, although for philosophical reasons they feel and present their activity rather as spiritual permeation than as missionary penetration.

SOME SPECIAL FEATURES

India is, amongst the great countries of Asia, in most respects the classical example of Resurgence. Nevertheless we can be quite brief, as in previous chapters this has already been treated more than once, and therefore in this section we will only examine some striking features of the post-war Resurgence.

The characteristic difference between Resurgence up to Independence (1947), and after it, is by and large the same as in Ceylonese Buddhism. The shock of Independence effected a still greater consciousness of needing, on the way towards a new destiny, a new allegiance to the religious and cultural heritage of the past in which India had its roots, and finds its self-identity and its self-esteem. In comparison with the strong evidence of Resurgence before Independence, these basic facts were the more intensified. Resurgence acquired a note of defensive aggressiveness or aggressive defensiveness. This accounts for the fact that, although the Constitution guarantees not only religious liberty, but also religious expansion (or in the usual terms missionary expansion to any religious body which is animated by missionary principles), the attitude towards Christian Missions and their evangelistic activity, even when carried out by representatives of the Indian Church(es), has become increasingly cautious and refractory, in many cases inimical. It has become more and more difficult for Western missionaries to acquire a visa to enter India. If it is granted they are not permitted to do any evangelistic work, but are only allowed to work in the fields of education or some branch of social service. Evangelistic activity should be performed—such is the motivation—by Indian Christians, who are children and citizens of the country, and not by foreigners.

The note of nationalism is unmistakable here, but even in the case of Christians who are nationals their whole work is often surrounded by suspicion, aversion, and an increasing watchfulness in order to limit and fight Christian expansion. Evangelism is proselytism and proselytism is *eo ipso* condemned. Many telling examples could be given,[1] but this book does not set out to analyse modern missionary policy and experience. The important thing in our context is to indicate a definite trend and attitude for the time being.

One of the most conspicuous signs of this tension is the controversy about "conversion", which in current discussion practically means the right or wrong of exchanging allegiance to one religious community for allegiance to another community. This is not a new thing. The controversy started with

[1] For example, the much-discussed Niyogi Commission Report in Madhya Pradesh.

Gandhi's pronouncement against "conversion" (which meant in practice that a Hindu should not become a Christian).

It is very difficult, if not impossible, to get the deeply religious implications of the biblical-Christian term "conversion" into focus in the religious and the cultural atmosphere peculiar to India. The Hindus take "conversion" as a sociological matter; allegiance to a community. To them, it is a category in the sociology of religion. "Conversion" as a religious act, that is, surrender to Jesus Christ as the sole Lord of Truth and Life, is alien to any sociological category. Christianity uses the word in this radical sense only.

The basic tenet (to which nowadays special emphasis is given) that all religions are equally true and should live in mutual respect and tolerance with one another, excludes at the outset any possibility of raising the primacy of the question of truth in all its sharpness and depth. The *Swadeshi* principle as advocated by Gandhi is a logical derivation of the assumption of the equal truth and essential equality of all religions. Its paradoxical effect is, however, that respect and tolerance are accorded only to those who submit, as an indisputable point of truth, to the line of "live and let live". Those who feel that truth and conscience will not permit them to take this line, though quite ready to respect and be tolerant as they understand it on the basis of their own premises, are in fact neither respected nor tolerated. This dilemma implied in *Swadeshi* in religiosis or the nationalization of religion and culture lies behind the controversy on "conversion", and is essentially another form of the identification of Ceylonese and Buddhist culture and religion, which was analysed above.

How naturally this idea leaps to the mind in the present situation in Asia is demonstrated by a tendency amongst Chinese expatriates, when reflecting on the Chinese cultural heritage and its significance, to take the attitude that a Chinese should culturally never become a Christian nor a Westerner a Confucianist. This is a doctrine of cultural *Swadeshi*, the logical conclusion of which would be the meaninglessness of spiritual and cultural exchange, which is the life-blood of true cultural progress. Wherever the question of truth and value is prejudged, as is done in religious and cultural *Swadeshi* theories, the logical outcome is not so much mutual respect and tolerance as mutual

isolation and alienation. Communism has drawn this conclusion, symbolized in iron and bamboo curtains.

However, justified as these fundamental reflections are, there
are many other reasons underlying these forms of Resurgence,[1]
which are at the same time aggressive and defensive. The
discovery, or at least the hope, that after a long period of submission one can again be one's own self or at any rate try to be
so, is a potent factor in all these Resurgence manifestations of
a more deliberate attachment to the Hindu heritage, and in the
manifold endeavours to revive, inculcate and popularize it. This
does not in most cases imply a revolutionary religious experience, but it signifies a greater conformism, among all classes, in
seeking one's way in the opaque and turbulent world of to-day
by taking one's place in the stream of the great historic tradition.

In India, as we observed above about Pakistan, it cannot be
said that the Resurgence shows itself conspicuously by a
heightened "religious" life in popular religion except that the
age-old habits of processions, pilgrimages, appreciation of holy
places and so on are, one might say, more consciously cherished
as emblems of the Hindu way of life.[2] It should, however, not
be overlooked, when paying due attention to the phenomenon
of Resurgence, that the secularist outlook which has penetrated
in India and everywhere in the East has an influence on many
minds, especially of course in the urban centres, which though
silent cannot easily be over-estimated. This silent but potent
factor will increasingly challenge the Neo-Vedantist and Neo-
Hindu re-interpretation to come more realistically to grips with
the fundamental and dynamic problems involved in the whole
issue between a radical secular outlook on life and a religious-
philosophical interpretation of human life and the world.

SCIENTIFIC HUMANISM IN INDIA

It is important to remind oneself that the planned upbuilding
of the country is undergirded by a programme of scientific

[1] Very useful information is to be found in the four booklets written by Dr.
P. D. Devanandan and published by the Christian Institution for the study of
Religion and Society, Bangalore, 1958. The four titles are: *Living Hinduism*;
Resurgent Hinduism; *The Gospel and the Hindu Intellectual*; *Our Task Today*. In what
I have said I owe much to Dr. Devanandan's lucid expositions.

[2] It is very interesting to note that in the Indonesian island of Bali, with its
peculiar form of Hinduism, there are signs of "Hindu" reassertion aided by Hindu
"theologians" from India.

humanism, one of the dynamic and veritably un-Hindu infiltrations of the West. Modern Indian secularism manifests itself clearly, with numberless urbanites of some "education", in a passive indifference towards all religion. Here India shows a phenomenon which is ubiquitous in Asia, whether one goes to Rangoon, Bangkok, Tokyo or any other big centre of urban and intellectual life. A total indifference to or a clear repudiation of religion everywhere is partly—indeed to a considerable extent—fostered necessarily by Communism. The more conscious trend of modern Indian secularism totally ignores the claims of Hindu spirituality, not even taking the trouble to enter into polemics with it. As the advocate of "emancipation" it calls upon the "emancipated" Hindu intellectual to "live in the conviction that what matters is to make the most of the here and now in terms of material goods and earthly joys for oneself and for others".[1] It tries, apparently, to interpret in concrete terms the second part of the definition of secularism as given for the first time in the 1850's by G. J. Holyoake: "Secularism indicates a positive and exclusive concern with this life as the only possible province of human action and interest."

From an historical point of view it is extremely interesting to see that the modern Indian secularists take hold of very ancient Indian philosophies of materialism and atheism which for more than two thousand years have been ousted by the exuberant development of Indian spirituality. These too have been unearthed by the labours of modern Oriental scholarship and now, after a long death, have been resurrected under the stimulus of modern secularism.

The aggressive form of Resurgence, which is embodied in such movements as the All-India Hindu Mahasabha and the Rashtriya Swayamsevak Sangh (R.S.S. = National Service Organization), betrays affinity with the Buddhist Resurgence in Ceylon, for these movements claim Hinduism as the national religion and culture of India and stand for the establishment of a Hindu State. These forms in which orthodox Hinduism is organized are, notwithstanding their affinity in aim with Ceylonese Buddhism and their militancy, not so explosive. They oppose the present structure of the secular democratic State, which amongst other things introduces much legislation,

[1] P. D. Devanandan: *Resurgent Hinduism*, p. 21.

315

especially in civil law, which displaces the orthodox Hindu framework of society and therefore arouses strong opposition.[1]

From the ranks of the R.S.S. came the act of supreme violence, for it was one of its members who assassinated Gandhi.[2] It is a natural consequence of the directive ideas of these movements that they are very antagonistic to Christian evangelism. From their ranks proposals have come to get rid of the clause in the Constitution which recognizes the right of all religions to propagate their faith, by demanding that the State should proclaim the Hindu dogma that all religions are equally true and that no religion should claim to be the only hope of salvation. "They are prepared to tolerate any non-Indian religion but only as a sect of Hinduism."[3]

AN AGGRESSIVE RESURGENCE

This aggressive-defensive mood and activity, annoying as it may be to the Government, to the victims concerned and to many sincere Hindus, is, well considered, nothing to be amazed at. Hinduism as a way and system of life is *not* endlessly flexible, as one would be inclined to think when listening to the philosophical apologists. Coupled with its indeed Protean flexibility it has also its undeniable rigidity. It is the latter which comes to grips with the inrush of the modern world and its totally different standards or absence of standards, and with the problem of making terms with alien cultures and religions which by their fundamental nature refuse to integrate on the basis of Hindu fundamentals. This cannot but engender conflict and tension. It would therefore not be fair to dispose of such movements simply by calling them conservative or arch-conservative. They represent, more unequivocally than the philosophical

[1] This aspect of the development in India, like many others, cannot be elaborated here, but should be borne in mind. In the fields of social legislation, education, economics, very important things are happening and will happen. Here in fact is the battlefield of secularism, religious apprehensions and ancient hallowed religious-social orders. To the two latter this means corrosion and dissolution or re-interpretation, and the undermining of age-old religious sanctions and key ideas (Karma, Maya, etc.).

[2] The R.S.S. was outlawed after this act, and the Mahasabha decided to dissociate itself from political activities. This does not mean that they have ceased to influence thinking. Cf. Devanandan, *op. cit.*, p. 24.

[3] Devanandan, *op. cit.*, p. 24. The same writer tells us that recently two new organizations have been formed to oppose missionary activity, namely the Bharatiya Adamjati Sevak Sangh (National Society for Service Among Aboriginal Tribes) and the Dharam Raksham Sangh (Society for the Safeguarding of the Faith).

apologists, the natural unwillingness of a great type of spirituality to question what is—to them—its self-evident fundamental outlook on the world and life. Because of their tendency to identify historic forms and basic assumptions, they are, in this present world of rapid and convulsive change and flux, necessarily retrograde and reactionary, and therefore are often objectionable and reprehensible in their methods of dealing with the situation. In the realm of ultimate ideas and assumptions they and the philosophical apologists are essentially one.

In the light of these reflections, their special quarrel with Christianity and Christian evangelism is (leaving on one side the methods and means of action often used) normal and understandable. The philosophical apologists and their followers have the same quarrel with Christianity—also with Islam—and Christian evangelism. Only their way of expressing it is different, because they differ from their more rigid co-religionists in the matter of the relation of form and content. They are aware, too, of the relativities of history; but are in the main less disturbed by the militancy of their orthodox brethren than their liberal philosophy might lead one to expect.

Moreover, in the case of Christianity one point must not be overlooked. In this first period of Independence particularly, which accentuates the exhilaration of being master in one's own house, a certain resentment easily gets a footing; resentment against an alien religion which by the dispensations of history implanted itself during the colonial era. From whatever angle one may look at the Resurgence and its implications in relation to Christianity, the most reasonable conclusion seems to be this: that it is mainly up to Christianity and those who stand for the Christian cause to find the right way and to prove their spiritual and moral value for the country as a whole, and to strive indefatigably after the most fruitful way of mutual communication in word and deed.

RESURGENCE IS NOT REVIVAL

This attempt to analyse the manifestations and meaning of the present Resurgence of the great religions invites, it seems to me, the conclusion that it would be misleading to take it as a religious "revival" in the sense this term has in the West. There, revival means what happened for example in the United States at the Great Awakening, which began in the 18th century in Northampton (Conn.) through the instrumentality of the great Jonathan Edwards, and what occurred in the Methodist Awakening under John Wesley in England. That is to say, the total religious renewal of life; a new seriousness in following the Truth and drawing the consequences, a new personal surrender to God, happening to thousands of men and women, and issuing thereby into a movement of renewed dedication and responsibility in their religious communities. Revival is a depth-movement. The new religious understanding and experience as something genuinely new—this is the primary factor in a revival, whatever other factors there may be.

Mustering the manifestations of the Resurgence under discussion, the conclusion must be that it cannot be equated with a revival. This is by no means to assert that it is not important. It is extremely important, as well to the adherents of these religions as to those who, not being adherents, dwell amongst them. But this importance, especially in the transition through which these religions and cultures are living, lies in the fact that it is a phase in their development in a turbulent world and in the process of reaction and adjustment, challenge and response they experience in their attempt to determine their rightful place in a world pattern and life pattern never known before. Therefore political and cultural factors play a preponderant rôle, far greater than that of the purely religious factor, which seems rather lacking.

If one insists on using the word "revival", then it is only legitimate to speak of a cultural revival or a revival of cultural-religious self-identification such as is happening also in American Jewry. Its importance lies in the fact that it is part of nationalism in the wider and deeper sense presented above. It reveals itself as an intensification of attachment or allegiance to a world of religious cultural values, which is the matrix of one's existence whether one is conscious of it or not. That is why it is accompanied by so many endeavours towards cultural and philosophical restatement.[1] It is a re-assertion which unavoidably develops strong self-assertive traits, and all the ensuing anti's (anti-Christian, anti-Western, etc.).

As we have seen above, this confronts Christianity in the East

[1] F. S. C. Northrop in *The Taming of the Nations*, 1952, makes an interesting proposal to speak of "culturalism" instead of "nationalism".

and in the West with new questions as to its expression, conduct and way of seeking real communication, for its own sake and for the sake of the other. As such, it is a great challenge indeed. This *re*-assertion is particularly strong in the realm of Buddhism and Hinduism, and sometimes assumes paradoxical forms through the need not so much to find *a* place in the sun as to acquire the certitude for claiming *the* place in the sun. Radhakrishnan, for instance, after having first absorbed a great quantity of Christian and semi-Christian ideas, then suddenly asks: "What new things have you Christians and Westerners to offer us?"

Tolerance and freedom from dogma, which are constantly proclaimed as the crowning virtues of Hinduism (and Buddhism), unexpectedly assume an aggressive face because many voices demand that everybody who is a child of the country in which Buddhism and Hinduism live should submit to the belief that all religions are the same; submit to it as an infallible dogma which is above discussion. The difficulty experienced by sincere Hindus and Buddhists (the problem is quite different in the Islamic world) with Christianity is that it baffles them. Infuriates, even, might be not too strong an expression in regard to Christianity. The word "unique" in the field of religion stands at present under condemnation because of its pretentious connotations. Taking this into account, it is perhaps legitimate to say (considering the things actually happening in the Resurgence under discussion) that Christianity's baffling effect in the world of the great Eastern religions is an indication and unsolicited testimonial, if not to its "uniqueness", then at any rate to its exceptional, incurably deviating character. It does not fit into the pattern of Hindu assumptions, and thus unintentionally refutes Hinduism's claim to be all-comprehensive. Christianity as it stands is plainly indigestible. Therefore it must be adapted to Hindu fashions of thinking in order to become digestible.

RESURGENCE DETERMINED BY NON-RELIGIOUS FACTORS

As the present Resurgence is so largely determined by factors that are by nature cultural, political and psychological, it seems to me that one must reckon with a constantly changing picture and also with a constantly changing evaluation of the

West and of Christianity. As long as the West, for instance, retains the lead in every realm of cultural and technical life, so long will the reaction and response to it always contain a recognition of its indispensability mingled with irritation. The more the Eastern world gains in self-assurance and world responsibility, the less will the irritation become and the more will relations become normal, as the relations of equals. The "coming dialogue" set out in this book will then get its real chance. The Resurgence itself is a phase in the great event of Transition in which all cultures and religions find themselves involved. A symptom of it—one amongst others—is the still unclarified antinomies that crop up, such as the claim to have a mission to the world and the proclaiming of World Missions, whereas the ideal which in fact is aspired after is religious-cultural autarchy, which logically excludes all Mission. Another example is that on the one hand a strong self-assertive aggressiveness seems to paralyse real communication; yet on the other hand inter-religious fellowship and co-operation are sincerely and emphatically advocated.

RESURGENCE IS CULTURAL-RELIGIOUS

The last consideration is that it seems misleading to speak of the Resurgence of the *religions*. It would be better, when looking at the facts, to use the term cultural-religious Resurgence; because this Resurgence is first and foremost cultural, a reaffirmation of one's own cultural world. It is a Resurgence of a vivified consciousness of common cultural solidarity and devotion, caused by the confrontation with the West. As these cultures are basically religious in orientation, "religion" is implied in a general sense. Everywhere independence and having one's own way of life, even with dire poverty, is ardently preferred to political dependence (in which there is no real self-determination as to the way of life) with security and prosperity. In the East, religion and culture have always been so fully united that the culturalism of the Resurgence inevitably moves in the religious orbit also, with all possible sensibilities implied; but the primary point in the whole matter of Resurgence is the *cultural* way of life, in which a religious aspect is included. The term "religious", however, must then be understood in the sense of religious apprehension and not of prophetic dynamism.

Chapter Eleven

"THE COMING WORLD-CIVILIZATION"

THE vast spectacle unfolded in the preceding chapters leads to the question of the interrelation of the "Western" and "Eastern" Invasion in their effect on the general cultural outlook. The Western Invasion has meant the intrusion of science, technics, dynamism, liberal-democratic ideas of freedom, justice, the place and significance of the individual in the Eastern hemisphere with all its liberating and upsetting effects. In this whole complex the penetration of the mood of Western secularism is very essential because of its uprooting consequences in worlds of a completely different orientation. It is impossible to foresee whither this will develop, especially as this feverish process of tearing down and building up, of seeking for new foundations, is happening in an atmosphere of conflicting political and racial passions and antagonisms. Communism, by its dynamism, operating unscrupulously in an immensely explosive situation of emotions and interest- and power-struggles, is one of the most incalculable factors. The permeation with Christian-tinged humanitarian ideals of social service and social responsibility has become everywhere an ingredient of the social mood. D. S. Sarma recognizes it[1] by saying: "There can be no going back to the evil customs and the harmful restrictions of our age of decadence. Thus the present Renaissance has made India pay more attention to life on earth and the well-being of society."

But our investigation has revealed the many signs of re-assertion of their own worth in their cultural-religious heritages; the widening into universalist claims with a renewed sense of world mission, in Islam, Buddhism and Hinduism. To quote Sarma again:[2] "From an ethnic religion Hinduism has become a credal religion, which invites everybody into any room of its

[1] *The Renaissance of Hinduism*, p. 637.   [2] *ibid*, p. 643.

spacious mansion credally, but demands with this conceptual-dogmatic freedom and tolerance the claim for conformity with rituals, usages, formulas of the sect one chooses, for this *sadhana* is his way to realize God and go forth to the attainment of the Formless."

THE WEST FERTILE SOIL FOR THE EAST

Looking at the West, it ought to be stressed that it is not only the effect of the Eastern Invasion in the West that should be put in juxtaposition to the Western Invasion in the East. This Eastern Invasion, which has been set in motion and will constantly increase in strength, is ultimately the West's own doing. The most significant point is that the West, by its contacts and by its efforts of understanding, has by its Invasion in the East made the Eastern cultures and religions an event of great purport in its own quest, and an important part of its own native crisis in religion and culture. So this involvement in the Eastern cultural and religious values and achievements has provided the West with ample material for its own cultural and religious doubts and self-criticism. The least that can be said about it is that the inescapable fact of the plurality of cultures and religions has not only become a weighty practical and social problem, but in the spiritual realm of either creates a spirit of relativistic indifferentism, a leaning towards the plausibility of a synthetic common denominator as the evident solution, or a propensity towards regarding the Christian heritage as irrelevant. De Lubac's words[1]: "Si l'Europe ne retrouve pas sa foi, alors elle est mûre pour une colonisation spirituelle", are not inappropriate.

A number of interesting facts illustrate these words and lend support to the impression that the modern Western mind is in many respects fertile soil for typically Eastern attitudes and fundamental notions. The more fertile, because it is often permeated by a feeling of resentment and even scorn towards the hard core of some fundamental assertions of the West's religion, Christianity, which seems to be offensive to the current supremacy of humanist conviction. In adducing these facts no value judgment is intended. They are meant merely as symptoms.

[1] *op. cit.*, p. 274. "If Europe does not recover her faith, then she is ripe for a spiritual colonization".

We are living, in regard to religion, in a paradoxical situation. The unique and unprecedented situation in our period of history is that the inner driving power of cultural and social development, as determined by post-Christian Western secular civilization, is tending relentlessly towards a religion-less atmosphere and world. This "objective power" wrecks whatever good arguments one may have for the survival of religion. The dominating tendencies of our time (scientific and technical mastery and manipulation of nature, society and men) constitute a mass-suggestion towards a religious Void. In this context religion can figure only as an historical category, an atavism. The one-dimensional world of scientific, positive, verifiable knowledge has no room for a different dimension of experience and knowledge. In other words, it does not leave room for the dimension of faith; because, as Sartre has expressed it, the Transcendent is silent (*se tait*). C. G. Jung states as a result of his therapeutic experience:[1] "The modern consciousness shudders at faith and therefore also at those religions based on it." This is an illuminating observation, as it is true that there is a strong strain of spontaneous aversion in the modern mind to the attitude of religious faith, particularly to Christianity. The underlying, unformulated dogma is the primordial conviction of the *aseitas hominis* (man's underivable self-subsistence), which has taken the place of the old doctrine of God's exclusive *aseitas*.

This is only one pole of the paradox. The other pole is represented by the fact, which seems to be contradictory to the drive for a religious Void, that our time is by no means divested of religiosity or of productive power in the field of religion. Distinctions have to be made here. The existing religious vacuum issues not only in irreligion, but also in the creation of a host of "pseudo" or "parody" religions, idolatries and mythologies. The "resurgence" of the Religions, examined at length in a previous chapter, is another sign of the irrepressibility of Religion. Again, another aspect is the proliferation of sects in the realm of the Christian Church. In regard to America Charles S. Braden[2] has published an interesting study

[1] *Seelenprobleme der Gegenwart*, p. 417.
[2] *"These also believe"*: *A Study of Modern American Cults and Minority Religious Movements*, 1953.

323

on this subject, showing that there are constantly growing "pseudo" Churches with a more or less strong Christian residue. They are marked, however, by new elements of emphasis: on healing, on peace of mind, on happiness, on prosperity, on success, on plenty, etc., attracting thereby hosts of people, the more so because they develop an enormous advertising activity. The stress is on longing for healing, peace of mind, security in regard to the good life *here* and *now*; that is to say, wholly *diesseitig*.

Although very different in mood and quality from the examples just mentioned of the activity of the religious appetite, the fact should be remembered that in the midst of the religious Void many thoughtful minds, not unaware of the general situation, have their private religiosity; and this, notwithstanding their detachment from organized or "dogmatic" religion, they cherish as a precious thing. They probably agree with Goethe's recognition of *unbekannte himmlische Mächte* (unknown divine powers) as the expression for their ultimate religious stand, but do not wholly accept Faust's famous phrase: "Wer Wissenschaft und Kunst besitzt, der hat auch Religion; wer diese beide nich besitzt, der habe Religion".[1]

Looking at these aspects it is undeniable that the great 19th century demolishers of religion (Marx, Nietzsche, Comte, Ingersoll) who predicted with prophetic certitude the speedy eclipse of religion and rang its death-knell, have been disproved in their diagnosis.

The paradoxical situation alluded to above is, however, not only constituted by this conjunction of the "objective power" which animates our secularist civilization, and of the abiding "subjective power" of human religious craving, whatever the quality or motivation may be. The symptoms of "colonisation spirituelle", mentioned above, are one of its most intriguing traits.

A MIGHTY CURRENT TOWARDS THE UNIVERSAL

The interest shown by the West in Eastern cultures and religions is in no respect a startling surprise. On the basis of all

---

[1] "Whoever possesses knowledge and art also has religion; whoever does not possess these two, may he come to have religion."

that has happened in the last 150 years, it is wholly understandable. The extraordinarily remarkable phenomenon[1]
which presents itself to us, however, is that one can perceive
through various signs in the modern mind a mighty current of
conscious and unconscious return to the universal, "natural"
religion which is strikingly expressed in the archaic systems of
life and thinking and which has found its sublimest expression
in the great Asian religious cultures. Especially in Hinduism,
Chinese "Universismus", and Buddhism. In other words, the
fundamental notions, shorn of the many appendages in rite and
custom characteristic of these Eastern systems of life- and world-
apprehension, seem to strike a responsive chord in many
leading modern minds.

In my book *The Christian Message in a Non-Christian World*
I have given this peculiar life- and world-apprehension[2] the
name of Naturalistic Monism, defining it more specifically as
"trans-empirical realization", meaning thereby that man conceives all his efforts of religious practices, asceticism, meditation,
concentration, etc., as means towards realizing and grasping
the identity of his real self with divine or ultimate reality.
Instead of "trans-empirical realization" one can say "God-
realization" or "Self-realization", which amounts to the same
thing. This is not to say that so-called "modern consciousness"
is responsive to this God- or Self-realization in the genuine
mystic sense of these expressions. But it is responsive to the
anthropocentric connotations which are inherent in this many-
splendoured "Naturalistic Monism", which is one of the first
great religio-philosophical intuitions and experiences of mankind, flowering into many cults, religions, philosophies,
mythologies, full of gnostic flavour.

The great attention paid by C. G. Jung to the Asiatic religions, especially in their gnostic and mythological aspects; his
endeavour to unveil the similarities of the phenomena in
modern neurosis with the wisdom of these systems; the widespread sympathetic interest in many quarters in this wisdom,
are therefore quite natural. It is not only a vogue for the exotic,
but most certainly a pointer to a mysterious happening in the
depth of collective modern consciousness. It affects one like the
working of a gulf stream under the surface of the ocean. It is as

---

[1] Here I return to a point only touched upon in the first chapter.   [2] p. 143.

if science- and technic-ridden man, void of all religion, instinctively returns to the origins, to the beginning. The anthropocentric connotations of the sublime notions of Naturalistic Monism suggest a kind of a-religious mystique, and at the same time a mystique-less sense of unification of the mind. This mysterious happening in the depth of collective modern consciousness reaches, moreover, further and deeper than religion in the strict or derived sense of the word. Indications are, e.g., also the spontaneous modern sensitivity to primitive art and music, jazz and dance. It is more than a ransacking of all cultures, being laid open to us by spade research and intermingling of races, for the satisfaction of a hedonistic consumption-drive. It is a return to buried elemental patterns, a liberation and new enslavement in one.

Some illustrations may shed light on this situation as I see it. In this respect the famous psycho-analyst C. G. Jung is of prime importance, as well in regard to himself as to the insights to which his psycho-therapeutic experiences have led him. To these I have already had occasion to refer in quoting his words: "The modern consciousness shudders at faith and therefore also at those religions based on it." In studying his writings one comes to the conclusion that, in spite of the fact that Jung has the honest conviction of being neither a *Bekenner* (confessor) nor a metaphysician, but merely an empirical psychologist and interpreter of religion, he is in fact a teacher and advocate of a religion wholly immanentist and representing a synthetic universal gnosticism. He himself uses the words: "the religion that is the sole true one and the only one that can be true". Martin Buber[1] is undoubtedly right in maintaining that Jung's real background is "the confession of an eminently gnostic God, in whom good and evil are connected with each other, and balance each other out". This gnostic God is a God-idea, not a real God who reaches into actual life. Jung's book: *Antwort auf Hiob* (1952)[2] which openly rejects all pretensions of being merely scientific, presents in its attempt to bridge the existence of Evil and of a "good" and "perfect" God, a daring modern form of gnostic metaphysic. In doing so he avows frankly his pose as the "accuser and arbiter of God and the religions" ("der

[1] In his book: *Gottesfinsternis*. (E.T. *Eclipse of God*, 1953.)
[2] E.T. *Answer to Job*, 1954.

Kläger und Schiedsrichter Gottes und der Religionen").

Turning to Jung's judgment (on the basis of his therapeutic praxis) on modern man, it is striking to find pronouncements in the same direction. He says for instance:[1] "modern consciousness turns to the soul and does so in a gnostic sense", explaining the meaning of the word "gnostic" by saying that it is "a fusion of opposites in an all-embracing unified form".

Extremely interesting too is Jung's statement that the modern "mandalas" appearing in the dreams of his neurotic patients do not symbolize, as the Asian mandalas do, the Divine in the centre, but have the centre in themselves, representing "the wholeness of man" (die Ganzheit des Menschen). Jung calls it das Selbst, which reminds one immediately of the Indian Atman or Self. Here is an unmistakable affinity between the anthropocentric, god-less Indian metaphysic and the subconscious data of modern consciousness. Jung's therapeutic doctrines aiming at showing the way of Self-release and Self-realization fit in with the aristocratic Ways of Self-release developed so richly in Hinduism, Buddhism and Taoism. Many names from different countries could be cited to substantiate the same conceptions of human dignity and ability to work one's own salvation, and the same predilection for the uncompromising, self-confident training towards Self-realization in whatever interpretation, of which the great Asian soteriologies are the most intrepid expressions in history. In Hinduism by its a-cosmistic Monism; in Buddhism by its radical phenomenological relativism and psychological positivism; both by their astounding psychological penetration as manifest in Yoga, that combination of fearless experimentalism and spiritual athleticism.

De Lubac has signalized the attitude bouddhisante. One could speak as well of the attitude hinduisante. One of the first names that come to mind is again Hermann Keyserling, to whom I have referred more than once. According to Keyserling, India has produced the profoundest metaphysic ever presented, and its pragmatist, relativistic conception of the function of religion is the perfect solution of the difficulty of religious pluralism.

Aldous Huxley's Perennial Philosophy with its immanentist,

---

[1] In Geheimnisz der goldenen Blüte, p. 73. (E.T. The Secret of the Golden Flower, with foreword by Jung.)

anti-personalist, anti-historical bias sees in certain Mahayana-sutra's the most perfect expression of the "philosophia perennis", just as René Guénon in his haughty way has been[1] the prophet of the "Primordial Tradition", the absolute Truth, preserved by India's faithful guardianship.

L. Ziegler in his many books has become the spokesman (for many) of one of the representative types of mystical-philosophical thinking, that is to say the doctrine of the "perfect man" (Ziegler calls it *der ewige Mensch*) as the central idea of all religion and the hidden meaning of all myth (Marduk, Purusha, Krishna, Adam Kadmon). It is evident in utterances of enthusiastic adherents of this view that its attraction lies just in this centrality of man with exclusion of God.

TOYNBEE—AN ASIAN SAGE

Arnold Toynbee, both in his Gifford Lectures[2] and in his *Christianity Among the Religions of the World*, notwithstanding his subjective faithfulness to the "Christian" tradition and his use of Christian terms,[3] reveals in his fundamental position exactly the Indian or East-Asian pragmatist attitude towards religion. In principle he can walk, like an Asian sage, all ways, but in practice for convenience's sake he prefers the accustomed "Christian" way, certainly also for reasons of genuine affection. His whole trend of expressing himself suggests an intellectual preference for the Asian conception of religion. As he is seriously concerned about good inter-religious relationships as a new issue and cultural task, he speaks repeatedly about the qualifications of the different great religions for good-neighbour-ship. In this respect there is in his opinion no trouble from the side of the higher religions of East Asia. By their innate tolerance they are admirably fitted for the "job". The trouble lies with Christianity, Judaism and Islam.

The innate intolerance and arrogance of Christianity and Islam, which they inherit in his opinion from the fanaticism inherent in the "jealous God" of the Old Testament, represent a formidable difficulty, necessitating a call to repentance and conversion. For this "intolerance", this "fanaticism", is a form

---

[1] Cf. his: *Introduction to the Study of Hindu Doctrine.*
[2] *An Historian's Approach to Religion.*
[3] "Original Sin" is one of the most precious to him.

of pride, of self-centredness, manifestations of "Original Sin". The only way to overcome this defect and to purge it out of Christianity is that the "higher religions" agree "to centre on a spiritual good, God or Absolute Reality", in which they find their unity. With goodwill this is possible, and in order to facilitate the solution Toynbee adds some "theological" considerations, based on Christian motives of thinking. If God is Love, says Toynbee, it is unthinkable that He should have given His revelation only to Christians and not "in some measure" everywhere "in different forms, with different facets, and to different degrees according to the difference in the nature of individual souls and in the nature of the local tradition of civilization".[1] All the higher religions may and do differ in the content and degree of Revelation given to mankind through them, but they too are light from the same source. "This must be so if God is the god of all men."

So Toynbee, pointing to God's Nature (love, *self-sacrifice*, not self-centredness) as his first and last court of appeal for his understanding of Revelation, pleads for the possibility and feasibility of keeping to the truth and rightness of Christianity and rejecting the arrogant thesis: I, *my* church, *my* people, have the sole and unique revelation. Toynbee expresses as his belief that "in a peaceful competition the best of the competing religions will eventually win the allegiance of the whole human race",[2] not by eliminating the others but by absorbing essential elements, as was done in the 3rd century. So we could have "conviction without fanaticisms, belief and action without arrogance or self-centredness or pride".[3]

I have devoted some space to consideration of Toynbee, without entering into any critical analysis of his reasoning, his presuppositions and historical assumptions, because he is widely read. He reflects in his representations widespread, modern religious feeling, which spontaneously rejects all that suggests exclusiveness, intolerance or the thesis of the uniqueness of Christianity. At the same time he is one of the main feeders of this attitude. The more so because Toynbee's way of reasoning, led by a simplistic rationalism and emotionalism in one, has an easy appeal to modern religious feeling. In our context the

---

[1] *Christianity Among the Religions of the World*, p. 96.
[2] *ibid.*, p. 110. [3] *ibid.*, p. 111.

main point, however, is that his method of equating and differentiating the religions is only understandable in Hindu perspective. Nor is it less important that the appeal it makes is an indication of the fact that the Indian pragmatic view of religion, although still motivated under typically Christian angles of view, has penetrated far more deeply into many minds in the West than is generally realized. Asian thinking achieves already many effortless victories in the West. Its claim to be undogmatic and tolerant chimes in with the modern mind. Panikkar (*op. cit.*, p. 447) quietly says that Hinduism knows its position is unassailable and that a doctrine of the monopoly of Truth and Revelation is absurd to the Asian mind.[1]

HERMANN HESSE AND W. T. STACE

Another writer who has, like Toynbee, a great audience, and who, also like Toynbee, reflects and feeds a mood at the same time, is the famous Swiss poet and writer Hermann Hesse. Some years ago a special study was devoted to the meeting of Christianity with the Asiatic religions as it appears in Hesse's literary production.[2] One of Hesse's most important works is his *Siddharta*. He characterizes it himself as a confession of his faith. In the person of Siddharta (Buddha) he tried to picture the mystical ascent of the soul towards oneness with God. Hesse advocates an "Indian-Asiatic coloured" religiosity, which is wholly animated by the idea of Unity. His personal object was to achieve a synthesis of Christian and oriental-mystical religiosity, which appears especially in his stress on responsibility in the world and personal immortality; two points which have no place of any significance in the Indian quest. But his chief concern was mystical experience and realization. The religions are dialects of the same ideal *Urreligion*. Therefore all religions are good and lead to an identical goal.

The importance of a figure like Hesse, who was a sincere God-seeker, is not whether he wrought a valid synthesis of

---

[1] As I abstain from critical analysis in order to let the facts speak, I abstain also from pointing out that such words as "monopoly" and the theses about tolerance and intolerance betray a deep misunderstanding of Christianity.

[2] Gerhart Mayer: "Die Begegnung des Christentums mit den asiatischen Religionen im Werk Hermann Hesses", 1956. In *Untersuchungen zur allgemeinen Religionsgeschichte*, Neue Folge, Heft I.

Christianity and Asian religion,[1] but consists in the fact that by his literary genius he created symbols of the all-embracing and all-identifying spirit of Indian religion. Being a man hungry for unitive mysticism, it is striking that Hesse, who was brought up in a Christian family in which religion was a living reality, did not turn to the great representatives of Christian mysticism, but to Buddha and the Upanishads.[2]

One finds even the wholly anthropocentric and pragmatic conception of religion, so congenial to East-Asia, in rather unexpected places as, e.g., in a collection of testimonies edited by Edward R. Murrow under the title: *This I believe*. This collection contains only voices of noted American writers or artists, and turns upon the ideas of the dignity of man, serving your fellow-man and belief in the intrinsic goodness of human nature. Rebecca West's definition: "religion offers a technique to get in touch with God", combining with it an agnostic attitude towards the possibility of knowing God, is fairly typical of the collection. This tendency to consider religion not as a matter of truth—that is the business of philosophy—but as a technique and discipline for attaining a goal by oneself, is pure Asian doctrine. Wing Tsit Chan in his *Religious Trends in Modern China* formulated the rule very aptly: "Truth is the domain of philosophy; religion of technique and discipline, either for the fulfilling of desires (lower level) or for peace, endurance, harmony (higher level)." These yogistic techniques can become wholly secularized,[3] a pure training in efficiency and self-reliance by self-mastery, or aim at peace and harmony of mind. The growing vogue of yoga training and Zen practice in the West serves both ends, the secular and the inner; either efficiency by self-mastery or self-realization in peace and harmony. To genuine Western feeling these immanent anthropocentric concerns have a strong a-religious flavour.

The most controversial topics in human history are solved by

---

[1] In my personal opinion, he did not.

[2] Romain Rolland, a writer of even greater power than Hesse, I mention only in passing, as his activity lies now too far back.

[3] The Eastern methods of yoga and contemplation as derived from Indian yoga, Buddhism in general and Zen in particular, as practised in the West are divested of all mythology and construed with an eye to Western needs, as rationalized means for self-realization and self-mastery. The many methods of self-education for acquiring the necessary qualities for success in life, so profusely advertised, derive many suggestions from these importations from the East.

contributors to Murrow's collection offhand by simple theses, all strongly humanist in emphasis.[1]

Although a lonely, scarcely known figure, W. T. Stace of Yale is by his book *Time and Eternity*[2] a notable illustration of the significant fact that every possible position can be combined with the spirituality of the East, whereas the case, e.g. with Christianity, is quite different. As I am convinced that there are many people, amongst modern mathematicians and physicists, who see in the Eastern way of speculative thinking an acceptable road towards combining a scientific view of space and time with spiritual conviction, I think it useful to dwell rather at length on Stace's remarkable book.

Stace pronounces himself to be a devotee of Naturalism, which logically includes atheism. But being interested in overcoming the antagonism between religion and science, he has contrived to write a fine book on the symbolic, intuitive quality of religion, following Whitehead's definition: "Religion is the vision of something which stands beyond, behind and within the passing film of immediate things, something which possesses the final good and yet is beyond all reach, something which is the ultimate ideal and the hopeless quest." Under this aegis, pointing in the direction of mysticism, Stace develops a *theologia negativa* (God is Non-being, Nothing, the ineffable, indefinable Mystery) as the true way, the way of all mystical experience and intuition in all ages. The classical expression of the idea that the essence of religion lies in religious experience, is, says Stace, to be found in the East. Conceptual differences in definition there (Brahma, Nirvana) are irrelevant. All theological and metaphysical thinking about God is mere elaboration made after the experience, and therefore symbolic. The mystic experience is identical with God. To speak of God as a person, as Creator, as Love, etc., is merely conceptual, symbolic speaking. The honour of Buddhism is that it declines this conceptualization.

Now, Naturalism (the look from without) asserts the sole

---

[1] Pearl Buck says for instance: "My faith in humanity stands firm." People like ex-President Hoover and Mrs. Roosevelt, both loyal members of a Christian Church, say: "There is one foundation common to all religious faith", and: "Develop the very best that you can develop". These utterances prove their confused syncretism in the matter of Religion and Christianity.

[2] Published 1952.

reality of the natural time- and space-order, denying the reality of the divine mystic order (the order of eternity). The moment of mystic illumination happens at the intersection which belongs to both orders. From within this moment is God, from without it is a passing stage. Both orders are self-contained but logically the intersection takes place at every time-moment and space-point. God is therefore literally omnipresent also in animals, plants and stones, though in entire darkness. The human mystical experience *is* God. It is also the justification of faith, revelation and religious intuition. These three are "one and the same thing". There is no natural theology, only mystical experience, intuition or revelation. "God is either known by intuition or by revelation or not at all." And in this mystical experience God is realized.

All religious language is symbolic. The only difference that can be made is that there are more adequate and less adequate forms of religious symbolism, which causes differences. Another cause of religious differences is the different geographic, cultural and historical environments that interact, nevertheless with the same basic religious intuitions. Philosophy of Religion (e.g. Hegel, Spinoza), with its natural rational bent, attempts the impossible, that is to say to justify rationally that God both is and is not in the world.

In fact, Stace has given in his book a crystal-clear exposition of the Ultimates of Asian thinking on immanent mysticism, but divested from its innate thirst for Salvation, Liberation (*moksha*), serene Peace and Tranquillity, and reduced to its kernel of intellection. His exposition is in this respect even more crystal-clear than that for instance of Radhakrishnan, with whom Stace shares the thesis on the basic centrality of mystical experience. For this Indian thinker as apologist of Hinduism has to devote himself to many concerns of synthesis and re-interpretation, which are irrelevant for the exclusive *sub specie aeternitatis* interest of Stace's.

EAST AND WEST—SPIRITUAL UNIFICATION

It is now necessary for the subject of this book to turn to a somewhat different aspect, namely, the more culturally inspired endeavours to think in the terms of a coming world civilization in which the fundamental notions and options of East and

West enter into a new dimension of cultural and spiritual unification.

One might characterize these endeavours, which by-pass the dialogue which according to the thesis of this book has still to happen, as individual prophetic dream-thinking. Even if this interpretation is right, the contributions to this line of thinking have real value. They are a useful kind of stocktaking, of diagnosis, of reviewing of contemporary history, and of self-examination.

The main samples selected for serious consideration are W. E. Hocking's *The Coming World Civilization*[1] and F. S. C. Northrop's *The Meeting of East and West*.[2] Stimulating, but without undue pretension, is L. Abegg's very interesting study *The Mind of East Asia*.[3] Miss Abegg does not aim at speculating on one unified world civilization, but tries simply to get a surer grasp of the difference in Eastern and Western mentality, profiting from what the *komplexe Psychologie* of Jung and others have taught us. Her simple thesis, deepened and enriched by illuminating illustration, is: the mental processes of the East-Asian mind are different from those of the Western mind. The Easterners (in this case the Chinese) are "total" and not intellectual as the Westerners. Their wisdom is mystical philosophy, equilibrium and self-control, resting in "the centre" of the Self in which everything is seen and felt. Self-realization, self-mastery and maturity of wisdom, *not* originality (as in the West) is prized. The Westerner is split, the Easterner unified. Miss Abegg's observations, which betray a great sympathy for the normative Chinese mentality,[4] are a good introduction to Northrop's massive book: *The Meeting of East and West*.

Northrop's concern is not the same as Stace's, viz., how to reconcile Naturalism = Science with religion = mysticism. The sub-title of his book is the phrase: "An Enquiry Concerning World Understanding", and expresses his object. It is to find a solution for the problem of formulating unified standards and a comprehensive theory, valid for the conflicting ideologies and

[1] Published 1956.   [2] Published 1946.

[3] Published 1952. Miss Abegg is an outstanding Swiss journalist, who has lived long in Eastern countries and manifests great powers of observation and insight.

[4] Cf. also Pearl Buck in many of her books. She carries her predilection to such an extent that, though coming from a Christi n home, she often misunderstands Christianity in its fundamental motives.

ideals of the East and the West. His ambition in this under-taking runs very high. Nothing is excluded in this unifying effort. It embraces the Western and Eastern philosophical, religious, political and economic theories, Communism, the Latin-American and Anglo-Saxon American worlds with their peculiar attitudes and philosophies.

Northrop's fundamental thesis[1] is: In human history the basic philosophical ideas of a society or a cultural province are always the primary, creative factors. Therefore World Under-standing requires a unified philosophy, which comprehends all existing "philosophies" in a transformed way. As it is urgently required in our world of to-day, it is possible. The unabated optimism expressed in this last part of the thesis characterizes the whole book and all his other writings. This enormous simplification, which reveals his blindness for history, and his axiomatic confidence in the power of theoretical reasoning, enables him to achieve a very acute analysis of Western and Eastern culture. It disables him, however, and hinders him from being awed by any incompatibility. In various cases he sees it, but overcomes it with ease by putting two incompatible attitudes in mutual relation to each other by declaring them "complementary".

In itself the approach expressed in the word "complemen-tary" is not at all despicable. It is one of the new ways in modern physics of accepting logically contradictory theories in regard to natural phenomena as equally and simultaneously true. It is also congenital to the tenor of Eastern thinking.[2] As will appear, Northrop is, however, too easily inclined to forget that the application of the idea of complementarity in the historical reality of human apprehension, option and decision is a far more complicated and subtle business than in the field of physics, where the matter of "consciousness and being", which is the crucial point in man's existence in the universe, is non-existent.

Without putting on the airs of a world reformer, Northrop

[1] It recurs in all his writings. Cf. *The Taming of the Nations*, "Toward a Religion with world-wide transforming power", in the 7th Symposon of the Conference on Science, Philosophy and Religion; "Comparative Religion in Today's World" in *The Christian Century*, September 14, 1955. Northrop's analysis of Mexican culture is very fascinating.

[2] Lily Abegg's book, treated briefly above, stresses this point more than once.

often falls into the tone of a universal philosophical Lawgiver and Reconciler of all opposites, as when he states[1] confidently that he intends to define the *correct*[2] relation between the basic beliefs and values of the East and of the West, and to resolve the difficulties underlying the conflicts between Democracy and Communism, Latin and Anglo-Saxon values, the mediaeval and modern world. Northrop's all-comprehensiveness, aiming at a conciliatory synthesis of all harmonies and disharmonies, reveals in its own way the spontaneous affinity to Eastern ways of apprehension of which I have already given many instances. It forgets, however, the rule—which inculcates modesty and soberness in this respect—that not everything that can, with goodwill, be *thought* into one, is necessarily able or ready to *live* in unity.

BRINGING EAST AND WEST TOGETHER

Northrop brings the West together under the denominator of the "theoretical component" and the East under that of the "aesthetical component". The first is scientific-rational, discursive; the second is intuitive and total.[3] Northrop notes that in the West it is more and more recognized that the true relation between intuitive "aesthetic",[4] religious and scientific is that of mutual supplementation. This idea is native to the East. Therefore the great task of the West is to understand the East.[5] This is indispensable for a correct (!) solution of its problems and a correct understanding of itself. The basic problem of East and West is the same, i.e. to determine the relation between the aesthetic and theoretical compound in things by combining the intuitive genius of the East with the scientific genius of the West, in order to found a world-civilization grounded in the equally primary theoretical and aesthetic compound[6] of things, which have to function in a complementary way. In Northrop's opinion it is a fortunate thing that the East already gladly welcomes the science of the West.

[1] *op. cit.*, p. 12.   [2] Italics mine.   [3] Cf. Abegg.

[4] Although not wholly consistently, Northrop does not use this term in the ordinary way, but he means by it in most cases the way of "knowledge" (gnosis) only by what is immediately "apprehended". The East is its great representative. But sometimes Northrop gives different senses to "aesthetic", meaning by it either "observed, sensed facts" or "immediately apprehended reality" in the philosophical or artistic sense.

[5] *op. cit.*, p. 311.   [6] *ibid.*, p. 434.

In religious respect the East has nothing to learn from the West with its limited determinate theistic ideas. The reverse is true. Western religious leaders should go to the East to acquire its intuitive turn and contemplative habits. Northrop evinces a deep admiration for China and its culture. He accepts China's keyword: "Tao", the equivalent of the undifferentiated Brahman of India, as the universal keyword, in which the lower-grade theistic conceptions of the West have to be integrated. Only if that has happened will there be occasion to speak of a perfect religion. It is the religion that conceives of God as embracing the Divine and the "True Self" as understood in the Eastern "aesthetic" component and the Divine and the Soul of the theistic religions. This perfect religion, representing a moral and religious *humanism*, can gain the response of the whole world as each religious group can preserve therein its integrity and self-respect.

It is impossible to give an adequate account of such a voluminous work. Fairness compels one to say that Northrop's analysis of Oriental culture is sensitive both to its "positivistic" bases, their inter-relation with intuitive natural truth and the fellow-feeling or social obligation between men in society.[1] Yet it is undeniable that his pacification and unification of ideologies and "components" is not so harmonious as the thesis pretends. Northrop, like Keyserling, Toynbee, Abegg, Huxley, etc.,—although in different tone and accents—harmonizes in theory only, as a point of programme. In fact, he, like the others, is a Western protagonist of the superiority of the East; the religion and philosophy he prefers is Buddhism, as so many other Western writers do.

This outspoken predilection for the East is not emphasized here for the sake of criticism or blame. It is here simply stated as one more example of an influential Western writer and thinker, who proves our thesis of the open gates in the West for the Eastern spiritual and cultural invasion. Justified criticism enters in at another point. Books such as Northrop's *The Meeting of East and West* in most cases announce, as Northrop does, a programme and thesis of cultural synthesis and philosophical reconciliation. But this in the course of execution

[1] The intractable exceptions to Northrop's unitary picture of the East are nationalist Shintoism and theistic, aggressive Islam.

breaks down on the intrinsic impossibility of the superhuman pretension of the thesis and on the ultimate, concrete content of the programme for a world civilization, built on the *complementary* combination of the "aesthetic" and "theoretic" compound as equally primary. Especially in the field of religion, this programmatic equating of cultural and spiritual contribution from either side turns out to mean that in the resulting perfect religion Eastern religiosity represents—to use Indian philosophical terms—*paramavidya* (higher truth), and Western religiosity *aparamavidya* (lower truth). This is quite logical, because the religious choice or preference is integral mysticism. Northrop himself says so at the end of his book, quite plainly.[1] "In tune with Nature" is the core of Chinese philosophy and of truth. Therefore when looking to the West, Northrop states that the priority of truth does not belong to the theoretic, doctrinal, orthodox religion of the male Moses, Christ or Muhammad and their determinate unseen Yahweh or God the Father, but to the intuitive, contemplative, indeterminate, "aesthetic" and emotional religion of the Western *theologia negativa*, the mysticism of John of the Cross and the cult of the Virgin at Guadeloupe in Mexico.[2]

This is neither reconciliation nor pacification, but a very definite choice. It is therefore logical that, in spite of his synthetic urge, Northrop shows no interest in the Hebrew component of Western culture, has a manifest aversion to Islam and a clear contempt for the Reformation and its background. Greek philosophy and modern philosophy since Locke and Kant hold his interest in accordance with his chiefly intellectual approach.

In his book *The Taming of the Nations*, Northrop on the background of his overall approach deals more specifically with the contemporaneous political situation. This political concern, in which Communism clearly does not fit into any comprehensive construction, in spite of his all-inclusive world philosophy,

[1] Cf. *op. cit.*, p. 462.

[2] To understand the insertion of the Mexican Virgin one has to take into account Northrop's stress on the Mexican departure from the standard Roman Catholic conception of the Virgin. In Mexico, he says, Mary is divine in her own right, the female Logos, who is in the countryside never represented as the Madonna with the Child (the male Logos), but alone. Likewise, in contradistinction to Roman Catholic custom, according to Northrop, the crucifix is absent from worship in the countryside.

turns his expectations of the perfect religion (see above) towards the idea of the *Civitas Dei* in its "culturalist" outlook. Its symbol is Cosmopolis, "that single earthly polity whose model is the unity of the Asians' intuition and the Occidentals' constitutional image of the Universal City".[1] World Peace can only be founded on the recognition of cultural pluralism, which includes religious pluralism, and Northrop takes great care to establish that on the basis of this policy all religions are safe within the American orbit and can live in quiet if they leave one another alone.

It is interesting to turn from Northrop to W. E. Hocking's *The Coming World Civilization* (1956). It is not such a vast, over-ambitious, intellectual synthesis as Northrop's opus, that starts from a fundamental syncretism and ends in a kind of static harmonization, from which the dynamic of history and man vanishes away. It claims to see *possibilities* for one world civilization and one world religion (though this latter in a qualified sense). It is in its treatment more diversified, more penetrating and more aware of the elusiveness of the whole subject. Whereas Northrop's book, in Eastern fashion, keeps "Religion" under the supreme judicial power and authority of theoretical thinking, Hocking has, although himself an out-standing philosopher, a different orientation. Religion is the indispensable, truly integrating factor, in all sectors of life, and also in a true world civilization. This point of view is in Hocking's case axiomatic.

HOCKING AND "CIVILIZATION"

In regard to the setting of his theme, his line of reasoning is clear and incisive. Though he (rightly) considers the distinction of East and West still valid, he starts from the fact that our period is one of genuine and reciprocal osmosis of thought, technique, art, law. The "Clean Universals" (science, mathematics, technics) are now no more borrowed by the East, but claimed as its own. So the era of civilizations (plural) has passed. That of civilization (singular) has begun. "Modernity", Hocking posits, is a fruit of Christianity. We have to do with the paradoxical fact that the outcome of empirical science is "a purposeless and meaningless Universe", and yet it

---

[1] *op. cit.*, p. 336.

has its moral origin in the Christian curbing of self-will.[1]

The vices of the West, however, can become the poison of the East and of the coming world civilization. At this point religion enters into Hocking's train of thought. He asks the question: Is Christianity, the parent religion of this whole happening, able to meet the emergence? The answer to this question leads him into a laborious argument on the "Westernness" and universality of Christianity. It is elaborated on the basis of the assumption that an incipient world civilization is a fact. Why? Because the inherently universal elements of culture (*vide* the "Clean Universals" above) are indeed becoming universal by spontaneous appropriation. The central problem is that the autonomy of all spheres of culture, characteristic to these universal elements, implies an emancipation from religion; especially in the Western case from Christianity. This situation cries out for a new rootage in religion. Hocking poses then as his conviction that this renewed rootage is possible, provided Christianity is willing to become purged into a universal religion.

ALL RELIGIONS—ESSENTIALLY ONE

This credo of necessary and possible de-secularization (I can't find a better word) is the pivotal point in Hocking's laying of the good foundation for the incipient world civilization. It is also the vulnerable point. Unlike Northrop he maintains a Christian bias and therefore everything hinges on a creative "re-conception" of Christianity; an idea already apparent in his former publications. On the other hand, he not only maintains that all religions have the intention of universality and the same address of prayer, but also that by assumption all religions are essentially one. The unacceptability of the doctrine of an "Only Way" is therefore one of Hocking's "postulates". This dual position of the prominent significance of Christianity in the whole matter of the incipient world civilization (as it is the parent religion of Western civilization which caused the rise of this world civilization) and the axiomatic assumption of the essential oneness of all religions, exposes Hocking to the

---

[1] Hocking rejects at this point Toynbee's opinion that modern man repudiates religion and substitutes for it man-made science. It seems to me that Hocking is right as to the question of origins, Toynbee as to that of results.

reproach of a too strong Western bias. This reproach would do no justice to Hocking's intention; but it is apt to arise.

Hocking's approach to the dilemma is that Christianity by its simple essence (i.e., the true nature of things is divine love for the created world, a love that suffers) is relieved of any burden of Westernism. At least logically, though not psychologically. The verification of the Christian faith happens in *experience*, that is to say the experience that this way is a way to peace and does not reject the vision of the true mystic, i.e. the person who has become aware of the nature of things as supremely good.

It deserves notice that Hocking in discussing this pragmatic method of his for the verification of Christian truth (a verification by the way that is claimed by all religions) suddenly introduces the "true mystic" as the universal, normative standard of religion. He presents this figure as one of his "postulates". The mystics in all religions understand each other and constitute therefore the concrete basis of essential unity. The essence of the religious world view, by which mystic recognizes mystic, is the perception of Being as Beatitude, of God's "is-ness and oneness". This final, universal truth is implicit in every religion. Salient differences between, for instance, Hinduism and Christianity are undeniable, such as the Indian conception of the world and history in the light of Maya and the Christian conception of man's participation in the historic work of the Kingdom of God. Such differences, however, are relative. They do not infringe the essential unity in the experience of the mystics.

These considerations make Hocking confident that the incipient world faith, indispensable for a healthy outgrowth of the incipient world civilization, is in principle, though not yet in the shape of positive religion, at hand and disposable.

This optimistic estimate of the situation does not prevent Hocking from expressing the sober opinion that the coming world civilization will be a civilization in which one has to reckon with the co-existence of at least a few of the great existing religions. Co-existence without displacement, but nevertheless with the acknowledgment of the right of Missions (!)[1]

[1] Hocking agrees here with Toynbee, just as he does on the point of "relatives" and "essentials" in the religions and the feasibility of disengaging them from each other. Cf. Toynbee, *An Historian's Approach to Religion*, pp. 263-399.

An extremely interesting piece of reasoning in Hocking's argument, to make at the same time a case for the essential oneness of all religions and for the rightful preponderance of Christianity, emerges for him from the facts of cultural history. "Modernity", by which he means the solipsist tendency which is implied in the path of Cartesian thinking, which generated scientific and technical civilization, has in its dynamism pressed on towards the stage of an incipient world civilization. Christianity is the religion which had to enter into an agonizing struggle with this emancipated, secularized titan, because it not only appeared in its territory, but the titan was also its bastard child. By this struggle Christianity has become the maturest faith. From this thesis Hocking draws (it seems to me, with rather too great ease) the conclusion that the coming world religion as the heart of the coming world civilization will be substantially Christian. He adds in good humanist style that he means by "substantially Christian" the viewpoint that the individual heart is the sole judge of its own peace.

So far Hocking's contribution to "prophecy", as he himself genially remarks in the preface to his book. Several more "visions" and "prophecies" concerning the coming world civilization could be discussed, but by taking the rather elaborated attempts by Northrop and Hocking it was intended to get a more concrete grasp of our cultural and spiritual situation, both in its realistic and its wishful thinking. As to the viewpoint of the present author himself, it is in many respects quite different.

It cannot be denied that by what Hocking calls "osmosis" of thought, technique, art and law and the universal dominance of his "Clean Universals", there are developing common lines of outlook. More than once this has been stressed in this book. They are the concomitants of the interdependence of the different parts of our present-day world. It is, however, quite a different thing to use them so confidently as stepping-stones towards a coming world civilization. Especially as the movement of things in our time is so dynamic, so volcanic, so incalculable, so pregnant of sudden change, that it is advisable to be cautious as to our powers of prediction. The more so as no one can calculate the consequences of the vehement passions and deep-seated resentments which sway the souls of millions in all continents, in the relations of men and the political and economic configuration. It seems to me that the problem of the relation of Orient and Occident, though at present crossed by the problem of "East" and "West" in the modern political sense, is not "antiquated" as many writers assert. It has changed, but is not *vieux jeu*. It is antiquated as a pure polarity, but it rather seems to enter a new dimension of depth and vehemence.

CULTURAL-SPIRITUAL HOROSCOPY

The chief difficulty with the efforts for outlining the contours of a coming world civilization lies, it seems to me, rather in the fact of the *historical* contingencies of the Eastern and Western cultures and religions each having their own marked physiognomy. The blue-prints of the bases and delineaments of a coming world civilization are not (or need not be) mere sterile speculations. They are laudable efforts to cast the cultural horoscope. They show, however, two weaknesses. First, it is the way of philosophical thinking to treat historical contingencies— which may nevertheless conceal as well as reveal fundamental, unbridgeable differences—on principle as "relative", "non-essential", and the intellectually construed fundamental agreements as "essential", as "unlosable essences". Leaving on one side the critical questions implied in this philosophical procedure, the so-called "relatives" can be, and often are, the most stubborn elements in the whole matter.

Second, the merit of these attempts at cultural/spiritual horoscopy lies usually more in the fact that one makes acquaintance with a brilliant and well-stored mind, which inevitably represents a definite value judgment on the cultures and religions under discussion and cannot refrain from using its ultimate philosophical and religious starting point as its divining rod. So it is clear that Hocking for instance takes a humanist stand with a Christian theistic bias, and Northrop takes a humanist stand with a Chinese bias of indeterminable Ultimate Reality. In saying this one simply states a fact; but this stating implies that other possibilities of approach are not only thinkable but actual, and have the same right to demand a hearing, if they put their case properly.

Many cultural anthropologists to-day maintain that the

process in which we find ourselves is not only one of osmosis, of cultural change and exchange, of acculturation, but of trans-culturation. They mean by this illuminating term, in which all West- or East-centrism is transcended, that there is going on over the whole world a radical change of culture. It means a gradual transformation, a process of diversified trans- and re-formation. This transculturation view has much to commend it, but it needs self-critical vigilance in order that the—in itself commendable—long-range view does not *obliterate* the equally necessary short-range view, instead of *elevating* it to a higher dimension. The short-range view presents us with the substantial fact (in the midst of a world-wide uprooting) of the deep-seated, irrational, *acquired* religious and cultural attitudes of the great cultures and religions, and their equally deep-seated affirmations on Ultimate Reality, Man and the World. These attitudes and basic affirmations, to be sure, are as much in a process of de-mysticizing and devaluation as of pertinent reaffirmation. Whatever may be the case, in a more conscious encounter of the different culture zones they will inescapably confront each other on the higher plane of *weltanschauliche Auseinandersetzung* (mutual confrontation of fundamental views of life and the world). Illuminating as the spectator attitude of the philosopher or cultural anthropologist may be—and it certainly is—one should maintain a deep sense of the dimension where the actual battle is fought in that half-blindness which is inseparable from our human confusion. The preceding chapters of this book provide many illustrations of this human condition.

Chapter Twelve

THE TERMS OF THE COMING DIALOGUE

THE title of this closing chapter takes the word "terms" in two different senses. One, a very wide sense, indicating the situation in which the meeting or dialogue has to happen, and which is common to all religions and cultures. To each of them, however (and this is the narrower sense of the word), this common situation has a different significance.

As we have seen, the contours of a world civilization are, according to some thinkers, appearing on the horizon. Their hopes are set on a peaceful co-existence of the great religions and cultures on the basis either of a universal humanism or on that of the recognition of the essential oneness of the religions. So universalism and self-preservation are both safeguarded. For the time being these projects are, however, thought-poems. They are visualized in an era which is living through a deep crisis of culture and religion. Of culture, and therefore of religion. Of religion, and therefore of culture. The thought-poems about a pending world civilization pay too little attention to this crisis.

WHAT IS CULTURE?

Although every informed person knows instinctively what culture is, it is difficult to define. In order to gauge the meaning of a "deep cultural crisis" the attempts at definition given by two famous students of cultural history may help. The first is by Sylvain Lévi in his booklet *L'Inde et le Monde*:[1]

A civilization is a system of beliefs, institutions, practices, worked out by a human community in the course of its historical development for the sake of guaranteeing to its members the realization of a special kind of happiness, considered naturally as that best suited to the instinctive tendencies and conscious traditions of

[1] p. 63.

345

this group, and therefore considered also as a form of happiness superior to those which other groups might pursue or attain.

This is a perfect definition of the most self-contained, static civilization that has ever existed, namely Brahman society, one of the two subjects of Lévi's booklet. Max Weber[1] has said about this society that it was the sole logically consistent form of "organische Heils- und Gesellschaftslehre" (organic doctrine of salvation and of society) that has ever arisen.

Quite different is the second attempt at a definition, by J. Huizinga.[2] It is bound to be different, because it deals with present Western culture, the most dynamic that has hitherto appeared, in its state of crisis. The passage is:

> Culture is richer and more powerful than ever before. But it lacks a genuine, proper style, a unifying faith, the inner confidence in its own validity. It has no standard of truth, no harmony, no real dignity and divine serenity.

On the basis of these pronouncements Huizinga speaks of the necessity for cultural sanitation (*Kulturgesundung*), and pleads for asceticism and self-limitation in the sense of limitation of inquisitive thinking, which produces the overwhelming and suffocating technical apparatus in modern life, as a measure of true wisdom.

It is evident that Lévi's magnificent definition of a static civilization in undisturbed equilibrium is not applicable to any culture of our times, whereas Huizinga's words, belonging to a reflective study of the present condition of Western culture, voice the crisis in which all cultures find themselves. Without exception, although in different grades, they are in jeopardy as to their cohesion, validity, and sense of direction. They are plunged into a welter of destruction and reconstruction, in which their original assumptions and certitudes are tested, questioned, thrown into the melting-pot, without any real clue as to whither it is all leading. The religions, as the bases and as specific expressions of the different cultures, are at present inescapably caught up in an identical crisis, the outcome of which is obscure. Yet, according to their different character, the cultures and religions meet and undergo this "identical crisis" each in a different way.

---

[1] *Gesammelte Aufsätze zur Religionssoziologie*, II, p. 367.

[2] *Verzamelde Werken* VII, p. 443, in a study entitled "Man and Culture", written in German.

The significant difference between the West and the Eastern religions is that in the West a deep awareness and merciless analysis of its own religious and cultural crisis is dominant. In the East this is not the case. Apologetic self-assertion has the upper hand over self-criticism.

The dominant and causal factor in this world-wide crisis of values, certitudes and expectations is the massive suggestion, dynamism and disturbance emanating from the Western-born secular outlook on and attitude towards life and the world. Its impact is irresistible and all-pervading. To get hold of its power and significance, to avoid the sentimental attitudes of cultural doom or utopianism, one should look at it from two different angles. From the angle of the logic which seems inherent in it, when taken in isolation from its setting in the concrete reality of man's native capacity for incalculable responses and the world's store of concrete, historical determinants. And also from the *pragmatical* angle, that is to say, not in isolation from, but in conjunction with, the two aspects of living reality just mentioned, elusive though they may be.

Logically speaking, secularism or secularity as the dominant trend of the modern outlook implies the atrophy of the religious constituent in human nature. By its inherent persistent drive to master the world and subject it to the quasi-omnipotence of human insight and manipulation, it impels at the same time towards a self-sufficient, purely profane anthropocentrism and towards a no less distinct self-alienation of man. It forces men automatically into an excessive preoccupation with the pursuit of worldly ends, with progress, with ever faster change. It generates a massive suggestion towards a purely immanent view of life. This *secular* immanentism must be stressed, because it presupposes and engenders (logically speaking) a religion-less world. A world in which God is superfluous, squeezed out and absent. Superfluous even as a decent hypothesis. Also a world in which mind and spirit, that same human mind and spirit which are the creators of this overpowering tendency, seem to lose true capacity for religious directness.[1]

[1] Pandit Nehru, who has himself to be an agent in introducing the dynamic and liberating forces of secularism in India, expresses in the midst of this inescapable stress his concern that "somehow it seems to me that the modern world is completely getting out of tune with what I might call the life of the mind". Cf. *Humanism and Education in East and West*, p. 194 (a Unesco publication of 1953).

347

Religious-metaphysical thinking, i.e. thinking which is by the nature of the case thinking in "images" (eidetical thinking), symbolic or mythic, and which belongs essentially to human nature, cannot thrive in the abstract formula-thinking to which the thought forms of the autonomously conceived world process are driven. The best proof of this tendency is that even many outstanding leaders of religious thought (in various religions) tend towards a "de-imagizing" and "demythologizing", more abstract language. The vital thing for religion is to sense God and His reality as an ever-present and ever-relevant reality. Utter remoteness and vagueness are the death-blow to it. At the same time the fundamental thought and image forms of religious thinking seem less and less compatible with the new thought forms arising from modern cosmology, biology, psychology, anthropology.

FUNDAMENTAL CRISIS FOR RELIGION

By this brief statement about the atrophying influence, on the religious nerve of man, of the secular atmosphere in which everybody has to live and is incessantly submitted to, it is not meant to suggest that this is the conscious programme of "secularism". It is simply its implied irradiation. The main object in accentuating the *logical* implications of "secularity" and its atmosphere is to bring into still clearer perspective the fact often mentioned already, that all religions, whether their adherents sense it or not as yet, have entered into a period of lasting and fundamental crisis. The more clearly and honestly their vocal representatives recognize this, the better it will be for the world, for religion and for culture. Such a recognition implies that not only do all religions find themselves, at least objectively, in a common situation of crisis, different as the terms may be in which each of them has to identify the crisis, but also that they all face the necessity of re-interpreting their unalterable, fundamental positions, without which they lose their self-identity.

Re-interpretation is, however, but one side of the picture. It habitually envisages the tremendous task of refashioning the intellectual and imaginative expression of the peculiar visions of every religion, the clarification and authenticating of religious experience, and the re-directing and re-inspiring of the religious will.

348

This is, however, probably still the lesser part of the total task of re-interpretation. The major part is perhaps the still more arduous task of integration into a quite new and unprecedented *social* structure. In this respect, again, all religions are in the same boat. Instead of integration, one could speak of adaptation or adjustment to a new social structure. In this case too, each religion has, by its peculiar character and history, to meet and solve peculiar problems of principle and of practical import. In general, however, for all the challenge for new integration, adaptation or adjustment is imperative. Ignoring or under-estimating it would mean loss of social vitality or even mummification.

Why is this so? All religions without exception are functioning in coalescence with forms of social structure which are frameworks of a society of the past, or at any rate of a type of society which is passing away. One of the main effects of "secularity" is the emergence of new world structures and social structures of high mobility. Therefore all religions face the same huge proposition of achieving a break with their own social past. The more huge, because the social forms created in the past, which the religions so to speak inhabit at present, were partly of their own making; whereas the emergent, religiously emancipated and *autonomous* new structures of our scientific-industrial society are not. Nor do they seem to offer congenial opportunities for "inhabitation". Yet, the inescapable task for the religions is to sow and sink themselves anew in this changed, autonomous world. This is a task for which the most convincing and profound philosophical or theological reasoning is not sufficient, but which demands hard work and great inventiveness. The words "adaptations", "adjustment," "integration", therefore easily lead to an under-estimation of the matter at issue. It is an emigration towards and an immigration into a wholly different world.[1]

What is logically implied in "secularity" should not be under-estimated as to its corrosive strength in regard to vital religion, i.e. religion not as a marginal force, but as a central vivifying reality. Yet the term "logical" (one could also say "objectival") must not be taken in the sense of working like

[1] For these socio-religious remarks I owe much to an article by H. Schelsky in *Zeitschrift für Evangelische Ethik*, 1957, pp. 153ff.

an inescapable fate. For two reasons. First, because, though the threat of religious atrophy is very real, man's nature is indelibly stamped with a *sensus divinitatis*; a *sensus religionis* is implanted in it, as ancient writers had it. To put it in a more modern fashion, human nature knows as one of its constituent factors the need for a transcendental order as the basis for meaningful life. This fundamental fact, blurred, distorted or effaced as it often may be, will always assert itself, even in the era of "secularity" and its inherent ignoring of it. This provides sufficient reason for refraining from a too facile indulgence in prophecies of nihilistic doom.

Second, the pragmatic angle of view offers abundant material to show that, however powerful the stranglehold of "secularity" on vital religion may be, its "logic" does not by any means reign supreme. Everybody knows that we are certainly not living in a religion-less world. On the contrary, we live in a world full of religious activity and spiritual searching. The "resurgence" of the great non-Christian religions has been discussed amply in this book. It cannot be maintained that (for instance) the Christian Church all over the world, although fiercely attacked, often condemned to death or considered irrelevant by many outstanding secularists and humanists, is moribund. The reverse seems more the case. This appears not too optimistic a statement, even when one is well aware of the loss of function and attraction which the Churches, as embodiments of institutional religion, plainly suffer. Outside the Churches there is in many quarters a religious productivity in fantastic proportions, often, though not always, of dubious quality.

In spite of all "demythologizing" and of many declarations as to what kind of religious representations a "modern" man can hold in all intellectual integrity and self-respect and what kind are impossible for him and therefore definitely outmoded, there goes on a great deal of mythological creativity and search for symbols.[1] Hosts of people, even very intelligent and sincere people, persist in living by concrete, "anthropomorphic" religious representations without any sense of injury to their intellectual or moral integrity.

To avoid misunderstanding, it has to be noted that the

[1] Even when one takes due account of the fact that the words "myth" and "symbol" are abused at present to such an extent that they often lose all intelligible meaning.

mythological creativity is mainly of the pseudo-religious, political variety, and rarely purely religious. Also I want to stress that this selection of features belonging to what I have called the "pragmatic" angle of view is not proffered in the spirit of a value or non-value judgment. It is done entirely for the sake of exemplification, to demonstrate that, in our universally "secularized" world of religion-less tendency, *all* religions are at present living and functioning in a twilight situation: on the one hand summoned to re-examine and re-interpret their credentials and establish a new *Sitz* in a new social structure, so gaining, if possible, a new validity; on the other hand continuing their course with piecemeal adjustments in self-expression and practice, but moving in an emptied Universe.

RELIGION IN THE SINGULAR

The vast and comprehensive over-all situation I have tried to suggest has, however, some additional features that need to be kept in mind when trying to gauge in what kind of atmosphere we find ourselves in an ensuing dialogue between religions and cultures, and what necessities confront us in the present world scene in regard to cultural and religious dialogue or multilogue.

Let us take, to begin with, a single point as an introduction to the wider subject of inter-cultural and inter-religious co-operation, which obtrudes itself increasingly upon minds occupied with international understanding in the interest of peace and a stable world order. This single point is the question constantly asked: What is the contribution that "religion" can make in the field of international problems?

The use of the singular in this case is significant. Everybody knows that this evasive entity called religion in the singular gets in fact its tangible meaning, especially in the sphere of relationship and understanding, only within each of the many existing religions. Religion in the singular is easily extolled or recommended as a bond, or cement, of unity. This kind of thinking and pleading is in our days much in vogue, but in practice it is, except for the reality-proof idealists, evident that problems like world peace and world stability are not yielding to noble wishful thinking. When religion in the singular is called upon

WORLD CULTURES AND WORLD RELIGIONS

to serve the great pragmatic ends of world peace and world stability, because of its depth and loftiness, the religions in the plural come immediately on the scene and have to define their possible common contribution to the service required. The disappointing experience then often follows that no intellectually construed universal religion, comprising all the necessary attributes for the unification of all minds, appears able to remove the fact that the concrete religions are more steeped in their peculiar habitus and consciousness than in these wishful fictions. It is, therefore, a recurrent fact that in meetings devoted to the search for unity and harmony in our sadly divided world, voices are heard saying that religion is a divisive and not a unitive influence. Therefore better no religion at all than one that is fanatical and intolerant. The fact of this alleged divisive influence of religion(s), in relation to each other or even within the same religious body, is patent enough all over the world.

This single point deserves specific notice, because it shows that the predicament in which the world to-day finds itself, the understandable longing for peace and harmony, are powerful instigations towards testing and evaluating the capacity of religion and religions for bringing men together instead of disuniting them, and for producing tolerance and forbearance. Not in theory, but in practice. It is indubitable that tolerance, creating unity, and the will towards mutual understanding, are very important tests as at present applied to religion as a viable power. The oft-recurring practical deficiency in this respect brings religion into disrepute. Particularly as the humanitarian principles of human solidarity and responsibility for one's neighbour not only have a universal appeal, just because they are "de-religionized", but also are often more effective than religious injunctions. Frequently such religious injunctions, although they are in fact of the same high moral calibre as the humanitarian ones and often even profounder, become somehow morally inoperative because some element of religious bigotry creeps in.

This prominence of the plea for tolerance as a symptom of right religious behaviour, and as a necessity in the tangled problem of human co-operation, is evident in many activities and pronouncements which contribute to the creation of what public opinion considers to be the desirable attitude in a dialogue or meeting of the religions. In this respect it is justifiable to say that a definite ethic of dialogue in the universe of religious intercourse is a real need because of the patent fact that inter-religious or inter-faith relationship and co-operation is a social requirement of the first order. One or two outstanding examples therefore may bear some scrutiny.

The many post-war publications flowing from Arnold Toynbee's fertile pen repeatedly return to the theme of the presuppositions and modes of right intercourse between the religions. Here Toynbee manifests a serious concern. Rightly so, because of the central place he accords to religion in the possibility of a renewal of civilization. In this context he incessantly reiterates the focal significance of tolerance, urging with real eloquence towards the seeking of this pearl of great price. Undoubtedly this appeal finds a world-wide echo and assent amongst all those who belong to the *bien-pensants*, the right-minded. Behind this appeal lies his conception of "religion in the singular" as the key to the mystery of existence. The religion*s* are various ways of approaching this self-same mystery, and, although he expresses himself in terms taken from his own Christian tradition, he is fully conscious of having abandoned the fundamental Christian position. He adheres to a view of religion which, as he says himself, was held by pre-Christian Greek and Roman paganism and is held by "that half of the human race that adheres to some form of Hinduism or Buddhism".[1]

INTER-RELIGIOUS AND INTER-FAITH

Another symptom of the same concern is the growing practical search for inter-religious and inter-faith relationships. How to further them; how to define their codes of behaviour and their standards of principle? American universities are particularly alert in organizing summer schools or other occasions to achieve the meeting of representatives of different religions, exchange of experience and thought, understanding of their peculiar situations and backgrounds. The World Congress of Faiths founded in 1936 by Sir Francis Younghusband, a venture to bring adherents of different religions

---

[1] *The Observer*, October 21, 1954.

into personal contact and exchange with one another, has its centre in London. The International Association for Liberal Christianity and Religious Freedom (I.A.F.R.) organized at Chicago, in August 1958, a Congress intended to bring together a world-wide variety of beliefs, traditions and practices that were willing to be included under the name "liberal". The Congress was clearly inspired not only by the desire to attempt a first contact of "true religious liberalism" from all representative religions, but also by the conviction that in the present world plight the "great religions" of the world have a responsibility for contributing to the solution of the problems menacing the future of mankind.

An important factor in this matter of inter-religious and inter-cultural relationships is Unesco with its many initiatives. Its natural task of promoting international understanding on the intellectual and cultural plane, as a contribution to world peace, has induced it to organize many international Congresses and Round Tables. To mention only one typical instance out of many: the international Round Table discussion in 1953 on "Humanism and Education in East and West". Unesco has always been very cautious as to getting involved in inter-faith or inter-religious relations, thereby in fact, however, making Humanism its standard value and working towards a kind of East-Western Humanism as a bond of unity and spiritual basis of co-operation; forgetting the simple truth that, in such vital matters, evading the choice of a standpoint is nevertheless a choice and a standpoint. This caution and this humanistic bias are understandable in so far as the multiplicity of religions and the practical workability of the hypothesis of a universal Humanism are an invitation to ignore the thorny field of religion. It is inherent in Unesco's position to pursue a policy of harmonization and reconciliation.

In 1956, however, the Unesco General Conference in New Delhi decided on a ten year East-West Project, which bears also the more explicit name: "Mutual Appreciation of Eastern and Western Cultural Values". It has been introduced to public attention as a Major Project. The word "Major" seems to imply that Unesco is groping towards overcoming its habitual caution and recognizing the point that "appreciation of cultural values" cannot be a real thing if the standards of

conduct, the fundamental social values, which belong intrinsically to culture remain artificially separated from their religious
matrix. So by a back door Unesco finds its way into the domain
of inter-religious relationships, though the over-all idea which
governs the undertaking is that of the absolute and irreplaceable
value of each culture as a part of mankind's common
patrimony.[1]

This development illustrates the fatuousness of "neutrality",
inevitably hiding a kind of Humanism, and the necessity of
trying the far cleaner line of impartiality. Yet, if I am not
mistaken, this project of Unesco's is on the one hand a laudable
attempt to cause different cultures to look on each other not
as separated provinces but as contributors to a common fund
of culture. On the other hand, however, it seems guided by the
humanist fallacy that any culture in the present upheaval can
escape a radical, unforeseeable reorientation and self-revision,
which leads to facing anew the question of truth. Mutual
appreciation of cultural values is a precious and necessary thing
in our multi-cultural world, but a higher good is a commitment, and a quest, which transcend our values.

The preceding examples have been mentioned in order to
show that the elevation of inter-religious relationships to the
rank of a world problem is a sheer necessity, arising out of the
ominous aspects of the world situation and also from the fact
that the great living religions of the world can no longer afford
to ignore one another. Sincere and sensitive minds everywhere
are scanning the whole horizon of human forces to find
resources that may and should tame the apparent dangers.
Many eyes are looking wistfully in the direction of the religions
as repositories of moral and spiritual power working to these
ends. There are many people entertaining the spontaneous

---

[1] Even the Congress for the History of Religions, held in August and September
1958 in Tokyo, had on its programme (in collaboration with Unesco's Major
Project) "a symposion on the rôle of Religion in Cultural Understanding between
Orient and Occident". The International Association for the History of Religions,
which organized this Congress, has as its aim, of course, scholarly research into
religions for its own sake. Nevertheless the urgency of inter-religious relationship,
in such a mixed East-Western gathering as the Congress of Tokyo, created the
"existential" situation for a symposion in which not so much scholars as human
beings of different religious allegiance met with one another. One of the most
famous speakers in the Congress, Dr. Friedrich Heiler, passionately expressed his
conviction that the final outcome of the study of the History of Religions, in spite
of its scholarly detachment, would be the unity of all religions.

conviction that religion as such, and therefore religion*s*, ought to be guardians and promoters of peace and happiness. This is undoubtedly a right intuition. Yet the experience of the divisive idiosyncrasy of religion(s) seems to belie this intuition. However, both the intuition and its belying co-operate in the drive for inter-religious relationships and a well-thought-out strategy for getting them under way. This well-thought-out strategy tends to be, in my opinion, the crux of the matter. It is necessary for a sound and responsible strategy of inter-religious relationships that those who work for it and in it should be themselves sincerely religious, and, above all, have a readiness to take a candidly self-critical view of the empirical reality of their own religion.

It is a dubious matter if world peace planners and world improvers, who are in religious respect rather indifferent, try to *use* religion and religions as reservoirs of resources or tools.

Another point of great importance in building up fruitful inter-religious relationships and contacts is to make a clear distinction in aims. There may be two aims: a pragmatic or a fundamental one. The pragmatic has to aim first and foremost at removing mutual misunderstandings and serving common human responsibilities. This may lead on to a deeper exchange of witness and experience, but if so it is a by-product. The fundamental aim directly involves this open exchange of witness, experience, cross-questioning and listening. The seriousness of true religion demands that one shall be really one's religious self and avoid the temptation—and this is valid for both cases, the pragmatic and the fundamental—of putting as an indispensable condition of dialogue and relationship the assumption that all religions are essentially one. As an axiomatic assumption it robs all true religion of its seriousness. This seriousness need not hinder participants from being open to new insights through the instrumentality[1] of contact with one another.

THE DISCOVERY OF AFFINITIES

Having delineated the great importance in "the coming dialogue" of the conception of tolerance and a right steering

[1] Cf. the striking article by U Hla Bu: "The Christian Encounter with Buddhism in Burma", *International Review of Missions*, April 1958, already referred to.

of inter-religious and inter-cultural relationships and contacts, we have to take into account yet another aspect if we are to arrive at a fairly realistic estimate of expectations. The "dialogue", increasingly occasioned by all kinds of contact, whether arranged or not—the latter will be more frequent and is by its very nature incalculable—will to a great extent not take place on the level of what is called scholarly competence. It occurs or will occur on many occasions between minds eager to learn or eager to communicate, or both. Minds often not well informed about the compass of what is said and about its validity, but simply interested.

This aspect of the "meeting" or "dialogue" between people who combine a certain amount of information with a certain amount of ignorance is, practically speaking, very important. The more so when we keep in mind the picture we tried to suggest in the preceding chapter of the spiritual atmosphere in the West in regard to what we have called the already ongoing Eastern Invasion. The central point in this picture is not the planned missionary activity performed more and more by the great non-Christian religions in the West, whether issuing from an Eastern initiative or from Western impulse and leadership. It is rather the significant phenomenon we have already referred to: that within the cultural and spiritual crisis native to the West there appear signs and symptoms of growing affinity with dominant Eastern ideas. An affinity deriving in the West from quite different sources and experiences, but in fact causing a genuine feeling of unexpected recognition. It is not a matter of regular conversion to Hinduism or Buddhism as a religion, but of discovering oneself somehow a "spiritual relative" of theirs.

Many of the writers discussed in the preceding chapter are voicing the inarticulate feelings of great multitudes, and are, in principle, exchanging Western "fundamental options" for Eastern or trying to integrate Western and Eastern fundamental options into a new whole. This statement of course is made from the cultural point of view in particular. It implies, however, implicitly or explicitly, in principle or in practice, a decision in respect of religion, because it often means a definite farewell to Christianity.

The affinities between present predilections in many Western minds and Eastern perceptions are to be found at several important points. I have already referred more than once to the relativist estimate of religion and religions, which is clearly not grounded in truly Christian self-understanding but is certainly akin to typically Eastern fundamental notions and options.[1] In the "dialogue" of the vaguely informed, vaguely ignorant "lay people" these notions respond to the need for broadmindedness, for equity and modesty of judgment. This solves at one stroke the thorny problem of the plurality of religions and so apparently paves the way for peaceful co-existence, mutual understanding and respect. It is an excellent way of escape from any suspicion of bigotry, which is one of the bugbears of the modern mind.

Closely connected with this is the point we have stressed so much: tolerance. It is precisely tolerance which in the West of the last centuries has become one of the hall-marks of true culture and broadmindedness. Nor do people forget that this progress has been wrung from the hands of a refractory Christendom. The expositors of the Eastern religious mentality present tolerance with great emphasis as one of its shining virtues. It is undoubtedly true that in comparison with Christian history the record of Eastern religions shows up favourably; and this naturally contributes towards recommending them as examples of humane and large-hearted conduct in the prickly problem of religion. The intricacies of the problem of tolerance and intolerance in human societies, whether Western or Eastern, are left on one side.[2]

The widespread agreement of many Western scholars and philosophers of religion as to the indubitable superiority and profundity of mysticism amongst the different types of religion has its antiphon in the fundamental position of Hinduism and Buddhism that the highest and truest religion is mystical. Many of their religious philosophies, and particularly the modern

[1] Although it is admittedly difficult to give a fair estimate of Goethe's attitude towards religion, the following saying of his has a relevant undertone: "Piety is not an end but a means to attaining the highest culture through the purest peace of mind."

[2] The degree of simplification of the problem of tolerance and intolerance in human societies is dismaying. Clear and equitable thinking in this field is rare. I regret that in the context of this page further elaboration of the tolerance-intolerance issue is not possible. In the "coming dialogue" great alertness in regard to this point will be indispensable.

ones, are a triumphant demonstration of this position, far more elaborate and subtle than the West itself has offered.

Again, it is an undoubted fact that mysticism represents a universal type of religious expression (different as its symbols and images may be) which has an identical structure and gamut all the world over. As Hocking rightly says: "Mystic recognizes mystic across all boundaries." The pathos of the modern self-understanding of man, with its stress on human dignity, self-sufficiency, self-respect and self-reliance, spontaneously averse to the need for "saviours," senses in the radical Eastern systems of self-salvation (*autosoteria*) a congenial attitude. The soil from which this stress on self-reliance in both cases springs is very different but the mood is essentially the same. Hence the appeal of Buddhism, the god-less faith of self-sufficient man, and of the Vedanta as intellectually more satisfying to the self-respecting élite than anything else. The man-centred naturalistic orientation of our secularized civilization cannot fail to recognize, or surmise, in the great Eastern systems an impressively intrepid justification of the man-centred, naturalistic apprehension of man and the world as the outcome of modern science.

Again, to be sure, their causes and the history of their growth are vastly different, but they meet each other in a hidden understanding. What seems in the West a modern conquest, appears in the East as an acquisition of ancient wisdom. Hence the easily understandable fascination of Chinese culture for many minds.

These examples could be multiplied. They are given only to illustrate in how many respects modern needs and tendencies, although entirely secularized, are met by Eastern claims and achievements whose spirit, notwithstanding their peculiar mythological or symbolic drapery, betrays affinity—and adds thereto a striking metaphysical and psychological penetration. They are also given simply as illustrations of mysterious interaction between two types of mind so utterly divergent in origin and goal and in "fundamental options" as the Eastern and the Western type, as a means to gauge the historical situation through which we happen to be passing and the two "worlds" that happen to be meeting. We leave on one side the wider question of how this "meeting", as a whole, of worlds of different fundamental options will lead them to interpenetrate, intermodify, and interact with one another, as forecast in Goethe's words:[1] "Orient and Occident can no more be separated".

"DIALOGUE" ON THE BORDER

But there is still another side to the fact that in the main the "dialogue" or "meeting" and interpenetration will happen, not on the level of the experts, but on the borderline between a certain amount of awareness and information and of unawareness and ignorance. It is this: that in books, in conversations and in public expositions these religions naturally present themselves in a way corresponding to the stage of self-reinterpretation they have at present reached, and which appeals to the Western mind. Both hang together, because, as we explained earlier, it is the Western "shock" which has led to these endeavours at self-reinterpretation. In being confronted by the peculiar ideals and stresses of the West they have formulated new approaches to their own spiritual heritage. Of these the most striking are the claims for dynamism, for due appreciation of the relevance of the personal and social element, for the importance of history as belonging to the fabric of the human adventure.

These new self-interpretations are in themselves quite natural and understandable in this period of revolutionary transition and adjustment. How far they constitute a lasting and decisive mutation in the fundamental structure of these religious-cultural systems nobody can predict. The important fact at this moment is that the most progressive reinterpreters present the endeavours as the adequate interpretation of their tradition, without troubling noticeably about the question whether it is a legitimate interpretation or a complete metamorphosis.

An interesting example is to be found in the *History of Philosophy Eastern and Western*, a work in two volumes sponsored by the Ministry of Education of the Government of India[2] on the initiative of the late Indian Minister of Education, Maulana Abul Kalam Azad. This book is an able performance, written mainly by Indian scholars of philosophy out of a sincere concern for the universal character of philosophy and the plasticity of

[1] *West-östlicher Divan.*   [2] First published 1952; second impression 1957.

Hindu spirituality. In the sections where Islam as represented in India comes in for consideration, the authors offer, as the right interpretation of Islam, that it advocates the fundamental unity of all faiths and the true reconciliation of religion, science and rationalism. The Indian portions are characterized by a new stress on the reality of the world, which implies a realistic interpretation of Maya and a positive attitude towards history.[1] Also by a distinct "recession" (to use again, as in the case of mutation, a term from modern biology) of the Indian concepts of *Karma* and *samsara*, which for centuries have been basic to Indian religious-philosophical thinking and are now reduced to general concepts in line with modern ideas (*samsara* for instance = dynamic change or flux).

These points are brought up solely in order to emphasize the fact that the "dialogue" or "meeting" will in practice be concerned, not with India's thought as pictured in the handbooks, but with an often drastic re-interpretation and recasting. The driving spirit in this whole undertaking is expressed in the closing words of the second volume: "It [philosophy] must inspire us with the faith to sustain the new world, to produce the men who subordinate national, racial and religious divisions to the ideal of humanity."

Another important publication, edited by the American professor of Religion at Colgate University, Kenneth W. Morgan, consists of three volumes: *The Religion of the Hindus, The Path of the Buddha, Islam the Straight Path*.[2] Their significance is that, unlike the ordinary run of books by Western scholars, they are the work of competent Hindus, Buddhists and Muslims. These volumes are well worth studying. They give a good idea of how well-informed intellectual Hindus, Buddhists and Muslims see and evaluate their respective religions. It is striking to observe that, although the way of presentation shows the influence of Western categories, all fundamental questions raised by modern thinking in regard to religious assumptions and symbolisms are absent. This has its advantages but also its disadvantages. The

---

[1] P. D. Devanandan in *The Gospel and the Hindu Intellectual* rightly observes (p. 26): "The responsibility of man for his action and its consequent effect on his nature and destiny have given new importance to world, life, and history in Indian thinking. Whether Hindus are conscious of this shift of emphasis or not the fact remains that modern Hinduism is evolving a new conception of history."

[2] Published by the Ronald Press Company, New York (1953, 1956, 1958).

main disadvantage is that, although one gets an impression of beauty and richness, any vindication or validation in the present critical stage of religion and of the human situation is, surprisingly, lacking. Only occasionally is this suggested, as for instance in the case of the caste system, which represents "the ethical organization of the social life of the Hindus"; its discountenance is frankly endorsed.

Amongst the three the volume on Islam, though undoubtedly useful, is disappointing and to a certain extent misleading in that it strongly vindicates a position as unassailable without giving any real reason why this is so. Therefore in some of its main sections it is more a piece of apologetic than of exposition. Of course, it would be unjust to find fault with this apologetic character. That might rather be an advantage. The difficulty, however, is that what is really apologetic is presented as an unquestionable exposition of incontrovertible fact.

In the case of Islam this is understandable because, in contradistinction to Hinduism and Buddhism, Islam has much to do with concrete points of history and dogma. Such points are the infallibility, incomparability and purely divine character of the Koran, and the historical personality of the Prophet. Both are points which still wait to be faced squarely in Islam for the sake of its own spiritual health and reconstruction. The divinization of the Koran and the idealization of the Prophet as the perfect embodiment of the divine law of Life incorporated in the Koran (as vindicated in some of the contributions) are quite acceptable as a testimony of honest faith and re-interpretation. They are, however, presented as problemless indisputable truth, and thereby run the risk of confusing the "dialogue" instead of helping it. Especially in that borderland of information, partial information and ignorance in which (as pointed out) the "dialogue" or "meeting" will mainly happen.

These considerations land us at a point of great importance. This is, that "dialogue" cannot possibly escape controversy and mutual cross-questioning, not in the interest of refuting an opponent but in the interest of straight thinking. The invigorating discipline of straight thinking as a service of mutual aid should not be suppressed by mistaken considerations of courtesy or generosity, or by concern for a reputation of broadmindedness. Serious interlocutors have to demand for the sake of true communication from each other whether a proffered re-interpretation, which often practically amounts to an important mutation, is justified or not by the basic outlook of a given religion.

THE ISSUES FOR CHRISTIANITY

It is time to turn now to the terms which define the Christian position, theoretically and practically, in this great encounter. That is to say to delimit the principal issues which emerge for Christianity in the midst of the modern spiritual cosmos (or chaos) in which the scientific spirit of the West has created a new kind of thinking, seemingly without any contact with the biblical view of man and the world, and in which the challenge of the great non-Christian religions jeopardizes its "allegedly" exclusive claim for religious truth. This "exclusiveness" is an offence not only to the Eastern mind and to philosophers in general, but to the modern mood as a whole, for which a strong leaning towards resigned relativism or the acceptance of a plurality of truth is natural and characteristic. The seeming "inclusiveness" and all-comprehensive hospitality to every religion, which are not only inherent in the Eastern religions and their religious philosophies, but are loudly proclaimed, cannot but meet with a strong preference in general public opinion. Christianity in its seeming stubborn "exclusiveness" and alleged "dogmatic narrowness" cuts a poor figure beside this grandiloquent "broadness" of mind.

Gandhi has called the unquenchable missionary temperament of Christianity "muscular" and "militant", clearly meaning this in a very critical sense, especially in regard to Christian Missions. Radhakrishnan[1] expresses the same mood in the words: "There is right through the imperialistic note that Christianity is the highest manifestation of the religious spirit." It is highly interesting to notice here the inability of Radhakrishnan to understand Christianity on its own terms. His use of the word "imperialistic", though wrong from the standpoint of the true biblical, apostolic spirit, is understandable because the practical behaviour of Missions has given ample occasion for the use of this word. To explain "the imperialistic note", however, by saying that Christianity regards itself as "the highest

[1] *East and West in Religion*, p. 24.

manifestation of the religious spirit" betrays sheer misunderstanding about the real motivation of Christianity's apostolic spirit. His remark is, unwillingly, a typically Hindu apprehension of Christianity, as Hinduism sees all stages of religion as *achievements* of the human spirit. The biblical view is quite different. Religions are in the Bible wrong or right ways of loving obedience to God, who reveals His holy will.[1]

To turn to another aspect; amongst many Christians, whether theologians or ordinary people, there is dominant an attitude (although somehow keeping to the conviction that the Christian Faith stands secure and supreme) of being deeply concerned about appearing humble and inclusive and avoiding any semblance of what *is called* religious arrogance or looks like "exclusiveness". This mistaken "softness" is in reality a spiritual disease. The increasing force with which the non-Christian religions press themselves on the attention as rival claims is—and this is a new feature—creating more and more a certain feeling of uneasiness and anxious questioning amongst hosts of ordinary Christians, who had been living till recently in undisturbed, naïve certitude as to Christianity's uniqueness and supremacy. The questioning that is going on in leading missionary circles about the real motivation and justification of the imperative missionary mandate of a Christian is, though on a different level, another symptom of incertitude. The new fact that the non-Christian religions are sturdily entering as factors in the world scene and putting their claims, contributes to this self-questioning in missionary circles. In short, this means a real summons to give an intelligible account of what is behind this "exclusiveness" claim of Christianity.

[1] An intriguing point in relation to the offence of "exclusiveness" is always that the Hindus especially, in the name of "inclusiveness", are thorough exclusivists in a concealed way. That is, by their claim in regard to "inter-faith relations and conversations" that "inter-faith relations" should mean that the "Christian arrogance" of offering by the Gospel the normative concept of religion should be dropped at the outset, and the tenet of the one, universal religion, hidden in all religions, should be taken as the normative concept. They have, of course, a perfect right to maintain this latter position, but it is really strange that they do not see how such a demand at the outset that one of the partners in the *inter*-faith relation should surrender his true position is arbitrary dogmatism and a frustration of genuine *inter*-faith relation; a flight from the real issue. This phenomenon, however, seems to be inherent in the position of the "inclusivists". E.g. the way in which the Inter-faith Relations between Christians and Jews are conceived in the U.S.A., and Karl Jaspers in *Der philosophische Glaube*. (E.T. *The Perennial Scope of Philosophy*, 1950.)

The Christian Church and the world at large stand in need of a new and unequivocal interpretation and elucidation of this exclusiveness. In this new interpretation and elucidation more care must be taken than has been in the past to maintain unashamedly this claim for exclusiveness, but to explain at the same time that it has nothing to do with religious arrogance, intolerance or dogmatic absolutism; that it rather includes a real openness to truth wherever it may be found, and an inclusiveness of its own sort, far more realistic and adequate to the human situation than the superficial, glittering universalist theories of the East and of theosophical and philosophical syncretists.

The implication of this whole situation is that the "dialogue" with the non-Christian religions should not only be the concern of a few so-called experts, who are as Christians professional students of one or more of these religions. The period in which that could be the case has definitely passed. The time has now arrived when all theological thinkers have to include these new worlds of thought and apprehension in their sphere of interest. Not only for the *theoretical* reason of joining issue in philosophical and religious respect with thought- and life-systems, whose key concepts were for a long time mainly marginal in the cultural and religious world debate, but for *pastoral* reasons. This pastoral aspect deserves special mention, because the "ordinary" people turn in their perplexity in the first place not to the leading Christian thinkers, but to their ministers and pastors. In other words it demands a re-orientation of the education of the ministry, a theology of religion and religions, which is more and something else than textbook or capsule knowledge of non-Christian religions.

We have got beyond the time when a Chair for the History of Religion in a Theological Faculty was sufficient to do justice to the new religious worlds which are interpreted by scientific inquisitiveness.

Another way of saying the same thing is that a new apologetic of the Christian Faith is an imperative demand. In this case, of course, it should be an apologetic arising out of a sincere and open dialogue with the non-Christian religions. It is simply a parallel to the other great *apologia nova* that Christian thinkers are called to in the present situation, viz. the dialogue with the vast new thinking on the Universe and Man by modern secularity (to which I have alluded already). I use the term "Christian thinkers" advisedly here, because it is by no means only the theologians who are summoned, but the great number of Christian lay people who co-operate fully in the vast enterprise of theoretical and applied sciences in every field. For they are not only intellectually but existentially confronted by the demand to spell out their faith in correlation with the new adventurous realm of apprehension of world, life and man, implied in the elusive term "modern world". The meeting with the philosophies and religions of the East is part of this complex. This two-sided dialogue or *apologia* is one of the greatest issues of the Christian world. In my conviction, if it is fearlessly met on the basis of well-considered ecumenical planning it is one of the surest ways towards a real regaining of intellectual responsibility and dignity.

TERMS OF THE "DIALOGUE"

An adequate treatment of the terms under which the dialogue between Christianity and the great living religions should take place requires at least a separate volume for each case.[1] The structure of such a volume should, in my opinion, be built up in four sections: history and growth of such a religion and culture in clear, compressed outline; a phenomenological survey of the creative mobiles in such a religious/cultural whole; a probing of it in the light of the biblical Revelation (theological evaluation); an outline of the ways of communication and of dialogue for defining the central points at issue between Christianity and the described religion.

In this closing chapter I can only indicate briefly with what issues Christianity is faced, in its meeting with the great religions, on the basis of its characteristic and authentic nature as embodied in its kerygma and ethos in the biblical record, without any concern about being liberal or orthodox. The observations are made almost exclusively with an eye on the Indian and the Far Eastern world of religious cultures, as Islam and Judaism are quite a different case. The former (Hinduism, Buddhism, etc.) are the most intriguing and

---

[1] The writer hopes, if strength and life are accorded him, to write them and offer them as a personal attempt.

challenging; the latter (Islam, Judaism) are, historically speaking, a family affair, but one characterized by great tensions and disturbing alienations.

The issues arising out of a fundamental confrontation with the Indian and Far Eastern realm are, essentially speaking, not new. They are, on close inspection, the same as were posed in the time of classical antiquity through Gnosticism, syncretism and the mystical philosophies by which the intellectual élite of the 3rd, 4th and 5th centuries hoped to vanquish Christianity, which was then a very uncongenial upstart. The similarity holds true also in this respect: that brilliant representatives of classical pagan Humanism, such as Porphyry (just like the true adherents of Indian and Far Eastern spirituality) cannot but consider Christianity as barbarous; at best as a form of *bhakti*-religion, that is to say, of relative (*paramarthika*) truth. Gnosticism and theosophy of the first centuries of our era were, just as the Eastern religions at the same time, soteriologies of the spiritual "aristocrats" (Max Weber speaks in regard to India, China and Japan of *intellektuellen-Soteriologien*) and ways for the common people to find salvation of a sort.

There is, however, also a great difference. The great Eastern religious cultures are distinctly superior to Gnosticism, etc., of the past, because in their quest for the liberating *jñāna* (gnosis) they display an unequalled, energetic concentration on the faculties inherent in man to work out, literally and radically, his own salvation; not "with fear and trembling", because it is God who in His good pleasure enables man to will this and achieve it, but with indomitable perseverance and singleness of mind (Yoga, Vinaya, etc.). Compared with this, the syncretistic mystery-cults of the Roman Empire are rather poor questing-grounds for "security".

At another point too they are far superior. The representative thinkers of Eastern spirituality, since the days of the Upanishads, the Buddha, Lao-Tse and Chuang-tse, have, in philosophical respect, thought through the problem of man as the agent of his own salvation with unsurpassed radicalism. As a result (although in practice taking a very broad and benevolently condescending attitude towards all religious representations and rites) they have, so to speak, thought to pieces, explained away, all religious representations, gods, demons and God included, relegating them to the realm of Maya. The Buddha is in this respect the most radical thinker. Others, like the great Indian thinkers such as Shankara, have maintained the sole reality of Pure Brahman, but combined this absolute Truth with a sincere participation in the lower-stage Truth of a Saviour God.

However, notwithstanding the great variety in metaphysical, ontological thinking among the Easterners, in one point they concur, viz. the centrality of man; his exclusive significance in the matter of understanding of Self and the Universe; his ability (long as the way may be) and duty to work out his own salvation by his own exertions.

Taking this into account, anthropology or the Understanding of Man will be in the future a crucial issue, arising out of the situation of modern secularism and of the Eastern Invasion. Karl Barth's anthropology in his *Church Dogmatics* may contain fruitful material for a real dialogue on this point.

It is therefore no exaggeration to say that the Eastern religious philosophies hide a formidable anthropocentrism, more formidable than has ever appeared on the Western scene. They are, therefore, in the realm of fundamental thinking a formidable challenge. One has the right to say, an unprecedented challenge.[1] The interesting thing about it is that they have by their own power reached conclusions centuries ago (especially in the field of psychology and mystical intuition) to which the modern Western quest for knowledge and for explanation of the enigma of Matter and Mind often seems to lead with compelling logic. For both (the Eastern philosophies and the modern "scientific" mind as the typical creation of the West), God and Revelation, His presence and activity in history, His relation to Man and Man's relation to Him, are irrelevant, at any rate when viewed in the light of their presuppositions and options; unattainable and non-sensical, that

---

[1] Fung Yu Lan, one of the contemporary Chinese thinkers (now pushed into the background in Communist China) who demonstrated clearly the proud Taoist self-consciousness of the East, says in his book *The Spirit of Chinese Philosophy* (1947), p. 219: "If philosophy can enable men to become sage men, then this is the usefulness of philosophy's uselessness. This kind of uselessness may rightly be called the highest form of usefulness. Philosophy can only make a man a perfect man."

is to say, making no real sense and therefore superfluous.

The Eastern religious philosophies, however, are again the most radical. They posit Self-Awakening over against Revelation as the true Way. In the realm of the Western quest for "scientific" knowledge the mood is one of metaphysical agnosticism, of pronouncing itself unable to proffer in regard to God as the prime, living Reality any judgment or light. Whereas in the realm of the Eastern philosophies God and Revelation in the biblical sense are discarded with victorious certainty. The "Man on the Cross" as *the* decisive revelatory act of God is as such, when compared with the awe-inspiring (they are really that) images of the Serene Sage Buddha plunged in meditation, revolting (in spite of all laudatory speaking about Christ) and hideous.

CHRISTIANITY'S FORMIDABLE OPPONENTS

It will be clear that in this light the meeting of Christianity with the Eastern religious cultures in their highest and most authentic dimension means the meeting with a formidable opponent. Christian theologians and thinkers will have to descend into philosophical depths and into the depths of the biblical message in such a way as never before. Philosophically speaking, the weakness of the Christian position is that it is founded on *historical* Revelation, especially in its central tenet of the Incarnation, God's entering Himself into history in a Person. Christianity will have to face clearly this "weakness", consisting in the point that the Absolute One has entered history, which is by definition relative. A *new* debate on the formula "Finitum non est capax Infiniti" (the finite cannot contain the Infinite) awaits us. New, because of the radical character of Eastern thinking.

This calls for some amplification by a few examples. In the "coming dialogue" it is the high duty of the Christian participants to *show openness of mind and eagerness to learn*, but not less *to keep uncompromisingly in focus the true issues*, for the danger of too great eagerness for harmonization and amalgamation, which means confounding of the real issues, is great. We stress this point not in order to minimize the necessity of openness and eagerness to learn. There is really much to learn. Teachableness is as necessary as firmness. The Christian participants therefore should be custodians of charity *and* clarity.[1]

Christianity in its basic character is, in its confrontation with modern reason and modern human experience, and not less with the basic tenets of the great Eastern religions, in a more complicated position than these great religions are (Buddhism, Hinduism, Taoism, Confucianism). The reason is not its inferiority but rather its peculiar dimension of depth, on account of which it has an innate irreducibility to a philosophy of religion, to "ideas" and "principles". It is not the case that within the domain of Christendom the reduction to a religious philosophy, to "ideas" and "principles", has never occurred or does not occur even at present. Far from it! The point I wish to make, however, is that this has occurred or occurs *contra naturam*. The *natura* of Christianity according to its true *natura* is to be irreducible to a philosophy, because its fundamental assumptions lie outside any philosophy.

This does not mean that Christianity is *per se* anti-philosophical (philosophy has always played an important rôle in its elaboration of doctrinal formulation), but it is basically a-philosophical, for its heart is God, revealing Himself sovereignly in and to His creation; God who is *eo ipso* unmanageable in philosophical thinking, because by the nature of the case He is not primarily *cogitandus* but *adorandus* and *amandus*.[2] Neither the philosophical "weakness" of Christianity's being irrevocably bound up with what must be called in secular language "relative" historical facts, nor the philosophical (also theological, unmanageability of the God who acts in the Bible, need necessarily mean their irrelevance or inferiority in the dialogue on Ultimates. However, Christian thinkers are challenged to maintain and interpret this with new power and lucidity. As against this, the Asian religions are ultimately religious intuitionist-rationalist philosophies. Therefore in a novel way the Pascalian distinction or antithesis between the God of the philosophers (and scholars) and the God of Abraham, Isaac and Jacob, the God and Father of Jesus Christ, is again, but now in an immense setting of secularist and Eastern religious thinking, at issue. The simple conclusion is

[1] E. W. Thompson: *The Word of the Cross to Hindus*, 1956, p. viii, reminds us rightly that "the Way of Jesus is not the way of some Hindu Sage. Their schemes of life differ at every critical point, and are even in opposition and contrast."

[2] Cf. the close of Chapter 1.

that many scholars and philosophically-minded people in the West are probably more drawn to the "Eastern" side than to intractable Christianity.

A good illustration is afforded by the perennial question of the relation of faith and science. In our Western "Christian" world this faith-science issue has been a real conflict, a shaking of the foundations. The conflict has gone through different stages of vehemence and quiescence, but it is and must be always there, latent or manifest. To be sure, a not unimportant part of the conflict was (and is still) due to the grievous misunderstanding, by the Christians and many of their spokesmen, of the true nature of faith and the true function of science. They had incorporated in their *credenda*, as matters *de fide*, views of the world in cosmological respect, about the age and evolution of man and the universe, about history, which were utterly discredited by the irrefutable results of the various modern sciences. Confusion and tumult were thus inevitable, and in the course of the ongoing scientific quest, reaching out in all directions, confusion and tumult will certainly arise time and again.

An important consequence has, however, undoubtedly been that this conflict has led Christianity into a purification of its own self-understanding and a truer grasp of its nature and of the possibilities inherent in independent and free pursuit of knowledge and truth. But, salutary as this may be, it should never be forgotten that (leaving aside Fundamentalism in various grades that will always refuse to acknowledge the purification, and the dogmatism of certain scientists who will always try to use their results for a combat against faith and religion) essentially speaking, there will remain, by the nature of the case, always a *disposition* for tension between *Christian* faith and science.

Why by the nature of the case? Because of the biblical conception of God the Creator, Sustainer and Lord of the universe, all three not as timid marginal annotations *to* a secularized world view, but as pivotal realities *in* a secularized world conception. Further, because of the biblical view of God's relation to history; God who enters into history by His Word and in the "Word" (Logos) *par excellence* in the historical person of Jesus Christ, and has a redemptive purpose for the world.

All these basic assumptions lie outside the competence of

z* 371

science; and they do not arouse any interest on the part of science. Rather, science's impersonal and immanentist bias engenders inevitably a feeling of uncongeniality, certainly not of harmonious compatibility. This points to a hidden tension, and for Christianity to a position of enduring vulnerability, even though on the Christian side the propriety and necessity of independent pursuit of knowledge is loyally acknowledged and science recognizes its limits and the modesty which behoves it. The so-called reconciliation of faith and science, often proclaimed, can only be a truce, not for enmity's sake but for the sake of truth.

THE CLAIM OF MAN'S AUTONOMY

At a yet deeper level, however, it rests with the Christian faith, with all due respect for science and its freedom, ultimately to challenge the principle of *autonomy* which necessarily is inherent in the endeavour of science and is therefore valid, and yet has to be challenged because it is only true in a relative sense and therefore ultimately not valid but invalid. This challenge to science is implied in the sentinel-character of the Christian faith; that is to say its having to be on guard against the *possible* (because inherent) claim for the complete autonomy of man, which can mean in concrete cases the flat denial (not only the ignoring) of the sovereignty of God's will. In other words: to be on guard against a world which is built unconditionally on the self-sufficiency of man.

When looking at Hinduism and Buddhism, one has to remark the absence of a real conflict between faith and science. This seems amazing when one thinks about their exuberant mythologies, their stupendous religious fantasies, their chaotic, unreasonable tangle of practices and ceremonies. Seen from a certain angle they seem to deserve the name of the most successful producers of superstitions and superstitiousness. Or one can take an example of far higher calibre, that is to say, their fundamental cosmic apprehension of nature and man, and of nature, man and man's orders of life as completely correlate; called by Northrop in his *Meeting of East and West* the "esthetic continuum" which differs totally from the Western scientific approach to Nature by methodical observation, experiment and reason.

And yet the statement about the absence of a conflict holds true. The penetration of Western science and its appliances has, no doubt, caused many upheavals in the realm of religious and social conservatism, but *in principle* there is no conflict. Though having canonical books, there has not been and will not be a "Babel-Bible" row, or a heated "Genesis-Evolution", "Man-Ape", etc., debate. Though overflowing with mythology, no "demythologizing" controversy will split their great spokesmen in parties, arduously and often acrimoniously labouring on the problem. Why is that so?

It is so because in the first place these great Eastern Religions are mystical ways of salvation, for which every belief and rite is a means to an end and in which everything, however important at times, is of *relative* (because only instrumental) value. The thing that really and solely matters is the supreme mystical experience of the goal of final and definite liberation (*moksha*). The rest is symbol and evanescent form. No clashes with science can arise, especially not, as we have seen, the thorny problem (in the case of Christianity) of God in history and the foundation of essential tenets of faith in *historical* facts. Self-realization and its quest is the supreme interest. It is no wonder that many great Western scientists feel drawn to these Eastern religious philosophies on the highest level. They sense an easier compatibility and harmony between scientific thinking and ultimate convictions than in Christianity's case. Within the realm of the Christian faith the way, indeed, is not so smooth, where the centre is not Man and his Self and Self-liberation, but God, the Holy, the Loving; which does not allow the conviction that true oneness and harmony is oneness and harmony with God, who is the Bestower of it, as Man has no wholeness in himself. Ramakrishna, the great inspirer of what became Neo-Vedantism and Reform Hinduism, said when speaking of the Absolute which "some call God, others the Self, the Whole, Being or Nothingness" that it makes no difference whether one calls Him or It "Thou" or whether one thinks: "I am He (It)". This utterance contains in a nutshell the radical identification of all Ultimates, the tenet of the limitless ocean of unqualitative, inactive Being (*Sat*) as the common Ground and Matrix of all religious Absolutes. It contains also the abysmal antinomy with Christianity confessing

373

the God and Father of Jesus Christ as the Eternal *Mover*.

Christian thinking in the "coming dialogue" will probably have to restate its relation to the philosophy of Being, to the inebriating *theologia negativa* and to mysticism at its apogee in terms clearer than ever before. This is in fact contained in the antinomy of Self-Awakening versus Revelation, to which I alluded before.

Another interesting thing is, in connection with the faith-science issue, that Eastern thinking has already in the past conceived categories in which opposites are not only harmonized but thought of as necessarily complementary. This kind of thinking belongs to the fundamental traits of Naturalistic Monism.[1] The problem of wave or particle, or wave and particle, which has confronted modern physics with the riddle of incompatible truths, is to Eastern wisdom neither a new nor an uncongenial experience, because with its passion for harmony as the keyword of the universe it has always been hospitable to the unifying of "contraries" or "antinomies". To be religious means to live in oneness of the entire life, which means to transcend both, man and God. This harmony principle, which pervades the thinking on all spheres of life (the Chinese have been its most able interpreters), is undoubtedly fascinating and certainly will fascinate in the future. It obscures, however, the inner core of the human condition in its brokenness, fragmentariness and guilt, and therefore is in fact deceptive.

Denis de Rougemont[2] aptly remarks: "A *real* dialogue cannot be set up . . . except at the level of the basic options, which are of the metaphysical order." The wisdom of the East possesses a great psychological virtuosity in analysing man, in order to teach him to manage and master himself by spiritual and other kinds of training. As is well known, Eastern wisdom and spiritual experience meet here with the great discoveries in psychology and psychotherapy since Freud. Likewise the supreme serenity of the mystics, especially of the Buddha, in

---

[1] See my book: *The Christian Message in a Non-Christian World*, where a full analysis can be found. A good example of this "opposite-complementary" category is the famous Chinese conception: yin-yang. Cf. also Lily Abegg's *The Mind of East Asia*, quoted above. She stresses this "complementary" point in Eastern thinking strongly.

[2] *op. cit.*, p. 189. See also the following pages on the difficulty of a dialogue.

order to rise beyond everything: man, god(s) and world, and achieve perfect harmony and self-contentment of spirit, impresses modern anthropocentric man visibly and satisfies needs in him that were dormant or frustrated. Though this Western anthropocentrism has a quite different origin and history, yet in meeting now the great Eastern type of anthropo-centrism and humanism it feels affinity, and the readiness for being invaded by and deriving enrichment from this Eastern wisdom is therefore natural.

CHRISTIAN HISTORY NOT MYTHOLOGY

Christianity stands in marked contrast to all this by its conception of God the Creator, Redeemer and Consummator. He incarnated Himself in Jesus Christ, who belongs to history (was born, died on the cross, rose from the dead), not to mythology as in the Hindu *Avataras*, inaugurating thereby the new creation. Man is His creature and His chosen partner in a common work, in and with the world. God in Christ is not a stage in the hierarchy of beings, nor the *mysterium fascinosum* and *tremendum* as if He were a specimen in the category of the numinous, but He is the Loving, Holy, Righteous God, the only One to be worshipped, adored and served. As a Dutch poet has said, who had the awe in his soul which measures up to His hidden majesty: "If Jesus Christ were really to pass through a street of our modern civilization, would the whole street not fall to pieces?"

When all is said and done, the two images that ultimately should arise out of the "dialogue" are the humility of God, incarnate in the humble suffering servant, Jesus Christ, with man as His worshipping disciple and apostle, and the sub-limity of the ineffable, indeterminate, unqualified Being (above *Sat* and *Asat*) with the Mystic/Sage triumphant through his victory in Self-awakening.

Besides the dialogue of the metaphysical order, the meeting of East and West in their religio-cultural manifestations requires a rethinking of the Christian faith and its meaning in contact and exchange with these Eastern religions. The meet-ing, the more tangible it becomes, contains inevitably many hazards, but in these hazards the opportunity arises for a salutary testing of the reality and substance of the Christian faith. The main response, however, in this dialogue is not the *thinking* but the *being* of the Church. To *be* a true Church, that is to say a Christ-centred, Christ-inspired, Christ-obeying community in word and deed, in solidarity with the world serving everybody without discrimination, is the only answer and authentication to be given in the present and the future, both full of challenges. The Christians of the West and of the East should, in the tremendous situation in which they are placed in this desperate but wonderful world of ours, be solely concerned about *being* and manifesting the people of God in and for the world, in and for the Occident and the Orient.

The meeting of East and West will assume, of course, various guises. One of them will certainly be that the "dialogue" of cultures and religions will also wear the aspect of a counter-agency to the world mission of Christianity, which has been so evident in the Asian (and African) scene. Another guise is its strong cultural aspect. Yet the Christian Church, though not losing sight of these aspects, should first and foremost set her own house in order, because the greatest service she can render to the world, the Western and the Eastern world, is by being resolutely the Church of Jesus Christ.

INDEX OF PROPER NAMES

INDEX OF SUBJECTS

Franciscans, 27, 32, 44, 49, 178
"Fundamental options", 126, 333, 357ff., 360, 374

Gaman period, 31, 56
Geographical factors, 26, 28, 263, 271, 333
Germany, 193, 231, 248, 251f., 258, 268, 285; East Germany, 227
Gnosticism, 24, 257, 325ff., 367
Greece, Greek, 11, 27f., 38f., 42, 45, 47, 54, 70, 114, 196, 199, 338, 353. See Hellenism
"Great Awakening", the, 88, 318

Harmony, harmonization, 23f., 369
Hellenism, 31, 34f., 46f., 50, 55; Hellenistic culture, 27f., 38f., 41, 114, 263. See Greece
Hinduism, Hindu world, 28, 70, 100f., 105, 117, ch. 6, 160, 233, 238, 257, 259, 280, 290, 299, 310-316, 330, 354, 358, 366, 370; Advaita-Ashrama, 149, 151; Arya Samaj, 145ff., 155, 278; Bhagavad Gita, 138, 140, 145, 252f.; Brahma, 24, 207, 238, 244, 246, 332, 337, 346, 368; Brahmins, 65, 131, 148, 150, 156; Brahmo Samaj, 132ff., 145, 155; and Buddhism, 163, 170f., 315; caste, 131, 141, 150, 156, 175, 311, 362; in Ceylon, 370f.; and Christianity, 132f., 146, 149, 312f., 316f., 319, 341, 364; and idolatry, 128, 155; Karma, 316, 361; Maya, 316, 341, 361, 368; minorities, 289, 307; missionary outreach, 311, 320, 357; multiformity, 127f., 148; Neo-Hinduism, 259; Neo-Vedantism, 259, 310, 373; no faith-science conflict in, 372ff.; outcastes, 90, 139, 300; pietism, 128; Prarthana Samaj, 134, 155; Ramakrishna movement, 90, 147ff., 150f., 258, 311; and reform, 132, 134ff., 145ff.; 373; resurgence, present-day, 310-316; sati, 72, 131; Shastras, 138, 141; survey by its own scholars, 361f.; and Theosophy, 147f., 256; tolerance, 128, 154, 156, 316, 319, 321; unity with Islam, possible basis for, 141, 146; universalism, 152f., 154f., 257, 321f., 364; University, 311; Upanishads, 145, 156, 235, 252f., 331, 367; Vedas, Vedanta, 145f., 150, 155f., 252f., 258, 359. See India
History, 26, 80f., 84, 99, 119f., 190, 198, 263, 317, 335, 343, 360f., 369, 371; Christian view of, 58, 368f., 373; Church history, 23, 95, 257; element

in Christianity, 235, 341; science of, 68f.; world history, 12
Holland, the Dutch, 57, 212f., 268, 273, 310, 375
Hongkong, 97
Humanism, 19, 23, 39, 55, 84, 176, 196, 259, 262, 304, 342f., 345, 354f., 375; Christian, 55; classical, 23, 367; scientific, 314f.

Iberian Peninsula, 32, 35
Idolatry, 227, 263. See Hinduism
Imperialism, Western, ch. 3, 189, 194, 363. See Colonialism
India, 28, 31f., 36f., 55f, 57, 59, 62f., 65, 70f., 72f., 76, 85, 90, 103f., 109f., 121, ch. 6, 156, 170f., 172, 174f., 197, 199f., 256ff., 269, 278, 280, 289, 310-316, 361, 366f.; Bengal, partition of, 137; Calcutta, 130f., 149, 151, 254; conception of religion, 327f., 330f., 341; cultural influence in Asia, 40, 101f.; East India Company, 129; education, 130, 136f., 142ff., 146, 316, 360; independence, 273, 312; influence on China, 173; on the West, 232f., 237f., 242, 251-260; on the world, 254, 256, 280; Institute of World Culture, 153; Islam in, 105f., 116-120, 129f., 266f., 361; Madras, 151, 246; Mahasabha Movement, 142, 315f.; and Muslim situation to-day, 153ff., 310-316, 321; Mutiny, 105f., 117; National Congress, 135, 138, 142; Niyogi Commission Report, 312; Partition, 116, 288; reactions to British rule, 72f., 76, 129f., 141, 147; R.S.S. (National Service Organization), 315f.; secularism, 315, 347; Swadeshi, 141f., 146f., 278, 306, 313; Swaraj, 135, 138ff., 141ff.; Tamils, 307. See Hinduism, Buddhism
Indonesia, 20, 28, 70f., 89, 157, 197, 209, 278, 290, 310, 314
Industrial Revolution, 59
Iran, 69, 105, 269. See Persia
Iraq, 69. See Mesopotamia
Islam, Muslim world, 9, 13, 24, 28f., 70, 100, 144, 148, 157, 199, 231, 259, 278, 317, 337, 366f.; in Africa to-day, 266, 288; Ahmadiyya Movement, 116, 266ff., 269, 288; art, 262, 264; "Bahamdun", 264; and Buddhism, 157; in Burma, 301; in Ceylon, 307f.; in China, 293, 298; Christian minorities under, 282, 289; Christianity, relations with, 24f., 30-58, 71, 114, 261ff., 295f.; Colloquium of

Myth, 328, 348, 350f., 359, 373

Nationalism, 69, 75, 80, 104, 134ff., 139, 143, 162, 189, 286, 307, 312, 361
Naturalism, 332, 334, 359; cosmic, 20f.
Neo-platonism, 35, 40, 46ff., 49, 269
Nepal, 300
Nestorians, 27, 38, 46
New Guinea, 20, 89
Normans, 41f.
Nuclear fission, 69

Oriental studies, in the West, 19f., 68ff., 71, 73, 80, 82, 163, 231, 234, 251f., 261, 264, 276, 300, 315
Original sin, 328f.
Osmosis, religious-cultural, 101f., 160f., 339, 342, 344

Pakistan, 121f., 143, 267, 285, 288-298, 314. See Islam
Palestine, 29, 35, 241
Pali, 233, 248, 302, 304
Pascal's antithesis, 370
Persia, 27, 29, 36ff., 41, 105, 116, 122, 262, 267, 288f. See Iran
Philippines, 64, 177
Philosophia perennis, 145, 150, 248, 252, 327f.
Pietism, 88, 128
Platonism, 46, 54, 253
Politics, political factors, 19, 24, 26, 59, 66, 69, 78f., 82, 91, 93, 98, 100f., 107f., 122, 136, 140, 144, 157, 161, 168f., 184, 190, 196, 203, 208, 212, 241, 261, ch. 10, 286, 288, 303, 307f., 309f., 318ff., 343, 351
Polynesia, 206, 209
Portugal, Portuguese, 31, 176f., 211ff., 304. See Iberian Peninsula
Prayer, 48, 340
Press, the, 105
Prophecy, 12, 20, 167, 320, 324, 342, 350
Psychology, psychological factors, 18, 46, 107f., 126, 171, 178, 204, 231, 238, 247, 249, 319, 326f., 341, 348, 359, 368, 374

Reformation, the, 84, 338
Religion; "comparative", 240f.; conversion, 133, 301, 312f., 357; fundamentalism, 371; future of, 12, 14, 323, ch. 12; Hesse's view of, 330f.; history of, 14, 18, 68, 355, 365f.; Hocking's view of, 339-343; International Association for Liberal Christianity and Religious Freedom, 354; International Association for the History of Religions, 355; and

international problems, 351-356; Jung's view of, 326f.; liberty, 227, 279; man-centred religion, 325f., 327f., 331, 340, 347, 359, 367f., 327f., 375; national, 313, 315; neutrality, not possible, 89, 355; Northrop's view of, 337ff.; not an isolated sector of life, 83; Parliament of, at Chicago, 150f., 154, 163, 258; philosophy of, 333, 358; plurality of religions, significance of, 16f., 260, 322, 327, 358; pseudo-religions, to-day, 323f., 351; resurgence of non-Christian, to-day, 77, 157, 162, 164, 199, ch. 10, 317f., 323, 350, 364; science of, 14, 17, 23, 48, 240f.; religion and science, 152, 166, 194, 332; sociology of, 313; Stace's view of, 332f.; and State, 90, 107, 212, 222f., 225, 227, 283ff., 289, 291, 293, 305f., 315; symbolism, 333, 350, 359, 361; syncretism, 332, 365; 367; synthesis, 168, 330; Toynbee's view of, 12, 328ff.; truth behind all religions, possibility of, 148, 260, 280, 313, 316, 319, 322, 330, 340f., 345, 358, 361, 363; Universal Religion, 259f., 325, 340ff., 352, 364f.; World Congress of Faiths, 353f.; world religion, possibility of, 12, 341f. See Bible, Buddhism, China, Christianity, Faith, Hinduism, India, Islam, Japan, Jesus Christ, Judaism, Mysticism, Secularism

Renaissance, the, 54f., 194, 233
Revelation, 20, 39, 46f., 48, 102f., 108f., 117, 120, 138, 153f., 263, 329f., 333, 366, 368f., 374; and Reason, 47-51, 58
Roman Catholicism, 18, 48f., 56, 82, 87, 92, 177, 212, 234, 252, 338
Roman Empire, 27ff., 30, 35, 54f., 57, 60, 101, 176, 353, 367
Russia, 105, 137f., 186, 194, 198, 219, 274, 286, 293, 298. See Communism

Sanskrit, 37, 73, 145f., 148, 156, 233, 252
Science, 38, 59, 107, 121, 125, 152, 166, 182, 190, 194, 196, 231, 247, 321, 323, 326, 332, 334, 336, 339f., 342, 348f., 359, 363, 365, 368f., 371ff.; biology, 348; natural science, 68f.; scientific method, 240f. See Faith, Islam, Religion
Secularism, 121, 210, 226, 229, 277, 314f., 316, 321, 331, 340, 342, 347-351, 366, 370
Semitic temperament, 116f.
Shantiniketan, 153, 254
Sicily, 32, 35, 40ff., 44, 49f., 53